Theology at the Dawn of the Twentieth Century

THEOLOGY AT THE DAWN OF THE TWENTIETH CENTURY

ESSAYS
ON THE PRESENT STATUS OF
CHRISTIANITY AND ITS DOCTRINES

Edited with an Introduction by
J. VYRNWY MORGAN, D.D.

BOSTON
SMALL, MAYNARD & COMPANY
MDCCCCI

Copyright, 1900, by
SMALL, MAYNARD & COMPANY
(Incorporated)

Entered at Stationers' Hall

Riggs' Printing and Publishing Company
Albany, U. S. A.

To
G. W. WATTLES, Esq.,
Omaha, Nebraska,
in recognition of many kindnesses
during the last days of my companion in life
who passed away from earth,
behind the veil into the unseen glory,
on January 1, 1900

PREFACE

THIS work is made up of original essays, prepared expressly in response to my appeal, by eminent theologians in England and the United States, for the purpose I had in view, namely, to show the status of great questions at this period and how far religion and theology have been influenced by the progress of scientific research.

President Faunce of Brown University had promised an original essay on Christian Science, but he subsequently felt compelled to substitute the one which he wrote for the *Chicago Standard,* and which is one of the series of studies published by the Fleming H. Revell Company, under the title " Search Lights on Christian Science."

My task has been a laborious one, covering a period of two years. There are sad memories connected with those years, and I wish to express my great obligation to my friend, the Rev. H. O. Rowlands, D. D., Lincoln, Nebraska, for the benefit of his varied and ample experience. I thank that noble-hearted man, Dean Hart of Denver, for his unfailing encouragement, and also the various contributors for their sympathetic co-operation. No eloquence of words can do justice to their confidence and affection.

The questions discussed represent almost all aspects of theology and of the ministry, and they possess an urgency to-day which they have never hitherto possessed. Care has been taken in arranging the subjects so as to give the discussion a systematic completeness. The discussion goes down to the roots of things and has high and permanent value. It shows the scientific drift of the century now closing, together with its bearing upon the intellectual and ethical movements which are now going on around us—movements that have changed not only our theories but the very spirit of our thinking. I wish to say that while I have been honored in presenting these authors to the public, it cannot be expected that I should endorse all their views. I have endeavored to be impartial, and to give an honest analysis of the trend of current thought upon these fundamental questions, as shown in this book. I have given special attention to two or three themes that seem to be absorbing public thinking at the moment. Want of space forbids me to call attention to every topic in full.

J. VYRNWY MORGAN.

December, 1900.

CONTENTS

	PAGE
INTRODUCTION	
The Reverend J. Vyrnwy Morgan, D.D.	xiii
CHRISTIANITY AT THE END OF THE NINETEENTH CENTURY.	
Frederic Harrison, Esquire, London	3
THE FUNDAMENTAL CONCEPTION IN CHRISTIANITY.	
I. *Sovereignty the Fundamental Conception in Christianity.*	
The Reverend Henry A. Stimson, D.D., Manhattan Congregational Church, New York	21
II. *Love the Fundamental Idea in Christianity.*	
The Reverend Frank Crane, Pastor Hyde Park Methodist Episcopal Church, Chicago, Illinois	31
IS CHRISTIANITY FOUNDED UPON A BOOK OR UPON A PERSON?	
The Reverend L. W. Batten, Ph.D., St. Mark's Church in-the-Bowery, New York	43
CHRISTIANITY AND ITS COMPETITORS.	
The Reverend Harry Jones, M. A., Prebendary of St. Paul's, London, and Chaplain-in-Ordinary to Her late Majesty, the Queen	51
THE DOCTRINE OF THE IMMANENCE OF GOD.	
The Reverend James Eells, Pastor First Unitarian Church, Boston, Massachusetts	61
EVOLUTION IN ITS RELATION TO MAN AND RELIGION.	
I. The Very Reverend H. Martyn Hart, D.D., Dean of St. John's Cathedral, Denver, Colorado	75
II. Rabbi Emil G. Hirsch, LL.D., Professor in University of Chicago, Pastor of Sinai Congregation, Chicago, Illinois	91
SCRIPTURE INSPIRATION AND AUTHORITY.	
I. The Reverend A. C. Dixon, D.D., Pastor Hanson Place Baptist Church, Brooklyn, N. Y.	101
II. The Reverend S. D. McConnell, D.D., Rector of Holy Trinity Church, New York	117
THE OLD TESTAMENT IN THE LIGHT OF HIGHER CRITICISM.	
I. The Reverend Professor Henry Preserved Smith, D.D., Amherst, Massachusetts	127
II. The Reverend Professor Meredith O. Smith, M.A., Nashotah, Wisconsin	141

Contents

WHAT HAS BECOME OF HELL?   PAGE
    The Reverend G. W. Shinn, D.D., Rector of Grace Church, Newton, Massachusetts 159

FUTURE RETRIBUTION.
  I. Future Punishment.
    The Reverend Charles A. Dickinson, D.D., Pastor of Berkeley Temple, Boston, Massachusetts . . . 177
  II. Is Punishment Everlasting?
    The Reverend James De Normandie, D.D., Pastor First Religious Society, Roxbury, Massachusetts . . . 191
  III. The Bearing of the Teaching of Jesus Christ on Man's Future Destiny.
    The Reverend Caleb Scott, B.A., LL.B. (London), D.D. (St. Andrews); Principal of Lancashire College, Manchester, England 203

UNIVERSALISM.
  I. The Reverend I. M. Atwood, D.D., General Superintendent Universalist Church, Rochester, New York . . . 215
  II. The Reverend David N. Beach, D.D., Pastor First Congregational Church, Denver, Colorado 229

THE PERSON OF CHRIST.
  I. The Reverend Frederick Wilkins Aveling, M.A., B.Sc. (London), Principal Christ's College, Blackheath, London 239
  II. The Reverend Charles F. Dole, Pastor First Congregational Society, Jamaica Plain, Boston, Massachusetts . . . 249

THE ATONEMENT.
  I. The Reverend Professor Franklin Johnson, D.D., LL.D., University of Chicago, Chicago, Illinois 261
  II. The Reverend James Muscutt Hodgson, M.A., D.D. (Glasgow), D.Sc. (Edinburgh), Principal of Congregational Theological Hall, Edinburgh, Scotland 277
  III. The Reverend Henry W. Pinkham, Minister of Bethany Baptist Church, Denver, Colorado 289

THE LORD'S SUPPER.
  I. The Reverend W. T. Jordan, Pastor Calvary Baptist Church, Denver, Colorado 303
  II. The Reverend George H. Hubbard, D.D., Pastor Congregational Church, Enfield, Massachusetts 311

THE SACRAMENT.
    The Reverend Robert Collyer, D.D., Church of the Messiah, New York 323

THE SACERDOTAL CONCEPTION OF CHRISTIANITY.
    The Reverend P. H. Hickman, B.Sc., Evergreen, Colorado 331

Contents   xi

DIVORCE AND REMARRIAGE.   PAGE
   I. The Right Reverend William Croswell Doane, D.D., Bishop
      of the Diocese of Albany, New York 345
  II. The Honourable D. V. Burns, LL.D., Justice of the Supreme
      Court, Denver, Colorado 359

CHRISTIAN SCIENCE.
   I. The Reverend O. P. Gifford, D.D., Pastor Delaware Avenue
      Baptist Church, Buffalo, New York 369
  II. Edward A. Kimball, C.S.D., First Reader, Christian Science
      Church, Chicago, Illinois 379
 III. The Reverend W. H. P. Faunce, D.D., LL.D., President of
      Brown University, Providence, Rhode Island . . . 391

THE CHURCH AND ETHICAL LEADERSHIP.
      The Reverend William E. Barton, D.D., Pastor of First
      Congregational Church, Oak Park, Illinois . . . 403

THE PLACE OF THE CHURCH IN MODERN CIVILIZATION.
      The Reverend Professor C. R. Henderson, D.D., University of Chicago, Chicago, Illinois 413

THE ADJUSTMENT OF THE CHURCH OF THE FUTURE TO THE LIFE OF
THE FUTURE.
      Charles F. Thwing, D.D., LL.D., President of Western
      Reserve University, Cleveland, Ohio 425

THE SABBATIC PRINCIPLE IN MODERN SOCIETY.
      The Reverend Albert E. Waffle, D.D., Pastor First Baptist
      Church, Albion, New York 437

REVIVALS IN THE LIGHT OF THE PRESENT DAY.
   I. The Reverend George A. Hilton, Superintendent Madison
      Square Church House, New York 447
  II. The Reverend Samuel McChord Crothers, D.D., Pastor First
      Parish, Cambridge, Massachusetts 457

THE NEW ORTHODOXY.
      The Reverend Daniel Evans, Pastor North Avenue Congregational Church, Cambridge, Massachusetts . . 465

THE TREND OF THEOLOGICAL THOUGHT IN ENGLAND.
      The Reverend R. A. Armstrong, Pastor Hope Street
      Church, Liverpool, England 481

THE MODERN TREND IN ESCHATOLOGY.
      The Reverend Hugh O. Rowlands, D.D., Pastor of the
      First Baptist Church, Lincoln, Nebraska . . . 493

PROGRESSIVE LIBERALISM IN THE CLOSING AND THE OPENING CENTURY.
      Charles W. Eliot, LL.D., President of Harvard University,
      Cambridge, Massachusetts 505

RELIGIOUS CONDITION OF THE ANGLO-SAXON RACE.   PAGE
  I. *The Effect of Recent Theological Discussions on the Upper Classes of the Anglo-Saxon Race.*
    The Very Reverend F. W. Farrar, D.D., F.R.S., Dean of Canterbury Cathedral, England 519
  II. *The Religious Condition of the Working Men in America.*
    Samuel M. Jones, Esquire, Mayor of Toledo, Ohio . . 529
  III. *The Effect of Recent Theological Discussion on the Lower Classes.*
    Brigadier S. L. Brengle, Salvation Army, New York . 537

INTRODUCTION

BY

The Editor, The Rev. J. VYRNWY MORGAN, D.D.

MY object in this work is to put in clear contrast the two tendencies in theology—liberal and conservative—and to show the status of great questions at the close of the century. It is apparent that the entire edifice of traditional religious conception has undergone a most remarkable transformation. It is unquestioned and unquestionable. Whether this transformation has been, or still will be, advantageous to true piety is a question upon which there is some conflict of opinion. The following is a review of some of the most prominent questions, as set forth in this book:

THE DOCTRINE OF THE IMMANENCE OF GOD

The belief in an Immanent Divine Will—that is, the indwelling of God in nature, in social and personal life, working out its purposes in humanity, has practically revolutionized the theology of our fathers. For the old legal conception of man's relation to God, and the relation of men to each other in God, it has substituted conceptions that are organic, progressive, educational and vital. The regulative conception of this doctrine of the Immanence of God is, that the Infinite is in the finite, and the finite in the Infinite. It is increasingly felt by a large constituency of the most cultured and reverent thinkers at the close of this century, that such a conception is at the basis of Christ's most memorable and loving utterances.

To the question: "What thus becomes of human freedom?"; the answer is, that the Divine Will does not exclude or overbear the human, neither does the human exclude nor overbear the Divine. Both are concurrent factors.

The chief difficulty, however, in connection with this doctrine is the necessity of teaching or of presenting it in such a way as to make it clear to those who are not professionally or technically educated. When so presented, and when shown in its bearing upon education, politics and economics, together with its ethical and religious application, it may be made a potent factor in the production of faith and hope.

What exact place this doctrine is likely to occupy in the religious thought of the twentieth century, it would be difficult to forecast, both on account of the different views which at present exist concerning it, and the fact that the doctrine is, as yet, in its infancy. This much, however, can be safely said: it has come to be the central doctrine around which all thought, religious and secular, is at present revolving. Theosophy and Christian Science are but the symptoms of this condition mind, as it exists to-day among multitudes of people, both side and outside of the church.

EVOLUTION

This is another aspect of theology which is daily gaining a larger, more thoughtful and reverent class of students. The subject is a very large, and a very difficult one. The new light which the hypothesis of evolution has shed upon preconceived ideas of man's origin and destiny, as well as God's method in creation and redemption, is simply astonishing. It has given us a new geology, a new biology, a new sociology and a new psychology; its influence is felt in the sphere of letters; it has shifted the emphasis from the deductive to the inductive method of literary study. Indeed, it may be said that the hypothesis of evolution has actually transformed the human spirit. That so many scholars of the class represented by Dean Hart should refuse to walk humbly in the illumination of this great doctrine, is not surprising; one is bound to respect their feelings, their training, their traditions, and indeed their intelligence; but it may be stated that at the close of this century, the growing tendency is to accept Evolution as the best, the most philosophical, scientific and satisfactory interpretation of God, man and religion that has yet been supplied. This means that man began his life, not in a state of large intelligence and innocency, but in a low, savage state, gradually emerging, under the Divine care and discipline, into a state of larger knowledge and better life, and that the revelation of God's character, purposes and saving grace moved along similar lines. Thus the tendency is gradually, but surely to withdraw the question of man's salvation out of the region of law and sovereignty and penalty. A belief in Evolution as the method of God in creation and redemption has been shown to be not incompatible with the profoundest religious faith, for the facts of Evolution are susceptible of no other than a theistic interpretation. As Prof. Hudson, the distinguished author of "The Law of Psychic Phenomena," says in his work on The Divine Pedigree of Man, "The facts of organic and mental evolution point clearly and unmistakably to a divine origin of mind and life on the earth, and that the atheistic theories of agnostic evolutionists are destitute of sustaining facts." To those who are in difficulties as to how to reconcile their theology with evolution, we commend this latest production of Dr. Hudson, for it presents a very satisfactory outline of the fundamental principles which manifest the harmony which exists between science and religion.

Mr. Herbert Spencer, who is not at all concerned to establish traditional religious truth, is the only one from whom we have had a comprehensive statement of evolution in its relation to all departments. He says:—"One truth must ever grow clearer and clearer—the truth that there is an Inscrutable Existence manifested everywhere." "This," says Mr. Eells, "is the witness of both experimental science and the latest researches of Psychology. Beyond this, men of science are precluded from testifying by the limits of their study." But the testimony they bear is enough for our purpose. It confirms our faith in God. The application of the testimony of psychology and experimental science to the truth of the Personality or Divine Personality is ably dwelt upon by Mr. Eells in his article on the Immanence of God.

RETRIBUTION

The idea of Eternal Torment, we are told, is not an original article of our Christian doctrine. Its incorporation into the authoritative creed of the church was accomplished in A. D. 544, at the instance of the Emperor Justinian. This is a question of considerable importance.

Among the numerous replies which I received to my letters, both from England and America, only one expressed willingness to go on record on the affirmative side of this important question, and even that distinguished writer was afraid his treatment of the question would not be conservative enough for my purpose. Whatever may be one's personal feeling, every thoughtful and candid student of current thought has to admit that there is a very remarkable degree of apathy, or intellectual suspense, concerning this doctrine, both inside and outside of the pulpit. Eternal punishment, as preached by Jonathan Edwards, is no longer accepted by Congregationalists. It is still retained by some minds as a scholastic theory, and even occasionally preached from a few pulpits; but they are very few, and not very influential. Generally speaking, it is looked upon as spiritually unthinkable—more so now than at any other period during the century now closing. There is a growing disinclination to believe that a soul can suffer forever, or that a God, such as the one Jesus Christ made known to us, can permit it to suffer forever. Very few are prepared dogmatically to affirm that the grace of God ends for all, or even for any man, at death, or that a creature will be kept in existence that he may go on in sin, eternally. Such ideas are regarded with abhorrence by an increasing number of minds cultured, minds reverent and minds religious, both inside and outside of the church. They are looked upon as dishonoring to God, antagonistic to the instincts of justice in humanity, and untrue to the Scriptures. The chief causes of this striking reaction are ably set forth in this book by Dr. Dickinson.

UNIVERSALISM

The exact question of the destiny of all men did not come up among Christians at the very beginning. Explicit Universalism was not taught in the church until the third century, though implicit universalism was taught much earlier. The universalist denomination dates from the preaching of John Murray, who came to the United States from London, England, in the year 1770; a compact and elaborate organization being effected in the year 1870. But like Unitarianism, it is still one of the small denominations.

The progress of the Universalist sentiment, and especially of the Universalist Church, during this century, has been much greater in America than in England. Referring to the Biennial Session of the Universalist General Convention at Boston, October 25, 1899, the *Outlook* observed:—

"One sees a significant contrast between the obloquy and persecution visited upon the Rev. John Murray, when he introduced Universalism at Gloucester, Massachusetts, a century ago, and the fraternal greeting given at Boston to the International Meeting."

Since that time, the Universalists have built seven hundred and seventy-six churches. In 1898, they had a membership of 46,522 and 760 settled pastors; though at the close of 1899, the Universalists of America could claim only 44,746 members as against 46,522 for the previous year, a decrease of 1,776. However, there are but few religious bodies in America that can claim an increase of membership at the latter end of this century. In fact, religious organizations have been losing ground for some years throughout the whole of the United States. The increase in membership in America during the year 1899 was about one per cent.; not a very vigorous growth. The relative decline of Presbyterianism during the last five years, is well known, though last year they report an increase in the percentage of growth. The Methodist Episcopal Church is busy seeking a remedy for declining membership. The Methodist Episcopal Church with three million communicants added only seven thousand to its membership during the year 1899. In addition to this it shows a decline of twenty-eight thousand, five hundred and ninety-five (28,595) in those candidates known as probationers. This decline is all the more ominous when we take into consideration the fact that the decline takes place in those territories where the population is actually increasing. The Unitarians made no gain, while the Universalists fell off three per cent. Dr. Atwood accounts for this diminished rate of increase in these two bodies, firstly, by the fact of the growth of Universalism and Unitarianism in evangelical communions, and, secondly, by the disposition in these churches to make Universalists and Unitarians comfortable in their fellowship. The first explanation is undoubtedly true, but the second is true only in part, and is unsatisfactory. Dr. Atwood says, " The more converts (to Universalism) the fewer the followers." Such a statement will not stand the test of denominational history. Christian Science can claim more adherents and sympathizers among religious bodies than any other sect, and yet it can claim a larger percentage of organic growth than any other denomination—being fourteen per cent. during 1899. The diminished rate of increase among Unitarians and Universalists has been largely due to the hitherto negative character of their creed and teaching. People are more anxious to know what to believe than what not to believe, though the Universalist teaching is not so negative as it formerly was, or is now generally supposed. This is also true of Unitarianism. But the chief explanation of the diminished rate of increase among the Universalists is to be found in the fact that its distinguishing tenet is generally regarded as being beyond the range of experimental knowledge. " In itself ", said the Duke of Argyle, " it is most fascinating—would God it were true." However, the growth of Christian thought and sentiment cannot be accurately gauged by the growth of Christian churches or denominations, for the largest proportion of growth in

Christian sentiment and thought has been, during this century, outside of the nominal church, and the twentieth century is likely to witness a larger growth in the same direction. It is no longer possible to persuade men to believe that they cannot lead Christian lives, or that they cannot be saved unless they join a church. Indeed, some natures can lead better lives outside of the church than in it. It is contended, however, that this decrease in church membership must not be taken as a sign of the ultimate decay or extinction of the organic church. Our industrial and economic conditions, which produce divisions among various classes, together with the suspense of judgment upon religious questions arising from our theological controversies, account for the present state of things. As the spirit of Christ will enable men to adjust these inequalities, and remove these difficulties, the social impulse towards meeting together for service and praise will, we are told, bring large accessions to the organic church.

The great German historian, Friedrich Nippold, passed this judgment upon the Church:—" The history of the church in the nineteenth century is less than ever before synonymous with the history of Christianity." Neither can the progress of the Universalist sentiment be accurately gauged by the number of churches or pastors. The sentiment has spread beyond the confines of the nominal Universalist Church, and while a large number of Christian pastors and believers do not feel disposed to be dogmatic, either for or against Universalism, there is a growing spirit of hope, that somehow God, in his wonderful Providence, may see a way to bring all men to himself. There is a large class of theologians, who, while unwilling to believe in Eternal Punishment, cannot accept Universalism; these are inevitably driven into the school of " Conditional Immortality." Those who reject the Universalist sentiment reject it because with them the ultimate fact in human life is the freedom of the human will, and they maintain the power of the will to stand out forever. Dr. Atwood says that he is a Universalist because God is. " God made everything for goodness, and purposes that goodness shall triumph. Every soul has in itself the evidence of the end for which it is made, and the destiny of that soul is to ally itself with its author and to co-operate with him in fulfilling the great end of its existence." The crucial question seems to be, how to reconcile this theory with the supposed freedom of the human will, for each man's destiny, it is maintained, is and ever will be, in his own hands, and God cannot force man to choose the good and renounce the evil—at least while man continues to be a free moral agent. So the great problem remains, "Can the most merciful God save all men?"

The main value of Dr. Beach's contribution is to show the trend of thought among Congregationalists, which is a very important consideration. He does not dogmatize, for there is much both in Scripture and in Nature that looks the other way. "The solution of the problem," says Dr. Beach, "lies in the ultimate capacity of man to respond to the Divine Treatment," so that at the close of this century, the question of how extensive redemption will be, both as to duration and number, is looked upon as being beyond the range of experimental knowledge.

Dr. Rowlands deprecates intolerant dogmatism upon the question of the fate of the impenitent, for the reason that in every age men profound in the history of Christian Dogmatics, men whose piety was unquestioned, differed in their deductions and conclusions. Moody did not preach endless torment. Dr. Rowlands would not make it a test for Church membership, and under certain conditions, not even a test for ordination to the Christian ministry or appointment to the missionary field. The question might be put here: ought we to make belief in certain theories of the Atonement, or of Inspiration, or of the Infallibility of the Bible, and especially of the nature and method of Revelation, a condition of Christian fellowship or of Church membership or of ordination to the ministry? The question of the fate of the impenitent is not the only question upon which the revelations of the Scriptures are not so con-

Introduction

clusive as to place them beyond controversy. President Eliot of Harvard observes that this age is the least presumptuous of the ages. This is well said. This modesty is likely to grow upon us. The old theologians thought they perfectly understood God's justice and what that justice demanded. But as Dr. Eliot says, the jurists and legislators of to-day are not at all sure that they understand what human justice ought to be. There is reason for greater tolerance especially concerning those problems upon which no definite, or conclusive testimony, has been left us by the prophets and apostles, not even by Christ Himself.

I have given a good deal of space to this subject for the reason that, notwithstanding the hue and cry over the gross materialism of the present day, there never was an age when so many millions were so much interested in the problem of man's destiny.

CHRISTIAN SCIENCE

The growth of Christian Science stands as one of the most remarkable facts of the nineteenth Century. In 1876, a Christian Scientist Association was founded in Boston; three years later it was incorporated as a church, with twenty-six members. Now it has a membership of fourteen hundred, and ten thousand non-resident members. In Canada and the United States they have a membership of three hundred thousand. Among them are men and women of unquestionable piety, of good social standing and considerable intellectual attainment. Mrs. Eddy's book has gone through one hundred and sixty editions; they have two thousand healers, and it is conceded that they have healed thousands. The quantity of literature distributed by them is simply amazing, and their generosity is such as to excite the envy of all churches. But the Christian Science spirit has gone beyond the confines of Christian Science Churches. They have sympathizers everywhere, so numerous and so strong, that but very few pastors deem it wise or prudent, for their own sakes and the peace of the Church, to stand up and denounce Christian Science theories and practices. There are cases on record which prove that the men who have done that have suffered.

What is the secret of the growth of Christian Science? Why is it that every convert to that faith immediately becomes a zealous propagandist? I have not yet seen a satisfactory answer to these questions. Like the Salvation Army, it is one of the most remarkable movements since the Apostolic Age, and its adherents are increasing both in number and in zeal, not only in America, but in Canada, England, China, France, Italy and Germany. What is the secret of this success? To my thinking Christian Science is but a symptom of a condition of mind which so largely exists to-day. What is that condition? It is the same condition which made theosophy possible;—It is the growing belief in the indwelling of God in nature, in man, in human society and in all life. Christian Science revolves around the great central doctrine of the immanence of God. The miracle of Immanuel is a continuous one, and is moving on to its grand culmination, as depicted in the book of Revelation.

Then, in estimating the growth of Christian Science, we must take into consideration the great passion for health among the people, combined with a growing revulsion of feeling against the ordinary medical practitioner. This is no reflection upon those members of the medical fraternity whose skill and discretion entitle them to the respect and confidence of the world. But such medical aid is accessible to only a limited class. It is highly probable that in the early years of the incoming century, evangelical churches will claim that the healing genius has always been in the Church from the beginning, and will seek to put it to greater use, and will also seek to emphasize the place of the mind in the making of both health and morality.

But how long will our country continue to cheat the criminal law by accepting the Christian Scientists' defense of some of their methods as the exercise of a religious right? No one questions their right to worship in any way they think fit, but one questions their moral and legal right to refuse medical aid to children suffering and dying from pneumonia and other diseases. This intellectual aristocracy has absolutely eliminated the term "sympathy" from its vocabulary. It has done likewise with the word "repentance". It is often said that "Christian Science" is neither Christian nor Scientific. However, Christendom owes a debt of gratitude to Christian Science for the prominence it has given to the great and important doctrine of the Immanence of God.

Dr. Faunce declares this to be one of the strong points of Christian Science—its clear realization of the immanence of God. "The average Christian Church," he says, "is still shy of the doctrine of the Holy Spirit leaving that to Northfield and Keswick, and believes only in a far-away Deity who occasionally has interfered with this world to work a miracle. The average Christian Church believes in an inspiration which ceased about 100 A. D., and in an interpretation of the Bible which makes it the story of what was, but no longer is." He bears witness to the personal ability and high-mindedness of many Christian Scientists, and he concedes that they have produced large results in bodily healing but with equal frankness he points out the fallacy and perils of Christian Science. Its philosophy, he says, is a rare collection of shreds and patches; many notions inconsistently united. While Christian Science has gotten hold of a great truth, still as a system it is, he contends, perilous to moral life. Its use of the Bible is unwarranted. It discredits all the prophets and apostles and makes the life and death of Christ farcical. It robs man of real freedom and responsibility. It dissolves God into a misty, unconscious abstraction. It confuses moral distinctions through the denial of the reality of evil, and he suggests that Christian Science is the path-way to atheism. "Beloved, believe not every spirit, but try the spirits whether they are of God."

REVIVALS

The thing that people generally understand the word "Revival" to signify was developed in America, but was never successfully transplanted to any other country. The preaching of Wesley and Whitefield, which produced such glorious and permanent effects in England and America, should not be classed with ordinary revivals. Neither should the preaching and the methods of Moody and Sankey. Though there was a strong undercurrent of prejudice in England against their method, one cannot mention their names without deep and sacred emotion, for they stirred England as it had not been stirred since the days of Wesley and Whitefield. They were no professional peripatetic revivalists, but men of God, who accomplished work of immense benefit to general morality, Biblical study, and Christianity in general.

Among the objections to revivals noted by Dr. Crothers, and which, it is alleged, have brought popular revivals into disrepute, are the following: The tendency of evangelists to sneer at culture, and to denounce learning; also their failure to realize the fact that there might be differences of opinion concerning religious work and religious topics among genuine Christians.

Dr. Crothers calls attention to the manner in which Evangelists discourage the piety of the intellect, or love of truth—doctrinal truth. The difference between the revivalist and the scientific man in this respect is very striking. The scientific man considers and weighs his statements, while the revivalist is much more concerned in impressing his audience than in emphasizing and elucidating the truth. While the evangelist never fails to expatiate upon the justice of God, and how that justice must be satisfied, very little, if anything, is said respecting the necessity of justice between man and man. Dr. Crothers calls attention to the failure of "evangelists" to discriminate between intellectual difference and moral obliquity. The chief objection however, urged against revivals is the lack of spiritual elevation. In seeking to popularize re-

Introduction

ligion, many "evangelists" succeed only in vulgarizing it; while creating religious excitement they fail to create a religious attitude.

Account must also be taken of the artificial life which is alleged to be the result of the emotional excitement consequent upon a revival season; and not least, the reprehensible methods resorted to by some revivalists, in order to stimulate religious excitement, mainly for the purpose of raising large sums of money. There is a growing disposition to regard the ordinary revival meeting as destructive of modesty, as well as injurious to the nervous system. Unquestionably, these excesses have brought revivals into disrepute among a large class of devout, discriminating, and even enthusiastic Christians. That genuine revivals have been a source of good, cannot be doubted. In proof of this we need only mention the fact that such influential denominations as the Baptist, Methodist and in some sections the Presbyterians have been built upon the results of revivals. But why is it that we have so few conversions at our modern Evangelistic Services? What is the cause that so many distinguished Evangelists have retired from the field? Major Hilton, a sane and a conservative Evangelist declared it as his belief that this decline is due to the fact that the "Holy Spirit" is withdrawing from the churches. This is a serious statement, especially coming from one who has had such wide experience, a man of undoubted piety and acknowledged ability. One wonders why the Spirit of God should withdraw from a sphere where, and at a time when, it is so much needed.

Major Hilton says that the very nature and environment of man demands seasons of revival, and that something more than ordinary is necessary to head off the on-rushing tide of humanity, and to bring it to a realization of spiritual matters. He does not plead for any special method, for the method is a secondary matter. Major Hilton very properly laments the fact that the Church has not yet recognized that something is wrong with the present church method for winning souls, and he calls attention to the shameful ignorance concerning the Bible prevailing to-day among church members. The reason why there are so few converts during seasons of revival to-day, Major Hilton says, is due to the fact that the Church is not equipped for this work, and also that ministers during their seminary course receive no instruction in this department of ministerial life. Major Hilton is discouraged over the outlook for revivals; present indications are not promising, and it is difficult to see what place revivals will occupy in the future life of the Church.

THE ATONEMENT

What the Atonement is or means; why the Atonement was made; how are we to believe in it—are problems that have agitated men's minds for ages, and yet the agitation continues. It is calculated that there are about fifteen or more theories on this subject. But in all these discussions, it is clear that Christendom is coming out and on to broader and higher outlooks upon the question of Atonement. The old ransom theory, or negotiations with Satan on the part of Christ, has been discarded as a hideous travesty. Likewise, the theory of negotiations with God has been repudiated by the majority of Christendom. These conceptions may be attributed to a misuse, or an over-emphasis, of certain portions of Scripture; it may also be attributed to the mental attitude of the race during the periods when they were conceived. That such theories, revolting as they may appear, did bring comfort to those who held them, cannot be doubted, but they also ministered to much popular error, and they have now yielded to simpler, profounder, and more vital conceptions. The blasphemy of representing God the Father as all wrathful, and God the Son as all mercy, is no longer preached. Dean Farrar says: "Men now accept no violent disintegration of the Persons of the Trinity in man's salvation." Men still believe that God forgives sin, not for Christ's sake, but in and through Christ. Creeds, with their scholastic phrases and damnatory clauses, have not added much to faith, and have alienated multitudes from the Church and religion.

The theory of absolute satisfaction, which at length followed upon Anselm's effort in the eleventh century to relate God's work in Christ to his holiness and high purposes, and the theory of satisfaction propounded by Grotius in the seventeenth century, are less and less preached, and are abandoned by the great majority of able and devout men. The theory of propitiation, which has met with wide acceptance, is also passing out of theology. Such a conception of the Atonement is now regarded as inconsistent with the whole trend of Apostolic teaching.

The substitutional theory, which in its essential principle is difficult of discrimination from those already mentioned, is a combination of the views of the school which followed upon Anselm, and of the Grotian school, and still largely prevails in Protestant Theology. It may be safely stated that the majority of Christian believers throughout Christendom still believe in this theory. It may also be stated that the substitutional theory no longer holds the same place as formerly in Protestant Theology. An increasing number of Christian believers, as well as of our theologians, regard, as unscriptural and purely Pagan, the theory that the justice of God must be satisfied by the infliction of punishment. The actual transference of the penalties of sin and of the Divine displeasure involved in the substitutional theory is regarded more and more as Dr. Hodgson puts it, "as utterly repugnant to the primary instincts of the moral sense, and really subversive of the very foundations of moral order." Dr. Franklin Johnson concedes that those who hold to the substitution of Christ do not regard as final or satisfactory any of the existing theories of the substitution. There is a growing feeling that these theories contain *glimpses*—only glimpses—of a truth larger than all. So that, while the majority of Christian believers and thinkers still accept the substitution of Christ as a fact, they accept it without a theory, and though it is not absolutely essential that we should have a theory, still Christian believers will never cease to search for an adequate one.

As to the moral influence theory, while it has considerable acceptance in some quarters, and while it is recognized as true as far as it goes, the trend of thought at this period seems to regard this theory as unsatisfactory, inasmuch as it does not seem to touch the vital spot. Dr. Franklin Johnson maintains that it is far too narrowly circumscribed. Such a theory, we are told, is not conducive to profound thought; and, so far as its effects are known, it tends to kill emotion. In conclusion, the opponents of the moral influence theory tell us that it is difficult to see how the preaching of such a theory can reach or influence the human will, and, if it cannot reach the will, it certainly cannot transform the life.

In answer to all this it may be said that the opponents of the moral influence theory do not seem to appreciate its true bearings. Bushnell was one of the great exponents of this theory and no preacher of this Century has been more vital. The same is true of those who were influenced by his thought.

The Rev. W. H. Pinkham observes: "A more advanced stage of spiritual progress requires a new theology." Mr. Pinkham's contribution is especially interesting from the fact that he was recently excommunicated for heresy. The editor is glad to bear testimony to Mr. Pinkham as a man of deep spiritual feeling. A broader and a better spirit, we are told, has taken possession of the churches; that is true; but they are still a long way off from the ideal of Christ. In Macaulay's essays (Hampden) the writer says: "It required no great sagacity to perceive the inconsistency and dishonesty of men who, dissenting from almost all Christendom would suffer no one to dissent from themselves; who demanded freedom of conscience, yet refused to grant it; who execrated persecution, yet persecuted; who urged reason against authority of one opponent and authority against the reasons of another."

Mr. Pinkham contends that if Christ bore the penalty of human sin, then there can be no room for repentance. He claims that the history of Christ shows not what we ought to suffer, but what sin really is—how deep the depravity of the human heart. The vicarious death of Christ was not a special or a unique act, as the old theologians have claimed, but an example—and the supreme example of a universal law.

THE HIGHER CRITICISM

It is yet too soon to gauge accurately the full effect of Higher Criticism upon our theology and preaching, for Higher Criticism has only just entered upon its constructive stage. This much, however, may be said, that Higher Criticism is fast overcoming the influence of ultra-conservative theologians who have claimed the exemption of the canonical writings from literary and historical criticism. It has succeeded in infusing a more scientific spirit into theological inquiry. It has also established for itself a reputation for wide scholarship and integrity of purpose. The position of Higher Criticism is that some of the books of the Scriptures are composite in structure; that some were written in times much later than the authors whose names they bear; that their incidental utterances are not necessarily infallible, and that the Old Testament teaching cannot be separated from its historical environment, and is ethical and spiritual rather than scientific—the method of parable and allegory being sometimes resorted to. Higher Criticism, while presupposing inspiration, seeks to determine the conditions under which it operates; but it contends that inspiration does not exclude the human element in the imperfect mediums by which it has been communicated. The question whether the Church created the Bible, or the Bible created the Church, has not a very essential bearing upon the conclusions of Higher Criticism. In all the Old Testament we are told not a word is said about itself as an inspired book, or as being a collection of inspired books. There is only one place where the New Testament speaks of itself as inspired, and, even there, the direct implication is that all scripture is not inspired; that is, that many of the things recorded in the Bible were natural, and not supernatural. Therefore, the Bible is in some respects a book, not of absolute, but of relative truth. It is adapted to certain men, certain periods and certain economies, while having at bottom immense moral weight for all times. Dr. McConnell defines the Bible as the literature of a movement. The movement produced the literature and not conversely. The movement is the master, and the book is the servant. The impulse of the spirit of Holiness is moral, not intellectual. The only authority which can decide which men, and what writings, have been inspired is the Christian Consciousness. As the Church lived for Centuries without the Bible, so the Church would not perish if the Bible were lost. The capacity to inspire is the only sufficient evidence of inspiration.

Furthermore, Higher Criticism maintains that creeds and theories should not be founded on isolated texts and misapplied metaphors; that the Bible must be interpreted as a whole, and interpreted in the light of our most advanced knowledge. Thus, and thus only, we are told, can reverence for the Bible be increased, and men of all classes be brought to realize the true worth of the Bible as the highest literary revelation of God ever made to man. But there is this criticism that might be passed; while the ultra-conservative theologians are guilty of over-using and of misusing isolated texts to buttress their theories, the liberals seldom, if ever, quote the Bible at all.

Higher Criticism claims that the New Testament knows nothing of systematic dogma; that infallibility can never be the quality of any known doctrine; that the very nature of Christianity makes it impossible for one generation of men to so formulate the truths of the Christian faith as to make them applicable to, or binding upon, another generation blessed with a larger mind and heart.

According to the famous formula of Athanasius's creed, intellectual acquiescence in what he at that period regarded as the truth constituted the way to Heaven, and the basis of salvation was submission to the authority of the Church. To these assumptions, Higher Criticism ascribes the alienation of so many thinking men from any outward relationship with Christianity. Some of them, like Huxley, have thus been driven into the region of scepticism, while others have been forced into the region of atheism.

Higher Criticism contends that some of the Old Testament books, such as Esther and Jonah, must not be taken as narratives of fact, and that the allegorical element plays a very prominent part in the Book of Genesis. Not that Higher Criticism claims to have been free from error, but as Dean Church said: "Those who make no mistakes make nothing." This is the position of the Higher Criticism and in this connection it should be noted that the more reasonable section of our modern conservative theologians, after much hesitation, have come to the conclusion that the interests of truth, of the Bible and of religion at large, necessitate the endorsement of the confession made by Mr. Moody, when he said: "It is not the authorship of the book that matters, but the contents." They now concede that the real question is, not whether the Prophets wrote the books which are called by their names, but whether they uttered the prophecies which have been recorded in these books; and that the whole value of the Pentateuch no longer stands or falls with its Mosaic or non-Mosaic authorship. Prof. M. O. Smith of Nashotah in his paper takes this ground, and it is the preliminary step towards the removal of the distractions which prevail at present in this field.

The most discouraging and lamentable feature in connection with these controversies is the uncharitable and unchristlike spirit in which many ultra-conservatives have received these criticisms. Why need we be afraid of the light? Christianity can stand the test of light from whatever quarter it may come. It has stood it for two thousand years. The truth is like a torch; the more you shake it, the more it blazes and shines. It is true, we have lost many darling phrases, and many of the Old Testament books have lost their supposed historical value, and our theories of inspiration have undergone considerable changes, and many of the books are no longer ascribed to the authors whose names they bear. It has been shown that there are in the Bible discrepancies in historical statements, but it has not been shown that there is any conflict in religious teaching. Inspiration, says Prof. M. O. Smith, is not so much the spirit of invention as it is the spirit of memory. The crucial point is not the date or authorship, but the relation which the legislation of the Pentateuch bears to the whole development of the history. The laws of the Pentateuch he maintains were actually tested before their insertion in the Bible. To say that Higher Criticism is symptomatic of a declining faith is not true. Higher criticism has compelled men to study the Bible in the light of our most advanced knowledge. It has emphasized the fact that Christianity is not religion, but only a form of religion—for there are many forms, Christianity being the highest. When Christianity fears inquiry its value falls. Higher Criticism it is claimed has given us a solution of great questions more satisfactory to the conscience, to the intellect, and to the teaching of science than any other.

It is alleged that the discussion of such questions has exercised a baneful influence, both upon the people and upon the critics. It has, we are told, alienated the people from the churches; and while it is possible for those who have had an inward experience of grace to hold such advanced views with impunity, it is not possible in the case of those who have not had such experiences. In answer to this, it is stated that the influence of these discussions upon the lower classes cannot be much, for as Brigadier Brengel says: " The lower classes do not and cannot take any intelligent or practical interest in these questions; the only two questions which concern them are, the Hell of the future and the Hell of the present, and even the Hell of the future has no terrors for them. They can be won by love, but they cannot be terrorized by fear. It was not always thus."

As regards the upper classes—our statesmen, merchants,

teachers and even the working classes, the influence of Higher Criticism upon them has not been shown to have been injurious. The weight of evidence is the other way.

As to the allegation that Higher Criticism has injuriously affected the critics themselves by withdrawing their sympathies and attention from missionary and philanthropic movements, the facts of the case refute it. Dean Farrar is one of England's most famous champions of the poor and degraded; he understands the condition of the lower classes, and never ceases to plead their cause before God and man. The same may be said of the late Professor Drummond, Dr. Clifford, Dr. Horton, and Dr. George Adam Smith, and it is stated that Dr. Charles A. Briggs, one of the most distinguished critics and theologians in Europe or America, made an application to Bishop Potter, after his induction, that he should be assigned to a church in a poor district of New York City. Many of the higher critics are men of deep and broad sympathies.

What has Higher Criticism claimed to have accomplished? In addition to the achievements already referred to it claims to have shown that the greater part of the Psalms, formerly ascribed to David, were not his productions. Dr. Preserved Smith says it is doubtful whether one can be ascribed to David. It has shown that the Pentateuch itself does not claim to be the work of Moses; that Isaiah had two, and probably three authors. It claims to have increased our sense of development in the literature and religious life of Israel; it has established the unity of the Bible to be the unity of an organism, and has pointed out the growth of Israel's religion, both ritual and institutional, which growth relieves us of the necessity of defending many of those customs and practices in the life of this ancient and historic people.

Furthermore, Higher Criticism claims to have made it unnecessary to attempt the impossible task of harmonizing everything in the Bible narrative, and it denotes the use to which such discrepancies should be put, namely: as marks of various stages of life and thought; and, in so far as Higher Criticism has been destructive, it has only destroyed certain traditions external to the Bible, which have been made to buttress its historical authority.

For the most notable example of its overthrow of tradition we are referred to the Book of Proverbs, which it is alleged, has been brought down to a comparatively late date; but the worth and power of the book has not been diminished thereby; indeed, we are told it actually enhances its value. Dr. Preserved Smith observes: "We should despair of the power of practical religion, if, after giving any man wisdom to utter so many excellent maxims of life and conduct, it should produce a life such as was led by Solomon."

Undoubtedly, Higher Criticism has come into theology to stay, for there is still more to be accomplished, both in the way of textual or lower criticism, as well as in the way of Higher Criticism, or, the examination of the internal characteristics of both the Old and New Testament. But there need be no apprehension for as Dean Farrar says: "Our reverence for the Bible has been increased by the criticism and the progressive enlightenment which have led us to a truer estimate of its place and meaning in the dealings of God with men." There is however a far more important question looming in the distance, a question which will engross our attention in the early years of the coming century, viz., what effect will these changes of opinion concerning revelation, inspiration and religion, have upon the future estimate of Christ's life and character? Pres. Eliot says that love for Jesus will not diminish, but that while the pathos and heroism of his life and death will be vastly heightened, Christ will be relieved of all supernatural attributes and power. There is evidence that the forward movement is carrying some of the critics farther than they anticipated, and indeed farther even than some of them desire.

PROTESTANTISM

The contest for supremacy between the Puritan and the Anglo-Catholic parties, which has been carried on since the

Reformation, has, now, in England at least, been brought to a crisis. For Rome, the prospects are encouraging; she has succeeded in covering the name of Luther with obloquy, and made the term "Protestantism" a term of reproach, and that among a large section of the clergy who live on the money of a Protestant Church, founded on Protestant principles for a Protestant end. The avowed object of the Papacy is to unprotestantize England, and judging by the introduction of those ideals and practices in vogue previous to the Reformation into so many of the Established Churches of England, there is a possibility that that object will be attained during the next century. Mr. Armstrong says: "Ritualism has come with a rush. The appeal to the senses by music, by vestment, by incense has fairly conquered the Church of England." But worse than the Ritualism is the Sacerdotalism which places the supernaturally endowed priest between the worshipper and God, holding the very Keys of Heaven. Side by side with this growth of Sacerdotalism is the decay of evangelicism. England at the close of this century, has no great evangelical scholars or thinkers. Indeed, England has no great intellectual leaders either in the field of science, of poetry, of literature, of philosophy or of romance.

This Sacerdotal movement began with the rise of the Oxford movement. Year by year it increased in power until to-day we find the pastoral conception of the ministry completely overshadowed by the priestly conception. By the act of uniformity of 1559, the limits of the Church to decree its own rites and ceremonies were clearly and definitely defined. But the high Church party contend that its application was limited to the reign of Queen Elizabeth. This contention has no foundation in fact. However, it seems to show the desperate character of the present movement to unprotestantize the English Church. This struggle has a political significance. The great middle or evangelical party within the Church is gradually arriving at the conclusion that the only remedy lies in the disestablishment of the Church, a result devoutly wished by the non-conformist section. Such an issue would be followed by the formal reunion of the sacerdotal party with the Church of Rome, and the formal recognition by the Pope of the validity of those re-ordinations which have been secretly performed by those English Episcopal bishops who act with the approval and under the inspiration of the Holy See itself. This is not a question of liberty of conscience or the enforcement of the Toleration Act. The essence of the struggle lies here; whether it is legal or moral for those clergy who sympathize with Rome to remain in the Church, to continue to receive Protestant money, to introduce Romish practices in violation of their ordination vows, and thus consciously to assist in destroying the Protestant character of the Church; a church which has been partly established, and is still partly maintained by the money of those citizens who were, and are, Protestants, and who are denied any vote in the appointment or dismissal of such clergy. These clergy remain in the Church, because, if they went out, they believe, England would be lost to Catholicism. There will be no improvement until the laity get the power of self-government. The bishops and archbishops are powerless, and Parliament is loath to interfere.

Cardinal Manning said that the most difficult task the Papacy would ever have to face would be the task of bending the neck of this imperial race (meaning the English) to the yoke of Rome.

If Manning lived in our day, he would probably withdraw or modify that statement, for there is a wave of Romanism sweeping over England at this period which is leaving abiding impressions in unexpected quarters.

Protestantism, we are told, has served its purpose. It has secured for us an open Bible, intellectual and religious freedom, and its mission is therefore ended. The obvious reply to this is that Protestantism does its work only so long as it survives. The power that brought toleration alone can preserve it, and the verdict of history is, that only under the Ægis of Protestantism can philosophy as a searcher after truth go its own way. Maclauchlin, a great Catholic writer whose book has received the approbation of the Pope, says: " The Catholic Church interdicts the use of private judgment in matters of faith. Free inquiry, liberty of mind, freedom of thought are words she will not and cannot listen to." On this ground, Rome burned Giordano Bruno, the great Italian thinker, and branded Galileo with imprisonment for proclaiming the most certain facts concerning the planetary system. The Roman Church claims a right through its alleged continuous growth and conscious unity, of explaining, formulating and restating truths and systems of doctrine. It therefore refuses and repudiates any knowledge which the Church itself does not possess or cannot sanction. The contention of Rome is, that the Bible itself is utterly incapable of supplying us with any system of coherent doctrine. This can only be done by the Romish Church, and as the Bible, as they allege, is the creation of the Church, and not the Church the creation of the Bible, it has a right to remake what it has made.

Another fact which is favorable to the spread of Roman Catholicism in England is the striking change which has come over the English character. Many of the qualities which contributed to England's greatness in the sixteenth and seventeenth centuries have passed away. Mr. Frederic Harrison states that England has lost much of that higher spirit which inspired public and private life thirty and fifty years ago. There has been, he contends, a gradual lowering, not only of intellectual powers, but of moral tone. With all the blunders and delusions of the earlier period of the century, Englishmen were characterized by finer aspirations and more generous impulses than at present. This deterioration is manifest in poetry, literature, science, philosophy and in national ideals, also in ethics and religion. There is a dying out of those high standards of life which characterized Englishmen in the sixteenth and seventeenth centuries. Moreover the English people, notwithstanding the temporary influence of the Cromwellian period, have instinctively retained that love of ritual which they inherited from the Middle Ages.

The Rev. R. A. Armstrong describes this movement to concentrate the consciences of Englishmen on the priest and his pretensions as an effort to hold back the public mind from inquiry as to the reality of the unseen God. It is unconsciously at bottom a movement of the profoundest scepticism which cannot trust the soul to find its pilgrim way to the breast of the living God. The nature of the movement, and the position of its sponsors, point to the conclusion that its prospects are encouraging. All retrograde movements begin at the top and go downward. All reformations begin at the bottom and go upward. The constant stream of perverts, making their way Romeward, come from the English aristocracy, the social leaders and the clergy.

Moreover, Catholicism in England has won a signal victory, in that it has succeeded in enlisting the Protestant sentiment of liberty on behalf of itself and of its methods, so that the man who opposes Roman practices, as a menace to national well-being, is certain to be put down as a bigot and an extremist.

Again, there are certain features in the closing years of this century which are favorable to the spread of Roman Catholicism. By these features, I mean slackened convictions, luxurious worldliness and self-indulgence. History shows that, in such times, and under such influences, Sacerdotalism becomes possible.

Then, there is the reaction from the lack of reverence, which has characterized the non-conformist system of worship. Faber went over to Rome, because of the " dreadful facility " of turning to God indicated by what he was pleased to call the " base theology " of the Evangelical school.

Lastly, in considering this Roman movement, we must take into account the perplexities and uncertainties which drove

Newman into the Roman fold, and which to-day press with heavier weight upon men's souls than at any other period. To such, Rome holds out her hand, representing herself as the only power capable of giving rest and freedom from doubt and distraction.

While this is a question which at present chiefly concerns the English people it is impossible altogether to ignore its bearing upon America. Here Cosmopolitanism is fast establishing itself. Here, if anywhere, the breaking up of nationality will take place, and it will be Rome's opportunity. She has always shown herself to be a bold, aggressive, proselyting Church, and she understands the American temperament thoroughly. In the sixteenth century the great opposition to Rome was the sentiment of nationality which was emphasized, or rather awakened by the Reformation. But the closing years of this century bear testimony to the decay, and approaching extinction of the sentiment of Nationality. What will be the attitude of the American democracy? This is the vital question. Democracy, we are assured in some quarters, is safe and can be depended upon. But can democracy be depended upon? It is too soon to prophesy for democracy is on its trial. Its success has not been established. There is a growing change of sentiment in the American democracy towards Roman Catholicism; there is a similar change among agnostics and even among men of scientific knowledge. The only people that appear impervious are the negroes. But this fact does not disturb Rome, for the reason that she knows, that notwithstanding the glamour and pride of the emancipation, the American people are as disinclined as ever, both north and south, to grant the negroes any substantial share in the development and guidance of their national life. The negro problem has assumed very grave proportions, and notes of alarm are already being sounded by the more thoughtful and reflective of the people.

THE LORD'S SUPPER

It is sad, but true, that what was meant to be a symbol of peace and fellowship, has been for well nigh two thousand years a source of contention and strife. Why? Because the Christianity of the Church is so different from the Christianity of Christ. The essence of Christianity is spirit, but the Church has sought to make it a thing of form; this means not only a contrast but antagonism.

The Rev. George Henry Hubbard says it is a mistake to suppose that Christ formed a church. The Church dates from the day of Pentecost—that is the Church of the New Dispensation—the Church as we know it. Matthew and the rest of the Apostles were not members of a church when they sat at the table with their Lord, for there was no organic church in existence at the time. There is no record that Jesus asked any questions before the bread was broken and the wine was poured. He imposed no conditions of belief, or indeed of character, for Judas was one of the twelve. So it was when He called them out of the world to be His disciples. He simply said "Follow me." Nothing was said about creed, or belief, or experience. Mr. Hubbard states: "We have no hint of a Churchly interpretation of the sacrament till some years had passed." "In fact we are informed in the Acts that the disciples went from house to house breaking bread with gladness and singleness of heart. Thus the family aspect of the old Passover feast observed by Christ the night before His death, was preserved by the apostles and Christians after His ascension." How, and by whom, was the Supper transferred from the home into the Church, and changed from its original simplicity to its present ceremonial form? Dr. McGiffert fixes the responsibility for this change on the Apostle Paul, whom he regards as the originator of the Lord's supper in its present form. The reason for this change was Paul's desire to avoid undue indulgence in food and drink on the part of the Christians. So he changed what was "originally a sacred family service, into a purely formal and Churchly ceremony."

Mr. Hubbard contends that by this transfer of the ordinance from the home to the Church, it lost much of its original significance and freedom. He further maintains that the theological fictions which have since been attached to the ordinance had no existence in the mind of Christ, certainly not in His utterances and example, and that to confine the sacrament to those who have submitted themselves to a certain form of baptism is to rob the ordinance of its original significance and to give it an interpretation absolutely unwarranted by anything Jesus said or did.

The ground upon which Mr. Jordan stands is that baptized believers constitute the Church. It was the practice of the apostles to baptize all believers before admitting them to the Lord's table. To this practice there was not a single exception; all orthodox churches or denominations agree in the practice of admitting none to the Lord's table until they become members of a Christian church, and none are considered members of a Christian church until they have been baptized. Such practice he says agrees with the New Testament. Mr. Jordan goes on to say that baptism constitutes membership; the Church being founded upon the ordinances. The New Testament recognizes no baptism except that of the believer. He further states that the scholarship of the world agrees that the original mode of baptism was immersion, that oneness of belief is the basis of fellowship and there can be no real fellowship at the table unless all who sit down together have the same views on spiritual truths. He asks if all Christians could consistently come together at the Lord's table, what justification would there be for maintaining separate denominations? It is clear he says from the Scriptures that the supper is not a family ordinance.

Which of these two propositions is " more in accordance with the example of Christ, with the spirit of the gospel, and with the reasonable demands of enlightened common sense," our readers will decide for themselves. The question is asked: " If the sacrament was not originally a family ordinance, how is it we are explicitly told in Acts ii: 46, that the disciples of Jesus went from house to house breaking bread?" "There can be no dispute as to the fact whatever may be our interpretation of it. There can also be no question that the Passover feast, which Jesus consecrated into a memorial of Himself, was eaten in the home; the members of the family being together and the father sitting at the head of the table as director of the feast." This is Mr. Hubbard's position. The battle cry of Christians during the closing years of this century, is "Back to Christ." "If we go back to Christ for instruction and inspiration upon the sacrament, we find that not one of those who partook of the supper was a church member; that we have no record that He imposed any condition of belief or declared that after its institution, there should be any condition." Jesus Himself, says Mr. Hubbard, never drew the lines of discipleship as sharply as the Church did after He had left them. Mr. Jordan declares that oneness of belief is the basis of fellowship, and that there can be no real fellowship at the table unless all who sit down together, have the same views of spiritual truth. This is a strong statement, and if that is so we must conclude that there never has been, and is not, such a thing as true fellowship, not in any church of any sect whatever throughout the whole world. Furthermore, it is a good thing that there is no such fellowship, and that the indications are that there never will be such fellowship. There can be no fellowship between man and wife, between friend and friend, or father and son, whether at home around the family altar or in the church, unless their views upon the Atonement, the Trinity and Inspiration are exactly alike. As to the contention that if all Christians could come together at the Lord's table, what justification would there be for maintaining separate denominations, the reply is obvious. The question of the Sacrament is not the only one that separates Christians; there is the question of organization, of discipline, of ministerial appointment, of a settled ministry and methods of worship. Mr. Jordan is mistaken when he says that all orthodox churches or

Introduction

denominations agree in admitting none to the Lord's table until they have become members of a Christian church. As a matter of historical fact, it may be stated that the Congregationalists invite non-members to partake of the Sacrament. Many Presbyterians do and the Protestant Episcopalians, and so do the Unitarians. There was such a theory, but it is not observed nor even recognized now.

Mr. Hubbard, we believe, is in error when he states that a "Church which insists upon one particular form of baptism, no longer refuses to fellowship churches that adopt other forms, nor denies to the members of other communions, the privilege of partaking of the Lord's supper in its circle." There are Baptist Churches in America which practice open Communion, but they are not numerous. There are also eminent ministers and a great number of Baptist members who believe in open communion. However, the great body of Baptists in America do not practice open Communion, and this is one of the secrets of their power. Generally speaking, the invitation is couched in such terms as to fix the responsibility of remaining or going upon the visitors.

THE OUTLOOK FOR THE FUTURE

Judging from the trend of the world's thought at this time, as shown in this work, the future does not belong to any sect or creed. James Martineau said: "The true religious life supplies grounds of sympathy and association deeper and wider than can be expressed by any doctrinal names or formulas, and that free play can never be given to those spiritual affinities till all stipulation, direct or implied, for specified agreement in theological opinion, is discarded from the basis of church union." We are evidently coming to that. Sect will mean less in the twentieth century than it does now, and it means less now than it did fifty years ago.

Those who think that religion consists in sprinkling, or in immersion, in denominational cliques, are growing less numerous as the years go by. True religion embraces all that is kind, or wise, or gentle, or pure in mankind. Such is the trend of the world's best thought at this period, and the indications are that many of the outward symbols, which now prevent intercommunion between different religious bodies, will be removed, and the churches will become more of missionary institutions, and less of doctrinal schools. The final test of salvation will be character. Uniformity of views upon such questions as the Atonement, or the Trinity, or Inspiration, is difficult, if not impossible.

The spirit of association, as Chevalier Bunsen called it fifty years ago, is upon us, and is one of the most signal characteristics of the closing years of this nineteenth century. There are but few signs of organic union; men still prefer to work on denominational lines, and it has not yet been shown that there is anything to be gained by a union of government. But there is a spirit of closer brotherhood dawning upon the world, and it may be safely stated that the one supreme question which is asked by the upper, middle and the lower classes is, not which of these denominations is the most primitive, but which is the most adapted to the needs and conditions of the incoming century. Service, and not creed, is now the test and qualification for honour. Character, not orthodoxy, will be the badge of honour in God's kingdom. Henry Ward Beecher used to say: "I would be a Catholic to-morrow if I thought the Catholic Church the best field in which to develop character." "The Church that is apostolic is the church that comes nearest to acting as the apostles did."

Under all the gusts and storms of human thought, there is developing a spirit of universal comradeship among believers in God. Comradeship in work and worship, the only comradeship that is possible. No wonder Walt Whitman, rapt in ecstasy with the vision of the coming union of men, said:

"What whispers are these, O' lands, running ahead of you, passing under the seas?
Are all nations communing? Is there going to be but one heart to the globe."

Christianity at the End of the Nineteenth Century

Christianity at the End of the Nineteenth Century.

BY

FREDERIC HARRISON, Esquire.

WE are entering on the last lap of another hundred years, as the centuries encircle the growth of nations in swift revolving eras. Let us ask, "Is life growing nobler and purer?" "Does religion inspire the heart?" "Are we coming nearer to the just, the loving, the beautiful, the true?" As we look back over the nineteenth century, is it so glorious an advance upon the eighteenth, or indeed upon the seventeenth? In population, in huge cities, in area of dominion, in wealth, in material prosperity, in mechanical inventions, in physical discoveries, in all forms of material resources—yes! in these the advance has been portentous; wealth beyond the dreams of avarice, dominion that would make Alexander of Macedon pale with envy, appliances that to our grandfathers would seem like fairy tales. But is humanity measured by these material things, by power, by wealth? Our great poet tells us that riches abound not in Heaven—but elsewhere:—

> "Let none admire
> That riches grow in hell; that soil may best
> Deserve the precious bane."

I am not making any barren comparison of one century with another. And I doubt if, even in the narrow limit of a single nation, the general progress of mankind can be turned back, unless in rare and exceptional cases. I am a convinced believer in the gradual improvement of civilization when we judge it by areas and epochs sufficiently wide and typical. In all progress there are oscillations, partial degeneration, and local or temporary ailments. But I must profess my conviction—and I hear the same confessed by the best men and women day by day, that our immediate generation has been sinking of late to meaner ideals, to coarser ways of life, to more vulgar types of literature and art, to more open craving after wealth, and a more insolent assertion of pride and force. The nineteenth century may be judged hereafter to be altogether as much superior to the eighteenth in moral progress, as it certainly has been superior in material progress. But to those of us who are well past the term of middle life there is a painful sense in these late decades that the moral currency has been debased.

I am old enough myself to remember distinctly the whole reign of Queen Victoria. And as I compare one decade with another I note how to-day we have lost much of the higher spirit which inspired our public and private life not more than thirty years ago; how to-day we make idols of things which were then the object of loathing and shame. I am not speaking of glaring examples of vice, of gambling in its multifarious forms, of public extravagances, delusions, nor of special acts of infatuation and greed in political adventures. There are plenty of such things in any age. And it is easy to found general and sweeping charges on specific follies and crimes. What I mean is a gradual lowering of moral tone in these recent years—an abandonment of the higher standard of public opinion, a deliberate acceptance of what is evil and base.

As I look back over the present reign, it seems to me clear that the later years have a lower tone of truth and of honour than that we remember in the earlier and middle years of this period. With all the blunders, wrongs and delusions of the earlier times, our people had some finer inspirations, and more generous impulses for ends which were not wholly selfish or mercenary. In my boyhood there began that long, complicated, and indefatigable series of movements to improve the condition of the people, to lift up the burdens of the poor, to reform our entire financial system, in the interest of the masses and by casting the burdens on the rich—the long labour to secure Free Trade, cheap food, factory legislation, legislation for the rescue of the young, for the education of the people, Poor Law reform, sanitary reform, financial reform, law reform—causes associated with the names of Peel, Cobden, Bright, Gladstone, Shaftesbury, Brougham, Russell, Stanley, Chadwick, Forster, Mill and many more. I am not referring to any special legislation or agitation, nor do I say that it was all wise, or wholly disinterested. I mean that all these various changes in our political and social system were pressed on with an unselfish desire to make the world better, with a genuine enthusiasm for what was good and right in itself which has more or less died out of us to-day. Enthusiasm and devotion to-day there is; but how deeply are they degraded to personal, material and national ambition?

The great religious upheaval associated with the name of John Henry Newman was a thing both deeper and more spiritual than the petty squabble to-day about vestments and incense. There was a generous sympathy with the independence of nations, and practical abhorrence of international oppression. We felt to the heart the griefs of Poles, of Hungarians, of Lombards and Venetians. The heart of the people was wrung to its fibre by a brotherly interest in the great crisis of the United States. The Crimean war, even if it were a blunder and an illusion, was entered upon with a genuine resolve to protect the weak against the strong. I am far from pretending to justify or extol all that was done in the first half of the present reign. But in those days what stirred the heart of our people were those strivings after well being, peace, and freedom at home and abroad, and not the ignoble passion to domineer and to grasp, to pile up wealth and to make a bigger Empire, to beat our rivals in trade and in arms.

Nor is it only that our national sympathies and enthusiasm have grown colder and coarser, but there has come over us a positive turn for vulgarity of thought, manners and taste. We seem to be declining on what the poet calls " a range of lower feelings and a narrower heart " than of old. It is a common observation that the widowhood and retirement of the Queen have been followed by a deplorable decline in the simplicity, purity, and culture which marked the dominant society in the days of her married life. Fashion, as it is called, is now at the mercy of any millionaire gambler, or any enterprising Monte Cristo from across the seas. Victorian literature is declining into the "short story" and the "problem play", taking its heroines from women with a past and its heroes from the slums. In prose and in verse the favourite style is the cockney slang of the costermonger, the betting ring, and the barrack canteen. The reek of the pot-house, the music hall, the turf, of the share-market, of the thieves' fence, infects our literature, our manners, our amusements, and our ideals of life. The note of the smart world is to bluster about guns, war-ships, race-horses, and Rand shares, in the jargon that is current at a race course.

Any general debasement of tone must have some determining cause. And the causes of this debasement are as usual somewhat mixed, and are partly material and partly spiritual. To begin with the material, it cannot be denied that a great change came over the world when it witnessed the triumph of the Bismarckian policy by which the map of Europe was transformed thirty years ago. The defeat and dismemberment of Denmark, followed by the defeat of Austria and the reorganization of Germany, and this crowned by the overthrow of France and the conquest of two of her provinces with 200,000,000 in money, raised Prussia in seven years from the fourth place of Continental Powers to the acknowledged primacy in the first rank. But it did much more. It started a wonderful development of financial, commercial, and colonial expansion. For the first time in this century war had been made "to pay". Industry had been nourished by war. A tremendous war was followed by unexampled national prosperity. It was a policy avowedly of "Blood and Iron", of force and ambition, of might without right. It mocked at moral considerations as foolish sentiment. Its creed was the good old rule, the simple plan—" Take what you can ". " To the victors the spoils!"

The previous wars in Europe, since the fall of Napoleon had all been professedly waged to protect some people from oppression, for defence against aggression, not of avowed offence and conquest. And they had all been the source of distress and heavy burdens even to the victor. But here was a series of three wars in succession which were hardly disclaimed as wars of conquest, which had been followed by prosperity in leaps and bounds, and had raised the nation in eight years to the primacy of Europe of a kind that might demand a century of progress in less violent ways. From the grossly material point of view, it was an astonishing success. Upon Prince Bismarck's death, the repulsive side of the reviews of his career lay in this, that no one thought anything of the question if it were right or wrong, just or unjust, beneficent or retrograde; to them all it seemed, however barbarous from the point of view of morality and civilization, a splendid and typical success. To doubt this was " unctuous rectitude ".

Bismarck set the fashion in statesmanship; he did not long wait for imitators and rivals. One after another the nations of Europe started rather poor copies of the Blood and Iron invention. It was taken up like a new machine-gun. Our own Disraeli was one of the first to try the new weapon. He started the Jingo fever in the Turko-Russian war, the " forward " policy in Afghanistan and Cyprus and he added to the historic crown of England the tawdry paste jewel of Empire. He founded Imperialism, which has grown since like a Upas tree, and has poisoned Conservatives, Whigs, and Radicals alike. Mr. Gladstone himself, with many reserves and various excuses, fell under the spell of it at last, and Mr. Gladstone's successor is now one of the chief prophets of the new Mahdism. British statesmen, to be just, were shy of resorting to the " Blood and Iron " weapon of Europe; but they made an excessive use of it in Colonial and Oriental regions. And in Egypt, the Soudan, in Central Africa, on the Congo and the Niger, in Uganda and Charterland, in Chitral, Burmah, and China they raised the cry year after year of Imperial expansion and trade profits, new markets and the Union Jack.

The whole world followed the Bismarckian lead. Russia, from whom perhaps the famous Chancellor originally imported his great idea, had an irresistible destiny in that direction, as the largest, most populous, least civilized nation in Europe. Austria even added to all her difficulties by another big annexation in the Balkan peninsula. Italy, in spite of her bankruptcy and dynastic weakness, must needs clutch at a province on the Red Sea. France could not be left out, and must make the tricolour wave over part of Siam, Tonquin, Madagascar, the Niger, and at last the Nile. Japan, and even little Greece, took up the Imperial mania. And at last the United States forsook their settled rules and policy, and are starting an Empire across the ocean. All nations, all parties, all statesmen are poisoned with this new microbe that one of them has named megalomania, and Disraeli, Gladstone, Rosebery, Ferry, Crispi, and McKinley took lessons from the great inventor of civilization and progress as based on blood and iron.

And then Mammon would not be behind Moloch; but resolved to show that blood and iron meant good business as well as glory. Gigantic speculations were started in all parts of the planet, railroads across whole continents, mines which produced the income and wielded the resources of an average State, plantations and settlements as big as many a great kingdom. And all these were put upon a footing that was half industrial and half military—like an ocean liner constructed to be used as an armed cruiser. Trade and business, war and conquest, were mixed up in equal shares. Under some charter or other guarantee of complicity from the State, the adventurers issued forth to fill their pockets, to beat down rivals, and extend the Empire in a kind of nondescript enterprise, which was partly commercial, partly imperial, partly buccaneering, but wholly immoral and perilous to peace. It was somewhat like those piratical enterprises under Drake and Raleigh, in the days of Elizabeth, when the Queen and her courtiers took shares in buccaneering adventures to plunder the people of Spain without declaring war.

The opening of the vast continent of Africa by missionaries, hunters, and prospectors set all Europe on fire much as the discovery of the wealth of the West Indies and South America led to the wild scramble for transatlantic empires in the age of Elizabeth. European nations rushed in to fight for the spoil and enslave the natives. And, as usual, our own people secured the lion's share of the loot with abundant jealousy and hatred from their distant competitors. Ruby mines, diamond mines, gold mines, ivory, rubber, oil, or cotton served from time to time to attract investors and to float gigantic adventures. As if the very spirit of evil had been commissioned to tempt our generation, like as Job was tempted in the poem, the era of this saturnalia of blood and iron in Europe was the moment when enormous discoveries of precious stones and metals were revealed to the gloating eyes of avarice and ambition. The pair fell upon the mines like furies, the one shouting out Gold, the other Empire, and aroused a national delirium for wealth and dominion. Already the spirit of Evil seems to have begun his work of slaughter and loss, as when Job in his distress cried out, " The Lord gave, and the Lord has taken away." But are we so sure that death and loss will be made good to us in the end as amply as it was made good to Job?

The various events all coincided within the last quarter of the century now about to end. If we needed a date for this great change in our national and industrial life I would take as a symbol the proclamation of the Queen as Empress of India. It was a mere form, without direct effect in itself. But it served as the baptism of the new Imperialism. The British flag henceforth represented an Empire of conquest and annexation, on the lines of that Russian Empire which, in the middle of the century, Europe had combined to check and humble. The Imperial title was a bauble in itself; but it symbolized the ambition of the men who arranged it. Cyprus was seized out of mere bravado. On the Imperial banner was inscribed the famous motto, *Peace with Honour;* on the obverse of which scroll was deeply graven, *War with Disgrace.* And the vulgar thing with a vulgar name, which is the new religion of the Imperialist, was bred in a cockney music-hall. The Transvaal was annexed by a snatch decree; the Zulu war followed; then the Afghan war and the " Forward " policy of our ardent proconsuls and the Young India party. Governments and parties changed; but not the policy. Egypt was seized; and in eighteen years it has cost us no less than six campaigns. Burmah was conquered and annexed. The rush to the diamond mines is hardly thirty years old; the rush to the gold mines about half of thirty; the Charterland is not ten years old, and it has led to two or three wars, including the Raid.

Analyze its degrading effects on the mind and temper of the nation. Compare the early and middle of the reign of the Queen with the last two or three decades. Who will dare to say that its close can compare with its promise and its maturity—in poetry, in romance, in literature, in philosophy, or in science? Allow what we will for the personal equation whereby the elder naturally looks back to the memories of the *temporis acti;* grant all the tendency we have to be slow to recognize latent genius in the budding, still it would be dishonest to claim for recent years an intellect as powerful and as solid as that which we knew in the middle of the reign. I insist on no particular writer, I rely on no special school. Names will occur to all—Dr. Arnold and his son, Wordsworth, Tennyson, Browning, Macaulay, Carlyle, Thackeray, Dickens, Bulwer, Disraeli, Hallam, Milman, Freeman, Froude, Ruskin, the Brontes, George Eliot, Kingsley, Trollope. All the work, or all the best and permanent work, of these was completed and had passed into the fabric of English literature before the Imperialist era began some twenty-five years ago. Have their successors quite equalled them?

It is the same story in more abstract things—in philosophy, in sociology, even in pure science, the special pursuit of our age. Charles Darwin, Stuart Mill, Herbert Spencer, Professor Owen, Thomas Huxley, John Henry Newman, Pusey, Keble, Grote, Whewell, Kelvin, Lyell, Thirlwall, Buckle, Wilberforce, Jowett, Maurice, Bagehot, Martineau. Three or four out of the forty names I have mentioned survive in extreme old age; but even of these their principal work was completed at the date now taken. I do not deny that many men of high distinction are living and working still, and that there are still with us men of great promise, of whom much is expected. But taking, as a test, influence upon the age and European reputation, the last quarter of the present century cannot compare in its intellectual product with the three earlier quarters of this century. Name for name, the intellectual leaders of our present day cannot be named with those that went before them, either in poetry, or in romance, or in literature, or in science, or in philosophy, or in ethics, or in religion.

It would be futile, of course, to admit the current nonsense about "decadence", or "the end of the century"; for the tone of a nation does not degenerate of its own motion, nor by the date of the calendar. It has a cause, and the cause is plain. No! When Imperialism set in about a quarter of a century ago, we all took to a much more practical, combative, and materialist view of life. We were told to get rich, to fight, to win the game, and the game was something solid and substantial. To be weak was to be miserable, as Satan told the rebel angels; to be poor was to be a failure; to make no conquests, no prizes, no fortunes, was to own oneself a poor thing. Competition ruled everything—education, sport, industry and literature. To win prizes we had to be up-to-date, and we grew year by year more up-to-date. We fell more and more under the rule of the newspaper press; and the press grew more and more noisy, braggart, bustling and smart. It got so furiously up-to-date that it even announced events before they had happened, and smashed books before they had been read. We all had to live in a perpetual rattle which was something like a fair or a race-course, and something like an army of volunteers on a bank-holiday. The reveries of the imagination became less easy, and fell out of fashion. The pace was killing. Stories became shorter and shorter, as no one had time for a long book. The "boss", the "gold-bug", the "syndicate" were terms imported across the seas, and with the terms came the things. The press fell into the hands of the "bosses", then "society" fell; and soon the State itself began to be run by the millionaires much as if it were a railway or a trust in the United States.

All this combined to materialize, to degrade the national life. It is not so much that we have glaring examples of folly, vice, extravagance, brutality, and lust. There are such examples in most ages, and they may be personal, independent of any general cause. The gloomy feature of our time is the wide diffusion of these evils amongst all classes and, what is far worse, the universal dying down of high standards of life, of generous ideals, of healthy tastes—the recrudescence of coarse, covetous, arrogant, and braggart passions. We who live quiet lives far apart from what calls itself the great world have no direct experience of these things; but we cannot resist the common testimony of those who know that during the reign of the Queen, wanton extravagances in dress, in living, in gaieties, have never been so crazy as now, with such sordid devices to scrape together the means for extravagance, such open sale of rank and person by those who claim to lead society and to dictate taste.

In such a world it is inevitable that the intellectual and æsthetic aims should become gross and materialized. The drama runs not merely to vice, but to morbid, sneaking forms of vice, to unwholesome melodrama, to a world of smart harlots and titled debauchees. The least vicious, the most vulgar, symptom of this decadence, is the prevalent fondness of men and women of fashion for the slang of the gutter and the slum. Popular novels, songs, and plays are composed in the jargon current amongst costermongers and thieves. Romance tends to vignettes of sensationalism, to the more cancerous forms of debauchery, and to prurient maunderings over sex problems. It may be true that there have been ages more vicious and brutal than our own; and no doubt the last years of the Victorian epoch are no worse than the Georgian epoch of Hogarth and Fielding. That is not my argument. My contention is that there is to-day, as compared with the middle of the present reign, a sensible debasement of tone. In a famous passage of declamation Edmund Burke committed himself to the dubious paradox that Vice lost half its evil in losing all its grossness. Be that as it may, it is in vain for Vice to hope that by covering its shame with an apron of vulgarity it will succeed in hiding its nakedness from sight.

I have spoken of the material and practical causes of this deterioration of the age. I will say a few words as to its spiritual and intellectual causes. All important changes in the world of action are preceded by profound movements in the world of thought. The intellectual " reversion " to a poorer type in these recent years is due to a certain despairing return to the cloudy intuitionalism, which fifty years ago had fallen into discredit. Forty or fifty years ago the schools of Bentham and his followers, as presented in the Westminster Review of James Mill and John Stuart Mill, of Professor Bain and George H. Lewes, of Herbert Spencer and his followers, of Grote and Cornewall Lewis, eminently that of Charles Darwin and the popularization of the philosophy of evolution, and finally the critical examination of Scripture, which was made common knowledge in " Essays and Reviews "—all these had established their ascendant in the world of serious thoughts, and raised hopes of almost indefinite progress and authority. It was an intellectual emancipation which had some kinship with that of the last century, in the age of Hume, Adam Smith, Voltaire, and Diderot. We may call it the Avatar of Evolution and of Logical Demonstration. And under it a brilliant efflorescence arose—in philosophy, in science, in economics, in sociology, and in real religion.

The philosophy of Evolution and of Demonstration promised, but it did not perform. It raised hopes, but it led to disappointment. It claimed to explain the world, and to direct man. But it left a great blank. That blank was the whole field of Religion, of morality, of the sanctions of duty. It left the mystery of the Future as mysterious as ever, and yet as imperative as ever. Whatever philosophy of Nature it offered, it gave no adequate philosophy of Man. It was busy with the physiology of Humanity; it propounded inconceivable and repulsive guesses about the origin of Humanity. It attempted no religion of Humanity. Charles Darwin thought that "he was generally, but not always, an Agnostic." Stuart Mill fluctuated between a religion of Duty and a very attenuated and sterilized Theism. And Herbert Spencer solemnly announced that the object of religion could only be the Unknowable. Hesitations, doubtings, double acrostics like this about the very central truths of Life and Duty, naturally caused plain men and women to turn away in disgust. Here we say that certain, intelligible, rational ideas about the religious problems of Man's highest nature form the very key-stone of philosophy; that the philosopher who fails to answer these problems so as to convince his questioners will convince them ultimately of little else. Evolution and Neo-Christianity failed to give any answer; called themselves "Know-nothings," prophets of the Unknowable; had not made up their own minds, and did not think it mattered much if they did or did not. The result was a wide and general discredit to the entire philosophy of Evolution and the entire Theology of Neo-Christianity.

No precise date could be given to this reaction, nor did it take any single or definite form. No new type of philosophy took the place of the discredited methods. Within the last twenty years these latter have been gradually losing their hold; and vague thin kinds of Spiritualism from time to time found acceptance. There was nothing like a new system, or even a definable tendency, unless a kind of metaphysical fogginess which uses grandiloquent phrases as if they were real things. If we took any date as a mark it might be found in the burst of welcome when Mr. Balfour's graceful book on " The Foundations of Belief " appeared about five years ago. There was nothing either new or solid in the book, except the pathetic dreaminess with which cynical pessimism and incurable doubt about all Truth was shown to lead up to practical support of the Orthodox Creeds. That the guides of public opinion announced this stale scepticism as giving new life to philosophy and religion, was indeed evidence how deeply the orthodox creeds were undermined, how ready was the philosophy of the day to clutch hold of any cloud that seemed likely to release it from sober study of the earth. All this was a sort of theological " confidence trick." The philosopher says to the simple inquirer: " You are so very little sure of any belief, and are so likely to lose it altogether in this Babylon of ours, that you had better trust me with your faith, and I will put it away safe in the Bank of the Church of England."

A maudlin philosophy based on nothing but vague aspirations, hopes, and possibilities, so that all the central problems of Life and of Man ended in the general formula, " After all, perhaps there may be "; this spread a dry-rot through the mental fabric. There is to-day plenty of activity, of ingenuity, of prettiness, of skill, as there is in any silver age, but of robustness, originality, inspiration, is there to-day as much as we have known and felt a generation or two ago? Take the decade which closes this century (1890-1900), can any man pretend that it equals in power either of the middle decades of the century (1840-1860) in poetry, in literature, in science, in philosophy? A shifty and muddle-headed kind of Spiritualism has mentally made cowards of us all.

And, finally, to take religion, which we are often told displays so striking a revival. In ceremonial, in ecclesiastical celebrations, in clerical organization and activity, no doubt the progress is manifest. The rites of the Churches, the dignity of worship, the parade of Church societies, are in full activity. The Churches were never more " in evidence " than they are to-day. Their pretensions were never higher; their rolls never fuller; their patrons never more illustrious. Is vital religion more general, more effective? Is genuine belief in the creeds more definite and clear? Is Christianity more truly a civilizing, a moralizing force? Who will dare to say so? By vital religion I mean not conventional phrases about getting to Heaven. I mean religion that can purify, direct, and inspire Man's life on earth. By genuine belief in the Creeds I mean literal acceptance of the three Creeds in the Book of Common Prayer in their plain sense. When I ask if Christianity is a civilizing and moralizing force, I ask if it prevents us as a people from injustice and oppression, and as men and women from the pride of life and the lusts of the flesh.

We have been dwelling to-day on the evil things in our modern life, on the chase after money, the rampant love of gambling, the extravagance, the coarseness, the materialist spirit growing on all sides. What have the Churches done to purify and check all this? Who would care if they did try? Who would believe them in earnest in doing it? What were they doing and saying yesterday? Offering up from ten thousand altars prayers to the God of Battles to bless our arms, *i. e.*, that he might enable us to slaughter our enemies and possess their land. Not a voice comes from the official Churches to raise a doubt as to the justice, good faith, and Christian charity of those who have thrust our country into a wanton war of spoliation. Not a word is breathed from their pulpits of respect for the brave civilians who are defending their homes and their freedom. These Republicans, we are told, gather round their hearthstones, whole families together, father, sons, grandsons, kneeling down in prayer—they do sincerely believe in their God and his readiness to hear them—and then wives, sisters, and daughters arm them for the front; and ere they engage in battle, their camp rings with hymns of prayer and praise. At home our own preparation for war is sounded in slang from drinking saloons, which is echoed back in pale and conventional litanies from the altars of the State Church. This is how Christianity works out in practice at the close of the nineteenth century.

This State Church and the Creed, to the husk of which it still clings, never seem so hollow or so corrupt as in the part they play in some national crisis such as an unjust war. Whilst sober men of all parties and opinions can feel some doubt or even searchings of heart; whilst soldiers, statesmen, and the public are open to remonstrance, the only order of men which is ever ready to supply the majority with hypocritical glozings is the official priesthood. It sinks till it becomes the mere domestic chaplain of the governing class—a sort of black police that has to stand by the Government—right or wrong. "Theirs not to reason why," as the poet says. It was an archbishop who told us the other day that God himself "made battles." Improving upon the old Hebrew war-songs about the God of Battles, we are now told that the God of mercy is the author of war, as a means of grace towards a higher morality. Why! No medicine man, no witch-finder in Central Africa, hounding on a savage chief to exterminate a neighbouring tribe, could utter a more atrocious blasphemy.

A church, a creed which can chant such a requiem as this over the grave of the Nineteenth Century need trouble us no more. It is left henceforth to faith in humanity to do what it can to curb the passions of the strong who are thirsting to crush the weak; to teach what is the true glory of civilized men; to preach the Gospel of Peace, which the apostate preachers of Christ have turned into a bye-word, and have made a war cry. These high priests of the New Imperialism have forsworn their own religion and forgotten their own sacred books. Let them turn back in their Bibles to the story of Ahab and Naboth, and reflect that it was the apostate priests who leapt upon the altar and called from morning even until noon, saying "O Baal, hear us." But it was the task of the true priest to say to the King in his pride, "Hast thou killed and also taken possession?"

Sovereignty the Fundamental Conception in Christianity

Sovereignty the Fundamental Conception in Christianity

BY

The Reverend HENRY A. STIMSON, D.D.

THE advanced fundamental conception, in both theology and philosophy, is that man is a unit. So long as philosophy looked upon man's mental and moral traits as so many accretions produced largely by outside conditions and forces—products which when taken together make up the man—it was inevitable that theology should discuss the attributes of God as so many distinct and separable qualities. But now that a sounder philosophy recognizes that man is not thus a product but rather that he exists quite apart from his environment and has a unity that is all his own, it is clear that strictly speaking no one attribute of character is prior to another or more fundamental. Logically speaking or for purposes of study, one may be held separate from the rest, but as in the body no organ can be completely known or its functions and diseases thoroughly understood without a study of the whole body, so, in a much closer and narrower sense, in morals, the elements of character, whether in God or man, are not to be known apart one from another. Confusion arises and fresh strife of words, when this essential oneness is forgotten and various traits of the divine character are set one over against the other or made exclusively the basis of any phase of theological teaching. Sovereignty and love, as justice and grace, are alike involved in the nature and character of God. Separation between them cannot occur, and appears possible only in our thought. They are simply God viewed in different relations and acting in certain directions. All of God is in each. As philosophy looks upon man as an original creation, a distinct personality, who exists apart from sensation and to whom sensations are referred, so theology starts with a conception of God as the one and indivisible source from which all character originates.

Having recognized this, it is still true that one side of the divine nature may be emphasized at the expense of another when a system either of ethics or of theology is constructed; and according as the one attribute or relation of God to His universe be so emphasized, the system will be one-sided, and in its acceptance will be found to produce types of character which, whether strong or weak, will prove to be more or less narrow and incomplete. This has occurred in regard to the sovereignty of God, in the theology of the past. Calvinism without doubt over-emphasized it, and the character produced was both strenuous and hard. That it has been the mightiest force in the production of the modern world, its enemies abundantly witness. When Unitarians like James Russell Lowell and Senator Hoar are heard boasting before distinguished audiences that they have Calvinistic blood in their veins, and saying —the one that "Calvinism has produced some of the noblest characters the world has ever seen, the very fibre and substance of which enduring commonwealths are made;" the other, "When you take out of the history of the last three centuries what has been wrought by Calvinists and those who have thought with them, there remains little else worth talking about;" when the glowing panegyric of Rufus Choate is still a part of our best literature, "I ascribe to that five years in Geneva, when many flocked to be taught by John Calvin, an influence which has changed the history of the world; I seem to myself to trace to it as an influence on the English character, a new theology, new politics, a new tone of character, the opening of another era of truth and of liberty; I seem to myself to trace to it the great civil war of England, the republican constitution framed in the cabin of the *Mayflower*, the divinity of Jonathan Edwards, the battle of Bunker Hill, the independence of America;" when one of Calvin's latest German biographers writes, "Seldom is human work so rigorously ordered according to fundamental truths as that accomplished by the Genevan reformers; it rested upon a marvellous simplicity, clearness and unshakable firmness of conviction;" when Guizot speaks of Calvin as "the great Christian of France;" when historians like Froude and Macaulay cannot write modern history without making their careful reckoning with John Calvin; when above all, enemies of the faith like Renan declare that "Calvin is but the shadow cast by St. Paul," and that the writings of Paul are the causes of what he calls the principal defects of Christian theology; surely the men who believe that Paul had the mind of Christ and spoke and wrote as he was moved by the Holy Ghost, are not the ones to cast disrespect on either the man or the theology which stands as the *fons et origo,* the source and abiding impulse of what we hold most dear.

But, for all this, that theology was incomplete, and there has been the inevitable reaction. We have now been living for some time under the influence of a theology which has delighted to call itself Christo-centric. It has violently repudiated not only the extreme doctrines of Calvinism, but also the conception of sovereignty as central in a theological system, and has substituted for this, love. The movement has not been without its distinctive advantages, and in its entirety constitutes an unquestioned contribution both to the progress of Christianity and to theologic thought. But it also has its limitations. We would give it all credit for its emphasis upon human brotherhood and the variety and amplitude of the philanthropic side of the Christian institutions which if it has not produced it certainly has developed. "Sweetness and light" may not be the most commanding or the most costly features of Christian character, but they are very precious and very attractive. The close of the century would give less evidence of the oncoming of the kingdom of Christ, would show far less of cheerfulness and of courage, if it were not for this gospel which makes so much of the divine love. But when this is said, there remains a necessity of pointing out the weakness of what is simply a reaction, and of compelling it as at best but an incomplete though valuable conception, to orient itself to the fuller and larger truth. The theology that would make love its starting point, can claim no more honorable distinction than its right to the term Christo-centric. But as Principal Fairbairn has well pointed out, a Christo-centric theology is a secondary and derived theology. For back of Christ is the conception of the Father from whom He came, whose message He delivered, whose will He did, and to whom again He returned. Upon whatever inductive study of man and of society it may rest, or from whatever philosophic conception it may proceed, any theology, whether calling itself new or practical or social, that eventually turns to Jesus Christ as its center and chief exponent, will find itself under the compulsion of going back to the same source from which He delighted to declare that He drew His own theology. This compels us to come to another fundamental conception than that of love. Without this, the descent from a true religion to what is only an ethical cult, is far too easy. Without it religion takes on the characteristic of a council of perfection. It loses its grip upon the conscience; it relaxes its vigorous and responsible restraints upon the life. The ethics that issues from it is at bottom a sentiment, and philosophy is seen resting on utilitarianism, or jauntily venturing a justification of hedonism. Under this protection we have had in these days not a few frivolous and superficial thinkers, standing alongside of Christianity, who as Dorner describes them, "being devoid of feeling for that which is lofty, can find no other way of dealing with it than dragging it into the dust, who, blind to the true light and intoxicated with a fancy of enlightenment, pronounce judgment upon the profoundest questions which have stirred and enriched the human mind for thousands of years.*

However we look at religion, whether at its source in God or at its result in man, character is the essential. A true theology cannot be narrower than this. Because character is the starting point and the end, sovereignty based on character is the consequent relation of God to the universe. He is to be loved

* Dorner, Person of Christ, Vol. V, p. 30.

and obeyed because He alone is worthy. He has the right, and no other has right in opposition to Him. The Bible declares that the chief end of God is to promote His own glory, but it also tells us that His highest glory is realized in redemption, and that redemption means the establishment of a kingdom in which God is supreme, a kingdom of love and grace, because a kingdom in which every member yields absolute surrender to Him. The emphasis of the Old Testament upon God's holiness is the foundation of the claim of God's supremacy. The Israelites were surrounded by heathen nations, addicted to degrading forms of idolatry. Their gods were like themselves, according to the conceptions of their own votaries, murderers, liars, adulterers, revengeful, cruel. Over against them was the God of Israel,—not simply the god of a henotheistic faith, a god who can tolerate other gods,—but the one God. That was the watchword of Israel. "The Lord our God is one Lord." To worship any other god was adultery, and the punishment death. He was a separate God, a being of perfect goodness; in this respect alone in the universe. Their conception of Him as dwelling in the light inaccessible, one whose pure eyes did not behold iniquity, before whom sinners could not stand, was fundamental and constant. From the first He did right, and men who would serve Him must do the same. "I the Lord am holy, be ye therefore holy." All the institutions of the Jewish Church were to emphasize this truth. The tabernacle, the temple, the consecration and service of the priests, the elaborate ritual, the anointing of the kings, the call and inspiration of the prophets, all turned the thoughts of the worshipper to the glorious holiness of the one God, whom to know aright is life and immortality. His present reign was the greatest blessing, His final dominion was to be established in righteousness and in truth. Justice and judgment were the inhabitants of His throne.

Love appears in all this. As Kittel says, "The religion founded by Moses knows its God not as the mighty potentate but as the life-giving helper in whom the love of God is involved; it knows Him as the God *sui generis,* who allows of the existence of no other, and in this exclusiveness involves His absolute unity; it recognizes Him as the dispenser of justice, and the Judge, from the loftiness of whose commands and judicial sentences it defines His holiness and covenant-faithfulness. It acknowledges Him as the non-sensuous and spiritual, and thus completes its protest against the prevalent forms of faith."*

God delights in His people, but that delight rests upon their allegiance to Him. It was a narrow conception of God, if you will, that filled the mind of the Israelite, who regarded himself as separated from all the rest of the world. And it is true that the distinctive mark of the Old Testament dispensation is its particularism, while that of the New is its catholicity; but that catholicity is obtained through the redemption of the world in which the gospel of the kingdom is preached and the world is won to a new and abiding allegiance, divine sovereignty is established, and men are blessed through the coming of Him whose right it is to reign. " God so loved the world," is the new gospel. And by that revelation, men who as sinners were without God and without hope, are brought into loving surrender to Him who died for them. He redeemed men in His death, but He saves them by His life. They are to live in Him as living in a kingdom the head and life of which is the living and reigning Christ. Thus love in its fulness becomes the revelation and the instrument by which and in which the right of God to His supreme place in the heart and life of man is established. This right lies back of the revelation. The divine sovereignty discloses itself in the divine love. Theologians contend to prove that the fatherhood and the love are universal, but there can be no question about the sovereignty. It can suffer no restriction. Rebellion only emphasizes it. The wantonness of sin lies in its attempt to deny it. Conscience is its herald, and death is the gate through which the self-accused soul passes tremblingly to its dread account. Rejected love is so

* Kittel, The History of the Hebrews, Vol. I, p. 249.

terrible because it is the love of our God. Love can at last be turned into wrath, because we are dealing not only with our heavenly Father but with our divine King.

To separate this conception of God from all that is loving and tender is to pervert and degrade it. The very idea of sovereignty rests upon the apprehension of the divine character in which all goodness and truth, all sweetness and light, no less than all righteousness and justice, are united. We are not content to limit our thought to that aspect of the divine nature to which our conscious need cries out; we cannot be satisfied with the thought alone of the divine and pardoning love. Our soul is of the nature of God. We look beyond our need, we grasp the future, we anticipate immortality, we long for the ineffable glories into which redeeming love shall at last usher us. There we behold the King in His glory. He is surrounded with the multitude of the redeemed, and their song, it is true, is of the Lamb that was slain. That is their especial contribution to the glory of the hour. It is their peculiar tribute of praise. But they are not the only worshippers, nor by any means the chief, in that great day. The angels and archangels, the principalities and powers in heavenly places give place in their praise but for a moment to hear and join in the new song. They recognize in it a transcription of the song they have been singing from the foundation of the world. The supreme glory of the hour is the delivering up by the triumphant Christ of His finished work, the glorified kingdom, to the Father. "And the Son also Himself shall be subject unto Him that put all things under Him, that God may be all and in all." Thus love accomplishes its work in the accepted sovereignty which has at last won all things unto itself.

Love the Fundamental Idea in Christianity

Love the Fundamental Idea in Christianity

BY

The Reverend FRANK CRANE

IS love or sovereignty the fundamental idea in Christianity? This is the question set before us, and it is one whose answer covers the entire history of Christian thought, from Jesus until now. The inner history of theology, indeed, has been but the story of the struggle of the human mind to shake itself loose from the cramping, regulative idea of God as a Sovereign, into the liberty and stimulative development of the idea of God as a Father.

The keynote of the intellectual system of Jesus, as far as He can be said to have had any intellectual system, was that our relations to the Creator are to be set right chiefly by allowing the idea of His fatherhood to swallow up the idea of His kingship. He taught that the souls of men are to come into direct communion with the Supreme Being in all the free affection of sonship. It was the apparent looseness of this notion, the supposedly dangerous freedom it allowed, that shocked the Pharisee and caused Jesus's rejection by the Jewish people. They could not see that sonship meant anything else than license. Puerile themselves, they felt that nothing could control them but law, and they were unable to comprehend how love could regulate. Love, in any degree, is but desire, and the world, until Christ—and alas! for the most part until this day, has failed to grasp the sublime truth that desire, which in the natural human heart is the cause of all sin and seems to be "set on fire of hell," can be cleansed, transformed into a divine guide and made to be the vicegerent of God in the life. The transition from law to love is so immense that, in two thousand years, mankind is still nonplussed, amazed, incredulous at the simple declaration of Jesus.

The apostolic church faced the same foe that confronted the Founder of their faith. St. Paul rapidly assumed the dominancy of the early church because he most clearly apprehended the meaning of Jesus and translated it into the brilliant dialectic of the Greeks. It was his main theme that the law had passed away, being superseded by the personal influence of Jesus manifested through the Holy Spirit, which fulfilled the law. Inspired by this conception, he flung open the doors of the church to the Gentiles, to "all men everywhere." In this he was met and opposed by the same reactionary spirit which had slain Jesus: jealousy for the system which governed by rules and laws lay in wait for the Master at every turn and at last had His blood, and the same jealousy dogged the footsteps of the chief apostle, sought to divide the church behind him by schism, and to stir up the heathen before him into riot. Everywhere the bitterest enemies of the new church were not the sins and passions of the common people, but the narrow zeal and literalism of those who clung to the outgrown legalities of Judaism.

Passing next to the church in the subsequent ages we find another great conflict, that of the East against the West, the Greek against the Latin. Underneath all the smoke and confusion of the theological battles of that day, down below the multitude of non-essentials that seemed at times to be the causes of dispute, lay this same issue which had been the root-cause of trouble in the days of Jesus and of Paul: to wit, Is religion the influence of the loving presence of God among men, or is it a rule given to men by a distant God? The Greek theologians as a rule stood for the immanence, the Latin for the transcendence of God.

The next great epoch in the life of Christian thought was the Reformation, a period which, roughly speaking, covers the time from Luther in the fourteenth century to Wesley in the eighteenth, reaching indeed until now, for our religious thought is still under the cast given it by the great controversies of the four centuries mentioned. Outwardly the Reformation seems to have been a revolt against ecclesiastical authority, to have been concerned mainly with matters of form and government. But, at bottom, there was the same old *casus belli* under new conditions. Luther had at first no thought of separating from the church; he sought only to throw off the unscriptural yoke of tradition and restore to the soul its immediate privilege of immediate access to the Father by faith, yet the reaction he awakened cried out against him as a subverter of authority, of law and of rule and he was forced out. In the reformed churches the same old zeal for the law and jealousy of God's sovereignty soon became manifested, even as in the church from which they rebelled, and before long the iron logic of Anselm and Augustine became the controlling idea in Protestantism, being revised and adapted by Calvin.

The next and last period was what is called the Revival of the eighteenth century, in which John Wesley is the central figure. His theme was holiness, which was but another phase of the old theme of Jesus—Fatherhood; of Paul—Grace, not law; of the Greek Fathers—God's immanence; and of Luther —justification by faith. John Wesley strove to remain a churchman—but they would have driven him out; just as Luther said: "*Ich bin ein frommer mönch gewesen,*" and would have so remained; just as Clement of Alexandria longed for unity with the Latin bishops; just as Paul loved and pleaded with Israel; just as Jesus "came unto His own" brethren in the flesh.

In all these succeeding upheavals in Christian history one can observe a single mighty idea now struggling up for recognition and again cast down, overwhelmed by the powerful reactionary force against which it warred. That idea was that God's love operating immediately upon the human soul is the essence of religion, is the dynamics of religion; as opposed to, or rather as superseding, the idea that religion has its power in God's sovereignty which imposes upon us certain rules of conduct and obligations of opinion. In each instance the reaction apparently conquered. Jesus was put to death and his disciples scattered. Paul and the Greek system he taught were utterly routed by the Latin bishops who deftly twisted the reasonings of the chief apostle into arguments for their own artificial framework of dogma; the protestant church after Luther was safely caged by Calvin in his iron box of thought; and the movement under Wesley, for lack of intellectual acumen or courage, speedily fell back into the use of the identical old materialism of theologic expression.

And yet the same spirit stirs to-day in the air. In a thousand ways it betrays its insistence. The warm and gentle words of the Master remain, the fiery protests of Paul remain; we cannot escape them; and more and more are men coming to see that the only thought which can win the world, and which can develop and not stunt mankind, is " Immanuel —God with us!" In the twentieth century will come the next upheaval and, it is to be hoped, the thought of Christendom will at length desert the " schoolmaster " and come to Christ, will at length lay aside the last hampering bands of Hebraistic, Latin, Puritanic legalism, and come out into the largeness and liberty of sonship with God, will at length be enabled to " stand fast in the liberty wherewith Christ hath made us free, and be not entangled again with the yoke of bondage."

Let us now take up, more particularly, the teachings of Jesus and of Paul, and see how their whole trend was from Sovereignty to Love, from Law to Liberty, from Bondage to Sonship.

In the Old Testament the prevailing words for Deity are Jehovah, Creator, the Almighty, the Most High, God, Lord and the like, all of which bespeak sovereignty and impress us with the idea of His power over us. Comparatively few are the times He is spoken of as a Father, Lover, Husband and Friend. The Hebrew notion of God was that of a Ruler who gives laws for His subjects and who rewards and punishes them according as they keep or violate His commandments. Occasionally there breaks out in David or Isaiah a pathetic cry of love; "My soul thirsteth for the living God;" "Doubtless thou art our Father, though Abraham be ignorant of us;" but the transcendence of God is the principal theme of the ancient scriptures. Turning to the New Testament we come at once into a different atmosphere. The transcendent God has come to live with men. The Word is made flesh and dwells among us and we behold His glory. With awe and with rising doubts we see Him, whom the heavens could not contain, going about doing good. When one of us speaks to Him of our perplexity He answers: "Have I been so long time with you, and yet hast thou not known Me, Philip? He that hath seen Me hath seen the Father."

This Man wins and governs His disciples by no laws, but by the attraction of His own person. He does not say: "Do this and that, and live," but "Follow Me, come unto Me and find rest, trust Me and receive life." The Christ-rule is not law, it is the power of character.

The notion of divine transcendence and majesty is still there, but it is suffused with the beatific conception of His immanence: the second half of the prophet's paradox is made plain: "I dwell in the high and holy place, and also with him that is contrite of heart."

The perfection of the law is not marred, but it is made to be no longer only a law from a God above but also a law from a God within: not a law regulating bad desire, but a law originating good desires that overpower the bad. The law shall never pass away: but it passes in.

Upon Jesus's lips the commonest word of Deity is Father; He teaches us to pray, saying: "Our Father;" He alludes often to "My Father;" He reminds us of "your heavenly Father." The argument from the lily and the sparrow gets its cogency from the subsumption that we are children dear to the Father heart. We are urged to do good to both friends and enemies "that we may be the children of our Father, whose rain falls on the just and the unjust." In fine, the whole regulation of conduct is to spring from a desire to please Him who loves us so. We are to do good and we are not to do evil because thus our love to our Father prompts us, rather than because we get rewarded on the one hand and punished on the other. For the woman taken in sin He has no word of condemnation, but only those of loving pity. He will not join in condemning the extravagance of her who broke for Him the box of costly perfume, but He perceives the love and ignores the error, and says: "Let her alone—she hath done what she could." Even when He meets the traitorous Peter, after that apostle's shameful denial of his Friend, He has no word of reproach, but only, " Simon, son of Jonas, lovest thou Me?"

In all this we cannot fail to notice that Jesus has put men upon an entirely different footing with God, a footing of loving friendship, not of timid service. "Henceforth," He said, "I call you not servants but friends."

The only instances in which the Master blazed in wrath were those when He came into contact with the Pharisees, who stood for the old literalism, who, in their eagerness to uphold the rulership of God, had extended the law into intolerable details, and whose pride as chief-servants would not brook the entrance of sons.

It is, however, in St. Paul's writings that we find the supremacy of love set forth with Hellenistic clearness and with passionate force. If the careful reader of Paul were asked, what is the pervading theme of the great apostle's preaching, he could but answer: "It is that the Law has been superseded by Grace." And what is grace? It is nothing but the "loving favor" of God, the helpful influence of His personality upon men.

God's relation to us as Sovereign is represented in the law. This law has been, according to Paul, "disannulled," and consequently our relation to God as subjects has been discontinued, its place being taken by a better relation, that of sons to a father, which works a higher and deeper righteousness than the law, preserving all the moralities of the law and giv-

Love the Fundamental Idea 37

ing to them power and life. "What the law could not do," he says, "God did in the person of His Son."

This is precisely the difference between the old "covenant" and the new. A covenant represents the condition or terms upon which the parties stand toward each other. The old covenant (or testament) was an arrangement by which God as Sovereign agreed to give certain blessings, provided that men as subjects obeyed certain rules. That covenant failed; it would not work; it was "weak through the flesh;" by it mankind failed to work righteousness. Consequently there was "verily a disannulling of the commandment going before, for the weakness and unprofitableness thereof." If that first covenant had been faultless, there should have been sought no place for the second. But finding fault with them, He saith: "Behold, the days come, when I will make a new covenant, establish a new relation, to the house of Israel: not according to the covenant which I made with them when I led them out of Egypt (the Sinaitic decalogue) : for this is the covenant that I will make: I will put My laws into their mind, and write them in their hearts, and I will be to them a God and they shall be to Me a people, for they shall all know Me, from the least to the greatest." (Hebrews 8; Paul is assumed to be the author of the epistle to the Hebrews. Even if he was not, its writer evidently had apostolic authority.) Over and over again Paul argues this same point, particularly in Ephesians and Galatians.

By his logic Paul forces us out of subjectship into sonship. We simply *cannot* be good subjects; sin is born in us; there is none that doeth good, no, not one; we have all gone astray; they that are in the flesh cannot please God (save they walk by an inner Spirit); He hath concluded all under unbelief, Jew and Greek, there is no difference; if we abide under the conception of God's sovereignty alone there is absolutely no hope, for only the utter keeping of the law in every particular can suffice, we must abide in *all* the deeds of the law to do them, and this none can do, for if we say we have no sin we deceive ourselves. We are thus expelled from servantship into sonship: " for we have not received the spirit of bondage again unto fear, but the spirit of adoption, whereby we cry, Abba, Father!"

It is not at all the New Testament idea that we are still subjects of God, deriving our obligation from His law, *and using Christ's oblation merely to make good our dereliction in keeping the commandments,* for that would be but a patched up Judaism: it would be *the same old covenant* with a new piece sewed on to an old garment; it would be putting new wine into old skins. The law is gone *as a source of obligation;* its place is taken by the indwelling Christ, who gives us a righteousness exceeding that of the Scribes and Pharisees. The law remains as a *yard-stick, a divinely given test or measure* by which we can examine ourselves and see whether we be in the love of Christ. As such not one jot nor tittle of the law shall ever pass away; it is an ever-perfect guide as to how the love of Christ will make a man act. The law was our schoolmaster unto (or until) Christ. But after that faith in Him is come, we are no longer under a schoolmaster; for ye are all the children of God by faith in Jesus Christ. (Gal. 3.)

From the very beginning men have feared to trust this love of God. It was deemed too faint, too weak. Paul's antagonists accused him of preaching a doctrine that would lead men to sin "that grace might abound." They thought his doctrine trusted so much to human nature and its possibilities that the flood-gates would be open to the iniquitous practices of antinomianism. This same distrust of the power of God's love to regulate man was the foundation upon which the Roman Church built its authority; people *must* have a schoolmaster, they must be given laws and rules; the law of love is too invertebrate! And even until this day the churches strive to keep authority over men's consciences and actions, they must play the schoolmaster. As a consequence, church life is more prolific in religiosity than in character. Unless the churches shall see their error and boldly come back to the liberty of Jesus and of Paul, preaching the power of the inner Christ to regulate all conduct, guided and advised but never commanded by churchly schoolmastership, it is probable that the next century will see the chief growth of Christianity outside of church life entirely, as a social movement and influence, while the churches dwindle more and more into Pharisaic cults.

Is Christianity Founded Upon a Book or Upon a Person?

Is Christianity Founded Upon a Book or Upon a Person?

BY

The Reverend L. W. BATTEN, Ph.D.

IN the period following the Reformation age a mistake was made which has cost the Christian Church dearly, and it will not finish paying the penalty for some time to come. With the enlightenment which came with the new era of learning there was bound to be a revolt from the bondage of the Church. The recent correspondence between Prof. Mivart and Cardinal Vaughn shows what that bondage was. The suspect is required to submit his judgment absolutely to the judgment of the Church, to teach what it teaches, to believe what it believes, and to condemn what it condemns.

The Reformation was in large part a revolt from such an abject submission to the authority of the Church. It asserted in the most explicit terms the right of private judgment. Especially it asserted this in regard to the interpretation of the Scriptures. But men cannot get along without an authority; at least most men cannot. The liberty gained at a great price was abused by some, and not appreciated by others. A new authority must be found just as infallible as the Pope, and satisfying to the minds of Protestants. With nearly one consent this new authority was found in the Scriptures. All the Protestant bodies did not make this authority an article of the faith, the Anglican Church and its American daughter never did; but all alike agreed that the Scripture was authoritative. With the ideas of the Bible which were held at that time this was very well. But when a new light was shed upon the sacred books these rigidly formulated ideas stood in the way of acceptance of new views, and so the Protestant Churches have been plagued by modern Biblical criticism, not on account of the criticism, but because they had set the Bible in a place of authority to take the place of the discarded authority of the Church. The Bible was looked upon as the foundation of the Church, the source of the faith, and the rock upon which Christianity was established.

If we go back to the teaching of Jesus Christ and His apostles, we can easily see that the Bible was never intended to occupy such a place. Moreover we can easily appreciate now what a great chance the men of the post-Reformation age missed, in that they made the Bible their fundamental authority instead of Jesus Christ Himself. Alike in the person of Christ, in the Holy Scriptures, and in the Church, we find both the divine and the human. But there is this difference. In the Scriptures and in the Church there is no assurance that the earthen vessels in which the divine treasure is contained are not of the earth, and so earthy; while in the person of Christ the divine so permeated the human, that the general human frailties find no place. However we may interpret the *kenosis*, we must and do hold to the absolute sinlessness of Christ. In Him, human though He was, there was no admixture of human error. But we have no such guarantee for the Church or for the Bible. There are and always have been errors in the Church, and there are errors in the Bible. Men may differ as to their amount and importance, but there cannot be two opinions as to their existence.

Now if we are to have an authority as the foundation of our religion, it must be infallible. All men have realized this necessity; hence the Roman doctrine of the infallibility of the Pope as the Vicar of Christ and the head of the Church, and the Protestant doctrine of the infallibility of the Scriptures. If the godly men of the post-Reformation age had fixed upon Christ as the foundation of their religion, and had valued the Scriptures because they bore witness to Him, they would have taken a position from which no criticism could have dislodged them, and the Church might have looked complacently upon the works of the scholars of the last century, knowing that their conclusions could not prove disastrous.

If the Bible were really intended to be the foundation of Christianity there should surely have been some hint of it in the New Testament. Jesus never wrote a single one of His utterances nor commanded any one else to do so. The first written versions of the sayings of Jesus have been lost, and there seems to have been no serious effort to preserve an account of His deeds and words until toward the close of the life of the apostles. The early preaching of the apostles was wholly oral, and the pen was for the most part only taken up when it was not possible to reach the people with the living voice. St. Paul wrote only when he could not be present in person, and he regarded the written epistle as a mere temporary substitute for the oral teaching.

Christ gave many commandments to His disciples, He bade them teach and baptize; but He never anywhere commanded them to write. There is no command anywhere in the New Testament to gather the writings of the apostolic age into a book, and to cherish it as the foundation of Christianity. Many of the apostolic writings have been lost, and there is no reason to doubt that those which were lost were just as valuable as those which have survived. But the writings which have been lost are a trifle compared to the oral teaching which was never put in written form. Think what a treasure it would be, if we had all the teaching of Christ, to say nothing of that of His apostles, of which we have but a few samples.

There is a fundamental difficulty about making the Bible the foundation of the Christian Church and the infallible authority in the Christian religion. The Church and the Christian faith both antedate the Scriptures. For some twenty years after the Resurrection of Christ, there was not a line of the New Testament written, and twenty years is a good while in such a critical time as the first period of the apostolic age. And it was a long time after the apostolic age before the various writings were collected and the collection declared canonical.

To assert that the Bible is the foundation of the Christian Church to-day is to deny that there was any foundation in the first Christian centuries, or else to hold that the foundation is different now from what it was first. Neither of these alternatives is very satisfying.

In the post-Reformation age very little stress was likely to be laid upon the historical facts concerning the origin of the Church and of the Bible. Many of the reformed Churches were recent organizations, and the Bible seemed old enough for them to rest upon. If I am not mistaken those same Churches now look upon their connection with the apostolic Church as real though they do not claim historic continuity. The question then of the foundation of the Church, before the New Testament became a recognized treasure of the Church, becomes important to them, as well as to us, who rejoice in a direct historic descent from Christ and His apostles.

The Fourth Gospel may be, as many claim, rather an interpretation than a statement of Christ's teachings. If so, the interpretation is apostolic, and it is remarkable for its insistence upon a personal attachment to Christ as the essential necessity in religion. "If I be lifted up from the earth, I will draw all men unto Myself." (St. John 12: 32.) "I am the Way, the Truth and the Life: no one cometh unto the Father but by Me." (Ib. 14: 6.) "I am the door: by Me if any man enter in, he shall be saved and shall go in and go out, and shall find pasture." (Ib. 19: 9.) "These things have I spoken unto you! that in Me ye may have peace." (Ib. 16: 33.) "Thou gavest Him authority over all flesh, that whatsoever Thou hast given Him, to them He should give eternal life." (Ib. 17: 2.) How sad that devotion to a book, however sacred and however infinitely precious that book is, should have taken the place of the attachment to the living Christ.

St. Paul expressed unmistakably his conception of the foundation of Christianity in a passage in the Epistle to the Ephesians: "Ye are fellow-citizens with the saints, and of the household of God, being built upon the foundation of the Apostles and Prophets, Christ Jesus Himself being the chief cornerstone" (2: 19 f). In another epistle St. Paul says that he himself laid a foundation as a wise master-builder; but lest he should be misunderstood as implying that it was competent for an apostle to choose his foundation at will, he hastens to add, "But let each man take heed how he buildeth thereon. For other foundation can no man lay than that which is laid, which is Jesus Christ." (1 Cor. 3: 10 f.)

With this I rest my plea. I do not for a moment desire to depreciate the great value of the Holy Scriptures. Thousands of struggling souls have found in them the inspiration of a new life. But I do hope the time is coming when the Scriptures will not be forced into a place which belongs to no other than to Jesus Christ Himself.

Christianity and Its Competitors

Christianity and Its Competitors

BY

The Reverend HARRY JONES, M.A.

BY the "Competitors of Christianity" must first be understood those religions which are still widely professed by mankind, and no notice should be taken of such as have dropped out of the race, though they might have taught another life and worshipped unknown gods, or as a cynic, might bow to the statue of Jupiter with a request to be remembered if he should ever sit upon a throne again. We cannot even glance at the cult of Babylon and Egypt, though a Coptic Church from its first, challenged decaying belief in the antiseptic land of the Nile. Nor will we make any account of African fetichism or any vague aboriginal worship of the "Great Spirit", for however much surviving heathen credulity may resist the pressure of Christian influence it is not "progressive." Nor can this be said of the unwieldy mass of Buddhism, though it is adhered to by more than can be counted in the Greek and Roman Churches together, with all professors of Christianity added to them. Of Eastern religions, indeed, there remains only Islam which deserves to be called a competitor of Christianity, though perhaps its vitality may be accounted for by the Christian tincture in its veins. But though we are told of some progress which it is stated to be making among black African natives, we hear nothing of its advance in civilized regions of the world. Where among them can we point to missions in the name of Mahomet?

Setting aside, then, aboriginal or ancient faiths, and those, however vast, which are still sluggishly alive, or continue appealing to the Oriental mind, we come to Christianity, which questions all forms of human religious belief in the name of One who came into this world twenty centuries ago not as a candidate for admission into the Pantheon, but as King of kings, and in the space of three years set up an action among men which has been more widely felt in our generation than by any in the world before. Like its Founder, it was once despised and rejected of men. It hid in catacombs and though a light shining in a dark place, its shine gave no more than that of an unheeded spark. But it now appeals to the simple and the wise in every land known in both hemispheres of our globe.

And who are its competitors? The thought of the Jews immediately presents itself. We worship the same God, read the same Bible, sing the same Psalms, and they are our colleagues in many good works dear to the Christian heart. But our prayers are put up "through Jesus Christ Our Lord". We look on Him as the Author and Finisher of our faith, and a religion which resents His predominance cannot strictly be reckoned among the competitors of Christianity. This is the more evident as now the Jews do not challenge the Christian, being persecuted rather than persecutors. They go their own way with surviving tenacity, and are content to await a Messiah who shall redeem Israel after their own fashion. Judaism cannot properly be said to compete with our Creed.

Far otherwise is it with Science, which professes no religion and does not even call itself a Society, though, as it were, it admits every one into its membership who is willing to learn. It recognizes no baptism except that by the spirit of inquiry and no revelation but such as follows experiment. Its gospel, that on which it rests for the rise and happiness of mankind, is all-pervading Law. This is no bloodless mortal code, but brims with progressive life, involving the use of human goodwill which is as much a result of creation or evolution as anything in the cosmos, and it is by many believed that as this Almighty Law is gradually discovered, man feels the ground firmer under his feet and takes his right place in creation, the kingdom of nature, or as we should say, the kingdom of God. And this kingdom it holds to be visible and invisible since in both it apprehends step after step, the things which have been hidden in the past. It admits no hell but that of obstinate ignorance, and no heaven but that of intelligent enquiring knowledge. And it turns its searchlight upon all claims of authority, including the religious.

It must not be supposed, however, that the scientific man always repudiates the title " Christian ". He uses its language. " Prove all things. Hold fast to that which is good." He quotes sayings of Jesus. He aims at the material and intellectual advance of mankind. Thus he latently influences many sincere Christians though he loosens the reliance of some on the Bible and occasionally takes the wind out of the sails of the Church. It is not that he despises Scripture and the stores of ecclesiastical learning, but they are no more to him than items in experience and history which no honest inquirer can disregard if true to his creed, and that is to learn what he can from any source, never to confuse opinions with conclusions, or mistake a station on the road for the terminus at the end of his journey. Meanwhile he is far from rejecting the hope of final definite instruction which is at the root of all good human desire, whether it be called religious or not. For this he craves, and sometimes is ready to forget the things which are behind, as fresh pages are opened in the book of knowledge.

It is not our business here to enter into the boundless field of competition between brain and heart, authority and reason, or objective and subjective, but when we talk of Christianity and its Competitors the gravest regard must be paid to the insistent world, and that influence of science which some good Christians (rightly or wrongly) look at as a challenger of their faith. This is the more suspected in these days when not a few devout and learned divines have recognized the necessity for taking new grounds in the study of the Bible and parting from some of its interpretations which have been long popularly accepted. The Christian, however, need not be dismayed at finding himself unable to give minute intellectual assent to what he hears, but he is imperilled if he resents that which is called the "higher criticism" even by pious truth-loving divines. Such an attitude changes what would have been a friend into a Competitor of Christianity.

Many, however, are sore let and hindered in the race by something quite different to the criticism of honest learned Christians who are only more anxious to shed a fuller light upon the Scriptures, and so utilize the present eager spirit of inquiry in support of their faith. Those I refer to as perplexed in their course are hampered by the exclusive requirements of some who repeat the same creed and say the same Lord's Prayer as themselves. But, unhappily, there is no truth more profound and far reaching than that seen in the saying of Jesus, " A man's foes shall be they of his own household."

I shall presently notice the drag upon Christianity which is caused, not by divisions, in themselves weakening, and thus mischievous, but by the procedure of some parties so influential that they do not so much compete together, as become hinderers, in what they should unite in advancing.

Meanwhile it must not be forgotten that without being ostentatiously or ostensibly Christian there are influences which rival those shed by our faith and may be called "'isms." Of course Christians hail every effort to forward the good of humanity by whomsoever made, and in the turmoil of religious dispute they may be disposed to say " Nevertheless Christ is preached." But that is just what some "'isms" don't do. They don't claim the spirit of Christ as the Mover of their souls. Some of them would eliminate anything distinctly "religious" from their creed, and thus in a sense must be reckoned as competitors, since they, nevertheless, desire the good of man, and they are intensely eager in the pursuit of their aims. Others may recognize Christianity as an ally, or count prominent Christians among their ranks, but frequently the apostles of an imperative "'ism," question the authority of any creed which claims to have a special revelation from God. Unlike cold-blooded scientists who listen for evidence all round, they pick out certain promising principles of life and squeeze them dry, professing to rely upon the great laws of Nature, as if one of these were not always balanced by another. They admit no compromises, forgetting that if centrifugal force were not met by that of gravitation we should all be whisked off the revolving globe like water from a twirling mop. Strenuous upholders of an 'ism are often one-sided as well as enthusiastic, but when enthusiasm (which governs the world) inspires a specialist in philanthropy who fails to realize the devotion of others, he is like a tree with one branch, and his 'ism becomes to him a small competitor of Christianity. Were he alone, his place in the race would be insignificant, but if he desires an end acknowledged by many to be radically good, his zeal is contagious and a multitude is swept into its stream hardly apprehending the aim of those who press towards the mark for the prize of their high calling in Christ Jesus. Thus they form a body which competes with the holders of our faith, for through the mind of Christ is all-embracing He requires the least good thing, such as the giving of a cup of cold water, to be done in His name in order that the doer may be reckoned as being " with " Him. In this sense Christianity is exclusive, but no more so than sunshine, shed on the evil and the good, but supporting no life in man or beast unless it be assimilated.

It is, however, among distinctly professing Christians that we find some of the most vital competitors of Christianity. For it knows no parties as such, and its spirit is damped by their exclusiveness, or by the substitution of something else for the supreme will of God which Christ came to do in the sacrifice of Himself. That which " competes " with this should be ⬚⬚ ly honoured among men and have a conspicuous place i⬚ ⬚en⬚ce. Indeed, it should have no mere worldly object ⬚ce t⬚ ⬚t one apparently Christian. We cannot sweep off t⬚ ⬚⬚⬚ subject before us simply by saying, " The competitors w⬚ ⬚hristianity are the World, the Flesh and the Devil." It is true that these powers appeal to man, but they address his lower appetites only, taking no notice of his aspirations except to sneer at them. They set his face the wrong way and offer a prize which is seen not unseen, bodily not spiritual. They are of those who glory in their shame, whose God is their belly, who mind earthly things. These three can hardly be called competitors, as even the last in their unholy trio is recorded, at a crisis of temptation, as seeking to divert the aim of Him who came preaching the kingdom of heaven by offering that of the world and its glory. They are enemies not rivals. And a rival should have some reputable aim, such as a worship of God or a hope of immortality, however tainted, mistaken, or superstitious. An avowed enemy is not in the race. He would hinder it altogether, not affecting to desire a prize contended for by rivals. Competitors of Christianity must all run, and run in the same direction, though they must needs appeal to some desire which reaches beyond this world. Possibly, indeed, this hope may be almost grotesquely mistaken, or rivals may so run that those best able to judge may wholly question their procedure though their professed intentions may be estimable. And that makes them all the more dangerous. To use an obvious illustration, a good physician reprobates the quack more than one who scorns any curative treatment whatever. An uneducated empiric may be quite sincere, and honestly desire to enter into the house of healing, but he may despise the door, trying to climb in some other way. So the apostles of Christianity are challenged and its advance hindered, not so much by declared enemies, as by one-sided adherents who would indignantly disclaim any opposition to its influence. They might, indeed, claim the greatest scriptural support to their " opinions " and " views " and profess to hold a leading place in the race divine, as the Pharisees did in the time of Jesus, and honestly enough, for they trusted in themselves that they were righteous, *i. e.* believed this confidence to be secure, and despised others.

But if any have been competitors of Christianity, they were. At all times such as these remind us of the saying or rather prophecy, " A man's foes shall be they of his own household." Jesus came to fulfil the law and the prophets, and who chiefly withstood Him? Not Gentiles, but Jews who in looking for a Messiah after their own mind based their hopes upon the scriptures which Jesus showed the true meaning of. And it was because He did that, and would not interpret them in a hard literal sense like the accepted theologians of His day, they opposed Him to the death, one of the chief charges against Him being that He blasphemed Moses and the law. And when we talk about the competitors of Christianity it is in the record of the Gospels themselves that we can find the initial fathers of such as can be rightly so called to-day. Some indeed of these early opponents saw their errors and may be likened to St. Paul, who thought verily, was quite sure, that he ought to be an enemy of Christ and a persecutor of Christians, but obtained mercy because he did what he did ignorantly, in misbelief, or, rather, misapprehension of what Christianity really was. Many have had their eyes opened from time to time as God teaches us and we are enabled to understand His will, but the old misapprehension of Christianity remains. The men of ancient days made the Word of God of none effect by their traditions and though the tradition be not now precisely the same, it is moving on, and thwarting the spirit of the Gospel as it once did the spirit of the Law. As the New Testament is the only book which tells us about the actual Jesus Christ Himself, though false Christs and prophets have arisen, those who handle it as the Scribes and Pharisees did the Old, are competitors of His faith to-day. He said " The words that I speak unto you they are spirit and they are life " but they are still " words ", and may be used to hide the spirit of the Gospel as well as that of the Law. The letter is nothing without the spirit beneath it, and Christianity is ever liable to be strangled by a punctilious insistence on verbal authority. The old Doctors in the time of Christ were sincerely esteemed as the most orthodox by the then religious world. So men may be credited now, and they may buttress their doctrine with Bible texts while they are really magnifying a sect till it veils the Christianity of Christ. And the smallest thing may block the widest view. A hand held before the face shuts out the world. Thus when the field of Christian vision is crowded with competing definitions and explanations of the Oracles of God and with forms claiming to represent the Christian faith, the sight of Christ Himself is blurred and those who are counted to be runners in His race might sometimes be perplexed at being asked what prize they expected to win.

Forms, in short, it is to be feared, are the chief competitors of Christianity. Of course they are valuable though not necessary, for it is the water, not the cup which satisfies the thirsty man. It may indeed be so beautiful, the giver cannot resist commending its beauty. Moreover, to pass from this obvious illustration, the Water of Life is not contained in a pool so that the ministers of religion can draw thence for their flocks and think that they can thus sufficiently supply their needs. Or, worse still, it is not stored in a tank fitted with pipes over which the sacerdotal officer alone has control. " The water that I give," says Jesus, " is a well of water springing up into everlasting life." The minister of Christ thus seeks to let his fellows know that they are, through Christ, in touch with God Himself, and there are those in every Christian Church and sect who have been and are enabled to do this. But if teachers of Christianity so magnify their office as to make their disciples think more of the " means of grace " than of the Spring itself, who can wonder at their coming to be reckoned among its competitors?

The Doctrine of the Immanence of God

The Doctrine of the Immanence of God

The Witness of Science to this Truth of Theology

BY

The Reverend JAMES EELLS

THE object of this paper is to examine the statements of the latest scientific researches, and to show that such statements really demand from theology the statement of the Immanence of God. It is proposed to show that science cannot be complete without this statement; and that no one can give due weight to scientific thought without being led toward this conclusion. Such is the large purpose, whether it fails or not, to solve the perplexity of the people honestly in doubt as to these things.

The history of opinion goes to show that whenever Experimental Science and Psychology agree in presenting any truth at any period, that truth soon controls the religious thinking of the time. Such a process is going on to-day, and accounts for the unrest and questioning and dismay which appall so many men and women. Religion is by no means overthrown; but it is shifting its theological point of view. We are living in an intensely religious time, howbeit in a time wherein a former theology is fast losing its control. Science and Psychology are in the lead; Theology must follow and be taught. Her gain will be transcendent if she be faithful to her God, and docile to her essentially devout instructors.

And now we must see what this process is. The first witness to examine is Experimental Science. Has this anything to say about God? The method of science is to observe material phenomena nearest at hand. It makes experiments upon these, it studies the way these act in various conditions, and how they can be modified, or their relations one to another be changed. Such study would be incomplete, of course, if it were confined to what exists now without asking whether it has always existed, and whether it existed in the shape in which we find it to-day. What made things take their present form and sequence? This study necessitates an examination of causes, and the fitting of fancied causes to the observed effects, in order to see if the cause and the effect belong together. When men push the method back from one cause to another behind it, at last they must be confronted with the tremendous question, —What caused the *World* in its complex entirety? and not only this world, but what caused the other bodies which we can see at night all round this world? Men cannot take their questions farther back than that. So when they get to this ultimate of observation they must begin to make their answers. To begin with, Laplace put forward the Nebular Hypothesis, which accounted for the facts not only of the existence of this earth, but also for the significant phenemenon that all the planets (all the bodies which belong to the solar system according to this theory) revolve in the same direction, *i. e.* from west to east. He accounted for this by assuming in the primitive fire-mist upon which his theory was based, the existence of various forces more or less contrary and disordered, but which eventually would settle down into directive forces among which the strongest would control. Then the query was put to him, " What caused the original fire-mist? " And the only adequate reply that could be made at that time was that " Matter is eternal; the fire-mist is only a new and transient form which has come from the wreck of former systems, perhaps." This answer men took, and based upon it the materialistic philosophy of the universe. But the old puzzle of the origin of force continued; it had not received a satisfactory settlement. Are there countless forces, or only one force with countless forms? If there are countless forces, how is it possible to change one form into another, and to make such changes according to man's will and ability? Motion for instance may be turned into heat; it may be turned into light; it may be turned into sound. The force of electricity may be turned into magnetism; or into a machine for overcoming gravitation, as in elevators; or into any one of a thousand contrivances which are simply machines, after all, for the better and more constant transformation of energy. Now, if forces can thus be turned into one another, how can the change be accounted for except on some theory, which would make them ultimately one single force? The reply of the last hundred years to this problem is that *all force is one,* which is the astounding and universally accepted theory of the Correlation of Forces, or the Persistence of Energy. This is a tremendous position to take, mainly because of the deductions which may be made from it, and which must be verified if the original theory is to stand. Science did not shrink from those deductions; in fact Science began to make them herself. She said that the only answer to the problem as to how the universe came into being was that Energy was the First Cause. See the step which has been taken. From the position that Matter is eternal, we have gone a little way into the region of the immaterial, and we have gone with our hand in the hand of Science, and Science leading the way. Must we stop now? Must we turn and go back? or will Science lead us on a little farther. If Force and Matter are different,—if one is the cause and the other the effect, what is the working of one upon the other? How do they stand related? In order fully to answer the question, Science must give her theory as to how matter is made. She states the Atomic Theory. In the very last analysis of Matter we find an atom, which is not material but is a combination,—a knot of entangled forces,—and forces are immaterial. This theory of the atom,—which is everywhere accepted as the only present explanation of many mechanical and chemical phenomena,—this theory formulated to show what is the relation between force and matter declares that matter is ultimately force, and that forms of matter which we have in visible, sensible masses about us, are consequently only manifestations of force,—the body which covers and yet reveals the —what shall we say, *Spirit?* yes; *spirit,* for that is the tremendous declaration of the present-day Science.

But there is another series of questions which forces itself into every observation of natural things. How does force work? or rather, how may motion be conveyed from one seat of operation to another? If light is a form of motion, how can the light from stars, millions of miles away be brought to us? If heat is a form of motion, how is it possible to bring the heat of the sun to us across the 93,000,000 miles of space? Light, sound, heat are all forms of vibration, we are told; but to have vibrations there must be somewhat to vibrate, of course. After making all sorts of guesses to meet this, it was finally declared that there is a subtle, pervasive medium called Ether, which fills all space, and all spaces; which cannot be felt, or seen, or submitted to any of the tests of the senses; but which is so elastic as to permeate all substances, and so tenuous as to admit of carrying sound through material obstructions, and light from the farthest star. If we cannot weigh or test or measure this medium, how do we know that it exists? What is the proof of it? "Because things happen just as if there were such a medium, and there is no other way to account for their happening." That is the reason which Science gives. Nothing more of proof than that. And this theoretic ether, is just like the theoretic atom,—immaterial, hypothecated, ultimately spiritual. Yet upon these two substantial theories has been reared the stupenduous and magnificent system of Experimental Science which is the glory of this century; the same which has been appealed to by those who would confidently lift materialism above spirituality.

These two great positions of scientific thought have established the orderliness and regularity of nature's workings. Because of the regular compounding of substances according to invariable formulæ chemists know what to expect when they wish to change the combination. Because of the persistence and the correlation of forces, observers know what will happen if they would modify the law by which any force operates, or would counteract one form of force by another. Immense advantage has come to the students of nature by reason of these. In fact, Evolution was made possible because these truths were at the bottom. It surely is not necessary that we should stop here to outline this marvel of the century, which has in fact revolutionized thought, and man's ideas of the world in which he lives. Let it be said, only, that the doctrine of Evolution is admissible only on a basis of a single directing indwelling Force. Mr. Herbert Spencer, who has the honor of being the only one thus far who has made a comprehensive statement of evolution as carried into all departments, asserts " One truth must ever grow clearer and clearer—the truth that there is an Inscrutable Existence everywhere manifested. * * * Amid mysteries which become the more mysterious the more they are thought about, there will remain the one absolute certainty, that we are ever in the presence of an Infinite and Eternal Energy, from which all things proceed." (Principles of Sociology, iii: 175.) Let us gather a bit of the significance of all this. The whole universe of material things is controlled by a single Force which operates under different forms; this force not only operates upon Matter, but because Matter is submissive to it, *it is manifested* through Matter. This one Energy, scientists affirm to be an Infinite Energy. The testimony of Experimental Science is then, that the world of substances manifests an immaterial Energy, which Energy is considered necessary to explain the origin and the present life and progress of all existing things. All of which is remarkably significant; in fact, it could not be more so, because Science could not go farther, and remain scientific. She has here led us to the limit of her possible seeking with the weights and crucibles, and measures of experiment. What else she might say would be outside her domain.

Turn now to the realm of inner nature, the region of thought and consciousness. Has there been any work there which is better than the old-time speculations? What have the students of the brain, and its activities to say about God,—anything?

The method of experiment has been employed here, as well.

Formerly psychologists dogmatized, because of the paucity of observations, and of the ignorance of how to make them. In Germany, the whole subject of Psychology has occupied the attention of some of the profoundest men. It was taken as a basis of investigation, that the senses in different persons vary appreciably; that is, one man is more sensitive in the matter of touch for instance than another. It took less time for the sensation to travel from his finger-tip to his brain. So with other senses. When this was perceived, laboratories were set up wherein measurements of such difference could accurately be made. It was hoped from a sufficient number of trustworthy measurements to deduct a law for guidance in further investigations. Experimenting continued very patiently, and with rather monotonous results, except to those specially interested. But the conclusion was most startling in its far-reaching suggestiveness. Early in the century the brain was said to "secrete thought as the liver secretes bile." This was the only way in which it could be understood that thought was a function of the brain. Physiologists had dissected the brain, and by many observations had concluded that consciousness was due to a "molecular change in the gray matter." Investigation was kept on this materialistic level. But within the last ten or twenty years a different idea of the brain's activities has come into favor. It starts with the old saying that to originate is not the only function known to physics or physiology. There is a *transmissive* function as well. That is, there is another way to get light—let us say,—than from the originating lamp; it may come to us through the window. This is a transmissive function. So, the brain may not only originate consciousness, it may just as truly be the organ to transmit it. What a tremendous step was taken when that theory was brought forward. As Prof. William James, of Harvard, says ("Human Immortality," p. 16): "Suppose the whole universe of material things should turn out to be a mere surface-veil of phenomena, hiding and keeping back the world of genuine realities. Such a supposition is foreign neither to common sense nor to philosophy. * * *

> "Life like a dome of many-coloured glass,
> Stains the white radiance of eternity."

Admit now that our brains are such thin and half-transparent veils, what would happen? Why, as the white radiance comes through the dome, with all sorts of staining and distortion imprinted on it by the glass, * * * even so the genuine matter of reality, the life of souls as it is in its fullness, will break through our severed brains into this world in all sorts of restricted forms, and with all the imperfections and queernesses that characterize our finite individualities here below." This sets forth the idea as clearly as anything. Our individuality is made by the varying elements of our life which we derive from heredity or circumstances, or mental attainments, or the material body itself. These factors all vary; and these factors restrain the full coming through of this outside consciousness in its amazing fullness. But what is this Consciousness outside ourselves? What is it that the brain transmits, if we grant that it transmits anything? We ask Spencer, again, because he has most liking for what is tangible, and can be demonstrated and examined. He says about this Consciousness: "The final outcome of that speculation commenced by the primitive man, is that the Power manifested throughout the universe distinguished as material, is the same Power which in ourselves wells up under the form of consciousness." ("Principles of Sociology," iii, p. 171.) So the witness of Experimental Science and the latest researches in Psychology come to the same conclusion: there is a power manifested in the world of things and the world of men; this power is one and the same under different forms of manifestation; and that is the "manifestation" of the Infinite and Eternal Energy, the spirit-reality behind matter, the spirit-reality of our own lives.

But the question may still be asked, and with reasonableness, How do these conclusions have any bearing upon the idea of God, as theology should declare that idea? There may be testimony to the prevalence of spirit, but is not that spirit so unlike the idea of God as to be almost foreign? Is there not a chasm so wide between this impersonal Energy and the personal God as to leave the problem still in doubt? The question is perfectly fair, and its answer must be attempted. But first it ought to be said that neither Science nor Psychology could say any more than they have said about this. They are limited by the terms of their study. They cannot go beyond those terms and remain Science and Psychology. What lies beyond belongs to another department of thought. In the domain of each, each has authority. Outside that domain the conclusion is shorn of that authority; it is speculation or logical conclusion. When either Science or Psychology steps outside its bounds, the statements made may be suggestive and illuminating, but they have no scientific or psychological sanction. When, therefore, I read of "an infinite and eternal Energy from which all things proceed' and recognize the description of the working of that energy as corresponding to what I should expect my God to do in the same realm; when in the matters of scientific study I see what corresponds to my idea of God, then I say that Science has borne what testimony she could to Deity, and for me, God is thus recognized through His operation whether the name be spelled " E-N-E-R-G-Y " or " G-O-D." And when Psychology declares that my brain transmits to my life the Universal Consciousness, I know that Psychology has said all that she could say as Psychology to establish my faith in God.

With reference to the question as to the personality of that to which such unflinching testimony is borne, only an outline can be given of an argument which all must develop for themselves. The problem is how to enlarge the truth of Energy into the truth of Divine personality?

Personality is too often confused with the form of an individual. A personal God is thought of by many, as only an enlarged man, as it were. Personality is often set aside because to some it is too anthropomorphic to enter into their thought of God. But impersonality is really as anthropomorphic as personality. "Force" is as much at fault in this as "Father." Both are terms of our cognizance, consequently both are anthropomorphic, essentially. Without making definitions, let us see if we cannot come to an understanding of this personality of God. Thus we shall be more scientific than if we make our definition and proceed to prove it.

Suppose you say that Force,—Power,—governs the Universe. Force cannot direct itself, any more than a wild-cat engine which goes thundering along the railway until it runs into something, or the fires burn themselves out. Force always runs along certain lines, and will keep on unless stopped, or directed. It cannot direct itself, nor does it know any modifications. It must always be the same, under the Scientific doctrine of the Persistence of Force. But the equally Scientific doctrine of the Transformation of Energy demands a power which can change. There must be a power to force, to make possible these transformations. We can see how that power works whenever we take a natural force and use it in inventions. Force can be set aside, or turned aside, or transformed by another power; hence Force itself, and *as* Force, cannot be the ultimate controlling agent in the universe. Scientists have seen that difficulty; and the later scientists have declared that Will is the ultimate agent. Will-power is stronger than natural Force. But is will-power impersonal? Is will an attribute of the stone, or of the cloud? Surely not: it is a personal power, *i. e.,* it belongs to people, let us say just now instead of to "persons." But this does not answer the question finally, because there are indications of something like will-power in animals. And there is room for debate on the question of an animal personality. Then, too, will-power may be arbitrary, capricious, unless itself is directed by a somewhat higher and still more powerful. We do not find caprice in the great movements of nature; on the contrary we do find a most astonishing orderliness, and a regularity which can be relied upon; which would be utterly impossible in a universe which should be under capricious or arbitrary or wilful control. Within ourselves we recognize the existence of a power greater than Will. Your will-power directs and controls your muscular power; but what directs and controls your Will? Your reason, or your love. There is nothing greater than the power of Love. It has inspired the noblest of martyrdoms; has made and unmade kingdoms; has swerved the determination of men hither and yon; and in all the world of men and women there is no force so masterful as Love. At the same time, there is nothing so intensely personal, which is so absolutely characteristic of personality as Love. Force cannot love; Will may not love; yet Force and Will are everywhere submissive to Love. Whatever it be that controls creation, must have in itself this element of love, or there is in the created thing a power vaster and higher than in the Creator. An inexorable rule of logic forbids that you have in the conclusion what is not implied in the premises. You cannot have in a part of creation anything greater than exists in the controller of creation as a whole. If personal power—as love—is in men, then the infinite Spirit which guides, controls, enables men, must have that same power, and consequently must be personal. When once we have divested our thinking of the crude idea that personality is form, then we can see that the Infinite and Eternal Energy must be personal, or man the created is greater than God the creator.

This is the line of argument, very imperfectly developed, which would go toward the establishing the personality of God as necessary even to the naturalistic interpretation of the world phenomena. All of this investigation, crowned by the insistence upon the personality of God, is simply, of course, the completed doctrine of Divine Immanence, of theology. To this doctrine, the age bears satisfactory and triumphant witness.

Certain conclusions must come from all this. We cannot stop in Materialism as the ultimate solution of things furnished by Science because Science herself is more than materialistic in her statements and irresistible deductions. We cannot substitute Science for a more complete and spiritual idea because Science herself is so spiritual as to cause us to be guilty of being unscientific if we stop before she has led us to the ultimate of her own declaring. We cannot take Experimental Science alone, because Psychology has a word that entitles her to be heard. We cannot rest in Psychology alone, because Science as well as Psychology tells of spirit. If we listen to what all say, and carry their statements out along the road which they point out but which they cannot pursue because they are simply departments of thought, we shall reach no conclusion other than that the ultimate reality of this universe is spirit; that this spirit wells up within each one of us in the form of consciousness; that this spirit is the infinite personal God,—immanent in all His works and in us men and women (who are thereby His children),—who is the Source of ideals, the Present Power toward their ultimate realization, and Surety of future existence, because he is the indwelling Eternal Power, which by the demand of the scientific doctrine of the Persistence of Force must last on past every change in its embodiment, even the stupendous change called Death.

Evolution in Its Relation to Man and Religion

Evolution in Its Relation to Man and Religion

Special Creation — Not Evolution

BY

The Very Reverend H. MARTYN HART, D.D,

THE race, in its mental phases, is well illustrated by the individual. A man of active mind and persistent endeavor finds himself absorbed at different times of his life with different subjects of investigation. So is it with the aggregate intelligence of the world; it has its mental phases. During this nineteenth century it has been in the scientific phase. Purely speculative philosophy has gradually waned until the field of mental energy has become wholly occupied with scientific quest.

The profession of science is to know. It observes and states; if it deduces it is only that experiment may give warrant to its theory and add another fact to the repertoire of certain things. Imagination is the scout of investigation. To account for what he sees, the man of science guesses, and then proceeds to observe in order that he may verify, or abandon his supposition. How the visible order of creation came to be what it is, has always been, to every generation, an interesting question.

Human intellect reached its highest development with the Greeks. Sir Francis Galton tells us that the Greek intelligence was as far beyond ours as we are superior in mental equipment to the African negro. And yet, with the exception of a few splendid but unsupported guesses, the Greek intelligence threw no light on the *raison d'etre* of the visible creation. For eighteen centuries of the Christian era, men were content not to enquire, and if any imaginative writer ventured to give some reply to the constant desire to know how these things came to be, he wrote arrant nonsense; it is a standing wonder how reasonable men could be found to copy, and at all preserve, such senseless guesses.

Then the mind of the world turned down the path to which Bacon had pointed, and a flood of light at once burst upon the processes and constitution of nature. Men traced with such success the links of the chain of cause and effect that by the middle of the century they thought complete discovery was within reach. Dr. Bastian declared he could produce life; that given a certain assemblage of atoms, life would appear. Tyndall, however, dissipated the theory of spontaneous generation; and the mysterious artificer remained as completely a mystery as ever. Still the very trend of the scientific disposition is to account for what is, by the operation of forces and devices which are in sight. It is the favorite assertion of the natural scientific mind, that we can account for the things that are, without appealing to powers that are beyond our ken; that we need not invoke the supernatural to explain the natural. This is the logical attitude of the scientific mind. When, therefore, Mr. Darwin published his theory and brought to its support such a vast array of observed facts, marshalling them with the skill of a consummate general to support his position, the scientific world shouted with one voice "eureka"! The whole multitude rushed down the newly opened path; a few of the more thoughtful stood on one side, but only a few, and their feeble protests were drowned in the universal acclaim—Evolution.

But the flood tide is past, and even Mr. Huxley was constrained to say "Darwin's theory is not satisfactory but it's the best in sight." Such a taking idea powerfully appealed to the ready, thirsty mind; it was gladly received; the scientific thought of the world became so fully occupied with it that it filled the whole outlook, and evolution was expected to account for everything; instead of listing evolution as one of the many agents detailed to fill the world with charming variety, it has been made to reign alone. Too much has been expected of it;

and as is always the case, it is beginning to fall into disrepute; only beginning, it is true, but evolution is stepping down from the throne.

From the very outset of the Darwinian craze there were men who kept their heads. They pertinently asked, "If environment and the struggle for existence are to be credited with the marvellous diversity of animal and vegetable life, why is it, that the process is not now in evidence? Why is it, that we have not presented to us, a whole gamut of creatures passing by easy gradients from one species to another?"

The reply that the intermediaries, not having reached fixed and valuable distinctions, were hipped in the race and died out, is a very feeble and unsatisfactory answer. Because even if this were so, we should have the process going on before us, and we should have the opportunity of witnessing the disappearance of some, at least, of these transition forms. But none are in sight. If the causes Darwin suggested are responsible for producing what we see, and if these causes are natural, and have been and always are in action, then the animal kingdom, instead of being divided into species, distinct and permanent, would be in inextricable confusion; by this time all dividing lines would have been obliterated and classification would be impossible. One would have thought that the single observation, that Hybrids are sterile would have thrown the gravest doubt upon the theory, that all had come from the same protoplasm and were therefore of the same sort. But so far from nature showing any disposition to mingle classes by evolving one class, by gradual changes, from another, and cross breeding would be presumed to be an eminent factor in the process, she puts her veto upon the first attempt, and even in the case of such neighborly animals as donkeys and horses she decrees that their co-habitation shall not be allowed beyond the first venture, and has ruled that mules shall be sterile.

Again, if evolution were responsible for the production of all the vast diversity of the animal and vegetable kingdoms, why should the best have appeared first? Or why should not the best be with us now? At the very dawn of life the Trilobite looked out upon his world with a wondrous eye—a pyramid of eyes, indeed, a far more capable and complex organ than the eyes now in use; curious, that at the very outset evolution should have made such bounding progress. And if evolution had achieved such masterpieces as the monarchs of the fish world in the Devonian times, and such glorious creatures as the pterodactyls later on, why should the kingly power have lapsed? Why should degeneracy have set in and evolution stayed its progress? Why should it not have produced still mightier monarchs, and not left us with their reduced and puny representatives? Or look at the butterfly nation. Who can for a moment believe that the interminable variation of color and design can, in any sense, be the product of utilitarian desires? If the gorgeous decorations of the flitting beauties be for the purpose of sexual attraction, or even for escape from birds when resting on flowers of similar hue, why should not all butterflies be more or less alike? Or why should the underside of the wings of some moths be exquisitely painted when the wing is only spread by night, and as far as we can comprehend, has actually no opportunity of exhibition? Evolution will not account for these things. Then what will? Let analogy lead to the reply.

There must be as many orders of life above us as there are below us. It is unreasonable, unscientific, to deny these mighty Intelligences less power over material organizations than we ourselves possess. We, by the use of processes which an empirical experience has hit upon, can work magical changes in the floral world without even guessing the cause by which our results are effected. If we, blindly groping, can work such wonder as to produce the American Beauty from the wild rose, what must be the capability of the Intelligence above, who can manipulate vitality at its very source and from its initial impetus direct the every detail of its future career? Once admit that the visible world is a working model of the invisible world, and all perplexity as to the peopling of the earth and the seas with an interminable variety of organism is at an end.

This new fountain pen, which I am using, is the latest development of this most useful article. This implement is the product of the inventive genius of a hundred men; each one of these inventors improved upon the work of somebody else. Use this analogy to account for the form and coloring of some animal. Some Intelligence, within whose capability it is so to manipulate vitality that it will secrete an organism of a certain design, starts such a creature on its existence; this same Intelligence, or another, observing the creature thus designed, conceives of an improvement or a variation in form; using the model to his hand, he produces another vitality which has the property of building up for its habitation and for the propagation of its kind, a body of a new design.

The variety of the world of life is no doubt produced in the same way as the variety of things with which we have surrounded ourselves. The inventive faculty of the Intelligences above us is accountable for the one, just as the inventive genius of men is the cause of the other. It is not sensible to object that the Spiritual has no capability of manipulating the material, for these bodies of ours are the work of that germ of vitality which was the contribution of each of our parents. That a protoplasmic cell should have in its inert matter the prodigious capability of producing my body which carries in it a memory of my father and mother, is a suggestion too absurd to entertain. That unseen, indescribable, and as yet wholly unobserved power we call "life" is the mysterious agent which builds up all organisms. That this "life" can have impressed upon it definite characteristics, is evident from the patent results. Take, for example, the cell of the bee. It is a problem many a mathematician has solved, what shall be the shape of a cell which shall contain the most honey and be of the maximum strength, with the least expenditure of wax. The answer to this question is, that the cell must be hexagonal, that the two angles of the rhomb shall be 109 deg. 28 min. 16 sec. and 70 deg. 31 min. 44 sec., that the cell shall have a certain slope in relation to its upper and lower attachments. It is perfectly clear that some Intelligence, whose mind works in the same way as our minds do, solved that problem; and when that Intelligence produced the bee vitality, this fact was impressed upon the character of the " life "; so that when that " life " builds up for its occupation a body, the organ which supplies the bee with intelligent direction, which we call instinct, causes this thought to come into operation, and the creature uses the result of mental acumen of the Intelligence which invented him, without being at all capable of following the reasons which led to the conclusion. There is no other feasible way of explaining the phenomenon of instinct. All those possible variations and rudimentary organs, triumphantly pointed to in support of the Darwinian theory are latent possibilities included in the original character of the " life ", placed there ready for emergency. Just as the modern loom is provided with apparatus which is called into play only when the shuttle thread accidentally breaks, in this emergency the contrivance comes into action and the loom stops.

There is no better proof that the world of life has been peopled by special creation, and if anything is due to evolution, the capabilities of change under certain circumstances were registered in the original quality of the " life "—than man himself. If man was the product of this gigantic Intelligence, Evolution, it was natural that the quadrumana, most of his build, should be considered his forbears. But it is a long call from the best of the monkey species to the worst of the human species. The brain of the largest ape is not more than half the size of that of the human infant. If we were the product of evolution it would require, to bridge this chasm, not one " missing link " but a hundred; whereas, not one has yet come in sight. As far as we are at present advised, man appeared suddenly and lately, upon the stage of mundane life. Mr. S. Laing in his " Human Origins " says that only a mind hopelessly prejudiced will any longer deny the existence of the Tertiary man; that is, that man was on this planet before the glacial epoch. But Mr. Laing is not a geologist, and his assertion is worthless when contradicted by such an array of authorities as Boyd-Dawkins, Prestwich, Page and LeConte; or to make a convenient summation of the series, Sir John Evans, from the elevation of the Presidential Chair of the British Association last year at Montreal, after surveying the whole field of enquiry, declared the Tertiary man was not yet in sight. Mr. Laing pins his faith to the Calaveras skull and the Nampa figurine. But these two dubious relics are the product of a country which still holds in keen memory Mr. Barnum's Muldoon. The astute showman befooled almost the whole of scientific society by making, baking, burying, finding and advertising a true fossilized man. The Calaveras skull, it is openly asserted in the neighborhood, was placed in a mine in auriferous sand which lies beneath a flow of basalt in Calaveras County, California; if the skull was a genuine find, its owner lived before the plutonic volcano belched forth the basalt, at a very early geological period. But even if this were the case, the skull would lend no support to the evolution theory, for it is similar to those produced by the Indians of the territory, to one of whom, without a doubt, the Calaveras skull belonged.

At Nampa, in Idaho, a well was being bored, the sand bucket brought up a baked earthenware doll about one and a half inches long. One of the oldest members of the U. S. Geological Survey, who has worked over the whole of that area, writes to me that he has no doubt one of the well sinkers dropped that "figurine" down the bore to "please the old man", who was extremely curious as to what came up from 150 feet below the surface. He was gratified and apparently so is Mr. S. Laing.

The human remains found imbedded in the floors of limestone caves in Belgium—of which the most celebrated are the Engis skull, the Neanderthal skull, and the skeleton of Cro-

Magnon, likewise lend no support whatever to the evolution theory. Whatever their age, and they are certainly later than the glacial period, they are no different from many skulls now in use. The "Old Man of Cro-Magnon" was over six feet high. Quatrefages, the French naturalist, compared his skull with that of a Bishop of Tours of the fourth century, and whatever might have been the peculiarities of the shape of the hunter's head, they were even more pronounced in the head of the Bishop.

All authorities, whose careful and unbiassed observation claim our respect, agree that the first appearance of man on our globe, as declared by his relics, is a line of men who lived close to the edge of the melting glaciers. In America and Europe the post-glacial drift, that is, the banks of the rivers formed by the sudden melting of the ice cap, which in those days came far down into our temperate zone, have furnished already some 3,000 flint arrow heads, stone knives and hammers, and culinary implements. There is no question whatever, therefore, that man saw the retreating ice and lived on the edge of the melting glaciers. Who were these people, and why were they here? The common sense reply would be, they were men who had migrated from the original stock, and to escape the intolerable heat which was melting the great ice fields, they had come so far north.

If the Biblical narratives of Genesis be history, this migration must have occurred in the four centuries between the Flood and Abraham's time; for the patriarch's days were times of literary activity; they were making and reading famous books, they had a postal system and were even translating from Acadian, then a dead language; these are historical times, and the glaciers must therefore have disappeared previous to Abraham, between him and the Flood; that is, not 4,000 years ago. That this was actually the case, we are now in a position to prove. The best measure of the time since the disappearance of the ice is the wearing of the seven-mile gorge by the Falls of Niagara; the Falls began their eroding work when the ice barrier was removed from the Mohawk valley. If, therefore, we can learn how long the Falls have been in existence, we shall know when the glacial period terminated, and when men began to appear in the neighborhood of the melting ice. This problem has engaged the attention of most of the eminent geologists; and the estimate has gradually grown less and less, from that of Desor, the French glacialist, of 3,500,000 years, to that of Dr. Julius Pohlman, of Buffalo, who has lately given conclusive reasons for believing that the Falls have not been in existence more than 3,500 years.

Some unwonted energy in the furnaces of the sun threw upon the earth such heat as to render living in the Euphrates valley uncomfortable. The meaning of the names in the "genealogy of Shem", in the eleventh chapter of Genesis, gives us a clear indication that this was the actual fact. Many people moved northwards to find comfortable existence. When the iron implements they had brought with them wore out, they were constrained to use flint. Necessity was the mother of their invention. The shortness of the time is no detriment to this theory. In three centuries a moving people, driven by a permanent cause, could go over the globe. One century, actual experience has shown, is sufficient for a colony, cut off from the mother country, to relapse into savagery. It is astonishing how rapidly human changes occur. It is only a little over three centuries since Queen Elizabeth was reigning over six million Anglo-Saxons, only one million of whom could read and write; and now see the dimensions and deeds of the race! Deterioration is naturally far more rapid than advance; Xenophon tells us, that in two centuries after the fall of Nineveh even all memory of the mighty city had disappeared, and the desert covered its once luxuriant site.

We are acquiring a more just estimate of the time required for geological and human changes; and a more careful reading of the early narratives of Genesis, with an honest appreciation of the geological history of early man, will yet convince the thinking world that man appeared suddenly on this planet six thousand years ago; that he was the product of special creation and not the outcome of a process of evolution.

If man be the product of special creation, and not the result of a process of evolution, then, if it does not follow of necessity, it becomes more than probable that his religion, the bond which binds him to the unseen Deity who called him into existence, was communicated to him.

The same inducements are to be found, on observing the variety of religious sentiments possessed by the families of the human race, for believing that these religious sentiments are the result of evolution under different environments, as are cited in support of the ascent of man from animal forms beneath him. Just as the palæolithic man is supposed to represent the earliest stage of his rise from the plane beneath him; so the crude conception of God and the primitive forms of worship belonging to savage tribes, are supposed to be the beginnings of that development of the religious idea which finds its latest and most advanced form in the Christian religion.

But we have shown that there is every reason to believe that the men of the stone age were descending, not ascending; that they were men who had been driven to the edge of the melting ice under the stress of the high temperature which put an end to the glacial epoch; that whatever civilization they had known in the Euphrates valley, they had lost; and compelled by the necessities of roaming life, they were reduced to an all but savage state. The religious history of the race has a similar record.

If man is the work of special creation, it is impossible to suppose he was turned out by his Maker in the shattered condition in which we behold him to-day—a bundle of possibilities without capability of their attainment; the sport of every chance; the victim of a multitude of ailments; with a heart biassed to evil. This cannot have been his pristine condition; at first, he must have been created as morally complete as he was physically. He has evidently fallen; but in the ruin that he is, he carries the memory of his former greatness. And one of the evidences of what he used to be, and one of the hopes that is with him of regaining the estate that he has lost, is the instinct of prayer that is natural to him. His heart has still an attachment to his Maker and his face is still turned toward the place from which he came. There must have been a time when the "religio", the bond that bound him to his Maker was very close. Then he could hear the voice of the Lord God daily. The entrance of evil separated between him and the celestial world; now he can hear no longer the voices of the other world; he has ears to hear but he hears not; he has eyes to see but he cannot see the kingdom of God.

It is impossible to suppose that the disobedience of the man made an essential alteration in his Maker. Sin affected the man. God was still his Father, and at once, with the solicitude of a Father's heart, undertook the cure of the desperate disease with which his child had become smitten. He communicated to him the process of cure. It is true the man supposed the effect of the cure was to be almost instantaneous. Eve called her first son "Jehovah", the deliverer. But the creator knew how vitiated had become the springs of human vitality and how that the race must have a fresh start by the importation of a new and pure vitality.

How this new life was to be produced, and how it was to be obtained by each individual of the race as he crossed the stage of human life, the Lord God must have communicated to the man, and He committed the story of this redemption to the symbolism of sacrifice. The proof of this rests in the universal practice of sacrifice.

If the idea of God be due to evolution, under the impetus of the instinct to pray, then it will be necessary to show some natural connection between the ritual of sacrifice and the relief of the sense of shame and fear consequent upon the knowledge of guilt. But there is no such natural connection. What the killing of an innocent creature, the burning part of it and the eating the rest, has to do with propitiating the Deity, enraged because of the violation of His supposed laws, it is impossible for the most fertile imagination to suggest. To account for sacrifice amongst savages upon this supposition would presuppose that the connection was so evident that the unintelligent could perceive it; whereas its explanation has taxed the philosophic mind to the utmost, and taxed it in vain. It has been urged that the basic idea of sacrifice was sitting down to meat with the Deity; but so many previous ideas must be predicated as present before that supposition could take form, that the application of the theory to the savage mind is untenable.

If, as is often the case, we found it universally held that the transgressor inflicted punishment upon himself to appease the Deity, it would have been no cause of wonder; but such a thought is by no means universal; whereas the notion of sacrifice is so widespread, especially among ancient and primitive peoples, that its presence can be accounted for only upon the supposition that its institution was a revealed command, and its ritual was constructed to tell to successive peoples, independent of the changes of language, the essential truths of the process of Redemption. It is impossible to see so enlightened a people as the Hebrews for 2,000 years persistently sacrificing, with scrupulous regard to a prescribed ritual, and not admit that sacrifice declared that religion cannot be the output of any process of evolution, but was definitely revealed to our first parents by their Creator, when he found that Redemption was necessary.

How degeneracy occurred; how variation from the original institution rapidly set in, St. Paul tells us in the first chapter of his Epistle to the Romans, and we have a pertinent illustration of the truth he advances in the sacrifice of Cain. When man, disliking the disobedience required by following the prescribed form of sacrifice; rebelling against the purity of its teaching that for a worthy sacrifice the worshipper must partake of the spotless innocence of the August victim the animal upon whose head he confessed his sins, typified; they invented a ritual for themselves, then God " gave them up to a reprobate mind ".

To this process may be traced all those crude notions which have been used as arguments for the evolution of religion. They are not steps in an upward movement, any more than the stone arrow heads are proofs of the dawning intelligence in ascending man, but they mark degeneracy.

The earliest generation had a clear notion of the moral nature of the Lord God and a plain revelation of His plan of salvation, written in the speaking symbolism of sacrifice; but not liking to have a God of such holiness and purity of nature in all their thoughts, they gave themselves up to " vain imaginations " and deliberately discarded the revealed for a human religion which should be more in harmony with their fleshly minds; and in the idolatrous worship they concocted they found excuse for giving reins to their filthy lusts. And religions are not proofs of the human mind beginning to grope after God, but of rapid departure from a pure and revealed religion.

Evolution in Its Relation to Man and Religion

Evolution in Its Relation to Man and Religion

BY

EMIL G. HIRSCH, LL.D.

THE year 1859 marks an incisive epoch in the history of human thought. The publication of Darwin's researches and the formulation of his hypothesis gave a mighty impulse to all studies concerned with the interpretation of nature's mysteries. And as a tenant of the circling globe man himself was asked to show the credentials to entitle him to retain the proud position which before had been conceded him as the chosen ruler and the appointed subduer of the earth. While the story of the planet was rewritten and life's ascending progression was traced by new co-ordinates, new charts were also demanded and drawn by those who would pilot man to the port of spiritual and moral certitudes. Religion in a degree no less intense than physics or zoology fell under the necessity of rearranging its household. The duty was laid upon its interpreters to reexamine its possessions and to reformulate its verities in the terminology of the new method.

Under the first shock of this urgency much alarm was expressed lest by the application of the hypothesis of evolution to the phenomena of religion God's altars would crumble. Many voices were raised in caution and in denunciation. Bold investigators were bidden refrain from lifting the curtain which had shielded against the intrusion of the profane the holy of holies of solemn and solid faith. On the other hand they were not few who triumphed that the new finds of natural science and the new key wherewith the runic signs of the rocks and the rills, the pebbles and the plants were deciphered had forever unmasked religion as an arrant usurper of the throne. Closer inquiry into the bearings of the theory of evolution and its results has quieted the early apprehensions and has silenced the boast of religion's detractors.

In the first place the hypothesis of evolution stands only for a method of interpretation of known data. As such a method it cannot affect the facts to which it is applied. The world is what it is whether we read its past in terms of evolutionary processes or hold it to have leaped into its present shape under the creative impulse effective in the very first moment of its existence. Man is the supreme fact and this fact is unshaken by the method to which resort is had in the curiosity to account for it. Religion is a force now vital and effective in the life of both the now existing man and the now organized society and this certitude is independent of our theories and hypotheses framed to explain the stubborn fact and persistent force. Science is always and in every department restricted to the "how". It is incompetent to deal with the "what". The line running from the source to the wave under investigation is under its inspection. The source itself is hidden from its view. Evolution is incompetent to answer the inquiry into origins. It outlines processes subsequent to the origin and leads up to the results through the processes grown out of the unexplained and unaffected origin. This inherent limitation recognized, religion's title is as secure as ever it was, the substantial acceptance by religion's expounders of the doctrine of evolution has removed or shaken none of the sanctuary's supporting pillars.

Furthermore the hypothesis of evolution as the one process which life employs in the successive unfolding of its phases postulates the necessity and legitimacy of whatever has come to be in the course of this evolutionary process. Religion is. Comparative anthropology has demonstrated that religion is one of the universal functions differentiating man from his predecessors and antecedents in the tenure of earth. Where man, there religion. This indisputable fact postulates religion's indispensability. Human nature then is so constituted as to evolve religion; religion must therefore correspond to a natural need of man. He would not have become religious had there not been in his composition something to which his religiousness is the corresponding answer. The very theory of evolution assumes that nature produces nothing which had not to be. Whatever is, had to be. Religion being, it had to be.

But when examined under the angle of view of the evolutionary hypothesis the rights of the higher religions to recognition will be found to be confirmed much more strongly than they are without the application of the method. The equivalence of the various religions is negatived by the very fundamental assumption of a development from the lower into the higher. The only classification which must be abandoned is that which divides religions into revealed and natural. This division is arbitrary. There is no religion but is credited by its devotees to own the higher credentials of a divine revelation. The Jew is convinced of this title of his faith and the Mohammedan is as strenuous as the Christian in this insistence. The new method saves us from the dangers of these quicksands of individual arrogance. By the fruits, the tree is known and valued. If certain religions have risen to higher outlooks and uplooks than others, their superiority must be due to an original dower of superior vigor, of deeper sympathy, of nobler spirituality, or to a difference in environment and historical experience. But science while enumerating and cataloguing them is incapacitated from explaining the reason for these original differences or subsequently differentiated experiences. It recognizes them and from them as its data it draws its inferences. And thus the evolution theory puts into a new form but with more definite emphasis the old contention worded in the phraseology of the old theology which attributes to the higher religions the authority of a divine revelation. Common in origin, rooted alike in a universally human need, all religions are authentic and authoritative but as some have grown to deeper potency than others the evolutionist thinker can have no hesitancy to press this fact and deduce from it the unavoidable inference that the religion which has attained to a higher outlook or carries the power of a stronger message has demonstrated its superiority beyond all doubt and dispute. In the valuation of religions before the forum of the evolution philosophy the inquiry into effects not that into origin is decisive.

Nor does evolution bear on the tenability of the fundamental tenets of the faith. God and Providence, redemption and Messianic fulfilment, sin and atonement connote truths which stand regardless of the media through which the mind looks at the impressive problems of human life. Human life has in its evolution run in a groove which for ever placed man face to face with the perplexity of his destiny and duty. The recognition of the want of harmony between his ideals and his conduct, the sense of weakness and imperfection which burns within him is operative in the mind and decisive in the soul of man whether we regard him as the last link in a continuous chain of evolving life or as a direct creation disconnected from any form of life antecedent to him. Religion retains its function as the organ through which answers are given to the searching and confiding heart and direction is given to the wavering will of man. Under the impulse to all studies by the proclamation of the theory of evolution the science of comparative religion was cradled. Its preoccupation is the investigation of the religious life in all of its manifestations. Its finds have lent new emphasis to the truth that religion is a vital force in the moulding of social factors. It is the bond which binding man to his fellowman leads the individual to the acknowledgment of the social will as the superior authority and from this as a basis proceeds to the recognition of the highest will in the universe. The truths of the highest dogmas are thus confirmed anew by the newest theories. They require only a reformulation.

DuBois-Reymond and other great thinkers have not been slow to admit the limitations of the analytic methods of the scientists. The origin of life, the evolution of thought and consciousness and the rise of conscience are gaps in the hypothesis which to fill or to bridge science is incompetent. Granted that man is a descendant of the simian, the fact that he is no longer a simian but speaks and thinks and progresses and controls the forces of life in a degree in which none of his supposed ancestors knew how, demonstrates his inherent distinction over all other beings and accentuates the exceptional position assigned to him in the economy of life. Not one single jewel has been taken out of his regal crown. To the contrary the theory of evolution has added new lustre to his diadem. He is but "little less than God." He shares the creative energy with the God who appears at every link of the chain as the power which is immanent in and directive of the long process and from whose mind whatever has come to be is derivative. For involution is the indispensable premise of evolution. Nothing can be in the result which was not potentially infolded from the very beginning in the germ. If at the end of the chain of evolution man appears as a thinking, conscious and moral entity, thought, consciousness and conscience must of necessity have been involved in the very first impulse and the primitive components of this process. And as matter cannot have begotten what is not material, as action and reaction of chemical elements cannot event in thought or conscience, the very theory of evolution leads infallibly to the reasonable assumption of mind and moral will as the ultimate and primary elements underlying all that has come to be or will ever come to pass. Evolution has merely replaced by a higher teleology the crude theory of purpose and plan as maintained by former thinkers. If evolution shows one thing it is this, that in the chain of being and becoming, one thing always is for another, by a law which admits of no deviations. We are because others were before us and therefore we must in turn live under the consecration of the solemn responsibility which is upon us for others. The teleology of the evolutionist is not mechanical but moral. Evolution thus lends a new potency to the idea of atonement through vicarious sacrifice.

One is for the other and through the other is the insistent text of this interpretation of life. An endless longing for greater perfection and deeper harmony runs in ever increasing pressure along the curves of evolving life. And this perfection and peace come to be realized through the sacrificial transmission of strength and power and enthusiasm and love on the part of the great and good, the "more divine" of the race whose life is indeed an uninterrupted dying that others may have a greater portion of life.

Evolution controverts indeed the theory of man's fall. It reads his career on earth in terms of a rise. Descended from others lower than himself he ascends to loftier altitudes. Sin is result of want of harmony between attainment and altitude. The sinner is he who willingly lags behind in the ascent. Moral progress is as insistent as is material and physical evolution. The morally strong draw the morally weak along in their upward climb. This from the view of evolution is the atoning function of the noble martyrs, the crucified. Their resurrection is real in the rise of their fellows to new and noble possibilities.

Evolution finally permits also outlooks into distances and immortalities unknown to the adherents of the older methods of reading God's signs. The process as now surveyed is of necessity only a part of the mightier process still unrun. In that process what now is will continue to be. What is cannot cease being. It may undergo a transformation. But it will be. Mind is, soul is. It cannot die. The messianic hope that at the end of time this evolution will culminate in perfection and peace is grounded and anchored in the very elements of the hypothesis. It is its necessary corollary. Without it, the theory fails at the vital point. It is suspended in mid air.

He who adopts the theory must modify his views on the value and character of the Biblical books. Daughters of evolutionary philosophy, Biblical criticism and the new Biblical scholarship, have thrown new light on the documents collectively known as the Bible. We have been taught to read these writings as literature. Genesis is poetry. Joshua is tribal tradition embellished in the colours of folklore. Israel's religion is itself the outcome of a long process of evolution. Analysis of the genius of the nation that produced the Bible reveals possession of moral intuitions in a degree not present among other men. National genius manifests itself again most strikingly in the nation's men of genius, the Prophets. These, not soothsayers but truthsayers, have been the first to apprehend that the only efficacious way of bringing self and God into harmony is the way of righteousness. They proclaim justice and equity as the pillars of God's throne the intentions of God's government and insist that human society shall be built on the same foundations. These ideas are vital. The form in which they were put is inconsequential. Religion is the parent not the child of religion. The application of the theory of evolution to religion and the acceptance of its principal contentions have not dethroned God nor refuted immortality. They have not weakened the function of the sacrificial life, nor robbed man of prerogative or eased him of obligation. A stronger foundation has been spread for the temple of the Highest; the ministry of the higher religions at His altar is confirmed and emphasized in a degree in which it is not under the old method of interpreting God's designs and formulating God's plans and purposes. Evolution reveals man and God as coefficients of one and the same force and volition.

And that force and will is Love.

Scripture Inspiration and Authority

Scripture Inspiration and Authority

The Bible a Revelation, not an Evolution

BY

The Reverend A. C. DIXON, D.D.

THERE is an evolution in nature, but not of nature; in the Bible but not of the Bible; in man but not of man. Life evolves along the line of its kind, and only that. God has created all things and put certain kinds of life and force in them to work as his servants, and he seems to have given to each kind very specific directions. Vegetable, animal, moral and spiritual life does his will without questioning.

The Bible claims to be a revelation from God, and its character sustains its claim. "The word of the Lord came expressly unto Ezekiel." (Ezekiel 1:13.) "The Lord said unto me," exclaimed Jeremiah. (Jeremiah 1:7.) "Hear the word of the Lord," says Isaiah. (Isaiah 1:10.) "Thus saith the Lord," rings through the Old Testament. And the New Testament puts the seal of inspiration upon the Old. "The Holy Ghost spake by the mouth of David." (Acts 1:16.) "All Scripture is given by inspiration of God." (2 Tim. 3:16.) "The prophecy came not in old time by the will of man, but holy men of God spake as they were moved by the Holy Ghost." (2 Peter, 1:21.) If the men who wrote this book were not inspired, they were liars, and we have to explain how the book which contains the highest morality ever given to earth could be written by a set of liars. And these bad men at the same time wrote their own doom, for there is no vice more severely condemned in the Bible than deception. To claim that good men wrote the Bible, and deny its inspiration, is on a par with the claim that Christ was a good man, while he pretended to be what he was not. Either horn of the dilemma pierces through the opponents of revelation. God speaks for himself through men whom he moves to write.

The purpose of the Bible is not to speculate or argue, but to reveal. It gives many facts that man cannot learn without a revelation. Men to reveal such facts must, therefore, be inspired of God. No other ancient sacred book claims to be a revelation from God. The Bible is often compared with the Vedas of India, and the Zendavesta of Persia. The Vedas, a collection of poems addressed to mythical deities, make no claim to revelation. The Zendavesta, a mass of speculation into the origin of things, makes no such claim. The Koran, and a few other poor imitations of the Bible, would hardly have thought of counterfeiting, if they had not had the genuine coin before them.

2. The make-up and style of the Bible mark it a revelation from God. One who is in the habit of studying flowers and trees and stars, as God has scattered them in nature, must be impressed as he reads the Bible that the God of nature is the God of the Bible. There is in the book little uniformity and plan; the book of truth is like the world of nature about us; we are invited to go in and gather and classify. To the devout naturalist the make-up of the Bible is a presumption that the God of nature is its author. And it has a style of its own. It is hard for us to realize that it is not a book, but a library of sixty-six books with more than forty authors. Each author retains his personality and writes as the man that he is. The style of the whole book is unique, shall we not say, Divine. John Randolph, in his mature years said, "It would have been as easy for a mole to have written Sir Isaac Newton's treatise on optics as for an uninspired man to have written the Bible." And he said this after he had read hundreds of other books. Disraeli describes Sebastian Castillion's attempt to improve the Bible by adding to it the best things of Shakespeare, and other eminent authors. The attempt was a failure, because even Shakespeare's best, in comparison with the Word of God, appeared poor and paltry. "What are you doing this morning?" asked the daughter of Dr. Charles Elliott. "I am reading the news," was his reply, as he held an open Bible

before him. Those who have spent their lives studying the old book, find in it news fresher than the monthly magazine or morning newspaper can furnish. It has a depth, and height, and length, and breadth, which the finite mind cannot fathom.

3. The unity of the Bible marks it as a revelation from God. It is made up of sixty-six books, written by at least forty different men. They differ in language, in nationality, in tastes, in surroundings. Among them were shepherds, kings, fishermen, priests, mechanics, physicians, theologians and law-makers. Some were learned, others were unlettered. It was at least fifteen hundred years in reaching maturity. With all this variety there is a marvelous unity. From beginning to end the doctrine of one God is taught. Where did these writers get the idea of one God? Certainly not from the cultured nations about them. Herodotus, who visited Egypt about five hundred years before Christ, said that the gods were more plentiful than men. In India there were three hundred million gods. The Persians worshipped well nigh everything that they could associate with fire and light. The cities, fields and groves of Greece were full of imaginary deities, all of whom Rome borrowed and worshipped. And yet all of these writers for fifteen hundred years taught that there was only one God.

Contrast the character of the Jehovah of the Bible with any of the gods of the nations. Jehovah is pure, just and merciful. Saturn, the son of Time, ate his own children, and, when Jupiter was born, his mother Rhea gave the hungry old father a stone wrapped in swaddling clothes. While he was gnawing on that, she succeeded in getting her child out of his reach. Jupiter was a licentious, vindictive, quarrelsome wretch. He flung poor Vulcan out of heaven and maimed him for life, because he took his mother's part in a family fracas. It was no uncommon thing for Jupiter and all his train to get drunk and make the top of Olympus hideous with their orgies. The scenes enacted in the worship of Baal, who kept thrusting his filthy presence upon the Israelites through the surrounding nations, and whom they were base enough at times to worship, ought not to be described. How different from these wicked, sensual gods is the God of the Bible who dwells in the "high and holy place," and "is of purer eyes than to behold iniquity."

There is also a unity of purpose running through the whole Bible. We see it for the first time in the curse upon the serpent in the first chapter of Genesis, and for the last time in the "Come, Lord Jesus, come quickly," of the last chapter of Revelation. Its purpose is to reveal God in Jesus Christ. The thought, like the rising sun, grows brighter and brighter until the perfect day of the gospels. Side by side with this revelation of Jesus the Saviour, we have in the Old Testament a dark revelation of man as a sinner. This unity of teaching as to the one God, and the holiness of that God, and the coming of Christ, running through so many minds and so many ages cannot be accounted for, except on the ground that the Book has one Author who moved men to write His thoughts, and kept them from falling into the errors of the time in which they lived. Stand by the foundation of Solomon's temple while it is building. Here comes a stone brought from a distant quarry, and it finds its place in the building without the touch of chisel. A second stone from another quarry fits exactly into its place. This continues day after day, until every stone is in its place, and the glorious temple stands there complete. Do you suppose for a moment that these stones have somehow by chance been prepared for their places, and that such a magnificent building had no mind to plan it and superintend its erection?

> "Whence but from heaven could men unskilled in arts
> In several ages, born in several parts
> Weave such agreeing truths? Or how or why
> Should all conspire to cheat us with a lie?
> Unasked their pains, ungrateful their advice,
> Starving their gains, and martyrdom their price."

What the Bible does not say is a presumption in favor of the claim that it is a revelation from God. It never stops to gratify curiosity. When men write biographies, they are careful to give details of boyhood and youth. We have but one incident in the boyhood of Jesus. He appears at twelve years of age, and then suddenly disappears. The Apochryphal writers, man-like, have filled the vacancies with marvelous stories of His childish pranks of power and wisdom. There is no attempt in the Bible at the marvelous. Its simple, straightforward tone in narrating the most wonderful things is a little more than could be expected of men trying to establish a false claim to the miraculous. The miraculous atmosphere about it seems to be its native air. Some one has truly said that Mohammed, Swedenborg, and Joseph Smith knew altogether too much. In their straining after the wonderful and the miraculous they showed the unreality of their claims.

5. The outspoken faithfulness of the book confirms the claim that it is a revelation from God. The Bible records without apology, the sins of its most prominent men. Abraham, the father of the faithful, lies, and the lie is recorded. David commits adultery, and though he is king, his foul deed is put down in black and white. Peter swears at the trial of Christ, and though he went out and wept over it, the record is there to recall his sin. Paul and Barnabas, apostles of good-will, quarrel and separate. The names of obscure sinners are not mentioned. No one knows the name of the poor thief on the cross, or the woman who was brought to Jesus for punishment. Man would have recorded them, and left out Abraham, David, Paul and Peter. Now and then a man like Thomas Carlyle admires this Divine way of doing things, and decides that he would like to have his biography written after the same fashion. Mr. Froude attempts it, with the result that no other man will make such a request for the next century; and Mr. Froude would not have done it, if he and Carlyle had been intimately associated in the establishment of an institution, whose very existence was to depend largely upon the character of its supporters.

6. The contents of the Bible mark it a revelation from God. There are statements in it which prove that it was far ahead of

the knowledge of its time. Compare the teachings of science to-day with the first chapter of Genesis. First, chaos: "the earth was without form and void, and darkness was upon the face of the deep." Then comes a period in which there was a separation of the gases from the liquids, clouds above, water beneath. That process is described by the words "God made the firmament and divided the waters which were under the firmament, from the waters which were above the firmament." The next process was the dividing of the liquids from the solids. "Let the waters under the heavens be gathered together in one place, and let the dry land appear." The first life that appeared was vegetable life. God said, "Let the earth bring forth grass, the herb yielding seed, and the fruit tree yielding fruit after his kind." Then comes the clear appearance of the lights in the heavens ruling the day and night. Next in order are the water animals, and then the fowl of the air, and the great monsters, wrecks of which are preserved in our museums to-day. This order of Genesis is the accepted geological order given in science to-day, and this first chapter of Genesis was written at least three thousand years before the present scientific knowledge existed. And in other parts of the book we find statements which were hundreds of years ahead of their times. Long before Maury was born Solomon gave a description of the trade winds. Thousands of years before the world ever heard of Copernicus and Newton, Isaiah wrote of "the circle of the heavens," and Job said, "He stretcheth out the north over the empty place, and hangeth the world upon nothing."

The prophecies of the Bible establish beyond a doubt that the Bible is a revelation rather than an evolution. There could be no evolution giving future events. I find in this book the biography of a person written hundreds of years before he was born. His name, and the place of His birth, over which He could have no control, are given. His character and His reception by the people are so accurately given by one of the prophets, that His enemies in their despair, have claimed that this chapter was inserted after His birth, though it is found in a translation of the Scriptures made over three hundred years before His birth. The manner of His death, even to the dividing of His garments among the soldiers, the piercing of His body, the kind of persons He would have as His companions in death, all this and more are given without any attempt at double dealing. How can we account for it? By simply accepting the claim that God, who moved men to write the Book, could see ahead and tell what was going to come to pass, and that He revealed to them what they as men could not possibly have known. This Jesus, whose biography was written by the prophets, is Himself a prophet, and tells His diciples that certain things would come to pass, while they could see no indications of their approach. He said of Jerusalem: " The days shall come upon thee that thine enemies shall cast a trench around thee and shall lay thee even with the ground, and thy children within thee; and they shall not leave in thee one stone above another; because thou knowest not the time of thy visitation." (Luke 19: 43-44.) Now has this been fulfilled? You have but to read Josephus and you will find that it was literally fulfilled, when Titus, the Roman general, laid siege to the city and utterly destroyed it. And His prophecy, " Jerusalem shall be trodden down of the Gentiles," was and is still fulfilled.

The prophets who wrote hundreds of years before Christ foretold the doom of their beloved city. Jeremiah had said " Zion shall be plowed as a field, and Jerusalem shall become heaps." (Jeremiah 36: 18.) The name of the Roman who ran his plowshare over the site of the temple is preserved—Terentius Rufus. Julian the Apostate tried to make it appear that the prophecy of Christ was false. He proclaimed his purpose to restore the temple, and it is said that Jewish women carried away in their aprons the dust and débris from the place of the old temple's foundation, weeping tears of joy as they worked, but the project failed.

While ancient Babylon was in her glory, a prophet wrote

her doom in these words: "Babylon, the glory of kingdoms, the beauty of the Chaldees' excellency, shall be as when God overthrew Sodom and Gomorrah. It shall never be inhabited, neither shall it be dwelt in from generation to generation, neither shall the Arabian pitch tent there, neither shall the shepherds make their fold there; but wild beasts of the desert shall lie there." (Isaiah 13: 19-21.) "I will also make it a possession for the bittern and pools of water." (Isaiah 14: 23.) We have but to turn to any authentic book of travels to read the fulfillment of this prophecy. The place is a desolation, shunned even by the wandering Bedouin. Owls hoot and wild beasts prowl among its ruins. The marshy pools of water and the bittern are there.

Nahum prophesied that Nineveh, then in her glory, should be destroyed by water and fire. History confirms it by stating that, after the swollen river had washed away a part of the wall, the besiegers rushed through the breach and set the city on fire.

Tyre, the queen of the seas, the Liverpool of ancient times, had her doom written for her, while there was no sign of weakness or decay! God said, through Ezekiel, "I will also scrape her dust from her, and make her like the top of a rock." (Ezekiel 23: 4.)

We all know that Alexander the Great demolished old Tyre, and with its ruins built a causeway half a mile long on which his soldiers might pass to new Tyre on the Island, and from that day to this her site has been like the top of a rock. Of Tyre, Ezekiel says again, "Thou shalt be a place to spread nets upon; thou shalt be built no more." (Ezekiel 26: 4.) That is the prophecy. Here is the history written by the infidel Volney: "The whole village of Tyre contains only fifty or sixty poor families, who live obscurely on the produce of their little ground and a trifling fishery." Bruce, the traveler, says that Tyre is a rock whereon fishers dry their nets.

Of Egypt, Ezekiel writes, "It shall be the basest of kingdoms." (Ezekiel 29: 15.) And no one who knows Egypt to-day will be inclined to deny the truth of that prophecy. It was written when Egypt was at the climax of her glory; as if some one should predict of England to-day that she is destined to become the basest of kingdoms.

Of the Jews it was prophesied by Moses and Ezekiel that they should be scattered among the nations, despised and persecuted, and yet remain distinct. (Deut. 28: 64; Ezekiel 6: 8; 36: 19.) We need not be told that this prophecy has been fulfilled, for we have the proof of it every day before us. When you meet a Jew you know him. They are a distinct nation without a nationality. The children of the Germans, English and French, who came to America a century ago have become Americans. No one can tell by looking into your face whether your great grandfather was from England, Germany, or France. But a Jew remains a Jew, wherever he may go, and whatever language he may speak. There is something about him that tells you he is a Jew. In China he has tried to become a Chinaman by adopting the Chinese customs, but the Jew with a pigtail is still a Jew. No one would mistake him for a Chinaman. Men like Baron Hirsch have advocated their mingling with the Gentiles, but all the millions they spend to bring it about only make the average Jew more determined to remain distinct. The Jew of to-day is a standing miracle in proof of the inspiration of the Bible and the divinity of Christ. Frederick the Great asked a learned man to give him in one sentence a good reason in favor of Christianity, and his reply was, "The Jews, Your Majesty." No candid man, it seems to me, can read what the Bible says about these people, and then trace its fulfillment in their history, without being convinced that a foresight more than human wrote the book, and a Providence more than human has preserved them a distinct people. Mr. Spurgeon says: " There was a man in Scotland who had a piece of cloth stolen. The thief was found with the piece of cloth in his house. The maker and owner of the cloth swore to it. The judge at the trial said: ' There are hundreds of pieces of cloth made in this district and put out in

the fields to dry; how can you swear to it as your piece?'
'Well,' said the man, 'I can swear to it by this: I have a number of tenter hooks upon which I hang my cloth, and there are holes in this piece which are exactly the same distance from one another as my tenter hooks. There are two hooks in a certain place and three hooks in another, close together, and the holes in the cloth exactly fit to these tenter hooks, therefore I can swear it is mine.' So we also can swear that this is none other than the Word of God, because we find that every historical statement given in the books fits in the tenter hook of absolute fact, which even profane writers do not venture to doubt."

7. The power of the Bible confirms the proposition that it is a revelation from God. It is the living Word. God's heart throbs in it, and his arm is felt in every chapter. It transforms character; it comforts in sorrow; it helps men to live and to die. It makes a revolution such as no book of human authorship has done. Pastor Hirsch says that in his parish visitation he gave a Bible to a seller of low literature. At first she refused it, and, when she consented to accept it she said, "I will sell it." "All right," replied Mr. Hirsch, "but read it before you sell it." When he returned to that book-store several months afterward, he found that all the low literature had been cast out. The woman, who had never read the Bible before, was so impressed with its truths, and her character was so changed, that she decided to run only a first-class book-store. The Bible thus cleanses and keeps clean every heart and business that will accept its teachings. After the battle of Inkerman, a dead soldier was found with his bloody finger pressing upon a leaf in his Bible. As they lifted his body, the leaf tore out, and one of his comrades read aloud the words upon which his finger rested, "I am the resurrection and the life!" While he was dying, he looked through these words of God into the future, bright as hope in Christ could make it. And no other book could give such an experience to a dying soldier on the battle field. A colporteur handed a Bible to another soldier of the Crimean War as the troops were leaving Toulon. He

said, "I will light my pipe with it." The colporteur regretted that he had given it to him, but prayed that God would somehow use it for his good. Several years afterward the colporteur stopped for a night in a peasant's home in France. He saw lying on the table a well-worn, soiled Bible. On opening it, he noticed the front leaves were torn out. The mother said to him, "I prize that book very highly. My boy was in the Crimean War and was mortally wounded in one of the battles. It was this book that led him to Christ, and gave him a hope of heaven." The colporteur recognized the book as the same one that he had given to the soldier at Toulon. He had torn out some of the leaves to light his pipe with, yet, when the hour of suffering arrived, he turned to the book which he had despised for light and comfort. And what took place in these special cases is the common experience of every Christian. The book is the voice of God, life and light and joy to every one who believes it. It brings about a revolution through the immediate agency of God. It introduces a new light, which grows and develops after its kind. There is no such thing as evolving flesh into spirit, and the natural into the spiritual man. The first birth is not the germ out of which the second birth grows. We become partakers of the Divine nature; it is God in the soul making all things new.

The attempt to make men Christians by a process of education has been tried with dismal failure. Bishop Colenso took a band of Zulu youth and gave them a good education in England. After they had advanced in their studies, he suggested that they now turn their attention to the consideration of the claims of Christianity; but, in the words of Dr. Gordon, "They kicked up their heels and went back to their former heathen practices." The good Bishop had to confess that his experiment was a failure. Hans Egede spent fifteen years in Greenland educating the people, attempting, as he said, to bring them to a point where they could be intelligent Christians. With a broken heart he preached his farewell sermon from the text, "I have laboured in vain; I have spent my strength for naught." Two years later, John Beck succeeded Egede on this field. He began at once to preach Christ crucified, and the result was the conversion of Karjanack, who became a flame of evangelistic zeal amid the frozen regions of Greenland. Christ's death and resurrection in their revolutionary power effected in him at once what fifteen years of training could not accomplish in others. Robert Moffat was told that if he went to preach to Africaner, the cruel chief would make out of his skull a drinking cup, and use his skin for a drum head. But Moffat, trusting in God, went to Africaner and told him the story of the suffering Christ and the risen Lord. The result was that the lion became the lamb; the cruel chieftain was transformed into an earnest Christian, so that Moffat, after years of association with him, wrote this testimonial of his Christianity: "I do not once remember having occasion to be grieved with him or to complain of any part of his conduct." Nothing short of the revolutionary power of the Gospel can explain the experience of Paul, Karjanack, Africaner, John Newton, Jerry McAuley and scores of others whose lives of wickedness have been won immediately and directly to lives of righteousness. Such has been the effect of Biblical preaching in many communities. James Calvert tells us that when he first arrived at the Fiji Islands, the first thing he had to do was to gather up the bones and pieces of flesh which had been left over from a cannibal feast the day before. Within less than half a century, which is scarcely less than a speck of time in the circle of evolution, these men once cannibals, were sitting at the table of the Lord. The death of Christ revealed in the Bible only, symbolized by the broken bread and the pouring wine, had wrought this revolution. On the island of Aneityum is the monument of John Geddie, bearing this inscription: "When he landed here in 1848, there were no Christians; when he left here in 1882, there were no heathen."

Some of us have heard from the lips of John G. Paton how the whole Island of Aniwa had been turned to Christ, so that among all its inhabitants there is not a single heathen. When

Mr. Darwin visited Terra del Fuego in 1833, he wrote: "The Fuegians are in a more miserable state of barbarism than I ever expected to have seen any human being." He thought it would be impossible to civilize them. On his second visit in 1869, he was astonished to find that these people, whom he had regarded as below the domestic animals, had been transformed into Christian men and women. In his astonishment he wrote: "I certainly should have predicted that not all the missionaries in the world could have done what has been done. It is wonderful, and it shames me, as I always prophesied failure. It is a grand success." In a letter to the London Missionary Society, enclosing twenty-five pounds for its work, Mr. Darwin said: "I shall feel proud if your committee shall think fit to elect me an honorary member of your society." It is evident that Darwin perceived that a revolutionary rather than an evolutionary force had been at work on Terra del Fuego.

Such is the Bible, because the living Christ goes with it and works as He will. As I went through Greenwood Cemetery the other day, I saw the evidence of abundant life clothing the hills in the beauty of shrub and grass and flower, but underneath the granite and marble shafts there was no appearance of life. Death is revolutionary. It soon destroys feature and form, and reduces our friends to dust. If evolution were my hope, I should stand in Greenwood full of despair. But I believe in the God of revolution. "In a moment, in the twinkling of an eye, at the last trump, the dead shall be raised." From underneath those heavy shafts of marble, shall come forth bodies of our loved ones, glorified and immortal: "Wherefore, comfort one another with these words."

Scripture Inspiration and Authority

Scripture Inspiration and Authority

BY

The Reverend S. D. McCONNELL, D.D.

TEN years ago Professor Thayer of Harvard spoke thus to his hearers:

"But inquirers, you tell me, demand certainties. They clamour for immediate and unequivocal answers.

"Doubtless, and overlook the fact that divine Wisdom rarely vouchsafes such. If God's Book had had the average man for its author, no doubt it would have abounded in direct and categoric replies to all questions. The most complicated problems of time and eternity would be solvable by a process as simple as the rule of three! But, alas, impatient souls. His people do not get into the promised land that way."

Nothing is more pathetic than the century long reluctance of Christians to admit the elemental truth of their Master's teaching. He came to set His people free,—but they shrink from the responsibility of freedom. He assured them that they were no longer servants but children,—whereupon they long for the minute directions which a master gives to a slave. In a word they have persistently sought for an "Authority." It is so much easier to live by rule than to live by a spirit. At least it seems to be easier. In point of fact the distinguishing feature of the religion of Christ is that it vacates all external mastership, turns the individual soul in upon itself and declares that by so doing it will find itself face to face with God. It has been well said that of the words which express religion, neither the verbs "to love," or "to believe" has any imperative mood. Christianity is loving and believing. In neither can any "Authority" coerce. One loves the things which he himself finds lovable: he believes the things which, for him, are believable. In the presence of an Authority he may be silent, or he may lie to the authority, or he may lie to himself, but the absolute situation remains unchanged.

There have been three conspicuous pretenders to the tyrant's throne,—the Church, the Bible, and Reason. To speak more accurately, they have not been pretenders so much as they have been worthy monarchs whose sceptres have been thrust into their reluctant hands by the prophets who have known the Master's wish in the case, but have yielded to the people's cry, "Nay, but we will have a King over us." Each of these has in turn played the tyrant, but it has always been because the people would have it so. Dr. Martineau has championed the cause of Reason as the legitimate occupant of the throne over against the claims of the Church and the Bible. Cardinal Newman has fought for the authority of the Church. A hundred Protestant champions have maintained the Westminster dictum that "the Scriptures of the Old and New Testament are the only rule of faith and practice." With all reverence I believe and say that the Master would have cried "a plague on all your houses"! I would not be misunderstood. The Church, the Bible, and Reason all have their necessary place and function in the economy of Christ's religion. But that function is not properly stated by the word "authority." Authorities they are not. Guides, interpreters, if you will, but masters, no. Four centuries ago a large and influential portion of Christendom revolted against the tyranny of the Church. They did not thereby cease to be Christians, nor did they cease to be Churchmen. They simply asserted that they who had been made free men in Jesus Christ were not to be brought into bondage by any spiritual master. A large portion of the Christian world believed then and believes yet that this revolt was a rebellion against God. They cannot think of it as a Reformation. They see in it a form of that same lawlessness which caused Satan to be cast out of heaven. This is fundamentally the question at issue between Protestantism and Papalism. Strictly speaking Rome has only one doctrine, that is, submit yourself to authority. Protestantism is essentially the assertion that the individual Christian is a *friend* of the Master, and no longer a servant who knoweth not what the

Master doeth. This position was consistently and valiantly maintained by the early reformers. So far as obedience to the Church is concerned they have not yielded. Obedience to the Church's commands, as commands, cannot to-day be secured in any portion of Protestantism. It is every year becoming more difficult to secure by Rome.

But the burden of freedom is very onerous. Before the second generation of the Reformers had passed away a movement had set in which had for its purpose to set the Bible upon the same throne of authority from which the Church had been rudely thrust. It was less fitted for that office than the Church had been, nor had it heretofore been regarded in that aspect by Catholic tradition. But the people had begun once more to cry "nay, but we will have a King over us." It was then that the doctrine of "*Inspiration*" began to be exploited. The Bible was first enthroned as authority, and thereupon its inspiration was urged to establish its legitimacy. The whole development of the dogma lies within the seventeenth and the first half of the eighteenth century, as any one who will take the trouble may read. During that time the *Literae Scriptae* were confirmed in a position which they have held until our own time. The Bible came to be called the "Word of God." It became a palladium and a charm. The theologian thought of it as a complete and final transcript of God's law and purpose. The common people adored it as a fetich. It came to be kissed in the court-room as the sacred thing which alone could invoke truth. It was appealed to as not only the ultimate but the immediate arbiter in every question of faith and conduct. Without its presence in its entirety it was believed that no people could know God. By its distribution it was believed that the Gospel could be spread abroad, whose Founder had decreed that it should be propagated by the contact of living man with living man. It came to hold the place in Protestantism which the Koran holds in Islam. And all this without its own consent, and even against its plain protest.

Just now a large portion of the Protestant world is disturbed by what it thinks to be a breaking away from the authority of the Bible. Is the apprehension justified? What has caused the fear? What will be the outcome of the movement? Of the ultimate issue there can be little question. The servant will be handed down from the seat of the King. The Scriptures of the Old and New Testament are the product of that long and wide movement toward God at the centre of which stands " God manifest in the flesh." The Church is that great company of faithful people, from every age and every clime, organized and unorganized, conscious and unconscious, who by thought, word and deed contributed to the bringing in of the Kingdom of God. The Bible is the literature of a movement. The movement produced the literature and not conversely. The movement is superior to the literature and controls it. The literature gains its peculiar character from the unique quality of the movement. The movement is the master and the Book is the servant. Within a certain very circumscribed area inside the Church, and within about three centuries of time, the servant has been unwisely elevated into a position to which it never claimed title. This action has been confined solely to a portion of Great Britain and to Protestantism within the United States. The task now is to remove the Bible from the unwarranted place assigned to it, and to do this in such manner that it will not suffer diminution of the honour which belongs to it of right and in its own place. But the task must be done.

Two classes of people within the nominal frontier of Protestantism fiercely oppose the doing of it. There are, first, the extreme Protestants whose whole fabric of religious thought is so based upon the idea of an infallible written revelation that they cannot conceive the fabric standing when the foundation should be withdrawn. The other is a comparatively small group of Churchmen who are so enamored of the very principle of Authority in Religion that they cannot abide question of any authority, even though it be one of which they themselves take small heed. These two join their voices in an outcry against the same kind of study of Scripture, which has been freely allowed always and everywhere within the universal Church, with the exception of the limited time and area above mentioned. But the majority is against them. All Catholic tradition is against them. The Bible itself refuses to side with them. The result is foregone.

But what then becomes of the "Doctrine of Inspiration"?

To this I reply, the Church Catholic has no doctrine of Inspiration. It has the fact. But it has never defined the fact or elevated it into a dogma. Only within the limited time and area before mentioned has this been done. Hence it happens that only within that area is the present perplexity felt. The Eastern Church cannot comprehend the difficulty. The Roman Church is untouched by it. The Anglican Church is only disturbed by it to the extent to which she has informally committed herself to a Protestant dogma. Officially she does not recognize any dogma of Inspiration. She is content with stating what books are included within the sacred writings, and with declaring that no belief is to be exacted as a condition of membership in the Church which is not recognized in them.

That the threescore little booklets bound up together in our Bible possesses a unique quality has always been recognized by those who were qualified to discern that quality. It is because they possessed this quality that they have survived while their contemporary writings have perished. But the name by which this quality shall be called is quite another matter. The word "Inspiration" suited the fact well enough so long as the word retained its original indefiniteness of connotation. It is a serious question now, whether it can be happily employed in the area where it has been so long misemployed. It misleads. By ancient and universal usage "inspiration" was credited to certain men who spoke or wrote. By local and modern usage inspiration is attached not to the writers but to the Book. A legitimate metonymy has created an illegitimate dogma. That certain men of old spake as they were moved by the Holy Ghost is beyond question. But the impulse of the Spirit of Holiness is a moral and not an intellectual one. It does not guarantee accuracy, but it is recognized by the moral sense of the hearer. This is why the words of some men have survived and are a living force in the moral movement of the race. The men were inspired.

But what authority shall decide which men have been inspired, and what writings possess the unique quality due thereto? I reply, no external decision can determine. No decree, no counsel, no *obiter dicta* can attach the label "inspired" to any book with the certainty that it will adhere. The appeal is to the Christian consciousness. When that has spoken a general council can but register its decree. It may be that in certain instances its voice has not been waited for, or that it has been constrained by ecclesiastical pressure, or that a judgment has been made by a passing authority against its silent protest. No doubt. But the simple fact that a literature fragmentary, incomplete, undistinguished by literary skill or intellectual brilliancy has remained through the centuries a constant, living stimulus and corrective to the world's conscience establishes its origin from the Spirit of Holiness. It is true that the Church lived for several centuries without it, that it would not perish were the Bible to be lost. This is but to say that salvation is not made contingent upon the ability to read and write. But when all is said, the fact still remains that the writings which we call sacred are sacred. Not because they burst into the world through any earthquake of divine visitation, not because they were sent forth by any mighty blast of ecclesiastical wind, but because in them speaks the still, small voice, at the sound of which every true prophet and man of God covers his face. What authority they possess rests upon this fact. The capacity to inspire is the only and the sufficient evidence of inspiration.

But this quality which they possess they possess in unequal degree. Whether or not any may perchance be included in the Canon which possess it not at all, only time can show. But this would require long time. Even a possession of twenty centuries' tenure does not establish an indefeasible title. And a general council in the thirtieth century would have just the same power to pronounce the Christian judgment in the premises, and if need be to reverse a previous judgment that a council of the fifth century had to reverse one of the third. There is no prescriptive right in the Kingdom of Christ.

If it be objected that this way of thinking vacates the Holy Scriptures of all divine authority, two answers are forthcoming. The first is that this *is* the way in which the Church throughout all the centuries and to-day has and does regard them. The only exception in time is the three centuries last past, and in space is a portion of the Protestant world of Great Britain and the United States. The other answer is, it does vacate them of all authority except this intrinsic power to inspire. It rests content with the doctrine of the Apostle that "Every God-breathed writing is profitable for teaching, reproof, correction and instruction in righteousness."

In righteousness: not in science, not in history, not in geography or ethnology. To this, which is essentially the Catholic doctrine of Holy Scripture, what can criticism or scholarship do? What if it should appear that the human race began ages before Eden or that Moses did not write the Pentateuch or that there were two Isaiahs, or that the Gospel which goes by his name was not written by the beloved disciple? Proof of these things would not touch the intrinsic quality by which the books live, any more than would the discovery that the alabaster box had been carved at Babylon and not in Jerusalem affect the fragrance of the precious nard contained therein.

We have come to a time in the history of the Christian world when nothing but realities will be tolerated. Only those things can be accepted as sacred which awake the sense of reverence. Only those things are inspired which can themselves inspire. There need be no fear to submit the Christian Scriptures to this test, nor need any one futilely imagine that they can secure them exemption from the test.

The Old Testament in the Light of Higher Criticism

The Old Testament in the Light of Higher Criticism

BY

The Reverend Professor HENRY PRESERVED SMITH, D.D.

THE nineteenth century has seen a thorough revision of our historical knowledge. This revision has begun with the study of ancient documents, and the science which concerns these documents—criticism we call it—has made very distinct advance during the hundred years. Historical criticism has developed along two lines; first, the settlement of the text of ancient documents on the basis of manuscript evidence. This is textual criticism sometimes called the lower criticism because it comes at the basis of all historical study. In distinction from this, the second branch (or higher criticism) concerns itself with the internal characteristics of a document after the text is settled. It asks about date, authorship, mode of composition.

When it was discovered that all historical knowledge is acquired by a critical process it became inevitable that the books of the Old Testament should be subjected to the same process. Both in textual criticism and in the higher branch there was evidently much to do. It is perhaps a misfortune that the textual criticism could not have been finished first, and so have prepared the way for the higher criticism. But one science does not wait for another—all the sciences are advanced simultaneously by a multitude of workers.

It would not be accurate to say that the whole critical study of the Old Testament is bounded by the limits of the nineteenth century. Slight beginnings of it are found as far back as the twelfth century in one or two Jewish scholars. In the period of the Reformation also we find a somewhat freer attitude towards tradition than had existed before. Luther is the most conspicuous example, and his contemporary *Carlstadt* raised some of the questions which have been widely discussed in our own day. As the Protestant theologians became more scholastic in their attitude, there was a reaction towards tradition, and the critical inquiries came to a stop.

The Jewish philosopher Spinoza may be called the first genuine Biblical critic. His attempts at a systematic examination of the Old Testament met with no favour among his contemporaries. With him should be mentioned Richard Simon, a Roman Catholic—like Spinoza he wrote in the latter part of the seventeenth century. In 1773, an epoch is marked by the publication of Astruc's *Conjectures*. This work gave a clue which was extraordinarily effective, in that it pointed out the different use of the names for God in the different parts of the Book of Genesis. The clue was followed up by Eichhorn, the first edition of whose *Einleitung* was published in 1780.

It is not the purpose of this paper to give a history of the higher criticism. The above names are adduced to show that critical science has been a plant of slow growth, and that its outlines were sketched before the century dawned. It remains to note that those outlines were traced again with a firmer hand, and filled in with the greatest conceivable fulness of detail during this century. Not only this—the new science has established itself with growing firmness, and its results are accepted with increasing unanimity.

There are no doubt a great many people still to whom the formula: *The Bible is the word of God* precludes critical investigation. But the number of such is diminishing, while the number of sincere Christian believers who accept the main results of critical inquiry increases daily.

The first stage of Biblical criticism was naturally concerned with the Pentateuch. Over the question of its genuineness or authenticity a long and pertinacious battle was fought. It is a misfortune that the question was put in the form in which it was actually presented. The Pentateuch in its entirety does not claim to be a work of Moses or of any other individual author. There can therefore be no question of genuineness to discuss. It is unfortunate also that the Pentateuch should be isolated from the other historical books. This isolation is a part of our inheritance from the Jews. To them the Torah, or Law, has a very special interest and importance. These five books regulate the life of the Jew, and as the result they were early treated as a code apart. But from a literary point of view they belong with the other books. There is no break between them and what follows. The inquiry should have started with the whole historical narrative stretching from Genesis to 2 Kings. When this is clearly seen, the way is open for some very simple truths. The first of these is that the whole group of books we are considering took their present shape not earlier than the Exile. Their final redaction may be later, but it cannot be earlier, because one of the authors knew of the release of Jehoiachin from the Babylonian prison (2 Kings 25:27). This took place in the year 561 B. C., and our inquiry should note the fact.

The whole debate about the Pentateuch has been bringing out a recognition of the fact just considered. It has also elaborated the theory which next claims our attention—the theory that the method of Hebrew historical writing is the method of compilation. This method is seen to lie on the surface when once it is pointed out. The difficulty of getting it acknowledged in the Pentateuch arose from the isolation of those books. The Biblical narrative from the Creation to the Exile is the result of a succession of compilations. The earliest prose author introduced into his work poems, like the song of Deborah, which were already in existence. The next in order of time enriched his history with a code of laws (the Book of the Covenant, Ex. 20:22-23:19) which had been written down by some one else. The obscurities in the account of Solomon's reign arise from the fact that the author put together sections from two early histories. The first great gain from the critical study of the century consists in insight into the method of Hebrew historical composition.

On the basis thus attained we may understand the detailed

documentary hypothesis, which has been worked out by long and patient inquiry. This hypothesis does indeed distinguish two groups in the historical books; it marks off the Hexateuch (the first six books) because this section of the narrative shows sources of its own. These sources are four in number. The oldest one is the work of an author usually called the Yahwist, because he generally uses the divine name Yahwist (Jehovah). His book was a collection of traditions concerning the Creation, the Flood, the Patriarchs and the Exodus. He is a brilliant and vivid narrator. To him we owe the account of the Garden of Eden, and the Fall of Man. He may be dated somewhere about 850 B. C. Next we have a kindred spirit who treated a part of the same material from a somewhat different point of view. He began with Abraham (instead of the Creation) and used the name Elohim (God) instead of the proper name Yahweh. Hence he is called the Elohist (E). He incorporated in his work a brief legal compendium called the Book of the Covenant—referred to above. His work was supplemented by other writers of the same school, reaching its final stage (say) 700 B. C.

These two books (at first circulated separately) were combined in the manner in which the four Gospels are sometimes worked into a continuous narrative. They were already thus combined before the incorporation with them of the Book of Deuteronomy. This book is the one which made such a sensation in the reign of Josiah. As we read in 2 Kings 22 the priest *Hilkiah* found in the Temple a book called the Book of Instruction. Its threats of God's wrath were so severe and its requirements so stringent that the King was much moved, and at once took measures to secure its observance. The way in which it is described, gives us reason to think that this book is some part of our Deuteronomy. When once in circulation it was supplemented and expanded, and at last it found its appropriate setting by being inserted into the history of *J. E.*

Deuteronomy is significant in view of its use of the name of

Moses. As a literary composition it cannot be much older than the date at which it was discovered in the Temple (623 B. C.). It purports however to produce speeches made by Moses who lived at least six hundred years earlier. No doubt the author made use of Mosaic traditions, but the only explanation which can be offered for his clothing them in the form in which we read them is that he boldly made use of fiction—a device which has been frequently employed in other times, both among the Hebrews and among Gentiles. In fact the book must be judged like the speeches so often put into the mouth of the hero by an ancient historian.

Deuteronomy is perhaps the most influential of the Old Testament books. It made a profound impression at the time of its discovery, and that impression was prolonged by the covenant into which the people entered to observe it. Especially after its threats were fulfilled by the destruction of Jerusalem, it became an authority for the faithful remnant. It was the first of the Old Testament books to become canonical in the full sense of the word. It became moreover the basis on which the earlier history of the nation was judged and partly rewritten.

The Exile gave opportunity for reflection. In the prophet Ezekiel we see the direction which the thought of the faithful took. It advanced along the path laid out by Deuteronomy. This book had aimed to give the people a rule of life more complete than they had before possessed. But a code of rules is capable of indefinite expansion. After the return to Jerusalem a priestly author collected all the legal traditions within his reach, and published them as the Law of Moses. He prefaced them with a brief historical sketch mainly made of genealogies. Thus came into being the Priest-code, the latest of the elements in the Hexateuch. A considerable part of the debate on Old Testament criticism has raged around the question of the comparative age of the Priest-code and the other documents. This document, from its formal and schematic character, readily furnished the compiler with a framework into which he fitted the other narratives. This gave the impression that it was the oldest document to which the others have been added as supplements. It was also thought that the interest in genealogical data was older than the interest in the narratives of events. But the reverse has been discovered to be the case. One of the latest of the Old Testament books is Chronicles; yet it is largely made up of genealogical tables. One of the permanent results of this century's study is the decision that the Priestly document is the youngest portion of the Hexateuch. This book seems to be the one promulgated by Ezra (B. C. 444) and of course its incorporation in the Hexateuch is still later.

These sources of the Hexateuch furnish also a part of the material for the other historical books (Judges, Samuel and Kings). To what extent this is the case is still under debate. Besides them we find evidence of a life of David, a life of Solomon, and a life of Elijah, large sections of which are preserved for us in Samuel and Kings. It is instructive to compare with these the Books of Chronicles. The latter cover precisely the same period as the older series. They are made up by compilation, as we see on comparing them with the others. The author of Chronicles took whole sections from the earlier history, incorporating them into his work without alteration. With them he combined other sections of a very different tenor. The result is a historical picture which it is impossible to harmonize with the earlier narrative. All that the critics have claimed concerning the composition of the Pentateuch is so plainly illustrated in Chronicles that no one can deny the possibility of such a process. It is the merit of present Biblical study that it recognizes these analogies, and also that it frankly recognizes the discrepancies between the two streams of Hebrew narrative.

Turning now to the group of books called the Prophets (but excluding Daniel), we easily discover that the group is an aggregation of fragments. The Book of Ezekiel indeed is a literary unit. The prophet Ezekiel himself seems to have been a writer rather than an orator, and there is no reason to doubt that he himself put his book into its present shape.* This certainly is of the greatest importance, for we are able to fix with accuracy the date of composition. The book is important as showing how the Jews in Exile were preparing the way for the later enforcement of the legalistic system of Ezra. Full appreciation of this fact has come only in the last quarter of this century, in the discussions on the age of the priestly legislation.

When we pass to the Book of Jeremiah we find ourselves less certain. A considerable part of what is there contained is Jeremiah's preaching, and there is no reason to doubt the accuracy of what the editor has written about the prophet's experience. But some of the prophecies bear a later date. If Baruch (as seems probable) put the original book into circulation, later editors have freely supplemented it with fragments from other sources. The most of the prophecies against foreign nations belong in the supplement. Here we find true what has so often been shown—that Hebrew literature is the result of a complicated process.

This is more conspicuously true of the book which bears the name of Isaiah. The book falls into two halves at once when we look at it. Isaiah the contemporary of Hezekiah is the author of a considerable part of the first half. But this half (Chapters 1-39), is composite and contains prophecies of different dates. The second half (Chapters 40-66) bears unmistakable marks of the Exile. But it also is composite, and the tendency is at present to find three different hands in the various sections of the Book. The debate is not yet closed. But substantial unanimity exists in recognizing the composite nature of both halves, and in ascribing portions of the first half as well as the greater part of the second half to exilic authors.

Among the books not yet considered, the Psalter easily holds the first place. Concerning this collection of hymns the cen-

---

*Much work has been done recently on the text of Ezekiel, which has been very badly preserved in the authorized Hebrew copies. But the account of textual criticism does not belong in the present paper.

tury shows a remarkable change of front. That the poems are not all by David has probably always been recognized, for the Hebrew titles ascribe some of them to other authors. But the progress of inquiry during the last fifty years has taken from David the greater part of those formerly accepted as his. At the present time it is a question whether even one can be claimed by him, and an increasing number of scholars find themselves unable to date any large number of the Psalms before the Exile. It is natural to suppose that the ripest fruits of the Old Testament Piety were produced in the latest period of Hebrew history. The four hundred years of silence that were assumed between Ezra and John the Baptist no longer puzzle the investigator, and it is a distinct gain to find the heroic age of the Maccabees expressing itself in the prayers and praises of the Psalter.

In like manner the progress of inquiry has brought down the Book of Proverbs to a comparatively late date. This is a conspicuous example of the overthrow of tradition which yet leaves the value of the book unimpaired. What value could be added to the aphorisms of this book by having them proceed from the luxurious and oppressive despot whose name they bear? No satisfactory answer can be given to this question. On the other hand, we should despair of the power of practical religion if after giving any man wisdom to utter so many excellent maxims of life and conduct, it should produce a life such as was led by Solomon. Ecclesiastes has long been recognized to be one of the latest Biblical books. It cannot be put very far away from Proverbs.

The most serious problems (for the defender of the older view of the Bible) are propounded by the Book of Daniel. The present century has carefully studied a variety of similar books which circulated about the beginning of our era. Acquaintance with them enables us to put the Book of Daniel in the same class. An apocalypse is a book which clothes history in the garb of prophecy up to a certain point, beyond which it looks for the consummation of all things. It is generally put forth under the name of some ancient worthy in whose mouth it will have greater authority. We have no difficulty in discovering that the author of Daniel makes his hero receive detailed predictions of the Persian and Greek domination over Israel down to the period of Antiochus the Great. After Antiochus he expects the Kingdom of God to appear, giving all power to the Jews. It is not difficult to see that he lived in the Maccabean period and wrote to comfort and encourage his contemporaries. The Hebrew canon places the book among the Hagiographa and not among the prophets. In fact two styles of composition and of thought could hardly be more unlike than that of Daniel and that of Isaiah or Jeremiah.

Among minor gains of recent Biblical study may be mentioned the recognition of the Book of Jonah as a parable, designed to teach a much needed lesson to the hide-bound Pharisees. The book of Esther also is better understood when discovered to be a piece of fiction. Its blood thirsty narrative may have a historical nucleus, though the present tendency is to find it made up from mythological material. In any case the believer must be relieved to find that he is not obliged to receive it as a narrative of fact.

The bible reader who has been accustomed to ascribe the Pentateuch to Moses, all the Psalms to David, the whole of Isaiah to the contemporary of Hezekiah, the Book of Daniel to the distinguished Statesman whose name it bears, and Proverbs and Ecclesiastes to Solomon the son of David, will doubtless find the results indicated in this paper disquieting and perhaps alarming. He will naturally accuse the higher criticism of being destructive and negative. It may not be superfluous therefore to point out that no criticism can destroy the Bible. We have it, we have the whole of it, just as truly as we ever had it. What criticism does is to destroy certain traditions external to the Bible which have been made to buttress its historical authority. Even here the work of criticism has accomplished less than is commonly supposed. The antediluvian Chronology in Genesis was not long ago accepted as a reliable scheme on which to build up universal history. Criticism has indeed shown that this Chronology is of later date than has been supposed. But the reason why its accuracy is now surrendered is not because of the change of view in regard to its authorship. If we had irrefragable proof that it was written by Moses, we should still find it impossible to defend its accuracy. The reason is that other sciences—biology, geology, archaeology, history, find themselves unable to adopt the Biblical scheme. For the most part, it is these other sciences which have made the old view of an inerrant Old Testament impossible. This is only saying that criticism is a part of the scientific advance of this century.

The gains which offset the apparent loss should not be forgotten. It is no small thing to be delivered from the necessity of harmonizing everything in the Biblical narrative. Criticism has enabled us to see the full extent of the discrepancies with which we have to deal. But it also enables us to make use of the discrepancies as marks of various stages of religious thought. By recognizing them we are able to appreciate the rich variety of thought and experience recorded for us in the Bible.

More to be valued is the increased sense of development in the religion of Israel. The unity of the Bible is now seen to be the unity of an organism. The growth of the literature registers the growth of the religious ideas. We frankly recognize the rudimentary nature of many of these ideas, and we are free from the obligation to defend the features which show this. The command to exterminate the Canaanites, the toleration of polygamy, the narrow exclusiveness of the priestly legislation, the imprecations upon Israel's enemies—these are no longer stumbling blocks to us. On the other hand, the originality and nobility of the prophets stand out more distinctly, now that we correctly estimate the back-ground from which they stand out.

The religious value of the Old Testament has always consisted in its being a record of religious experience. This value can never be affected by criticism. The Shepherd Psalm may not have been written by David. It is surely no less precious to us that it came from the heart of a humble believer—perhaps one sorely tried by the enemies to which he briefly alludes. And the same is true of all those parts of the Bible in which the soul finds comfort and help. Criticism does not affect them. They are still the bread of life to the hungry soul.

The Old Testament in the Light of Higher Criticism

The Old Testament in the Light of Higher Criticism

Revelation and Inspiration

BY

The Reverend Professor MEREDITH O. SMITH, M.A.

DR. DALE in his treatise on the Atonement gives an excellent illustration of what we conceive to be the nature of Revelation.

"Although," he writes, "as a Teacher of religious truth, the Lord Jesus had a unique power, we misapprehend the character of the supremacy which he claims, if we suppose that it is to be illustrated and vindicated by placing his mere words side by side with the words of the Prophets who preceded him. I doubt whether he ever said anything about the Divine compassion more pathetic or more perfectly beautiful than had been said by the writer of the hundred-and-third Psalm: "Like as a father pitieth his children, so the Lord pitieth them that fear him. For he knoweth our frame. He remembereth that we are dust." It is not in the words of Christ that we find a fuller and deeper revelation of the Divine compassion than in the words of the Psalmist, but in His deeds.

"There came a leper and worshipped him, saying, Lord, if thou wilt, thou canst make me clean. And Jesus ('moved with compassion:' Mark 1:41) put forth his hand and *touched* him'—touched the man, from whom kindred had shrunk:—'touched him'—it was the first time that the leper had felt the warmth and pressure of a human hand since his loathsome disease came upon him;—'touched him,' and said, I will, be thou clean!"

To which in a foot-note, Dr. Dale adds the remark, "that every one of the Synoptical Gospels notices the fact that our

Lord 'touched' the man." See S. Matt. 8: 2, 3; Mark 1: 40, 41; Luke 5: 12, 13.

The importance of this incident for the purpose in hand is found in the manner in which it enables us to emphasize the truth that the Revelation which our Saviour imparted, *did not entirely consist in his teaching.* For really, he was himself the revelation. Thus when he "looked round about on the Pharisees with anger, being grieved for the hardness of their hearts," that was a revelation of the Wrath of God; when he took little children up in his arms and blessed them, that was a revelation of the Benediction of God.

Quite different from this is the function of Inspiration, which is to be sought, not in the actions of our Saviour himself, but in an appropriate activity evoked by his presence among certain who encountered him. Its purpose is the preservation, and fructification, of the appointed lesson to be obtained from such encounter. The lesson itself is regularly regarded in the capacity of a *seed,* or a *germ;* which seed searches out the response of its corresponding *spirit;* and by that Spirit is, in the first place, kept from perishing, that is to say, from being forgotten or overlooked, in the rush of human life; and, in the next place also, is quickened, or *developed,* towards the gathering round about itself of body and substance, and the production of the fruit that was held in view in the very act of its bestowal. The lesson, or the revelation, in Biblical language, is referred to as a λόγος, or Word; and the position that it occupies as the *germ,* or the *seed,* from which the fruits of Christianity develop, is expressed in a single utterance of our Saviour himself,—"*The seed is the word of God.*" Meanwhile, the various kinds of Soil that the Sower encounters, explain the need for the operation of the Spirit, in its double duty of quickening and preserving the seed which has been sown; since with the Trodden Ground the word is taken away, or the Revelation, to put it more plainly, has been forgotten; whilst with the Thorny Ground no fruit has been brought to perfection,—that is to say, that the Revelation has been thwarted in the process of legitimate growth.

Thus primarily and originally our Saviour's desire was simply that his words and his actions, so far as practicable, might be *remembered.* S. Luke, 8: 12.

For example, the Mother of our Lord is said to have " kept all these things, and pondered them in her heart "*, that is to say that, in a certain peculiar manner, she was the person who remembered them. " The comforter, which is the Holy Ghost," were the words of the promise, " He shall teach you all things, *and bring all things to your remembrance,* whatsoever I have said unto you."†

So that the Spirit of Inspiration is the spirit of memory, rather than the spirit of invention. This high esteem in which the memory was held by the first disciples lasted down to the age that followed the Apostles;—thus we find it in that remarkable expression of Papias, " I did not think that I could get so much profit from the contents of books as from the utterances of a living and abiding voice; "‡ i. e. the voice of those who rebered the Revelation; and in the fervent language again of Irenaeus in his letter to Florinus, where he calls to mind S. Polycarp as relating those things which he had heard from the Apostles concerning our Lord, " and about his miracles, and about his teaching, as having received them from eye-witnesses of the life of the Word, . . . altogether in accordance with the Scriptures."§ In fact, this appreciation of the memory continued until circumstances made it only too apparent that by itself it was no longer sufficient for the task imposed upon it, and that our Lord's life must be preserved to us in writing, if it was really to be preserved to us at all.

It may seem, perhaps, at first sight a strange thing,—and, in point of fact, with our modern habits, it does seem a strange

---

* S. Luke, ii. 18.
† S. John, xiv, 26.
‡ Eusebius. H. E., iii, 39.
§ Ibid., v, 20.

thing,—that God's Revelation should have been primarily entrusted to so frail and uncertain a keeper as is the tenure of human memory; seeing that our Lord might have acted readily as a Scribe to himself, during the course of his own lifetime, and either committed his teaching to writing in person, or else have allotted to his disciples the task of recording it, under his immediate supervision. Yet he left it apparently simply to take its chances, during the thirty or forty years intervening before the date of the composition of the Gospels. And doubtless also, we trace a similar phenomenon concerning the prophets of the Old Testament before our Lord; in that there intervened in each case an analogous interval between the pronouncement of the prophecy itself, and its preservation at last in the form of a written volume. St. John the Baptist was the chief of the prophets, and yet the prophecies that he uttered have not been written. And Baruch put in writing the prophecies that Jeremiah had pronounced. So that the real question is not so much as to whether the Prophet *wrote* the book which is called by his name; but as to whether he *uttered* the prophecies which in that book have been recorded. And thus, to press the matter farther back still, the real question is not so much if Moses was the *author* of the Pentateuch, but as to whether the Giving of the Law, $\dot{\eta}\ \nu o\mu o\theta\epsilon\sigma ia$* did actually take place on Mount Sinai. Because, exactly as our Lord left his Gospel to be recorded by his followers, after his Resurrection, so Moses may have left his legislation to be collected by the Israelites after his death. Dr. Robertson, of Glasgow, has put the case plainly; the books of the Pentateuch ought rightly to be regarded as " anonymous compositions." " Although other books, which are also anonymous, are accepted as materials for history, although the books of the Pentateuch, with supreme indifference, say nothing about their authorship, it has been tacitly assumed that their whole value stands or falls with their Mosaic or non-Mosaic authorship. A broad distinction is evident between the questions. By whose

---

* Rom. ix, 4.

instrumentality or authority was law given? and, by whose hands were books written which contain the law? The essential question is not as to the early or late date of the books of the Pentateuch, *but as to the relation in which the legislation of the Pentateuch stands to the whole development of the history.*"* And this latter point we do account crucial.

Fragile as the human memory may easily seem for the position which has thus been assigned it, yet from another point of view, it is in each case the interval, between the recording and the event of the Revelation, which constitutes its pledge of reality. For it means that the Word was actually put to the test, and proved itself of value, *before* it was entrusted to writing; and that the recognition of its value itself stirred the Spirit, which animates the books of the Bible. " I am come," said our Saviour, "that they might have life, and that they might have it more abundantly;" or, to put it otherwise, our Lord was the Word of Life, ὁ Λόγος τῆς ζωῆς and it was the fact that its life-giving energy *already* had been recognized, which ensured the perpetuation of the Word in the Gospels. So of old time, the word that Baruch had inscribed in his roll, was found *in the actual test* to be "quick and powerful, and sharper than any two-edged sword" which Jeremiah could have employed against King Jehoiakim; and it was the fact that in application it had proved so effective, which roused the determination that by taking another roll, and writing in it all the former words that had been in the first roll, they would provide that it should not be extinguished.† Again, the laws that fill the books of the Pentateuch are not, as it were, mere ambitions, or ideals, or speculations, or experiments, but they had actually met the test of their reception *before* they have been inserted in the books; and because they were seen to be of such primary importance, they found a place in the pages of the books. This principle, that the Word all along has been introduced into the works of the Bible as something which had

---
* Early Religion of Israel, ch. xiii.
† Jer. xxxvi.

already been exposed to a trial, *before its introduction,* is our constant guarantee of its truthfulness. As will be seen at once, the interval that we find interposed between its first enunciation and the commitment to writing, was not too long for a satisfactory test to be made. Thus, the fact is that the veneration which obtains for the teaching that occupies the Biblical pages, far from being the upgrowth of later centuries, existed while the doctrine was still held in memory, and was the ground that rendered its writing a necessity. Where, for example, have we a deeper veneration, which has been felt at any subsequent period, for the *doctrine* taught by St. Paul to the Corinthians, than is implied in the expressions which he uses himself? which doctrine up to the moment of his writing he had kept simply by remembering what he had received; " by which also ye are saved," he writes, " if ye hold it fast," or as it is not inaptly rendered in the Authorized Version, *" if ye keep in memory,* τίνι λόγῳ, in what words I preached it unto you;" whilst the letter that he was writing was but an assistance towards holding it fast still further. Still, we grant that in one particular direction it does remain the fact that the Bible has appreciated in the value that it holds for us; namely, in that esteem which always must appertain to a treasure which, if once it is lost, can never be replaced; and whose function there is nothing in the universe to correspond to, in its stead; only in its actual authority there has been no accretion since the time of its production. In the lapse of time, our *dependence* for information, as to what constituted the Apostolic teaching, has been concentred more than at first upon the Epistles; but no greater deference has been developed since then for the teaching of the Apostles itself, than had already been before pen was put to paper. Unfortunately, most modern scholars, for instance, do not read the First Epistle to the Corinthians with a greater reverence than did those disciples at Corinth, who were the very first to hear it.

" The fundamental error," writes Green, " which underlies

all the arguments of the critics, . . . and vitiates their conclusion is the assumption that the books of the Old Testament " (and for that matter the New Testament as well) *"were not written with the design of being held sacred and divinely authoritative; but that in course of time they came to be treated with a veneration which was not at first accorded to them."* * Because the truth is that their subject matter was already held sacred, before they had been written.

Along these lines, we have to trace a remarkable contrast, as existing between the Bible and the Koran; and which by no means has obtained the attention that might well have been bestowed on it. Yet it throws a highly interesting side-light upon the argument before us. The opening words of the Koran, for example, are these:—

"That is the Book! there is no doubt therein; a guide to the pious, who believe in the unseen, and are steadfast in prayer, and of what we have given them expend in alms; who believe in what is revealed to thee, and what was revealed before thee, and of the hereafter they are sure. These are in guidance from their Lord, and these are the prosperous."

As to the opening clause, "That is the Book," Mr. Palmer has the following note:—

"Although the Arabic demonstrative pronoun means 'that,' the translators have hitherto always rendered it 'this,' forgetting that it is not an address to the reader, but supposed to be Gabriel's words of inspiration to Mohammed while showing him the Umm al Kitâb—the 'Eternal original of the Koran.'"

Or, in other words, the Revelation is viewed as passing directly from the mind of the Archangel Gabriel, through the inspiration of Mohammed, to the pages of the Koran. Contrast this with the incident of Baruch, who is first sent with the message to Jehoiakim, and after the word has actually proved itself ἐνεργής determines, in spite of all, that it shall be preserved by his pen. So, too, the interval that all through the Bible is interposed between the κήρυγμα, or the actual procla-

---
* General introduction to the Old Testament. The Canon, p. 26.

mation of the message, and the γραφή, or written record of the same. St. Matt. 12:41. Thus what the Koran claims is to be the organ of revelation, or the way that the revelation is imparted; whilst what the Bible claims on the other hand is to be the *record of revelation,* or the way that the revelation is remembered. Therefore, in the one case, the inspiration is conceived as that power which enabled Mohammed to produce his revelations; whilst in the other it is the fact of revelation which has kindled the inspiration of the Biblical writers. Practically this implies that the claim of Mohammed was the privilege of dictating revelations at his personal discretion, and that he regarded this as the characteristic function of one who held the prophetic office; since the same inspiration as guided his first pronouncements could easily enable him to continue indefinitely making additions to the Koran. Thus to all intents, to acknowledge his claims as prophet, was to surrender to him discretionary powers over the guidance of mankind; and abandon oneself at random to the tide of Mohammedan advancement. Such was not the case, however, with the Old Testament prophets. They never are found seeking to exercise discretionary control over the policy of Israel; but only emphasizing that particular message which they had been sent to deliver, which message they spoke directly in the first place to the ears of a stiff-necked people, and, not till it first had been spoken, undertook, or even left it to their disciples to undertake, the additional task of reducing it to writing; so that far from the collection of their prophecies constituting a claim to an undefined sphere of discretion in the future, it represented in the first instance but the attempt to be faithful to, and to give its due effect to, and to preserve from being entirely forgotten, the message which they already had delivered.

Quite possibly one of the reasons why the prophets seem originally to have avoided the pen, as a medium for the announcement of their message, and to have reserved it rather for the purpose of recording it, was precisely that they were anxious that by speaking it, it should be implanted in the memories of men, and through the memory lying embedded in their hearts, should be retained in the daily life as a living seed, and prove the basis of an appropriate development. Yet still there remains the fact that the resulting development furnishes us no good guarantee for the preservation of the original revelation; viewed as a seed. Upon the contrary, it is nearly certain that it will not so preserve it. According to that deep word of the Apostle:—" That which thou sowest, *thou sowest not that body that shall be.*" " But God giveth it a body as it hath pleased him." Thus while it is the fact that the development is in a sense the outcome and product of the Seed; in a way, it is something different from the Seed, to which, externally and apparently at least, it need not even bear a resemblance. And the consequence is that the Seed itself is buried under, or, to put it otherwise, it perishes for the sake of, the wealth of its own development. Thus, doubtless, it was a purpose of our Lord's ministrations that he might institute a certain development; to run its appointed course in human history; and this development was the natural outcome of his activity and presence; yet, at the same time, the very forces which he himself had set going would never have kept the memory of our Saviour's own life, except in a very vague and uncertain way,—so that it could be constantly re-sown, as seed, in each successive generation,—nor could the details of the original Life be afterwards recovered from the results that it had accomplished. So that, unless its features were preserved in some special and appropriate way, by the side of, and along with, the development to which it gave the impetus, it was destined gradually to fade away from memory, and at last to be almost entirely forgotten. Thus we arrive at what we conceive to be the function that the Bible plays in the structure of Christianity, viz:—

The Bible preserves the record of the Divine Revelation, specifically in the form of seed—truth.

"Thus is the Lord's Prayer," writes Dean Goulburn, "a

seed of prayer, containing in germ every petition which the human heart can send up to God, even as the Decalogue is a seed of precept, containing in germ every rule which can be given for human conduct."* And yet the Prayer, if lost, could hardly be recovered again, out of that exuberance of Christian devotion, which its own petitions have done so much to stimulate; nor could the Decalogue, if once forgotten, be collected again, out of the multitude of succeeding regulations, which attempt to ensure the fulfilment of its precepts.

Whilst it will not come amiss, as an Anglican theologian, to remark that along such lines I understand the Sixth of our Thirty-nine Articles, "Holy Scripture containeth all things necessary to salvation; so that whatsoever is not read therein, nor may be proved thereby, is not to be required of any man, that it should be believed as an article of the Faith, or be thought requisite or necessary to salvation." Not that, by such language, we imply that the very depths of the Christian religion lie *unfolded* in the Scriptures to every casual reader, or that we undervalue the place of legitimate leadership in developing their teaching, what we insist on is that a doctrine which calls itself Christian should be *rooted* at some definite and ascertainable point in the account of revelation and maintain through its development the appropriate type which has been started by the word *as the germ*. This, however, we would regard as fundamental.

No writer, upon the contrary, of the critical school, will be found in this way, proposing a revelation, *as the starting-point* of a system of religious development. The place to which they uniformly assign it can hardly, perhaps, better be stated than in the words of Dr. Driver.

"Criticism", he writes, "in the hands of Christian scholars does not banish or destroy the inspiration of the Old Testament; it *presupposes* it; it seeks only to determine the conditions under which it operates, and the literary forms through which it manifests itself, and it thus helps us to frame truer

---
* The Lord's Prayer. E. P. Dutton & Co., p. 18.

conceptions of the methods which it has pleased God to employ in revealing Himself to His ancient people of Israel, **and in preparing the way for the fuller manifestation of Himself in Christ Jesus.***

The italics, the reader will note, are Dr. Driver's. Observe that the criticism *presupposes* inspiration; whilst it helps us to frame conceptions of the "methods" which have been employed in revelation; or, in other words, that the revelation has been moved down the line, out of its original position as the starting-point, to a new place as the consummation. No longer regarded as a principle, it has now come to be considered a climax. In the meantime, Dr. Driver neglects to inform us, upon what ground it is of scientific method that he makes this presupposition; and what it is exactly that he means by his use of the term "inspiration"?

"The central question", as a recent writer has put it, "after all, is this, Is the Word of God the creation of the Church, or is the Church itself created by the Word of God? . . . . . . If the history is not sufficiently authenticated, then . . . . . the supposed Word of God is the creation of the Church. And it is the thinly disguised purpose, or at least effect, of the Higher Criticism more and more to approximate to this position. . . . . What the Church has made, it can, of course, unmake. Hence the unsatisfactoriness of (these) methods and results."†

Pascal, if I mistake not, has somewhere a question, to the effect that if the same words and phrases once have been joined together in a different order, they make a different sentence; and so, he asks, why should not the same sentences, if only I have joined them together in another order, produce another treatise? thus the parts of the Bible, placed in another order, compose a different Bible. It may not seem a great alteration to change the sequence of the Law and the Prophets into this new arrangement of the Prophets and Law; but what it comes to mean is, that the prophets have invented the commandments

---
* Introduction to the Literature of the Old Testament. Preface p. xiii.
† Church Quarterly Review, Oct. 1899, p. 81.

of the Law, instead of being invigorated by them. So, again, to connect the Pentateuch with Ezra, rather than with Moses, simply transfers it from the time of the entry into the Land of Promise, to that of the exile to a strange land; or, in other words, you neatly have changed it from the beginning to the end of Israel's national history. Consequently the νομοθεσία, the giving of the Law on Mt. Sinai,—not necessarily the Pentateuch as we have it to-day,—but what was actually *spoken* by Moses instead of lying embedded at the very heart of the nation, all along the course of its history, emerges at the close as a legacy. But, then again, the Jews have left us the ideas of the Pharisees, as another sort of legacy. So, if the law is viewed as the outcome of their history, still the system of the Pharisees is an outcome as well; whether the true and proper outcome, of course, is the question; but at least it is a state of things that really was reached. Thus, after all, if Ezra the Scribe was the composer of the Law, what more natural supposition than that the religion it teaches is that of the Scribes and Pharisees? So that we find a German writer coolly pronouncing that, "The Pharisees were the truest disciples of Moses." (Die Pharisäer waren die treuesten Diener Mosis, ihre Theologie ist aber nicht die Christliche.*)

Such, then, is the conclusion to which the critical arguments appear to have ultimately brought us; they have simply given away the whole case to the Pharisees. Far from acknowledging the Pharisees as the true exponents of Moses, our Lord Himself insisted that they did not really know Moses. "Had ye believed Moses, ye would have believed Me; for he wrote of Me." In view of this, I can hardly say honestly that I am prepared to accept altogether the protestations of Dr. Driver that all "apprehensions" about the effects of these critical results on religion are entirely unfounded. It appears to me, that coolly to make a present in this way of the

* Prof. Sepp of Munich; in the Revue Internationale de Théologie, Jan., 1899.
† Introduction; Preface, p. xi.

whole Old Testament to the cause of the Pharisees, and quietly to allow them the whole argument, justifies at least some apprehensions on this score.

Writing, however, from quite another point of view in last November's "Nineteenth Century", Mr. W. H. Mallock, whilst engaged in forecasting the "Future of Catholicism", among sundry other depreciatory statements, has this remark to make on the Bible. He estimates that the "scientific study of history . . . . . . is exhibiting the Biblical books as utterly incompetent, in themselves to supply us with any system of coherent doctrine." " The Church of Rome, on the contrary, by a process of continuous growth, has developed, ... an increasingly conscious unity, and a single organ of thought *and historic memory,* constantly able to explain and re-state doctrine." The reader will observe that our present contention has not exactly been that the Scriptures furnish us a " system of coherent doctrine ". Such systems, doubtless, share in the limitations which appertain to all things human; but it does not therefore follow that they are quite without value. Meanwhile, what we have tried to do, is to make clear that their truest value depends upon their real derivation from some original λόγος, or seed, implanted by God's Revelation, and preserved to our own days, *in its germinal form,* only in the Bible. Now, it is not so much a feature of germinal truth that it should be systematic. System appertains to a stage of maturity. Yet, so far as concerns this "increasingly conscious unity", and this "single organ of thought and historic memory", *from what starting-point* is it, we would ask, that the Church of Rome has been developing these things? Upon what foundation and basis do they rest? Surely not on these same singularly incompetent Scriptures which have already been referred to. However, this plea of Mr. Mallock's for the Papacy, rests exactly on a disbelief in any Divine Revelation, as existing *at the outset.* He insists that whatever truths were believed at the first, were such truths as were at any rate " embedded in a mass of error ", but that upon the other hand this " organ of thought and memory ", and this " increasingly conscious unity ", have been developed after the close of nineteen centuries, as the outcome of intermediate advancement. But, more than this, just as Mohammed viewed the Koran, as being the *organ* of revelation to mankind rather than its record, so Mr. Mallock, as well, is disposed to view the Papacy as an " organ " of truth to the world, and not as its depository. Here, perchance, we have disclosed the real barrier between ourselves and the claims of the Papacy. It is, that it distinctly asserts itself to be an *instrument* for the revelation of God's truth and will; were it only that it was glad to be its guardian, things might, perhaps, be very different. But, through this claim that it can bestow on its own decrees the force of utterances from the mouth of God Almighty, it clusters human life round itself, instead of our Saviour, and enters into a kind of competition with our Lord as the Word of God, so that His own teaching must be kept in the background that the policy of the Vatican may escape interference. Therefore, what room can there be for a choice between the two?

" Say not in thine heart," we find the apostle writing in the epistle to the Romans, " Say not in thine heart, who shall ascend into heaven? (that is, to bring Christ down from above); or, who shall descend into the deep? (that is, to bring up Christ again from the dead). But what saith it? The word is nigh thee, even in thy mouth, and in thy heart, that is, the word of faith, *which we preach;*" that is to say, that the word of God was the apostolic teaching. Set over against this, the apostle sees the thought that the word still remains to be uttered, in the times that were yet in the future, perhaps even in the twentieth century; in the one case proclaimed like a pæan from the heights, *as an achievement,* or wrested with laborious drudgery from the very depths, *as a discovery.* So, on the one hand, there arises before us a proud Authority, propounding its *dicta* as the Word of God, from the summit to which it has climbed in its ambitions; and, on the other, we meet a disdainful so-called science, which trusts to be able to grasp a like position, for its own asservations. Whilst I must say, that the simple Christian seems left standing between them, much in those straits which have been described in the Pilgrim's Progress, on a road between Giant Pope and Giant Pagan, who are neither of them dead yet, and for the present he must just trudge along with Faithful at his side. I can see no good reason why they should prevent him from reaching the Heavenly City, here at the change of the centuries, more than in those preceding.

What Has Become of Hell?

What Has Become of Hell?

BY

The Reverend GEORGE WOLFE SHINN, D.D.

THIS title has been selected, not because of any leaning it may have toward sensationalism, but simply because it states precisely the purpose of this inquiry.

There has been a remarkable change of late years, in religious teaching with reference to future punishment. Whereas formerly in theological papers, in sermons and books of instruction, much was said about hell, now it is but rarely mentioned. In fact, by many an accredited teacher, it is not mentioned at all. It is pertinent to ask, therefore:— What has become of Hell?

We still use the word " hell " in the Apostle's Creed, but we are always careful to explain that there it does not mean the place of punishment, but simply the place of departed spirits; that it has no reference to their condition as happy or unhappy; but simply refers to the separation of soul and body, and to the residence of the soul in an intermediate state or place until the resurrection day. We are not concerned with that use of the word in this inquiry. We have started out to find what has become of hell as a place of punishment. We hear very little about it except in the profanity of the day. Now and then, a man in his wrath, tells another to go to this place. While not approving the profanity, it may be suggested that perhaps this angry brother, who would send his enemy to torture, may boast sometime that but for him a great many people would have known nothing about hell. Or if they had ever heard of it, he revived what feeble recollection they retained. You do not hear of it in the pulpit, or see any reference to it in the religious press, or in the modern theological book, nor is it often brought up in religious conversation. It is tabooed by the pulpit generally. When, under stress, the preacher has to refer to it, he may adopt the euphemistic method of one who spoke of "the place which could not be named in the presence of cultured people."

It was not always thus, as we may learn by taking up almost any book of sermons delivered fifty years ago; or if we read the diaries kept by people who lived in the days of our grand-parents; or if we read the history of religious controversies. In a day not very long past, men argued with each other, concerning the place and the people who were on their way thither. Some of us are not too old to remember the terrible appeals made by the revivalists to flee the wrath to come, and so to escape the pains of hell. The stories which have been handed down to us concerning the great revival movements in this country, show that the prominent theme, which was repeated again and again, and in every possible way, was how to escape from hell.

We know, for example, that so superb a thinker as Johnathan Edwards, the author of "The Freedom of the Will," was also a revivalist of the most intense type; and that he had such power in portraying the dangers of the impenitent, that men screamed out during his sermons.

Go back still farther, and we find that religious literature is full of allusions to hell. We need hardly refer to Milton's Paradise Lost, and to Dante's *Divina Comedia*. The theology of the Middle Ages, was so full of it that men have sometimes thought that hell was a creation of that period.

But go back into Patristic literature and you find it there in large profusion. St. Polycarp said to the pro-consul, "With fire which burns for an hour or so and is extinguished, thou dost threaten me, but dost thou not know of the fire of the future judgment and of the eternal punishment reserved for the ungodly?" St. Augustine took pains to refute the opinions of those who thought that the torments of hell would only be purgatorial, and therefore only of limited duration. St. Chrysostom described the miseries of the future of the lost.

With the exception of Origen and a few of his followers, there was an outspoken belief in hell by all the Fathers.

When we turn to the Sacred Scriptures, we certainly find the recognition of hell in those writings. Unhappily in our English Bible the word hell is made the equivalent of four other words:—Sheol, Gehenna, Tartarus and Hades. It is going over ground very familiar to many to say that "Sheol," the Hebrew word in the Old Testament, usually refers, in an indefinite way, to the grave or the place or condition of the dead. "Hades," the Greek word in the New Testament, has a similar meaning, with perhaps a clearer recognition of continuing life under new conditions. It is the word "Gehenna," also translated hell, upon which so much depends. The name "Gehenna" was taken from the Hebrew word by which the valley of Hinnom was known. That was the valley near Jerusalem where the great sanitary fires, kept up day and night, consumed the refuse of the city and the bodies of unclean beasts, and sometimes the bodies of criminals. From being the name of a locality near the city the word was adopted to refer to that place or condition in the unseen world where punishment would be meted out to the impenitent. And so you find the word used in such passages as:—St. Matthew 5: 22; "shall be in danger of the Gehenna of fire." 5: 29; "and not that thy whole body shall be cast into Gehenna." St. Mark, 9: 43; "into Gehenna, into the fire that shall never be quenched." St. Matthew, 10: 28; "Fear him which is able to destroy both soul and body in Gehenna.

We are not seeking for explanations now, nor are we considering the nature of future punishment and the character of those who are to be punished hereafter. We are simply trying to establish the fact that there is an unbroken chain of testimony to the belief in the existence of hell down to a comparatively recent time. The fact is surely well established. As a fact it cannot be contradicted. Even Origen, under whose arms every heretic seeks refuge now, believed in hell. But he thought it was not to be eternal. He looked for a final restoration. Origen is never to be cited as denying future retribution, but as only disbelieving the eternity of torment.

The belief in hell as a place or condition of punishment, with varying explanations as to the nature and continuance of that punishment, has been the belief of Christian people from the beginning of Christianity to our own day.

Now, almost suddenly, certainly with remarkable unanimity, men have well nigh ceased to talk about it. Whereas they once said much about it, now they say but little; some, indeed, nothing at all. It has ceased to be urged as a motive for good living here in this life, and men are not told to prepare themselves here to avoid it there in the future. In other words, there has been, if not an actual denial of hell, a very thorough change of emphasis.

What has become of hell? Here is surely a very notable change in theology at the close of the nineteenth century. How did it come about? It is claimed by some friends of the late Henry Ward Beecher that he did more than any other man in this country to change the style of thinking of many preachers and of many laymen who admired him. If he did not begin the change he certainly helped on the revulsion from the old doctrines which had been preached, and he dealt some very effective blows at the narrow theology which had been accepted by many as orthodoxy.

The movement, however, for the dissolution of hell began much earlier in this country. The Universalist body came into existence here as early as 1770, as the antagonist of the intense views which were held by the old Calvinists. Universalism has gradually pervaded the country, and has done much to tincture the thought of the religious world. Crude and ignorant as were many of the efforts of the first Universalists, they directed their blows at one point and made their impression.

Perhaps, however, nothing has had so widespread an influence in this direction over intelligent minds in America as

Canon Farrar's book on "Eternal Hope." It found a sympathetic audience prepared for it in different parts of the land, and in different grades of society, and his views were very readily adopted. It was in vain that replies were made, and that Dr. Pusey issued his book entitled, "What is of the Faith?" Evidently many in the religious world wanted to get rid of hell.

A very curious compromise was attempted by some who could not quite accept Farrar and retain their old orthodoxy. The compromise is in the suggestion of a second probation. That is, if one has not had a fair and full chance to know the truth here, he will have a second chance in the other world.

Believers in a second probation retained their belief in a place of punishment. One antagonist of this view of a probation after death, says that to him it seems to be groping for "a new probation, not for the culprit but for the Judge, as if they were apprehensive that, according to their scheme, He would not do the exactly right and infinitely kind and merciful thing the first time." They would give Him a chance to do better later on.

Now, although this is a "smart" way of replying to views of another side, it does not by any means sweep away the foundations on which some build up a belief that the future (before the final judgment) brings not only a growth in goodness for some, but a growth toward goodness for others.

It is very curious how Purgatory, formerly condemned as one of the errors of Romanism, is yet adopted in other forms by the ultra Protestant. Substitute such an expression as "is trained by the bitterness of experience past and present, warned by judgments yet to be fulfilled, in clearer light beholding things in better perspective,"—substitute this sentence for Purgatory, and do you not have the same thing? Purgatory may carry with it gross materialistic conceptions of purifying fires, but the essential thought is the same as that contained in the expressed hope that somehow, when men in another world see what sin is, and how it harms them and dishonours God, they will want to have it purged and done away, and so will welcome the purifying pains. But even if we adopt this view of reparation in a future life we do not get rid of retribution. Nor do we by such a view necessarily get rid of eternal punishment. May there not be some incorrigible ones left over after the last chance of reparation is offered? And if there are any, we are back again to the old thought of an eternal rebellion and hence an eternal penalty.

The usual plan, however, for obliterating hell has been to explain away the language in which the doctrine of eternal suffering is supposed to be set forth. There can be no doubt that figurative language is used. It has been simply impossible to set forth the truths of religion without the use of figurative language. Happiness is declared under the figure of living in a beautiful city,—the city of God. The opposite of the happiness of heaven is the misery of hell. To express this, fire is used as the dominant figure. Fire is a symbol of painfulness, hence of punishment. Then to render fire more horrible, another destructive agent is added,—the suffocating fumes of brimstone; and to express the acme of punishment we have the figure of fire and brimstone, and are told of the lake of fire and brimstone where the smoke of torment continually ascends. When such expressions are used are we dealing with material facts? Is there a city whose streets are paved with gold and whose gates are of pearl? Is there a lake whose waves are liquid fire? The language is figurative. If figurative in one case, figurative in both.

But the figurative language of Scripture has been added to by the efforts of men who have tried to deter their fellowmen from vice by elaborating the horrors of hell. So we have been told of red hot gridirons attended by shrieking demons who have kept the gridirons well filled with broiling victims. We have heard of huge cauldrons full of boiling lead and brimstone to be poured over new comers as the ceremony of welcoming them to the society of the lost. We have heard of a pestilential atmosphere laden with concentrated diseases, and men driven by demons to breathe this disease-laden air. We have heard of horned and cloven-footed demons goading their victims around circles; up and down steep heights; onward and onward, simply for the gratification of their hatred and to add to the sorrows of the lost. We have been told of the great chorus of dreadful shrieks that issued from prisons into which special victims had been driven for special enormities.

What ingenuity men have used to describe the life lived by men in hell! As an illustration of how the materialistic views of hell were kept before the people some centuries ago, think of that strange fresco in an old parish church in England. It is a sample of many like adornments which were once common. Over the chancel arch, where it is continually in sight, is a picture representing the doom of the lost. Some very agile demons with pitchforks are shoving poor wretches, men and women, down the throat of an awful monster. They do not seem to like it, but the monster does. His appetite is insatiable and he has room for them all in his capacious maw. A nice thing to look at every Sunday! Weather stains mercifully obliterated the worst of it after awhile and would have got rid of it all, but along came the restorer,—the ecclesiologist—and he brought it back in all its hideousness.

Figurative language has been taken literally; translated into the grossest materialism and then added to until its very extravagance suggested revolt. But when the revolt came those who would get rid of the materialistic views of hell have so completely explained away all the figurative language in which reference is made to hell in the Scriptures that nothing is left. Or, to state it in other words, because they objected to the views held, they have tried to deny the reality back of even the figurative terms in which that reality was set forth.

Another effort has been made to relieve some of the awfulness associated with the idea of hell, by making explanations of the words "eternal," "everlasting," and whatever seems to imply the changeless condition of the sufferings of the lost. One of the most ingenious is that which requires us to observe that "eternal" is not always the attribute but the result. Thus "eternal redemption" means eternal in its results. The act of redemption was accomplished on the Cross in a day; the results are eternal. Sodom and Gomorrah are spoken of as the prey of eternal fire, yet the fire does not continue. It is the result of the fire which is spoken of.

Again much is said of eternity as relating to this age, this æon, and it has the idea of completing a circle; but there may be, according to some who hold this view, other circles beyond. This is an æon, and eternity has reference to this period over which the gleam of revelation is thrown. There may be æons and eternities and eternities beyond.

Then the philosophers come along and tell us that we know nothing at all of time when we get beyond the present material facts. Time is the succession of events. When we get out of the region of material things there is no time. And here comes that old monastic story to illustrate what the philosophers mean. The monk, delighted with the singing of the birds one summer morning, roused himself upon thinking he had lost a few moments in an accustomed enjoyment, and discovered that he had been listening a thousand years. And so the philosopher says that such expressions as "everlasting," "eternal," are to be regarded as the blue haze which ends our view as we look over the horizon. Everything shades off into this vaporous nothing and ends there; that is, so far as we know. We are carried thus far, and then we are told that that is the end of time.

One of the most ingenious and earnest efforts in the way of explanation of what is involved in the doctrine of hell is called "conditional immortality." The leading idea is that all men are capable of survival in their spiritual nature, but that not all will survive eternally. Some may cease to be after death of the body; others may live after death and be punished for awhile, but they are finally resolved into nothingness. Men who do not possess the sanctifying, renewing, immortal spirit must perish, either at death or some time after death. According to this view, immortality is a special gift to those who are united to Christ by faith. All those souls not brought into union with Him lose their power, and eventually lose all conscious individuality. That is, they cease to be.

The doctrine of conditional immortality makes it necessary to deny the natural immortality of the human soul. This is a most important point, for if the soul may cease to be, then eternal death means a dissolution which continues eternally. It is boldly declared by those who hold this view that the Scriptures speak nowhere of immortality apart from Christ; that there is no permanent life except for the believer.

There are many things connected with this doctrine of conditional immortality which would make almost any one wish he could accept it.

These various theories,—denials, explanations and the like—indicate a most unsettled condition of Christian eschatology at the close of the nineteenth century. There is no agreement among Christian people on these points, but on the contrary there is great divergence of view, as is very evident in sermons and newspapers, in trials for heresy and in the discussions of ordinary people. It is most seen in the uncertain sounds which proceed from the pulpit, and in the almost entire cessation of the appeal to fear. Appeals to fear now!—How seldom are men warned of the judgment to come! Hell has lost its terrors. What has become of hell?

The appeals to fear have well nigh ceased, and yet there is no fact which we are so compelled to see as the fact of retribution. The law of retribution works in our present life. We become aware of it in earliest infancy, and we never become developed in character until we have learned to fear that which is evil and to shun the consequences of sin. There is a sense of righteousness in all men, and all men know that unrighteousness brings punishment. It is fair to assume that what holds good in the present life,—that what is a part of man's very structure here, will continue hereafter. We may give up entirely the notion of a material hell, but we cannot give up the doctrine of retribution. Suffering must follow sin, and therefore to appeal to fear is not only legitimate but it is in accordance with the structure of man's nature. Let us grant that the descriptions of hell are figurative. Let us admit that men have blundered in accepting as literal what was intended to be figurative. Let us grant that there is no material lake of torment. Yet after all there is something back of the imagery. There is something real: so real that men may well strive to escape it. It cannot be well with him who passes hence in his sins.

If we are asked for reasons for believing in future retribution we need not dwell upon the thought of Divine sovereignty showing its detestation of sin by punishment. That view has been brought out with frightful distinctness in Puritan theology. Rather let us call attention to the fact which forces itself upon the notice of even the less thinking men. It is this:—*Men are condemned by themselves.* They must recognize at some period that they prepared themselves for their own place and for their own condition. A rather grotesque illustration of this point is suggested by a once popular preacher. It is the story of a man who got into the wrong boat. He was a prize fighter, and, rushing in a hurry to embark on an excursion boat, got into one filled with a company of enthusiastic Methodist people bound for a camp-meeting. When the boat started he found out his mistake and offered the captain all the money he had if he would land him somewhere. He was out of place. His character did not accord with that around him. He was a most unhappy man.

Feeble as the illustration is, it suggests that each man is making his own future along the lines of his own character. Now if this be so it is perfectly legitimate to appeal to fear. There is, however, such a tone of uncertainty about this matter of retribution that people almost gain the impression that religious teachers are trifling with them. The dread of speaking out boldly causes many a sermon to lose its point. The preacher seems afraid to say what he believes, or appears to be in great doubt whether after all it makes any difference how people live. Some lay people have great reluctance in hearing anything about hell or retribution of any kind. It is a distasteful topic. Awhile ago a clergyman was requested to resign his parish because of a difference between his vestrymen and himself upon this subject. He warned his hearers in some sermons that unrepented sin must be punished in another world. His vestrymen informed him they did not believe in hell any longer and they seemed to think they had abolished it by ceasing to believe in it.

But however distasteful it is to men, as there is such a thing as retribution it must be set forth. There is no need of falling into the error of those who delighted in describing the doom of the lost; nor into the error of others who mistake what is figurative for what is literal. No need of allowing the imagination to run riot over the mysteries of the future. In a straight-forward fashion they who believe in retribution must declare the difference between the righteous and the wicked.

The pulpit is losing some of its power because it so seldom appeals to healthy fear. It has been taken for granted that men could always be reached by appeals to their better nature. The fact has been overlooked that the better nature is often hidden from sight by the encrustation of worldliness and sin. The conscience of men must be aroused, and the most effectual quickening of conscience is through the dread of the judgment to come.

It is not for any of us to explain the thousand difficulties that spring up just as soon as we think of the separation of men by character in the world now unseen. It is not well to discuss them in the pulpit, for we have so little to help us in the formation of opinions. The contention is that as there is future retribution, so men must be warned against it now, and there must be an appeal again and again made to the motive of fear.

It is this failure to appeal to fear which accounts in part for the decline of interest in personal religion by so many. It is the seeming willingness of so many Christian people to give up all reference to retribution that is making it difficult for some to know what course to pursue. We may talk as we will about the evanescent nature of fear, and we may talk about its being an inferior motive, but in all other things in life it is appealed to. Take it out of life and chaos comes in ordinary matters. Because it has been taken out of religion—out of the religion of our time—there has been the weakening of the force of religion. If we had perfectly normal beings to deal with—and that is a modern way of saying, if we were all without sin—then might there be no reference to fear, but an appeal to everything high and holy within us. We have to do with beings who are sinful and who must be led up to the higher motives by the exercise of the lower.

What then has become of hell? It has not been obliterated. It cannot be obliterated. Retribution exists as an awful fact back of all figurative language. Men in our day have overlooked retribution in seeking to get rid of materialistic notions concerning hell. The time has come to recall the awful fact of retribution. But it must be done discreetly, and always with those exceptions in mind which so greatly modify it.

There are allowances to be made when we consider the working out of retribution as it pertains to the future. First of all, it cannot include children in its penalty inasmuch as not inherited sin but wilful sin is punished, and children are irresponsible. And we read one of the reasons why there has been such revolt against the doctrine of retribution. It has been taught that men are to be condemned for original sin. One of the thirty-nine articles of the Anglican and American Churches has a clause which has often been misunderstood in favour of such teaching. "It deserveth God's wrath and damnation." What? Not the being who has come into this inheritance of sin, but original sin itself. Certainly God hates sin. But there came One who was without sin. He came to be the Lamb without spot, who by the sacrifice of Himself once made, should take away the sins of the world.

Here then, on one hand, is an universal fact,—the infection of sin in every human being; and sin deserves God's wrath and damnation. On the other hand is another fact as universal,—that Christ has tasted death for every man;—died that He might pay the penalty for every man. Does not one fact overbalance the other? If so, there can be no wrath or damnation now for the infection of our nature. Punishable sin is the conscious violation of law.

Then, in the next place, in thinking of future retribution we must always think of the large number of people who are as irresponsible as the veriest infants. They may have intelligence enough for the purposes of daily life but no more. The religious nature, existing somewhere in every human being, finds but imperfect modes of manifestation, or is altogether hidden. We are not speaking of idiots or of the insane, but of many people who, while belonging in neither of these classes, are no more responsible than are children. We cannot think of their being consigned to penalty in the other world.

Then as we think of future retribution we come to the great bulk of those who have never had the opportunity to hear the Gospel,—the vast multitude of the heathen. Are they all condemned for the infection of their nature, if Christ died for them? Are they all condemned for rejecting a Gospel of which they have never heard? What of the heathen, then, in the life to come? We can know very little about their future condition except that they will be judged righteously according to a standard which they themselves must admit is just.

Part of the perplexity with reference to the heathen arises from two errors,—first, in thinking of them as all equally condemned to perdition, and then thinking of eternal happiness as alike for all the saved. Since the sacrifice of Christ the heathen stand as all other men. They come within the merits of that sacrifice although they are unconscious of the fact. If they are condemned it will not be because of original sin, but because they have not lived up to their own laws.

When a correct view is taken of responsibility—responsibility according to knowledge—it relieves the doctrine of retribution considerably, inasmuch as it narrows down the number of the lost to those who consciously and wilfully reject the offer of salvation.

When, beside all this, we take a correct view of future bliss and of future woe we find still more relief. It cannot be that all the redeemed in the future will be equally happy and that all the lost will be equally wretched, for there are varying degrees of capacity. There must be an immeasurable distance, for example, between the saintly martyr whose whole life was a conflict and whose death came as a happy release,—an immeasurable distance between his experiences in the eternal kingdom and those of a little child whose coming into life and whose departure hence were on the same day. There must be infinite grades of happiness there, as there must be vast differences between those who are driven into outer darkness.

And what of those who are driven from the presence of the Lord? What are their experiences? How long does their expulsion last? Is it forever and forever? Or is there some limit? If they learn obedience through their sufferings, will their sufferings end? And is there in some far off future some final restoration so that the last vestige of rebellion shall be removed?

What answers shall be given to these questions? No man can answer them except to express the hope that somehow the justice of God may be satisfied, and the sinner's rebellion cease. But we know nothing clearly upon these points. We do know that there is retribution for sin,—for sin unrepented of and unforgiven. Whether that retribution continue for one year, or for a thousand years, or for eternity is not material to decide. He who dies in sin passes on to be judged for the deeds done in the body. Having rejected the offers of mercy here he must meet penalty there. The man who dies impenitent and unforgiven finds his retribution.

Judgment, like the gift of life, is immediate. It is not to be looked for only in the future. It is now. The soul that sins dies. If one would know what sin merits, he sees in the cross of Christ a costly sacrifice for its cancellation. There God has registered His estimate of sin, and there we are to read what sin is, from what sin has done. Future judgment is no arbitrary act. It is not something which springs from laws to be set in motion hereafter. It is the working out of laws under which we are now living. If we sin wilfully now, we must suffer for it. If we pass hence with a load of unrepented and unforgiven sin, judgment must surely follow us wherever we go. But it is not a new judgment. It is only a continuation of a judgment begun here; something inseparable from sin. Why should we fear to speak of a judgment to come when we know that a judgment has already come? True, the present judgment is not in every instance that which brings bitter anguish, but it is just as real as if men groaned in agony. It is a separation from goodness; a loss of spiritual power; a falling below the ideal. When men's eyes are opened they may see that the loss of what they might have been and their degradation through sin, is indeed the visitation of penalty. Judgment consists quite largely in deprivation. Such a judgment has begun here and it points to the awful issues of the future when the day of earthly probation shall have ended.

We must admit the moral government of God in the present life. What reason is there to think that it will cease in another life? If sin be the corruption of man's nature, and that corruption be not checked here, then the man goes hence with an inward condition that seeks to conform itself to its surroundings. What can they be? Surely whatever they are they are different from the surroundings of those who have received that corrective of evil which is provided by the incarnation of Christ and the indwelling of the Spirit.

When we think of an evil man seeking to find his place in the other world, how can we object to the use of expressions of Scripture such as "fire", "darkness", "chains"? Do not these figurative words enable us to catch a glimpse of wretchedness such as other words could not express? Figurative though they may be they point to some fearful reality. Suppose it to be the ceaseless wailing of regret:—" This is my doing. I brought this on myself." Can we fully understand the agony of such iteration? Over and over, " I brought this on myself." No shifting of responsibility. Nothing but a clear-eyed view of what he has done, and of what he has lost. And that to go on and on! Why, whoever has felt here in this life one hour's remorse knows what hell is, for he has experienced it in his own soul. To endure it for a day, or a year, for many years, for an æon! God help us, we cannot even grasp the thought! We struggle with words that tell us of fire and darkness and demons and chains and torment, but with the result of knowing only that there is some frightful reality far beyond our present human experiences. One of the most solemn questions asked by our Lord of certain hypocrites was, " How can ye escape the damnation of hell? " The damnation of Gehenna! He who warned men against speaking idle words, could He himself use words that were idle? There must surely be something to dread else He had not warned men to escape it.

Future Punishment

Future Punishment

BY

The Reverend CHARLES ALBERT DICKINSON, D.D.

UNQUESTIONABLY the doctrine of future retribution does not hold the place in religious thought that it held fifty or even twenty-five years ago. Theologians do not emphasize it as they once did; preachers do not make as much use of it as a warning; and it apparently has very little influence as a working belief in the lives of the laity. This is especially true of Protestants. Among the Catholics the doctrine has a stronger hold, but even among the more intelligent classes of that faith it seems to be weakening.

This change is not peculiar to any one country, but is general throughout Christendom, being more pronounced, perhaps, where intelligent progress is more marked.

Prof. Joseph Angus, D.D., a leading Baptist of London, said within the last decade: "The doctrine of future punishment has become within the last fifty years a subject of grave discussion; and not a few writers think that the evidence of a state of eternal conscious punishment has been greatly shaken." Bishop E. R. Hendrix, D.D., of the Methodist Episcopal Church, South, says, "That the doctrine of future retribution after death is less frequently a theme of the pulpit than was the case a generation ago is doubtless true." And says Dr. Washington Gladden, an eminent Congregationalist, "It seems to be generally believed that the opinion of the church with respect to retribution has been greatly changed within the last century. As to the forms by which the doctrine is set forth, this belief is well founded."

The question occurs to the thoughtful mind, is this change in the direction of a final elimination from our creeds of the doctrine, or is it tending toward such a restatement of the doctrine that it will eventually have a more vital effect upon life and character than formerly? Has the new century found us, as some think, drifting carelessly into an indifferent materialism, or is it true as that eminent German scholar, Dr. C. F. Kling, affirms, "that our age enters with an earnestness and intensity such as no earlier one has done, into the eschatological examination, and presses forward in the complete development of this doctrine—one sign among the many that we are hastening to the great decision?"

I am inclined to agree with Dr. Kling, and to see in the changes in theological thought and statement which have made the end of the old century notable, an epochal transition of the human mind from ecclesiastical error to Gospel truth, and from the slavery of literalism to the liberty of the Spirit.

In 1889 an interesting volume entitled *That Unknown Country* was published, in which some fifty of the most able representatives of religious thought in this and other countries expressed their views upon future retribution. The volume has a special interest, not only because it brings together so many divergent views concerning the form of the doctrine, but because it reveals the fact that even the most liberal thinker seems forced by reason to admit that there is some kind of retribution after death. On the one hand, we have set forth by Dr. Hewit, Superior of the Paulist Institute of New York, the extreme penal theory which originated with the Latin Fathers, and which for twelve centuries has prevailed in the Roman Catholic Church and among the orthodox Protestants; and on the other hand, we have the milder theories of God's dealings with the impenitent, as presented by such thinkers as Dr. Lyman Abbott and Dr. Edward Everett Hale.

The striking feature of the volume is the conscious or unconscious attempt of nearly all of the writers to break away from, or to mitigate the stern logic of the old Latin system, and to repudiate the aspersions cast upon the divine character by the Latin conception of hell,—a feature which is evidently indicative of the general tendency of modern religious thought.

The feature of the old theory of future retribution which

most offends modern reason, and antagonizes modern Christian sentiment is that the impenitent soul is tortured by an almighty wrathful God to satisfy His justice. The Presbyterian Confession of Faith teaches that the punishment of sin shall be "most grievous torments in soul and body without intermission in hell-fire forever." Spurgeon said, "In fire exactly like that we have on earth thy body will lie asbestos-like forever unconsumed; all thy veins roads for the feet of pain to travel on." And President Edwards taught that hell is like a red-hot oven in which the wicked are to be eternally roasted for the glory of God; all of which ideas are but somewhat exaggerated echoes of the literalisms of the Latin Schoolmen, one of whom, who flourished A. D. 300, declares that in hell "the intelligent fire burns the limbs and restores them, feeds on them and nourishes them."

While such representations might impress, and perhaps frighten into an unwilling penitence the ignorant masses of past ages, they could in the long run only repel the intelligent thinker whose conception of God is derived from the words of Christ as interpreted by the Christian consciousness of the nineteenth century, and so the last few years have witnessed many notable attempts upon the part of theological and religious leaders to rescue the doctrine of future retribution from the odium into which it had fallen, and reinstate it as a power in modern preaching. While many of our ablest thinkers have been thus employed, and while there have been several hot controversies like that which nearly rent the American Board asunder some years ago, the rank and file of the clergy have hesitated to preach upon the subject, the average churchgoer has grown more and more skeptical concerning it, and the unchurched masses, if they think of it at all, only make light of it. The doctrine, like a dilapidated sanctuary, seems to be temporarily closed for repairs, and although skilful builders are at work upon it, there is evidently danger that the present generation will not be able to make much use of it. The time has not come, as it must come, when the truth that the wages of sin must inevitably be moral and spiritual death will make such a potent appeal to the enlightened reason that men will act as instinctively and continuously under the influence of it as they now act under the influence of the simple proposition that fire burns.

Any opinion upon the exact status of the doctrine would necessarily be relative, and dependent not only upon the view point of the observer, but upon his theological predilections. We are at present in the whirl and dust of the transition period, and what we see are doubtless very imperfect parts of the rehabilitated truth. With the proneness of the laity to do their own thinking, and the inability of theologians to agree in their thinking, it would be rash to attempt to say what any considerable body of people really do believe upon this subject. The very fact, however, that the church universal has not yet given its sanction to any definite statement of the doctrine would seem to indicate that it is not within the purpose of revelation, as it certainly is not within the power of reason, to state it in clearly defined terms. The advocates of diametrically opposed statements think that they are sustained by the Bible, and reason has as many theories as there are theorists. From my own standpoint I can see as it were certain shapes in the air which suggest at least whither the thought of the day is tending.

The doctrine of the Fatherhood of God with its correlate the Brotherhood of Man is to be, I think, the working centre of the theology and anthropology of the twentieth century. From this centre, where Christ Himself evidently stood, we are to derive our views of God's character and administration, and our conceptions of the future life. It might almost be said that the chief characteristic of modern religious thought is the emphasis which it gives to the Divine Fatherhood. It is doubtless due to this conception of God's character that the old doctrine of retribution has been so seriously shattered, and that from its fragments so many new and modified forms have appeared. Taking the three classes into which Christendom may be roughly divided, the theological teachers, the professing believers, and the unchurched masses, it is doubtless true that a vast majority of them are to-day bringing all of their religious beliefs and ideas to the test of this central doctrine. The masses outside the churches, so far as they think at all upon the subject of a future life, rest consciously or unconsciously in the belief that God is a good Father, and are either Agnostics or practical universalists; the churchgoing people, while they desire to be loyal to their creeds, are nevertheless very restive under the old-time retributive clauses, and either insist upon their revision, or interpret them in the light of God's love in a way that would have incurred the charge of heresy fifty years ago; while the theologians, influenced to a greater or less extent by this all prevailing conception of the Divine Father are, as has already been said, doing their best to restate the doctrine of future retribution so that it shall be true to Christ's thought upon the subject, and at the same time shall not violate that universal Christian consciousness, which is the century's most glorious product of His other teachings. Among the attempts in this direction which have already won many advocates may be mentioned the following:

CONDITIONAL IMMORTALITY

The teachers of this theory, one of the ablest of whom is Rev. Edward White, D.D., of England, insist that natural immortality is taught neither by reason nor by primeval tradition, nor by Revelation, but is denied by the Scriptures both explicitly and expressly; that everlasting life is the gift of God through Christ; and that everlasting death is just what the terms imply,—the eternal non-existence of the soul. This view finds wide acceptance in England, and it is gaining ground in this country.

II. UNIVERSALISM

This perhaps is the tacit belief of the greatest number of those who think of a hereafter. It has many forms, each of which admits that sin is punished, but all of which teach that all men everywhere will be saved. Some Universalists believe that salvation begins before or at the time of death; others think that there are penalties beyond the grave, but that in the " restitution of all things "

> "—— Not one soul shall be destroyed,
> Or cast as rubbish to the void,
> When God hath made the pile complete."

In one or the other of these theories, annihilation or restoration, multitudes of earnest religious thinkers find it possible to reconcile the Scriptural declarations concerning the final state of the impenitent with Christ's representation of God as a loving Father. Some unable to believe that any soul can ever cease to exist, and convinced that all sin must have its fitting penalty, admit that that penalty may extend beyond the grave, but deny that it is eternal. Assured in their own minds " that *aiovios* does not by any means always or necessarily connote endlessness," they accept the doctrine of restoration. Others, convinced " that the most awful fact in human life is the fact that man can resist all the sympathetic pleadings of God, and that it is not within the power of omnipotent love to save a soul against its will," find no ground in human nature or the Bible for a belief in universal salvation, and so take refuge in the theory of the final annihilation of the wicked. Both schools, convinced that a good God *will not* suffer any sentient being in His universe to remain in eternal agony, and that an omnipotent God *cannot* suffer an eternal rebellion in His universe, come, by opposing hypotheses, to ultimate agreement in the Scriptural passage: " It pleased the Father that in Him should all fulness dwell; and having made peace through the blood of His cross, by Him to *reconcile all things unto Himself* . . . whether they be things in earth or things in heaven."

Now while this is the trend of much of the modern thinking when unhampered by ecclesiastical traditions and expediencies, there is, apart from these and all other hypotheses, a growing conviction in the consciousness of the age as to the real seriousness of sin and its penalty. The old penal and governmental statements concerning future punishment were so unreal and confusing, that they had little grip upon human life and character; and it is perhaps too true, as an eminent writer has said: " A sign that the received philosophy of retribution has ceased to represent any real belief is seen in the scarcely concealed tendency everywhere observable among the champions of the old theology to treat the whole subject lightly. The theme is one around which humour is often suffered to play in ministers' meetings; many facetious allusions of one sort or another are made to it; if it must not be said of some of them that hell is a huge joke, it is certain that it cannot be regarded by them as an awful reality. And yet if Christ's words are to be accepted, hell is an awful reality; it is something more awful in its destructive possibilities and pathetic impossibilities than any physical burning of fire and brimstone. It is the awful alternative to heaven in a world of moral beings whom infinite love has endowed with the power of choice; and the awfulness consists not so much in the pain of him who chooses hell, as in the sorrow of God and all good creatures who are obliged to witness the choice, without the power to avert it. The moral degeneration and ruin attached to selfishness, and which will forever be attached to it, is a condition which grows more awful and impressive as the race becomes more enlightened spiritually: the new century will be impressed with it as no former age has been. This doctrine lies at the root of all of Christ's teachings, and as has been well said, " It can be preached with the demonstration of the Spirit and with power. No man who understands this view of the subject will ever be heard treating it facetiously, and he will feel that the terrible fact must continually be kept before the eyes of transgressors."

In connection with this general review of the status of the doctrine of future punishment in modern religious thought, I have been asked to give my own view concerning it. Perhaps this view has already been unconsciously foreshadowed in what I have written. I believe that the moral consequences of sin are inevitable and awful, but that they are perfectly consistent with the love of God as a Father. God works in and through His universe according to what we call natural laws. These laws are nothing more nor less than God's method of expressing Himself. They are the ways in which He creates the world, the human body, and the human spirit, " and adjusts one substance and form to another in the infinitely complex relations of matter and spirit to attain the purposes of His love." These laws are "the hands of the living God," with which He holds up, preserves, and controls His universe. They are the hands which swing the constellations along the blanks of space, which hold Arcturus and Orion in their orbits, which hurl the thunderbolts, spread out the clouds like a canopy, and gather the waters of the ocean into their hollow. They are round about us everywhere. They are the hands of the living God, who is working here and now in every blade of growing grass and every falling drop of water. They are the hands which sustain and keep us as long as we conform ourselves to their guidance; but it is a fearful thing to fall into or against them either in a physical or a spiritual sense. Some time ago in a Southern city a horse which was tied to an iron post was seen to fall suddenly dead. A man seeing him fall rushed across the street, and putting his hand on the iron post stooped to take hold of the horse's bridle, when to the amazement of the spectators he too fell dead beside the horse. A second man rushed to his assistance, and, in stooping to lift him, brought his head near the iron post. There was a flash and he too fell upon the pavement unconscious, but not dead. What was the secret of these terrible phenomena? The horse and the men had fallen into the hands of the living God. They had unconsciously violated a law of their physical being and made their bodies the conductor of that subtle and awful force which we call electricity. An electric wire had fallen upon the iron post and had surcharged it with death which, under other circumstances, would have been light and life giving power. Nobody thought of blaming God for this calamity. People in spite of these constantly occurring accidents still consider electricity as one of the most beneficent and useful forces of the physical world.

Now what is true physically is true in a larger sense spiritually. The violation of a spiritual law brings spiritual pain and suffering. God has made us so that we can be happy only when we are in harmony with Him. It is a part of the very nature of things that sin and selfishness shall bring their own punishment, for they put us out of harmony with God. They make us so that we do not love the things which God loves or desire the things which He desires. They shut us up to ourselves so that we keep growing smaller and smaller spiritually until what ought to be a large happy soul becomes a miserable little thing incapable of loving anything.

But God loves us for all this, and His mercy never ceases. Stricken as man is with the disease of selfishness, God makes every provision to restore him, and when man refuses to be restored, and persists in turning his back upon divine love, and going out of the world in selfish impenitence, still I believe he will meet with no experience in after life that will in any way reflect upon the divine compassion.

I will illustrate what I believe to be the Biblical view of this man's hereafter. A wealthy father has a son, who through some violation of the law of his being has become hopelessly insane. The father is plunged into the deepest sorrow and does everything within his power to bring his son back to his right mind, but all in vain. The father becomes deeply interested in other insane people, and finally his love and sympathy for this unfortunate class which no skill can relieve or cure, prompt him to build and endow a magnificent hospital wherein every convenience and comfort are provided for those who have lost their minds. Go into that hospital with me and walk through its various wards. Here you see a poor woman who thinks she must figure up the number of grains of sand on the seashore. Love has provided for her paper, slate and pencil, and there she sits day after day intent only on that endless maze of figures. Here is a man who thinks that he must pay the national debt; he is frantic and desperate whenever he is not counting his money. Love has provided him with a box of coppers, and he is counting them out over and over again from sunrise to sunset. Go farther and open that door. It is very dark within, and you shudder when you are told that a human being has to dwell there all the time. She has a peculiar kind of mania, and withal her eyes have become so sensitive that she cannot bear the least ray of light without excruciating pain. Love has made for her a separate room and drawn the curtains close. Go a step farther and look in through that grated door. There sits the son of the wealthy founder of this hospital. His hands are manacled, his eyes are bloodshot and restless. There is the look of a demon on his face. Love has put him behind those iron bars and manacled his hands, for without these barriers he would take the life of his best friend. He has even conceived an intolerable hatred for his father. He is madly beside himself; beyond the possibility of ever knowing or realizing that his father loves him.

What have these unfortunate people in common with you and me? They cannot mingle with us, or sympathize with us, or work with us. Their direful misfortune has put them out of the sphere of rational humanity, and all that human love and sympathy can do, is to make them as comfortable as possible till the end shall come.

There is nothing which so exactly defines sin in the Biblical sense as madness. The prodigal was beside himself. His return to the father is spoken of as " coming to himself," to his right mind. A man's true self is that which is always kept in harmony with God. When he turns from God and gives himself over to his selfish appetites and desires he is much like those unfortunates who, imprisoned in their one weary idea, were trying to reckon up the sands on the seashore, or pay the national debt. This one idea which isolates a man from God and from his fellowmen, this selfish figuring for one's own interests, this habit of selfish thinking and selfish loving, man must take with him to the isolation of the world to come, and it must be to him his world in which he must live, and move, and have his being. Though infinite love may surround him even there with the tokens of its compassion, though it shall do all that Omnipotence can do to mitigate his sufferings, yet the probability is that there, as here, he will remain in stolid unconsciousness of the divine yearning and care, and possibly with manacled hands, think with hatred of the holy and loving God. This is what he sometimes does in his madness here upon the earth before he has entered the great asylum which love itself has provided for them that are lost.

You ask me how long this asylum shall stand in God's universe. I answer, as long as one mad, unhappy soul needs the restraining power of omnipotent love, so long shall it be true that God shall " make the wrath of men to praise Him, and the remainder of wrath will He restrain; " so long shall all heaven wonder at and adore that marvellous mercy which provides even for its enemies an asylum to mitigate, so far as in Omnipotence lies, the wretchedness which they have brought upon themselves and in which they choose to remain.

But how long will they choose to remain? As long perhaps as they shall have the power of choice. Dives does not ask to go to Abraham's bosom. There are no attractions for him there. He simply wants Lazarus to come to his place and relieve his thirst. "Unrestrained appetite was his sin on earth, unsatisfied appetite is his punishment." All he wants in Hades is to have his appetite appeased, and the thing which he most wants is the thing which he cannot have. It is not in the power of infinite love to give it to him any more than it was in the power of the father to take the burning fever out of his mad boy's brain. Love could surround Dives with external comforts. It could perhaps make for him a mansion in Hades whose windows would look out upon the sun-kissed hills of Paradise, but it cannot relieve him of his selfish self or compel him to covet a place in Abraham's bosom.

This is the best solution I can give of the dark mysteries which surround our subject. I have no arithmetic by which I can reckon the duration of retribution. I have no philosophy which proves to me that sin is necessarily immortal. I would that the conviction of my mind were as strong as the desire of my heart that

> "Good shall fall
> At last, far off, at last to all,
> And every winter change to spring."

"So runs my dream." I wish it were more than a dream. I blame no man who tries to find in reason and in Scripture this *Ultima Thule* of the world's hope. If I cannot conclude with him that the consummation of Christ's work must be the final restoration of the entire race, it is not because I do not sympathize with him in his attempt to solve the dark problem of human sin and misery, but because my reason and my interpretation of the Scriptures prevent me from reaching this conclusion. I cannot be a Universalist because I do not believe in the power of Omnipotence to save a soul against its will, and because everything which I can see here in this world among men indicates that there is a point beyond which evil character becomes fixed and unchangeable.

If, however, a man should tell me that in the far-off æons of eternity the vast asylum of the lost shall be depopulated because the madness of sin has spent itself and its victims have dropped away into that eternal unconsciousness which is "the blackness of darkness," and "the second death," I should be more willing to agree with him, for I am more and more convinced that the final end of sin is death, and that life and immortality are the gift of God through Jesus Christ our Lord.

My own struggle has been in reconciling the divine love with the fact of a future retribution. This done, I am willing to leave the times and seasons in God's hands.

Is Punishment Everlasting?

Is Punishment Everlasting?

BY

The Reverend JAMES DE NORMANDIE, D.D.

THE view of the Christian church upon the subject of punishment is unmistakable. For many centuries it has been quite commonly held that, for the vast majority of souls, punishment was in a realm of fiery tortures, and it was everlasting.

From the time of Origen, a few voices, here and there, have been lifted against this view; but they have been feeble and almost unheard amidst the loud and consenting testimony of the great body of believers. Those who are predestined unto life were chosen unto everlasting glory, and all others were bound over to the wrath of God, subject to death, " and most grievous torments in soul and body, without intermission, in hell fire forever."

All through Christian literature one meets passages which show that, as if by common consent, this view was held without question. " How shall I admire," says Tertullian, " how laugh, how rejoice, how exult, when I behold so many proud monarchs groaning in the lowest abyss of darkness, so many magistrates liquefying in fierier flames than they ever hurled against the Christians, so many philosophers blushing in redhot fires with their deluded pupils, so many tragedians more tuneful in the expression of their own sufferings, so many dancers tripping more nimbly from anguish than ever before from applause!" A modern theologian says " Should the fire of eternal punishment cease, it would in a great measure obscure the light of heaven and put an end to a great part of the happiness and glory of the blessed." Another writes, " that the saints may enjoy their beatitude and the grace of God more richly, a perfect sight of the punishment of the damned is granted to them." The American Board of Commissioners for Foreign Missions says. " To send the gospel to the heathen is a work of great exigency. Within the last thirty years a whole generation, of five hundred millions, have gone down to eternal death." Occasionally in some official way we find that this view is still emphasized. Canon Liddon of St. Paul's, the leading preacher and theologian of the English Church in the present generation, in a sermon of ordination, wherein he pleads with the candidates to declare the whole counsel of God, refers to a decision where it was ruled " that it is permissible in law for a clergyman to express a hope for the final restoration of the lost ", and then adds: " The question is a question not of the inclinations of a sinful creature, but of the revealed will of a holy God. May we consistently with that will indulge that hope? Assuredly not." " For nothing is more certain than that by the terms of the Christian revelation any such hope is delusive and vain, since it is opposed to the awful truth that they who die out of favour with God and are lost are lost irrevocably, lost forever. If Holy Scripture is still to be our rule of faith, Scripture, I submit, is decisive. If endless punishment could be described in human words, no words could exhaust the description more absolutely than the recorded words of Christ. They admit of no limitation, they are patient of no toning down or softening away; in the page of the evangelist they live for all time before the eyes of men, in all their vivid, awful power. If Jesus Christ has taught us anything certain about the other world, we cannot doubt that the penal fire must last forever."

Of course Canon Liddon ignores all the results of modern Biblical criticism, which probably he was unwilling or fearful to study, and takes his stand upon the old idea of the literal inspiration and infallibility of the scriptures; and for those who take this view there are many passages to substantiate it. " Scripture ", he says truly, " is no less explicit as to the endlessness of the woe of the lost soul than as to the endlessness of the scene or instrument of its punishment."

We find the words " eternal ", " everlasting ", and " forever and ever " associated with torment and destruction and fire. "The vengeance of eternal fire." "They perish forever without any regarding it." "O God, why hast thou cast us off forever?" "The everlasting burning." "Lord of the everlasting fire." Jude speaks of "a blackness of darkness" which is reserved forever. Revelation says of the penal woe of the lost, that it lasts "unto ages of ages."

One may put over against these a multitude of expressions which utterly deny and make impossible the idea of any everlasting wrath of God being visited upon His children in the form of eternal fire or punishment. How can we reconcile with any such doctrine passages like these:—"His anger endureth but for a moment"; "He will not always chide, neither will He keep His anger forever"; "the Lord is merciful and gracious, slow to anger and plenteous in mercy"; "the goodness of God endureth continually"; "like as a father pitieth his children, so the Lord pitieth them that fear Him"; "God is love"; while the whole life and teaching of Jesus and the whole spirit of the gospels and epistles have a great overweight against the idea of eternal punishment in any place of fire. It has not, however, been usual for theologians to take the general or the highest spirit of the Bible as the substance of doctrine, and while they taught that even a few texts were sufficient to justify the most awful views of God or the future, it is not strange that the view common to the church for centuries about everlasting punishment found its authority. It has been accepted thoughtlessly, unconcernedly, as the teaching of Scripture, without any effect upon the multitude, and as a nightmare upon many beautiful and gentle souls. It has not deterred from worldliness and sin, and it has not been of much efficacy toward truth and righteousness. It has, however, for centuries been regarded as essential to Christian faith, and even the greatest English preacher of this generation is found solemnly declaring that a Christian may not even indulge the hope that there can be any final escape from eternal punishment in the fires of hell.

Nevertheless it is quite evident that the close of this century bears witness that if the authorized declaration of the church has not changed, an entire change has come over the better part of Christendom in regard to this doctrine. The emphasis upon it has greatly softened, its prominence has been lessened, its gloomy and lurid pictures are not longer portrayed, and by more and more of the leading preachers of all sects it is kept out of their discussions, while they freely speak of other views, which, perhaps without thought of the issue, make the old doctrine of eternal punishment entirely untenable.

Among those views the first and most evident one is the result of modern Biblical criticism. It may be said that among scholars, while searching investigations are still being made, upon many questions, and further light is sought upon single books or events, there is substantial agreement upon the errancy of the Scriptures. Plenary inspiration, literal infallibility, has vanished. Upon many subjects we know that these authors spoke with limitations and in agreement with the current theories of their day. When Moses, David, Jesus Christ, and Paul speak of hell and eternal fire and everlasting punishment, it is with the idea of illustration, or in keeping with the general views accepted by their hearers. When Jesus, in the Oriental and tropical style which belongs to much of his teaching, says at the conclusion of the allegory of the sheep and the goats, "these shall go away into everlasting punishment, but the righteous into life eternal," the picture is of a paradise and a Gehenna, two realms separated by an impassable barrier. The higher and more spiritual thought of the day gives us a universe so full of God that there is no room for a hell where He is not. The most profound scholars of the Bible and the liberal sects of Christendom have long accepted these views of inspiration and interpretation which have brought relief and joy to so many anxious hearts, and made easy and grateful the rejection of some of the most awful doctrines of the past theology. But now, at the close of the century, when we find a halting consent won to them by leading preachers like Dr. Munger and Dr. Gladden and Dr. Abbott and Dr.

Briggs, we know the victory is gained, and to uphold the doctrine of everlasting punishment by a few quotations from the Scripture is quite as outgrown as the Ptolemaic system of the universe. Says Dr. Munger, " The theories of the past generation are fast disappearing; verbal, dynamic, plenary, and inspiration covering all scientific and historical reference,—none of them are any longer insisted upon." Says Washington Gladden, " God never designed to give us an infallible book."

The growth of the humanitarian spirit which has been very great during the century now drawing to its close, has had much to do with overthrowing the old views about everlasting punishment. In spite of the vast preparations of the principal nations of the world for war, in spite of the wars that are now being waged with such seeming injustice, as the intercourse among the nations has rapidly increased, as the old prejudices and enmities and ignorances have disappeared, there has been a vast increase of the spirit of human sympathy and helpfulness and brotherhood. This has always been a marked feature of Christianity. The impartial historian must admit that it brought a deeper and wider idea of sympathy into the world. It emphasized charity as its cornerstone. And however far we have fallen from the whole Christian ideal, no other truth of Christianity has had such a constant declaration and no other truth has been as nearly approached in its practical fruit. The early churches began their life by contributions to the poor. Christendom blossomed into institutions of every kind to relieve the suffering. But never as in our own century have there been such wise and consecrated efforts everywhere to solve the great problems of social inequality and social degradation. The best and most generous lives are devoted to the relief of every kind of suffering. The work extends to the brute creation If a man belabours a dumb beast in our streets, we arrest him on a charge of cruelty. The laws which permitted whipping at the post have been repealed almost everywhere, as unworthy of our humanity. If we see a father beating his child, we turn away from the inhuman spectacle. We look with gratitude for our escape from the day when man put his brother man upon the rack or in the dungeon. And yet the Infinite Father, whom we profess to worship as just and merciful and good, is to inflict the most agonizing pain upon the most of His children, and we are to behold them and rejoice at them, not only for a short time but as one of the most eminent theologians of this country said, " not for one minute, not for one day, not for one age, not for two ages, not for a hundred ages, not for ten thousands of millions of ages, one after another, but forever and ever, without any end at all, and never, never, to be delivered."

Now the humane spirit of this age, ignoring all bodies of divinity by men however able or consecrated, casts away all such reasoning, and falls back upon the larger, older, wider truth of the Fatherhood of God and the Brotherhood of Man. No man who accepts God as a Father, with all the sweet, divine, far-reaching significance of that word, can really believe that His children are to be tortured in some realm forever, beyond His vision or reach or recall. No man who believes in the brotherhood of man with all the promise and possibility and duty which such a belief implies, can for a moment believe in everlasting punishment in some realm of local torture, for his brothers. The two beliefs cannot co-exist, however much some may have thought they could, and as the doctrine of God's fatherhood and man's brotherhood grows, the doctrine of everlasting punishment declines.

The old ecclesiastical and inhuman view of punishment overshoots its mark. It makes the sentence out of proportion to the deed, and it makes it possible to escape the sentence by too easy a process, and to have persons believe that the divine law is set aside and even the consequences of sin escaped. The old view of punishment has been so tenaciously clung to because it is so favourable to a life of meanness, dishonesty, and sin, and makes heaven purchasable at the close of a degraded career at so cheap a rate. And, on the contrary, our higher view of punishment still slowly finds acceptance because it requires a life measured by a standard so just, noble, and advancing. The common doctrine of eternal punishment may justly be held responsible for many of the worst evils which have afflicted humanity. It has kept the world in darkness, it has hindered civilization, it has aroused the worst fanaticism and cruelty, and it has been the secret inspiration of the worst religious persecution. Give to any body of men the power of holding over their fellow-creatures the keys of the future, of opening the doors to eternal wrath and torture, or to eternal happiness, as they deny or accept certain schemes of salvation or dogmas of the church, and you give to them the most dangerous power man can wield. And it will be wielded, as it has been wielded by the church for centuries, to corrupt and degrade humanity.

The mystery of the eucharist, instead of a life of righteousness, drew the line between the regenerated and the lost; and so long as that was the tribunal there was no hope for the world. The lost were lost forever, doomed to torture forever, not because they were not as good as others, but because they could not accept certain doctrines which persons nowise superior to themselves had made the arbitrary condition of salvation. All that is passing out of the better religious life of the closing century. The future takes its cast from the present: rewards and retributions depend upon the real spiritual character which has been struggled after or attained here. That judgment belongs only to the Infinite to pronounce. Such is the complexity of human nature, in its hidden temptations, its secret aspirations and resistances, that it is not for us to say with any dogmatism what the rewards or punishments shall be. We only know, as the final law of morals throughout the universe, that they shall be in accord with infinite and eternal justice, and that they shall be according to the actual quantity of righteousness in the life. Man can draw no lines which shall run straight across humanity, as the lines of latitude cross with undeviating exactness the earth's surface, and divide the elect from the lost. You have noticed

198 Theology at the Dawn of the Century

on some maps the isothermal lines, which represent the places which have the same temperature. What crooked lines they are! How they bend and sway and curve, affected by an ocean current here, or a mountain range there, and show us what strange and distant places have the same genial air. So any lines which shall apportion eternal suffering and eternal happiness must wind in and out among this mass of humanity, more mysteriously than the isothermal lines, making of the same company lives which to our present measuring are far asunder.

The old theology taught us that the least sin a mortal could commit was so awful in its nature as against the infinite majesty and purity of God, that it deserved eternal punishment. The new theology would teach us that no sin a finite can commit deserves infinite wrath and torture, but it deserves and will receive what the Infinite knows is sufficient punishment, to show to the sinner the evil of his way and to turn him to virtue.

Here, then, lies the idea of eternal punishment which is far truer and far more helpful than the old theology has taught. Not that the Infinite condemns us in wrath to a realm of tortures, for the universe has no such realm; nor that He is wearied of our failures, or disgusted with our weaknesses, or punishes us in anger; but that every transgression bears with it a divinely appointed punishment which is everlasting in the sense that it is a loss of opportunity, a loss of spiritual power, a loss of divine companionship. And whatever we may attain to, that loss remains forever, just as consequences are everlasting. All punishment in which the divine law bears a part is not revengeful, but remedial, not vindictive but corrective. It is precisely the punishment necessary to preserve the order of the universe, and to lead man to learn it, to obey it, and to rest in it.

When we come to such a view of God's government we shall have no fears of eternal torment, nor shall we ask to escape any punishment which we most justly have deserved. We will not ask the Infinite to withhold the corrective, the punishment, He sees is necessary to heal our lives and turn them into harmonious ways of forgiveness, which is not the remission of the penalty, and of peace which is not the escape from just retribution. Such petitions can only be born of a poor conception of this universe and its rules or of the good of humanity. It must be a low stage of the moral life which desires, or of the intellectual life which reasons, that it is possible to set aside what we have justly deserved. A higher and truer reflection is, I have transgressed and I must bear the infinitely just punishment for my wrong, for the sake of justice throughout the universe. Instead of praying for any forgiveness which takes away the sins and the punishment we most justly have deserved, we must cry, even though it be out of the depths, " Even so, Father, for so it seemeth good in Thy sight!" He who once turns to the side of virtue and righteousness finds all the laws of God at work for him in the struggle, but they remit nothing of the punishment which is justly his due. And our everlasting punishment is the loss of some spiritual power which might have been ours.

The Bearing of the Teaching of Jesus Christ on Man's Future Destiny

The Bearing of the Teaching of Jesus Christ on Man's Future Destiny

BY

The Reverend CALEB SCOTT, D.D.

IT is not the object of this article to enquire into the meaning of the sayings attributed to Jesus Christ on the subject of eschatology either in the synoptists or the 4th Gospel. The difficulties which gather around many of those sayings both as to their genuineness and interpretation are apparent from the diverse views which have been taken of them by scholars equally competent and devout. A recent writer (Dr. Stalker, Contemporary Review, Jan. 7, 1900, p. 130) has said "It is more than possible that within the next decade the Gospels may be issued from the press printed in all the colours of the rainbow to indicate the different documents by which they are composed, as is happening to the Old Testament at the present hour. The materials already exist in abundance for such an effort; and only a bold hand is required to appropriate them." Whether such an achievement will be accomplished in the early years of the forthcoming century may well be questioned: but when it is, the colours in which the eschatological discourses ascribed to our Lord are printed will testify to the remoteness of much of the matter contained in them from the period of His life and ministry.

But it is possible to approach the question of the bearing of what Jesus taught on man's future destiny in a wholly different way. There were some truths which were so incorporated into the very warp and woof of our Lord's life and teaching that they cannot be destroyed or altered by any process of destructive criticism to which the records we have in the four gospels may be subjected. Of these truths the most important is the revelation He gave of who God essentially is. Our Lord spoke of this revelation as being the object of His life and ministry, and of the attainment of a true knowledge of God as constituting eternal life. Now there can be no doubt that the whole of the revelation which Jesus gave of God is comprehended in the Fatherhood of God. The Fatherhood of God is as Bishop Moorhouse entitles it "the Master thought of Christ's teaching", "the secret of Jesus" or as Dr. Clarke (in his outlines of Christian theology, p. 267) puts it "the heart of His message". It occupies a place in His life and teaching such that we may be quite satisfied that any truth which cannot be formulated in terms of the Divine Fatherhood is not one of the truths taught by Christ. Especially it were absurd to assign to those "long eschatological discourses which read like a Christian version of some Jewish Apocalypse" a place of importance equal to that which we give to Christ's doctrine of the Fatherhood. No inference from those discourses as to Christ's teachings can be compared with an inference which necessarily follows from what is the very essence of our Lord's teaching,—the very centre of the whole.

Anything like an adequate exposition of the fact that this doctrine of the Divine Fatherhood occupies this regnant place is impossible within the limits of this paper. The Church of Christ has emphasized the physical and intellectual attributes of God: but our Lord emphasized His moral and spiritual attributes. Commonly God has been thought of and spoken of as a King, and the attributes which that word suggests have been made most prominent. Never once did Jesus Christ speak of him as King.* He very often spoke of the Kingdom of God but invariably represented Himself to be the King of that Kingdom, never God. In the addresses of the Church to God no phrase is more common than "Almighty God". Such a phrase is never once ascribed to Jesus in the Gospels. That in the words of Paul, 1 Tim. 1: 17, "God is the King Eternal, incorruptible, invisible, the only God" is indisputable, but the

* It may be said that Matt. 5: 35, where Christ says of Jerusalem, "It is the city of the Great King" is an exception. But surely the reference is to the Messianic King Himself.

truths thus set forth were taken for granted, not accentuated by our Lord. His one word for God was Father. Apart from the words "the" "my" "your" the only attributes He added to the word Father were "holy" "righteous", "Holy Father", "Righteous Father".

This teaching is rendered the more significant by the fact that as has been well said "its material or constructive principle is the consciousness of Christ." We have in what He taught about the divine Fatherhood the ultimate deliverance of that consciousness. He did not unfold the truth in reasoned discourse or in well sustained argument every step of which compels our assent; or as a deduction from a wide survey of the works of God looked at in their true perspective through the atmosphere of holy thought and devout feeling; or as a reproduction of the divine image from the broken reflections of Him on which different ages and nations have looked. But the truth as He taught it was simply a transcript of His own consciousness of God.

The prominent place which the truth occupies in the 4th Gospel, especially in the discourses in the 14th and three following chapters is well known. In those chapters the word "Father" is ascribed to Christ some fifty times whereas even the word God is only ascribed to Him five times. It is being more and more largely conceded that we have in the words ascribed to Jesus Christ in this gospel a correct transcript of what He really taught. See the Hubbard Lectures by Dr. Drummond, Principal of Manchester College, Oxford, entitled "Via, Veritas, Vita," who argues that the "profound sayings" in the chapters in question are a true expression of Christ's doctrine. In the synoptic gospels the doctrine of the divine Fatherhood is hardly less prominent. The agreement between the three and the one in this respect has been cited as a proof of the "identity of Christ's character" as taught in both. No words more accurately express the way in which it is taught in the first three Gospels than the words of Jesus "neither knoweth any man save the Father and he to whomsoever the Son will reveal

Him," Matt. 11 : 27. It may be said without any fear of contradiction that alike in the 4th Gospel and the other three there is no truth about God which is coördinated with His Fatherhood. He plied men with considerations drawn from this doctrine when we might have expected He would have made His chief appeal to other thoughts about God. To secure obedience to the laws of the Kingdom of God laid down in the sermon on the mount, He appealed not to God's omnipotence—omniscience and omnipresence, to His prerogative as the searcher of hearts, but to manifold aspects of the relationship which, as the Father, God sustains to men. It was so on the one hand when He insisted on that right attitude toward God which is the prime condition of membership of the Kingdom of God, in the directions He gave about fasting and prayer and about the uselessness and folly of gnawing anxiety about the morrow. It was so on the other hand when He insisted on that right attitude towards man which is the obverse side of a right attitude toward God, as exemplified in love even for enemies and persecutors, generosity in judgment and action and conspicuousness in good deeds.

Further Christ's teaching about God's Fatherhood assumes that the relation it sets forth is *not metaphorical* but *absolute* and *essential* and consequently *universal*. The Hebrew Psalmist had said, " Like as a Father pitieth His children " making human Fatherhood the reality and divine Fatherhood the metaphor. Christ's teaching was the reverse of this. " Fatherhood is the essence of God " says Dr. Fairbairn. The archetype of fatherhood is not to be found in the human relationship but in the divine. The human relationship just in so far as it approaches its ideal shadows forth the divine. Paul simply expressed the necessary implication in our Lord's teaching about God when he wrote " There is one God and Father of all ". That the whole of that multitude who listened to the sermon on the mount had " become the Sons of God " through faith and love is an impossible supposition, yet there is not the remotest hint either there or elsewhere that when Christ proclaimed the divine Fatherhood He was only speaking of the relation sustained by God to some of those whom He addressed. It is true that He repudiated the claim of the Pharisees to be the children of God but in the same breath He repudiated their claim to be the children of Abraham. Manifestly the words were no denial of the Universal Fatherhood of God but a strong assertion of the fact that by their conduct they were spiritually and morally denying their Sonship. Sons may be prodigal, they may be so far alienated from their Father's house and home that only through the love of God as expressed on the cross can they be won back to their true position, and become in heart and life the Sons of God,—but however prolonged and stubborn their rebellion, their Father remains their Father still. His relation to them as Father is unchanged and unchangeable. So whilst the phrase to become the Sons of God often used in the New Testament is easily understood in consistency with the essential and universal Fatherhood of God, such a phrase as *God becoming our Father* is never found, and is contradictory to such teaching. God always has been, always is, and always will be our Father. He cannot become what He essentially is.

Our contention then is that the teaching that God is essentially the Father, and the Father of all men is the very centre of our Lord's teaching, of His system of Doctrine. Dissociating from the word Father all that is sensuous and earthly, it implies something much more than that God is the Creator and the Supreme Ruler of men. It implies that there is a community of nature between Him and us that He communicates this nature to us, that we are partakers of the divine nature. It implies further that the whole of His dealings with men are compatible with the assertion "God is Love". In idealized human Fatherhood we have the purest love we know on earth. The love of a child for its parent has in it necessarily an element of selfishness. So has the rapture of married love. But the love of a Father for his child when it at all approaches its ideal is simply free from all such admixture. A true human

Father is ready to endure any suffering which may be needful for the highest welfare of his child. Further he is ready to inflict any suffering which may be needful for that welfare. Precisely so is it with the Father. The cross is the age-long expression of the one truth. All the pain of the universe, the pain which is inseparable from sin and which can only cease when sin ceases is the expression of the other truth. If there is any utter misconception on the subject of God's Fatherhood, it is that it is equivalent to weak indulgence. The most terrible message of the Gospel to the man who is living in determined alienation from God is " God is your Father ". The language of that man's heart is depart from me, I desire not the knowledge of thy ways. The language of the Gospel is God is your Father. He will never leave you alone in your sin. He will pursue you with its shame and remorse. The worm that dieth not will never cease to gnaw; the fire which is not quenched will never cease to burn with ever fiercer flame until you return to God. The " dread machinery of sin and sorrow " which is grinding always and everywhere is devised " at most expenditure of pain by Him who devises all pain ".

" to evolve
The moral qualities of man,
To make him love in turn and be beloved,
Creative and self-sacrificing too,
And thus eventually Godlike."

And what is the bearing of this upon the final destiny of mankind? The assumption that the destiny of every man, be he never so much handicapped by heredity and environment is fixed forever by the use he makes of the few short years he spends in the world, the $\pi\rho\tilde{\omega}\tau o\nu$ $\psi\varepsilon\tilde{\upsilon}\delta o\varsigma$ of much popular theology—is utterly untenable. God is the Father, and whatever worlds may succeed this world, however the conditions of existence may vary hereafter He always will be the Father and as such will always deal with every child of His. This we may regard as an indisputable corollary, God's essential Fatherhood being conceded. The doctrine of eternal damnation in the mechanical and unethical form in which it has been commonly held cannot possibly live together with that of the Fatherhood. Of it, Dr. Charles (Jowett Lectures for 1898-9 on Eschatology, p. 311) well says, " It is a Judaistic survival of a grossly immoral character, and originated in Judaism when monotheism had become a lifeless dogma . . . and when a handful of the pious could not only comfortably believe that God was the God of the Jew alone, and only of a very few of these, but also could believe that a part of their highest bliss in the next world would consist in witnessing the torment of the damned ". Equally untenable is the doctrine of conditional immortality, if God is the Eternal Father. Both these doctrines imply " that the intention of God may be perpetually frustrated. In the one case He dismisses the rebellious beyond the limits of His grace; in the other weary of opposition He shatters resistance by simple annihilation." Christ's doctrine of God's Fatherhood is utterly irreconcilable with both these doctrines. Neither of them can be held unless the Fatherhood is denied. It assures us that as long as any child of His is alienated from Him He will never cease to ply that child with all the resources which omnipotence places at the disposal of His love in order to bring him to himself,—that true self which in all his wanderings the prodigal never lost. It matters not what ages may elapse. It matters not how terrible and how prolonged the discipline needful to effect God's purpose may be. That purpose can never throughout the ages be relinquished. It must be pursued until it be accomplished. The Eternal Father must go after that which is lost until He find it.

But it may be said, and it is undoubtedly true, that no exercise of physical omnipotence can crush the rebellion of the heart. Human freedom is such that whatever God may do, in whatever form He may bring truth to bear upon His child, however vividly He may show him that it is an evil and a bitter thing to sin against Him, however the divine love may use the resources which unlimited power and knowledge and wisdom place at its disposal to bring the prodigal to repentance, all may be unavailing. Throughout eternity some rebellious children may say " no " to God and so may continue rebellious still. If such is the case and God foresaw it, then assuredly such rebellious children would never have been created by Him. That the Eternal Father should foresee that one child of His would forever rebel and in consequence be forever lost in the misery of alienation from Him, and should still create that child is an impossible conception, indeed a monstrous supposition. It is monstrous if we think of ideal human Fatherhood. It is infinitely more monstrous when we think of Him " from whom every Fatherhood in heaven and on earth is named." Eph. 3 : 15.

But it may be contended that whether or not divine grace will ultimately overcome sin in any child of His is not an object of the divine prescience; that as Dr. Martineau puts it (Study of Religion, Vol. 2, p. 279) God by " lending us a portion of His causation refrains from covering all with His omniscience ", that He so limits His own " foresight that He cannot read all volitions that are to be ". Now if this is the case we are compelled to the conclusion pointed out by Darner, when he writes (System of Christian Doctrine, vol. 2, p. 60, Eng. Trans:) " if divine foreknowledge of the free is to be absolutely denied, inasmuch as the entire accomplishment of the divine counsel is still conditioned by freedom, there *will be no certainty of even one* individual being led by his spontaneous decision to the desired end. . . . God then would have created the world at a mere guess ". If this position be taken in spite of the tremendous difficulties in which we are landed by it, then as in the previous alternative we are forced back to the conclusion that the Eternal Father would not have created man at all. If His omniscience could not beforehand tell whether a single child of His would remain loyal to Him, then surely in face of such terrible possibilities, creation were impossible.

The position taken in this paper is then as follows. What was the direct teaching of our Lord on the subject of eschatol-

Teaching of Jesus Christ on Man's Destiny

ogy it is extremely difficult if not impossible to decide. But there can be no doubt that the eschatology of any religion must be finally decided by its central conception of God. Now our Lord revealed God to us in no ambiguous terms. He taught us as plainly as words can teach that God in His unalterable nature is our Father. This was the centre of His teaching,—its master thought, the pivot on which it all revolved,—God's Fatherhood, not metaphorical but essential and so universal. This doctrine occupies a place in our Lord's teaching such that we may be perfectly certain that no doctrine incompatible with it is a doctrine of His. Applied to the future destiny of man the doctrine forbids the supposition that by the decrees of God any of His children are condemned to everlasting punishment; it is equally inconsistent with the contention that annihilation will be the ultimate doom of any; and it cannot be harmonized with the supposition that " God will never be reluctant though man may forever refuse ", as Dr. Fairbairn phrases it. The only conclusion which is compatible with the regal place which the Fatherhood occupies in the teaching of our Lord is that to which the Apostle Paul comes when he writes, " God hath shut up *all* unto disobedience that He might have mercy upon *all*. Romans 11 : 32. " It was the good pleasure of the Father . . . through Him (*i. e.* Jesus Christ) to reconcile *all things* unto Himself." Colossians 1 : 19, 20. " That at the name of Jesus *every knee* should bow . . . and that *every tongue* should confess that Jesus Christ is Lord to the glory of God the Father." Philippians 2 : 10, 11. That which underlies the assurance that " God sent His Son into the world, that the world should be saved through Him," John 3 : 17; that which is plainly stated in the words of our Lord " And I if I be lifted up from the earth will draw all men unto myself." John 12 : 32.

Universalism

Universalism

BY

The Reverend I. M. ATWOOD, D.D.

UNIVERSALISM is primarily a theodicy. It is a theory that seeks the explanation of present discords by predicating future harmony. It is not a dogma nor a science; it is a faith and a philosophy.

All persons who have looked into the human situation with any degree of penetration have been more or less perplexed. The race exists in many branches, of very unequal capacities and possessions. It is one race, palpably; but of widely variant types. Some tribes are found at a stage not much above brutes. Others display powers and attainments that warrant the encomium of Shakespeare,—

> What a piece of work is man;
> How noble in reason, how infinite in faculty!

So differently conditioned are the various divisions of mankind as to induce wide differences of occupation, development, usages, aims, character. In all branches, at whatever stage of evolution, are marked family and individual differences. So soon as organization, labor, traffic, government begin, the tendency to greater inequalities, to tyranny of the strong over the weak, to conflict of interests, to strife and misunderstanding, to greed, untruthfulness, cruelty and crime, appears. The struggle that ensues leads to every form of excess and is marked by every variety of evil. True, the same ordeal brings out virtue, magnanimity, self-sacrifice. But in these excellences all do not share. Heroes and saints are always few and far between. Concede progress, admit improvement and amelioration; yet the fact is patent and undeniable, that hitherto in its history mankind, taken as a whole, or in the great representative races, has made a record which no enlightened and humane soul can contemplate without horror and shame.

Whatever may be justly said for the restraining and refining influences of religion, it is a truth too abundantly confirmed by all history, that no form of it, not even the highest, has yet been able to do more than modify in a small degree the general unsatisfactory result. No religion has been able to so curb ambition, allay greed, transform desire, infuse a spirit of fraternity, as to bring any considerable number of any tribe or class under the beneficent rule of the law of love. I mean not to exaggerate. I believe students of this phase of the subject will agree that I have made a statement which might be much enlarged and intensified.

The Christian doctrine of human immortality, that the spiritual and real man survives the event of death and in another state of existence continues the moral ordeal which began here, raises all the questions concerning unequal allotment and diversity of character into what may be termed acute significance. Do matters improve in the new state, do they go on as before, do they get worse? The circumstance that an affirmative is given to each of these inquiries by as many schools of theorists, does not tend to clarify mystery. It is seen by all, that if the earthly scene is initial to another, that fact must reflect an explanatory light on man's beginning and may possibly illuminate the darkness of his days that are so few and so full of evil.

Thoughtful men and women have been asking in every age, what shall we say to these things? Is there any rational and satisfactory solution of the human problem? Is it Providence or Fate?

Various replies have been framed, from Plato's time to our own. None of them, I suspect, have been entirely satisfactory, even to those who formulated them. Rather than give up in confessed impotence or in blank despair, they have tried to see a little way into, if they could not see through, the intricate maze. Those who have felt constrained to say that there is no God, and those who have concluded that there is no plan and hence no solution, are practically in the same case, and need not be further considered.

Those who content themselves with saying that God chose some men and angels for a good destiny, to which He will bring them, and other men and angels for a bad destiny, to which He will leave them, do not pretend, I believe, to be satisfied to have it so. They simply affirm that it is so, and there rest.

Those who say the choice lies not with God but with men, and adopt a sliding scale of possibilities, running all the way from the salvation of a tenth to that of nine-tenths of the human race, would, they assure us, be glad to tell a more cheerful story, if facts warranted. Some of them admit with entire frankness the dark and awful alternatives to which their view forecloses them. Others contrive to be tolerably comfortable by persuading themselves that the issue which their theory involves is, on the whole, the best which "the system of things" makes possible. As matter of fact, they say, men are to determine their destiny; it cannot be otherwise. Let them know the worst and prepare for it.

It is really a variety of the view just stated which supposes that a portion of mankind,—how large can only be conjectured, but vast in any event,—will fail to maintain themselves in existence through failing to cultivate the germ of spiritual life. Here, as before, it is a disastrous choice that at length closes opportunity and finally ruins the soul. Some relief is obtained, no doubt, from the appalling thought of spirits forever kept in being only to be forever wretched, by the hypothesis of ultimate extinction or of the sudden termination of life for the unfortunates. But in both cases the insoluble problem is, to reconcile an outcome so undesirable, and as between the preserved and the perished, so unequal, with wisdom and goodness.

Now Universalism is believed, by those who prefer it, to be not only a much better view but a real and rational solution of the dark problem. Not by ignoring the perplexities but by recognizing them in all their solemn significance and yet finding a way out into light, is relief brought to the perturbed mind. This is what the Universalist theory accomplishes. It makes room for all the facts, takes the full measure of the apparently irreconcilable antinomies, gives free play to the tremendous alternatives of human choice and to the terrific force of retribution, yet sees through all, the natural superiority of truth and right and goodness, and after all, a triumphant, harmonized, unmutilated humanity.

Evidently this is what all enquirers have sought after. Whether conscious of it or not, they have wished for an issue of the human scene on which no shadow rests. Argue with ourselves as we will, multiply words as much as we please, the naked, solemn truth is, that no hypothesis which sacrifices some to save others, or which bluntly ascribes to the Divine pleasure what satisfies no good man; or which allows a reasoned and ordered universe to end in catastrophe, ever was or will be acceptable to the unperverted intelligence. It leaves the difficulty larger than it found it. The problem is not solved.

But if we are permitted to believe in a program of progress, in a purpose and plans that from seeming ill are still educing good, in a universe so solidly based on beneficence that the better thought and course are sure of final advantage, no present darkness can shake our confidence in the coming dawn. And if this program be conceived of as including in its one far off, divine event, the victory of every human spirit over its foes and its bonds, and its final establishment in rectitude, our problem is solved; no ireducible residuum remains.

So far, I suppose, all will go with me. They will admit that this issue would be desirable. Said the Duke of Argyle to Erskine of Linlathen, "No objection can be urged to your view of final universal salvation, except that there are not sufficient grounds for believing it. In itself it is most fascinating. Would to God it were so!" The late Col. Robert Ingersoll is on record to the same effect. "I have nothing against Universalism," said he: " if I could believe it I should be happy." Among the many that I have met who feel themselves called on to oppose this theory of religion, I have never found one who would not concede that the end it predicts is desirable. Most of those who reject it admit that it escapes all the more serious difficulties with which Christian theology is encumbered.

Is Universalism, then, believable? Is it probable? Is it true? The scope of this article does not permit me to go into this inquiry so thoroughly as I could wish. A sketch of the argument must suffice.

The fact that the Universalist view clears up the difficulties and vindicates the ways of God to man, is a powerful presumption of its truth. What more conclusive affirmative can be made for any hypothesis?

If I were asked to state in the shortest phrase, why I am a Universalist I should put it this way: I am a Universalist because God is. As I understand Him, God has made man, any man and every man, to be like Himself. He has not only made man capable of that, but to be that. He has not made one soul to be vile and filthy and fiendlike. If He has made any soul to be bad there is small use of that soul's trying to be good. But He has not made any soul to be bad. God does not delight in badness, but in goodness. And that shows God to be a Universalist. He made His children to glorify Him and enjoy Him forever. He wishes them to do so and purposes that they shall do so; and there are no exceptions. When, therefore, I range myself along side God and seek what He seeks I become a Universalist.

It has been said, in every human soul is a longing for moral perfection. I am not sure that we are authorized to affirm this. In many souls there is such a longing: there may be in every soul. But it is a larger assumption than I feel warranted in making. We may, I think, assume that every soul is conscious of a desire to be better and worthier than it is. If that soul should take one step towards the attainment of its desire it would be still less satisfied with itself and still more desirous of attaining a better estate. To this law of advance there is no limit and in this race there is no halting place. The meaning of such a phenomenon must be that the human soul has in itself the evidence of the end for which it is made. And since each soul has it, the prophecy is unmistakable. Its destiny is to ally itself with its Author and to coöperate with Him in fulfilling a great end of His creation.

The spirit of man is never content nor at peace until it is conscious of walking in the path ordained for it. The disturbance that ensues, and inevitably, from a wrong course is both a warning and a prophecy. It means that the soul was made for a good use and a good end, and that the whole moral order is against any other use and end.

The torpor that follows repeated sinning, the death in trespasses and in sin, is itself proof that the soul cannot abide in that awful trance. For if the death were literal and absolute there would be no sense of guilt, no possibility of condemnation, no ability to sin. So long as we can sin, we can repent. This is the exact meaning of a Saviour. He is a Saviour only because there are sinners. And sinners exist not to be damned: they are damned already. They exist to be saved. That there were sinners, and sinners of a deeply depraved type, presented no obstacle to the mission of Jesus. He came to seek and to save these very classes. That there are sinners now, and sinners of an inveterate and hopeless grade, does not militate against the Universalist conclusion. If it did, it would make Christianity impracticable and the mission of Jesus Quixotic.

No one can deny the final triumph of good over evil in the case of all souls unless he is willing to dispute human immortality or to abrogate the moral order. If souls persist in conscious existence and remain subjects of the moral realm no one is authorized to say that some of them will never attain the end for which they are created. For to do so he must take his stand at the conclusion of the trial, when the ordeal is finished and the books are closed. If it be said, that far off era is not open to the Universalist for prediction, it must be replied that it is still less open to any one to dispute his prediction. Especially must we say this when we remember that the only glimpse vouchsafed us of the final scene in the human drama, intimates unclouded victory! *Then cometh the end, when He shall deliver up the Kingdom to God, even the Father; when He shall have abolished all rule and all authority and power. For He must reign till He hath put all enemies under His feet. The last enemy that shall be destroyed is death.* That the conquest referred to is moral and not physical and involves the loving obedience of the subjects, is shown by the fact, that in the consummation " the Son also Himself shall be subject unto Him that did put all things under him, that God may be all in all."

I am persuaded that the destiny of man, including the after-death life, hinges on his natural relation to God. Origin concludes destiny. If man is a child of God, in such sense that he shares the spiritual nature of God, that fact insures his survival after the death of his body. If he is not thus naturally and spiritually related to God, no weight of probabilities, no arguments from analogy, and no supposed prophecy of Scripture can supply a solid base for the doctrine of human immortality. The idea that any man, by any kind of favour, can confer on himself a possession so infinitely transcending his natural endowment as an endless life transcends mortal life, appears to me an unfounded fancy.

The logic of these facts runs irresistibly, as it seems to me, to a foregone conclusion. If a man is really the child of God, if it is more than a flourish of mocking rhetoric for us to say, " Our Father," we are authorized to believe that the child will come to his intended and proper estate in the divine family. I feel strong here, and willing to stake all, for myself and for mankind, on the natural relation which we sustain to the Author of our being. If we do not belong to Him we can expect no Spiritual inheritance: if we do belong to Him, who can pluck us out of His hand?

The Universalist denomination dates from the preaching of the Rev. John Murray, though there were other preachers of Universalism in various parts of the country before him. Mr. Murray came to the United States in 1770, from London, where he had been a disciple of James Relly. He itinerated through New Jersey, Pennsylvania and Massachusetts, finally establishing a church at Gloucester in the latter State, and also in Boston, for each of which he served some years as minister.

For some time after Mr. Murray founded the denomination it was supposed that Universalism was a modern heresy; and its speedy downfall and disappearance were predicted on the ground that it had no historic root. But the researches of more recent years have shown that explicit Universalism was taught in the Church as early as the Third Century, and implicit Universalism much earlier. The exact question of the destiny of all men did not come up among Christians at the very beginning. But in the course of their missionary labours and their fruitful discussions it was bound to come to the surface ere long. We know that it did, and that for three hundred years and more it reckoned among its advocates the greatest names in the schools and pulpits of Christendom. The facts in relation to this interesting historic question are not now disputed anywhere and may be ascertained as readily from other sources as from Universalist writers. I may refer the reader, however, for full information on this point, to *The Ancient History of Universalism,* by President Hosea Ballou; to Dr. Edward Beecher's *History of the Doctrine of Retribution;* and particularly to a work issued within a year, by the Rev. J. W. Hanson, D.D., entitled, *Universalism in the First Five Hundred Years of the Christian Church.*

Universalism

The means by which its condemnation was procured and by which the names and memories of its great advocates were attempted to be dishonoured, are the same by which so many of the fairest pages of Christian history have been stained.

But Clement and Origen and Didymus and Diodorus, and the Gregories and Titus and Theodore and Jerome and Chrysostom, with other Fathers of great learning and piety, are none the less the treasures of the Church.

From very small beginnings in the last years of the eighteenth century and the first of the nineteenth, the Universalist denomination in America made steady but slow headway. The denominations already in existence were pretty unanimous in their hostility to the new sect and often very violent in their methods of opposition. In 1870, after a hundred years of varying fortune and incessant struggle, a compact and quite elaborate organization was effected. The Secretary of the General Convention, Rev. Dr. Demarest, a high authority on the statistics of the Universalist denomination, said in 1899, that it was not until 1884 that, " we were able to present a reasonably accurate table of our statistics. Comparing those of fifteen years ago with the present year we find:

	1884	1899		Increase.
Number of Parishes	875	1,003	14	5-8 per cent.
" Families	35,791	47,411	33	1-3 per cent.
" Church Members	31,709	52,177	64	1-2 per cent.
" S. S. Pupils	50,069	59,179	18	1-5 per cent.
Parish Prop. (Less Debts)	$6,724,079	$9,623,762	43	1-8 per cent.
" Expenses—Contributions	853,490	1,105,869	29	1-10 per cent.

This table shows that while the Universalist Church in America is still one of the small denominations, and while its rate of increase has been slow, it has steadily gained in all the elements of power that are capable of tabulation. Many attempts have been made to furnish the reason or reasons why denominations like the Universalist and Unitarian, which certainly are in accord with the progress of religious opinion in the whole Christian world and are not behind others in the quality and capacity of their ministerial force, should, in the comparison, make so slow progress. There are without doubt, many minor reasons; but the principal cause of the diminished rate of increase in these bodies is, beyond a question, the growth of Universalist and Unitarian sentiment in evangelical communions and a marked disposition in those churches to make Universalists and Unitarians comfortable in their fellowship. It thus comes to pass that the more successful Universalism is in winning assent to its propositions the less opportunity does it enjoy to secure denominational adherents. The more conversions the fewer followers!

The Universalist Church has organizations in thirty-one States, in the Provinces of Ontario and Quebec and Nova Scotia and in Japan. Two or three churches of that name in Scotland hold relations with the Universalist General Convention. Four colleges, three theological seminaries, five academies, have been founded and are maintained by the denomination; besides a theological school and two other schools in Japan, and a recently started " Industrial College " in Alabama. Two missions, with schools attached, are supported among the coloured people in Norfolk and in Suffolk, Va.

The legislative bodies of the Universalist church are the conventions, State and General. The former are composed of delegates from the parishes in any State; the latter of delegates from the various State conventions. The General Convention is the highest tribunal. It meets once in two years. The State conventions meet once in each year. At the recent session of the General Convention in Boston, Mass., the basis of representation in that body was enlarged so that delegations are now twice as numerous as formerly. In the interval between sessions the affairs of the General Body are managed by a Board of eleven trustees, and the executive officers are a General Secretary, a General Missionary, a Financial Secretary and a General Superintendent.

Since the reorganization of the body in 1870 nearly all the funds possessed by the denomination have been accumulated.

The General Convention now has funds amounting to $314,523; the Woman's Centennary Association a fund of $14,393; the Woman's Missionary Society a fund of $6,890; the Woman's Alliance a fund of $791; The Woman's Association of Illinois $1,500; the Universalist Sabbath School Union $11,201; the various State conventions funds aggregating $414,202;—a grand total of $783,555.

The historic Profession of Belief, adopted at the session of the General Convention in Winchester, N. H. in 1803 contains three articles as follows:

Article I. We believe that the Holy Scriptures of the Old and New Testaments contain a revelation of the character of God and of the duty, interest and destination of mankind.

Article II. We believe that there is one God, whose nature is Love, revealed in one Lord Jesus Christ, by one Holy Spirit of Grace, who will finally restore the whole family of mankind to holiness and happiness.

Article III. We believe that holiness and true happiness are inseparably connected, and that believers ought to be careful to maintain order and practise good works; for these things are good and profitable unto men.

By the action of the two last biennial sessions another statement has been substituted for the Winchester Profession as the authoritative one of the Church—it runs thus:

" The conditions of fellowship in this Convention shall be as follows:—

" First. The acceptance of the principles of the Universalist faith, to wit, The Universal Fatherhood of God; The Spiritual authority and leadership of His Son Jesus Christ; The Trustworthiness of the Bible as containing a revelation from God; The certainty of just retribution for sin; the final harmony of all souls with God. The Winchester Profession is commended as containing these principles, but neither this nor any other form of words is required as a condition of fellowship, provided always that the principles above stated be professed.

"Second. The acknowledgment of the authority of the General Convention and assent to its laws."

The Women's Auxiliary societies, of which there are several, and one with organizations in nearly every State, are an integral and potent part of the forces of the denomination. And the National organization of Young People's Christian Unions, with a total membership of 15,000, enrolls a body of young men and women who, for intelligence, capacity and high religious purpose, are not excelled by any similar body in any Church.

What is here set forth may serve to show, that the Universalist denomination has a definite theological and religious basis, a compact and complete organization, missionary enterprises and means of church extension, institutions of learning, a considerable literature, a liberal provision of permanent funds, a progressive and popular policy of administration, a record of growth of which it has no need to feel ashamed, and a prospect of usefulness and so of permanence calculated to stir the enthusiasm and enlist the active energies of its adherents. It is in no invidious sense a competitor for place among the Christian forces of the times. It is rather in a large and true sense a co-worker with all other churches in the great business of emancipating the minds of men from error and establishing their characters in righteousness and love. It would be glad to maintain relations of fraternity and fellowship with all other followers of our Lord Jesus Christ.

Universalism

Universalism

BY

The Reverend DAVID N. BEACH, D.D.

AT the Universalist General Convention of 1899, held in Boston, one of the speakers of "Interdenominated Evening," October 23d, was the Rev. Dr. Lyman Abbott. He undertook to say "Why liberal Congregationalists are not Universalists." "I think it very clear," he said, "that modern Congregationalism does not accept the doctrine of eternal punishment as it was preached by Jonathan Edwards or even by Charles G. Finney. It may still be entertained as a scholastic theory by a few minds, it may be occasionally preached in isolated pulpits, but it is not found to any extent in the ministry of even the more conservative pulpits of to-day, and certainly not in the pulpits of liberal Congregationalists. Personally I absolutely disown it." Dr. Abbott's central reason assigned is the freedom of the will. He maintains that life is approachable by the study of phenomena from without or by the interrogation of consciousness from within. If we approach it by a study of the phenomena without we come to the irresistible conclusion that not only physical nature but human nature is under great Divine Laws and under a great Divine Lawgiver. But we may also interrogate alike from within, and if we do, the first and fundamental fact that confronts us is the fact of our own freedom. We come back to Samuel Johnson's utterance "'All argument is against the freedom of the will. We know we are free and that's the end of it.'" "By omnipotence in the moral realm," he continues, "I mean that God can do all things in that realm consistent with preserving the freedom of the free moral agent whom He is making in His own image, —so making him that he may be righteous as God is righteous by choosing the right end and eschewing the evil under no compulsion. If it were possible for God to hypnotize the race so that under His hypnotic influence every man should choose his crown of glory, I would not have him do it, for then all the virtue would be in the hypnotizer and not in the hypnotized, and the glory of humanity is this that when the last man is completed he will stand in his moral nature independent, holding the helm of his own destiny and directing his own course."

"Sometimes" he proceeds to illustrate "you see a child sitting on the seat by his father driving the span, the father holds the reins in front of the child, the boy thinks he is guiding the horses, but he is not. So some believe in the freedom of the will. Sometimes you will see that your Father is allowing the boy to hold the reins but sitting by his side ready to snatch them the moment any peril arises. So other men believe in the freedom of the will."

Giving his own point of view, he continues "The most awful and the most splendid fact in human life to me is this that God puts the reins of my destiny into my own hands and neither holds the reins before me nor behind me."

Then he proceeds "So preaching the illimitable love and the infinite grace of God our Saviour unto men, repudiating all particularism in theology, repudiating the notion that the grace of God ends for any man at death, believing with all my heart that all the resources of God's love and life and power are pledged to the restoration of all men to righteousness, holiness, and happiness, still my last message to the men and women to whom I speak this, I set before you life and death, therefore choose life that thou and thy seed may live."

Giving his judgment of the Congregational body in the United States he summarizes: "Any man who believes that the God's law is inviolable, that punishment follows its infraction, that remedy follows repentance and never follows or can follow without repentance, and that this remedy is revealed in and through Jesus Christ will receive ordination though he believe as some Congregationalists do that some men will never repent and will live in sin and misery forever, or as some other Congregationalists do that some men will never repent and will therefore cease to exist, or as still other Congregationalists do, that under the persuasions of Almighty God all men will at last repent and through the door of repentance be brought back to holiness and happiness and God, or, as I think the majority of Congregationalists do to-day, decline to be dogmatic on that question altogether. The Congregational Church, thank God, is large enough for them all."

The purpose of this article is not to argue the case, nor to give individual opinion, but to indicate,—with some suggestion of its ground,—what is the dominant view among devout and intelligent persons. Dr. Abbott expresses this view justly, and its main ground. He knows, and the present writer knows, Congregationalism in the United States well, and Congregationalism which has the temper just summarized in this regard, is an index in no small degree of the state of intelligent opinion on this subject because on the one hand it is evangelical, Christ-following, and dead-in-earnest, and yet on the other hand historically and, in virtue of its character, it is also broadminded and inclusive.

Without desiring to be personal, the present writer ventures to adduce one evidence of what is the Congregational temper in this matter, when put to a signal test on his installation, October 27th, 1896, as Minister of Plymouth Church, Minneapolis. He said, speaking of man in his inherent condition "Man is God's child; man always will be God's child. He may alienate himself never so much from God, and in such a sense be a child of wrath, speaking in the figurative language of Scripture, and in such a sense in this still figurative language he doubtless needs to be adopted back again by his Father, but none the less he can never cease to be unless he can cease to exist, a child of God, nor pass beyond the yearnings of God's love. This, as I believe, is a clear indication of scripture, as certainly it tends to be the deepening conviction of most persons who have had revealed to them in any fulness how God is Father and how Christ is elder brother."

Under the head of redemption, he said "Toward man's redemption from that individual fall, which has come for all intents and purposes to him universally,—all the energy, love, and power of God the Father, God the Son and God the Spirit are ever directed. The redemption is not a forensic matter. It is not an adjustment of laws and courts. It is the only redemption that can find a human soul. It is the redemption of life, of love, of suffering. The cross was always set up, the Lamb was slain from the foundation of the world. What happened on Calvary was the outward manifestation in time and space and terms of human anguish of the always bleeding heart of God going out to His children. Scripture expressly speaks of Jesus as the " Same yesterday, to-day and forever," and of " crucifying Him afresh." That is the way of our redemption. We are redeemed through the love and suffering of God. These find us, enable us to see how, even before we ask, we are forgiven, and how we need but to come to Him and we shall have Life."

The candidate in expressing his primary theological conviction said: "From what I have said about the manifold means used of God for the redemption of men, and particularly though so briefly about the Church and the Sacraments, and the living life of our Lord, running through them, you will have perceived that I believe in the absoluteness of Jesus. I do. And I am very little concerned about the definition of Him or any like thing about Him, being sure that ere He is done, whoever and whatever He is, He will command all life."

Coming to the last things, the speaker declared, "I do not think that the universality of redemption is able to be dogmatically affirmed either with regard to all persons in its application or to all duration. As I intimated, there is too much scripture looking the other way and too much in human life. Therefore, I am not a Universalist, though I believe that Universalists have witnessed to an important truth for our time. On the other hand, on grounds which I implied earlier, I have faith to hold a very strong, a living, and an inspiring hope that the hundred sheep will yet be found, and that as God has shut up into disobedience it has been in order, as St. Paul says, that

"He might have mercy upon all." To put it a little differently I believe that the world and the universe are God's world and universe and the whole of them God's. And that the mystery of the condition of sin and the permission of suffering has its roots in that moral and spiritual education of the universe which is its *raison d'être* of the eternal purpose of God. What shall we say then? Shall we sin that grace may abound? God forbid. In fact, the more in my judgment one entertains such a hope, the more hateful and intrinsically sinful will sin seem to the person holding, and the more will he desire to bring men whether in Christendom or in heathendom or in that third and worse category, the domain of Mohammedanism to the knowledge and the love of God in Christ.

Whoever conceives that this hope works the other way does not know what this hope is, that has got hold only of its terminology.

By way of summarizing, the speaker said: " Concluding this part of my statement, let me say, that I have a gospel for men. It is a gospel of the divinity and beauty and glory of the whole creation of God and in particular of every child of God that is to say of every person,—a gospel of the awfulness of sin, of its terrible consequences,—a gospel of the infinite, bleeding, suffering, forgiving love of God, and effort of God from eternity in Jesus Christ through His spirit to redeem men to Himself,— and of the presence and power and love and grace of the Man of Nazareth, the Lord Jesus, my brother and theirs, and my and their All in All. And this gospel I expect to see or begin to see applied to everything, to me even and to you, and to everybody, and to every side and aspect of life,—to the family, to the community, to society, to civics, yea, to all the thinking and poetry and arts, and wonder and manifoldness of existence. I expect soon to be seen in this world no longer, but I do not expect to die. I expect to live. I expect to see His face and that His name,—not letters which would disfigure, but His very look,—shall be in my forehead. I do not expect there except in the scriptural sense to rest, but in scripture phrase, " to rest not, day nor night," to work, to sacrifice, to know the fellowship of His suffering there as well as here, and to join with Him in His mighty purpose to redeem the world and the universe to Himself."

The installing council was the largest ever convened for Congregational purposes in the Northwest. It proceeded to installation, and expressed itself regarding the candidate thus "We record our assured confidence that in his preaching and living he exalts Jesus Christ as Lord and Saviour and as the world's only hope. We declare that the fellowship of Congregational Churches, though never given without regard to intellectual conceptions of truth, is not tied to them alone, but is rather given upon the spirit and temper and proportion in which views are held. On these grounds therefore we advise the Church to proceed with Dr. Beach's installation, and profess our readiness to assist in the same."

The action of this large council shows conclusively the temper of the denomination in the matter of inclusiveness in this regard.

In conclusion, a brief summary may be made of reasons for holding the question open, even though—as does the present writer—one cherishes the larger hope.

First: There is much scripture that looks the other way.

Second: There is much in life that looks the other way.

Third: The analogy of failures and destructions under physical evolution may hold here.

Fourth: Dogmatic Universalism, the affirmation that "God is a Universalist," falls under the suspicion of being too easy a solution of a most complex, intricate, and mysterious problem. Universalism's true field is to indicate the benevolence of the Divine character in this range,—not to end the problem.

Fifth: The whole subject includes data not as yet accessible. It transcends the present bounds of knowledge.

Sixth: If excessive generalization is perilous in any department of knowledge or life, it is peculiarly so in this matter of a soul's destiny, even faith, hope and love are bound not to issue in presumption. "Thou shalt not tempt the Lord thy God."

One word more, the base of the larger hope whereby—if that hope be well grounded—the freedom of the will will not be infringed and the reins neither held before him nor behind him by God, but be left in human hands, is the Divine image in man. God on His side will never cease to pity, love and yearn after His children. His persuasions will be infinitely beautiful and strong, and will weary not. If the Divine image in man is of such a nature as to be ultimately responsive to this beauty and strength, Universalism is true. The boy, not muscular nor skilled enough to drive as yet will become so. The Divine power will not hypnotize, but vitalize, persuade and win. It is the growing hope of multitudes of devout and thoughtful men and women that such prove the fact, but who can tell whether the free will will not shatter the Divine image? May not pervert it so that even the Divine beauty and strength shall be impotent to lay hold on it? What discreet person will deny this possibility? Who will dogmatize about a hope?

The Person of Christ

The Person of Christ

BY

The Reverend F. W. AVELING, M.A., B.Sc.

THE Christ of history is admitted to be the most wonderful moral phenomenon in the world.

His supernatural entrance into life, His early wisdom, whereby at the age of twelve He conversed with the doctors of the law, yet displays no pertness. His hold upon the poor, though He is the poorest of all. His magic influence on sinners leading them to give up their evil life. His resurrection, His supernatural exit from life, mark Him out as above all other men.

His marvellous career is shown in,

(1) His wonderful wisdom as a teacher.
(2) His wonderful innocence and sinlessness.
(3) His wonderful influence over others.

(1) As a teacher we note, (a) His *originality*. Without any special educational advantages, coming forth from mental and social obscurity, He stands out as the greatest teacher of the ages. He did not prove His words, He spoke and men *felt* the truth of His sayings. Again though living in an age of superstition He was free from any taint of that folly. Once more, while Socrates and Plato taught an inferior morality to a limited few, Jesus taught the highest ethics to the multitudes and made virtue " current coin."

(b) His *boldness*. From the carpentershop He comes forth to inaugurate a kingdom that shall be universal and unmoved. He, the world's greatest reformer, in an age when brute force was triumphant, based His kingdom on love, with all the world against Him He was ever calm and sure of the issue.

(c) The *consistency* of His life with His doctrine. He alone of ethical preachers lived up to what He preached, in Him are found all virtues, balanced and harmonized.

(2) His sinlessness. " The holiest souls are most alive to

personal sin," but the heart-broken utterances of the saints are never reached by Jesus. He has no sins to confess. Those who knew Him best and could have pointed out flaws, had there been any, unanimously call Him sinless. He claims to be sinless (John 8:46). If He was not sinless He was a great hypocrite. Could a hypocrite move the world as Christ has done? " I find no fault in this man " (Luke 23:4).

(3) His influence over others.

(a) No one has yet gone beyond Christ's moral teachings. Indeed no other instructor has come up to it.

(b) His followers totally changed their life, under His magnetic influence.

(c) The Christian Church with its mission of healing and elevating, with its martyrs in all ages, is the offspring of His wondrous influence. And His religion, with no sword like that which spread Mahometanism, by peaceful means has entered every land.

Again, all through the Jewish Scriptures of the old Testament there are predictions of and aspirations after a Messiah (anointed), who is to unite the office of prophet, priest, and king. In Gen. 3:15, 22, 18, 49:10; Deut. 18:18; Psal. 2, and 110; Is. 9:6 and 7, 42:1-4,53; Mich. 5:1-5; Jerem. 33:5 and 6, 15:16, something more than a hint is given that the coming one was to be divine as well as human. The great lesson for the Jews to learn, one they never learned properly till after the captivity, was that of Monotheism. Had the triune nature of the Deity been revealed to them in early times, they would inevitably have run into tri-theism, and then to polytheism.

The teachings of the New Testament distinctly assert the Christ to be the Son of God. We are sometimes told that only the fourth gospel, and not the synoptic ones, state their doctrine. Let us look then at the synoptics first. The angel informed Mary that the holy thing which should be born of her should be called Son of the Highest, and should have an everlasting kingdom (Luke 1:32-33). Matthew (11:27) tells us

The Person of Christ

that Jesus said " all things are delivered unto Me of My Father, and no man knoweth the Son but the Father; neither any man the Father, save the Son, and him to whom the Son willeth to reveal Him." Christ here asserts a knowledge and intimacy with the Father, which no created mortal would dare to claim. Again in Mat. 28:19-20, we read that Christ commanded His disciples to teach all the nations His gospel, and to baptize them in the one Name of the Father, the Son, and the Spirit.

Mark (1:11), says that, when Jesus was baptized, a voice from heaven said, " Thou art my beloved Son in whom I am well pleased." Peter confessed " Thou art the Son of the living God " (Mat. 16:16). Note the words, " the Son," not a Son. Peter in the Acts (10:36) calls Jesus " Lord of all." If Christ were only a good man, such language would be blasphemy.

Jesus declared Himself to be greater than the temple; for He is the object of divine worship (Mat. 12-6).

The fourth gospel is full of declarations of the divinity of our Lord. Christ and the Father are one, in essential being, power, worship, will, love. He can do nothing (morally) without the Father, because they are one in will and nature. The world and man were made by the Logos (John 1:3; Colos. 1:6).

Jesus forgives sins (Mat. 9:2). He gives life and quickeneth whom He will (John 5:21). The Logos humbled Himself to be a man, and possessing an intimate knowledge of our struggles, through the bitter experience He bought in the hard market of human life, He becomes the Judge of the world. The Father giveth all things into His hands (John 13:3; 5: 22-23; 1 Cor. 15:25). I cannot support the unscriptural expression " eternal generation," but the meaning of that formula is that the Sonship of the Logos is eternal. God was not a hard unit, but for eternity a being uniting three distinctions, Father, Son, Spirit.

We speak of God as our Father; Jesus speaks of Him as My Father (John 20:17; Luke 2:49).

Jesus was worshipped on many occasions, as a babe (Mat. 2: 11). By a leper (Mat. 8:2). After His resurrection by His disciples (Mat. 28:7-9).

"In the beginning was the Word, and the Word was with God, and the Word was God" (John 1). The Word become flesh. The divine Word entered in time, into our human state. The Word was God (in essential being), and became (not man but) flesh. That fact destroys Docetism. The Word revealed God's thoughts.

I take it that the Scriptures declared Jesus to hold a unique relation to God. The incarnation is a stupendous miracle. The full comprehension of it is beyond our faculties at present; for we know not enough of the nature of Deity to understand it. Some theologians speak of the incarnation of God, just as Romanists speak of the Virgin as the Mother of God. Both these terms seem to me as unphilosophical as they are unscriptural. The Bible teaches the incarnation of the Logos. Again the expression, "God the Father, God the Son, and God the Holy Ghost," is unscriptural, and I think misleading. It savours distinctly of tri-theism, not trinity.

Some have maintained that Christ was a man with body, soul and spirit, plus the Logos. Such a doctrine gives our Lord two spirits, a divine and a human one; two wills, the human obeying the divine. On such a view I cannot see how our Lord would differ essentially from a good Christian full of the Holy Spirit. It represents Christ as a union of God and man, but not the God-man. This is the error of di-theism, which bases its view on the fact that there were struggles in the spiritual life of Christ. But there are struggles in our spiritual life also; yet we have but one will.

Has not the error arisen from failure to grasp the doctrine of the Kenosis, the emptying Himself of His glory, while on earth? To say that Christ knew some things in His divine nature which He knew not in His human nature seems frivolously like juggling with sublime truths. May we venture to make the incarnation more comprehensible by putting it thus:

—Jesus had a human body, a human soul (the seat of desire and appetites), both received from the Virgin, while the Spirit came not from humanity but was the eternal word the Logos.

A man consists of (1) body, (2) soul, which gives life to the body and creates desires and appetites, and (3) spirit, his true self. The Logos took the place of spirit in Jesus. Then He divested Himself, for the time He was on earth, of His equality with God, submitting to human limitations and all the conditions and experiences of humanity,—sin duly excepted.

Jesus was the Son of God before He came on earth, the Logos held a relation to the Father so close, so affectionate, that the best way to express it, in our poor human language, is to call Him the Son of the Father.

On earth, His powers were limited. He says " My Father is greater than I." After His ascension He resumed His glory. Why should it be thought incredible, that God should become incarnate? Man, made in God's image, is not so essentially unlike God as to render incarnation impossible. It is *sin* which separates us from God, but sin is not an essential characteristic of man. That the incarnation is a mystery, we cheerfully admit, all great ultimate truths are mysterious. Scratch beneath the surface, and you will soon come upon the rock of mystery. *And all mysteries are divine; all contradictions human.* The incarnation is not a contradiction like a round-square, as Spinoza said, but a mystery eluding our comprehension.

As to the procession of the Holy Spirit from the Father and the Son, I must admit that I cannot understand what it means. As to the Athanasian Creed, to say nothing of its uncharitable condemnatory clauses, I confess I cannot understand it; but it does seem to contradict itself. We had better keep to the words of Holy Writ.

There are many texts which point to the Holy Spirit as something more than a mere influence. " The Spirit searcheth all things " (1 Cor. 2:10). " I beseech you by our Lord Jesus Christ, and by the love of the Spirit " (Rom. 15: 30). " The

Holy Spirit said separate unto me Barnabas and Saul " (Acts 13:2). Again the Comforter, the Spirit, is spoken of as He, not It. (John. 14:26; 16:8.)

In man there are three distinctions, viz., Feeling, Intellect, Will, but man is a unit. So we read of the " grace of our Lord Jesus Christ, and the love of God the Father, and the fellowship of the Holy Spirit." But these are not the emotions or influences of three Gods; they are the working of a triune Lord.

The great difficulty men have had in believing the incarnation, arises from that doctrine having been misrepresented. They have regarded God as a magnified man, and so regarded the Trinity as three magnified men—Witness those representations of the Godhead, sometimes found on the continent, where on the Cross is Christ (the Son), on the top of the cross is a dove (the Holy Spirit), and above all, the head of a benevolent man (the Father)! The Godhead is not a magnified man with a big body. We are made in God's image, not as to our body, but as to our mental and moral nature, our feelings, thoughts and volitions.

Those who knew Christ best declared Him to be the (not a) Son of God. That doctrine was no myth, growing up in later years. Is it not less marvellous that Christ should be Deity incarnate, than that an impostor blasphemously claiming equality in essence with God should have set before the world the sublimest, noblest, purest character in history? Paul admits, emphasizes, the Kenosis. (Phil. 2:6-8.) For thirty-three years Christ on earth was inferior to the Father, not in holiness or love, but in office, in knowledge, in grandeur. On earth Jesus underwent development (Heb. 5:8), was tempted as we are (Heb. 4:15), was dependent on the Father (John. 5:30), knew not when the day of judgment would come (Mark 13:32). But all this temporary subjection was voluntary. When on earth His divine functions and honours were largely handed over to the Father, and again bestowed upon the Son by the Father after His resurrection from the dead.

And this Kenosis was necessary. He could not have been in all things like His brethren, if He had retained all His divine prerogatives. "And here, O Father, glorify Thou Me *with* Thine own self, with the glory which I had with Thee before the world was." (John 17:5.) Belief in the incarnation has been the cherished tenet of most of the Christian Churches from the days of the apostles. Disbelief therein seems to me to have the following serious consequences:

(1) It tends to destroy the fatherly character of God, allowing Him to be a father only after man was created—and it tends to Deism or Pantheism.

(2) It lessens the perfection, or the beauty of God's character, not allowing Him to have always had fraternal instincts.

(3) It robs us of the one infallible teacher the world has had, for if Christ is not what He claimed to be, *the Son* of God, how can we acquit Him of false teachings.

(4) It robs us of the sublimest example of condescension and self sacrifice (God sending His own Son, who voluntarily came, to live and die for us).

(5) It robs humanity of the honour put upon it by the incarnation.

(6) It spoils both Jewish and Christian history.

(7) It takes away the very life-blood of the Christian faith.

Looking up into the face of the sinless Jesus, we believe His words assuring us that He lived with the eternal Father before He came on earth, that He was, and is, the eternal Son of God.

The Person of Christ

The Person of Christ

BY

The Reverend CHARLES F. DOLE.

IT is inevitable that men should take up the old question: "What think ye of Christ?" in the light of modern thought, with reference to new conceptions of the Universe, with the help of the clew given by the idea of Evolution, and with the flood of illumination that comes through modern Biblical criticism. The problem is not merely intellectual; its issue is ethical and spiritual.

Our question to-day has obviously become twofold. The first part touches a matter of historical fact. Who do we modern men think that Jesus of Nazareth was? What do we make of his character and personality? At least, what is both true and important for us to think about him?

The second part of our inquiry is entirely different. It is this: What do modern men, and especially the most thoughtful and representative men mean, when they speak of "Christ"? It may be, of course, that men mean the same thing by "the mind of Christ" and "the mind of Jesus". But these are certainly different expressions, and they are likely to offer somewhat different interpretations. Let us take the historical subject first.

Have we the means to-day to draw near enough to the historical Jesus, to become acquainted with him, and to determine his rank in the scale of being? I do not see how this is possible. Even when men imagined that they had an inerrant Bible, the task was difficult enough. Knowing what we now know of the nature of the New Testament writings, we can only guess, each for himself, as to the moral and spiritual features and stature of Jesus. We surely seem to see the outlines of a grand and noble figure. But we are obliged to clothe it mostly in the forms which our own imaginations furnish. Some tell us that they can distinguish in Jesus no human limitations; others think that the limitations of the man and the age are as obvious as anything to be found in the meager fragments of the biography. When, however, the practical questions have to be put: "Do you purpose exactly to imitate the actual Jesus? Is it safe to adopt all his ideas? If he drank wine, shall we drink wine? If he cried woes upon the respectable Church members of his time, shall we too venture to call down woes upon modern Pharisees? Shall we, like him, believe in Satan and his devils? Shall we expect the speedy end of the world? Shall we turn the other cheek to the smiter and resist not evil?" I find the barest minority of the believers in the authority of Jesus, who do not wince under such questions as these.

What, now, is the use of saying that Jesus was God, if it is not safe exactly to imitate him? Or, if the absolute truth is lacking, in things which he said? Or, if we never can know for certain what he did say? Who to-day is willing to accept the old belief in eternal punishment, on the strength of Jesus' authority? Accept it, and you have not only hurt Jesus' ideal character as a man of love, but you have cast a doubt upon the moral integrity of the Universe. Reject it, and there is no teaching of Jesus which you can urge as authentic.

I have purposely raised insoluble difficulties. I do not believe that you can ever demonstrate how great in the spiritual realm the nature of Jesus was. I cannot see that this is even important. You do not insist upon settling this part of the question with any other figure of history. You do not insist that men shall agree that Homer or Shakespeare was supreme in the realm of letters. You do not agree that Columbus was greater than David Livingstone. You let men think what they will, as to the rank of all great historic characters. I plead for the same freedom about Jesus.

This brings me to speak of the only facts upon which we can depend, and which alone seem to me important to-day. Reserving all matters of dissent or criticism, it remains that Jesus stands as the historical type, as well as the teacher, of a new order of human life. In the Beatitudes, the Golden Rule and the parable of the Good Samaritan, the world is made to face the ideal of the life of the true children of God. Grant that these teachings were not original with Jesus. Nevertheless, he is the conspicuous figure of the man who adopted them, trusted them and went to his death for their sake. The teachings took his name, because somehow he contrived to give them reality and working power. They are the teachings which underlie all modern civilization. The spirit of them, released from bondage to the letter, means to-day friendliness, humanity, faith in the divine universe, and life eternal. It is a very impracticable question to ask, whether a man believes that Jesus was God. The worst men may believe this and tremble. They are no better for believing it. It is a vital question to ask any man: Do you believe in what the good Samaritan did? And will you go and do likewise?

I have already suggested that, when men speak of " Christ," they do not necessarily mean Jesus of Nazareth. They are not even thinking of him. They do not know him well enough to think of him. They might not be sure to like his permanent company, if he were suddenly to come for a month's visit to their house. Whom now do men mean by Christ, " the living Christ," " the present Christ? " Have the men of the Christocentric theology discovered a new God, of whom others are ignorant? I answer, without fear of intelligent contradiction, that the name of Christ has come to be, for many, simply another and somewhat dearer name for God. Under this name is the thought of a Presence, infinite, full of power, of boundless intelligence, absolute in His goodness. Here is all " the fulness of the Godhead." What is there lacking? If there is a mystic threeness, or any species of manifoldness in the Deity, there must be this threeness or manifoldness in " Christ." For all that can be conceived is in Him. In other words, if there is a Trinity, the modern Christ is that Trinity. You have so described Christ that you have left nothing to say about God. Do you say that Christ is the

"Son?" What new word of differentiation can you add for the conception of the Father? What new word can you add to describe the Holy Spirit? What does the Father do, which Christ has not done? What is the office or function of the "Holy Ghost," alongside of the immanent Christ? There are not three divine presences! If there were three, each would be exactly identical with the others, and each would have its threeness or manifoldness. Is not one infinite and perfect Presence, in whom are Power, Wisdom and Goodness, Lover of all the souls of men, with whom men can come into communion, surely enough for all purposes of thought, worship or noble conduct?

Those who make the person of Christ identical with their thought of the fulness of God, ought to know that this is a new extension of the meaning of words. Paul, for example, never confounded Christ with Almighty God. In Paul's thought, difficult and mystical as it appears, Christ and God were evidently two distinct persons, in the ordinary and natural sense of the word "person."

Neither did the makers of the Nicene Creed conceive of Christ as the modern Christocentric theologians conceive of him. Their thought may be vague, but they at least fancied that they had some use for the Father, and the Holy Ghost, as well as for Christ, the Son. Though they strained language, they made an attempt to persuade themselves that the first and third Persons of the Trinity had offices to perform which the Son alone could not perform. It was left for our modern theologians to arrogate to the Son all divine offices.

I have already insisted that, in modern thought, "Christ" cannot possibly be identified with Jesus of Nazareth. Let us leave no doubt here, for it is on this point that our Christocentric friends play fast and loose with language. If we use "Christ" to stand for God, we all agree that God was revealed in Jesus, as He must, by parity of reasoning, be revealed wherever goodness shines. Grant, if you please, that Jesus held all of the Deity that a human life can hold; this is not

The Person of Christ

saying that the fulness of the infinite God dwelt in Jesus. We to-day know better. We know that he felt the limitations of a Jewish education and environment. No modern man can believe that the historical Jesus was present in Capernaum and in Rome at one and the same time, as men now say that "Christ" is present at once in London and New York, and in the Pleiades as well. On the contrary, Jesus possessed his own proper human personality, differentiating him from God, or Christ, so far as any soul can ever be differentiated from the Giver of his being.

This brings me to say a word as to Jesus' own reported sayings about himself. Does he not claim a certain identity with Deity? Does he not put himself above all common humanity in the terms of some kind of spiritual sovereignty? We must make allowance here for the mystic ideas of Messiahship, floating in the minds of all Jesus' contemporaries and followers. We must make allowance for the oriental mind, especially in the prophetic order of person. With moderate allowance for the difference of colour and point of view between Jesus' age and ours, I make bold to say that Jesus claims nothing for himself which is not universally true of the ideal or divine nature inherent in all of us. If we may call God our Father in any real sense of the word, let us not be afraid of the consequent dignity of our common human nature. Let us carry the doctrine of our divine Sonship as far as it will go. If we live in God, He lives in us; that is, "the eternal" or immortal nature is in us. What higher things can we say? No fear that this will make us arrogant or immodest! The conception empties us of all egotism and selfishness. What is the divine and sovereign nature which sets man above the stars and gives rule over all the works of God? It is love or beneficence. The lower sovereignty was to crush and subdue; it was to get, with the idea of self as a center. The divine sovereignty is to give, to serve, to uplift. This is the kernel of the gospel; it is a new order of life. Keep this clew in mind and you may say of yourself whatever Jesus said. You will not think of yourself in what you say; you will think what is true of the divine nature, which you simply share.

See now what an extraordinary and interesting development the word "Christ" has taken on. Even the word "spirit" has not marched further from its original meaning. Christ, first, was simply an adjective, to describe the anointed one, whether a king or a priest. Then it became the title wherewith to call the hero-king who should come to save the Jewish people. Then Jesus changed the ideal of the hero from the man of force to the man of good will and peace. Then Paul took the word for the idealized Presence of his visions, the celestial man, the head of the race. Then the title, getting further from the historical Jesus, went over to describe a metaphysical Being, a sort of an emanation of the Deity,; now, lastly, the title has come to stand for the Deity Himself.

The new use of the word Christ covers two opposite tendencies. One is cowardly and superficial. There are those who desire, by means of familiar words, to get the advantage, prestige and popularity of the old faith. They are shy of telling the frank truth, namely, that old words have developed into new meaning, which would not be altogether recognized or understood by earlier men. For want of frankness, they are willing to appear to worship a different God from the God of James Martineau or Dr. Hale or President Eliot. They are content to go on misleading and confusing the minds of each new generation of children by a semblance of teaching which simple people have never yet been able to understand and which separates good men from one another's company.

The other tendency in the use of the word "Christ" is thoroughly respectable. A religion wants a name, a motto, we might say a flag about which its adherents may rally. "Who are you?" the world asks of the followers of any religion. "Tell us in one word what you stand for and what your faith is." The tenacity of earnest and progressive men in holding upon the words Christ and Christian, is here explained. We believe in the old flag, men cry. True, the flag no longer floats over a king's palace; it is over market-places and schoolhouses. It does not represent loyalty, but the welfare of all the people. All men love it; it is the symbol of their common country. So the name of Christ seems to a multitude of people to be inseparable from their common faith in a good God and a divine humanity. As theists take up the word God, that once carried and that still carries to some the thought of a distant, austere, jealous artificer and despot, and adapt the word in spite of its crude old associations, to convey the most modern and philosophical conception of the present and beneficent Life of the universe, so men adapt the name "Christ" to carry their faith in this same good God, incarnate in the life of humanity.

The practical question in religious thought to-day is this: Can the word Christ be honestly used, with a still fresher and frank adaptation of meaning, to express a perfectly rational conception of a great reality, which is slowly coming to consciousness in the religious experience of our race? This conception is the divine nature in humanity, the higher potentiality in all men. We call this by various terms:—"The higher nature," "The better self." It is by virtue of this quality or nature in us that we have real personality. At our best, goodwill possesses us, flows in us, dominates our conduct. This good will is the highest expression of the life of God. It is through this good will ruling us that we venture to call ourselves the children of God. We are God's children as we are like Him in His highest attributes. At our best, God's power, intelligence, justice and goodness are incarnate in us. There is now a law of unity in us, co-ordinating all the experiences of our lives into their orderly place. There is now no dissonance between the body and the spirit. Spirit possesses the body. There is inward, moral and spiritual health, of which the nice adjustments of the bodily health are but a parallel. This sort or order of life seems to have been precisely that which the Jesus of history preached and lived. The Beatitudes set it forth. The key to it was in Jesus' thought that the true or ideal man, that is, the moral man, is not here to be ministered unto, but to minister and to pour out his life for the welfare of all. In other words, in the truest human life, the divine law holds that a man lives not by getting, but by giving and doing. Life is at its maximum of power, peace, joy, efficiency, to the man who gives himself utterly to be the channel, the voice, the minister, aye rather the Son and the sharer of the divine beneficence.

This was substantially the secret of Paul's gospel. Underneath his somewhat obscure and rabbinical philosophy was the idea of a life, as he says, " hid with Christ in God." He could " do all things through Christ." When he was weak, then was he strong. What did he mean? He meant what we mean to-day at those times when, without thought of reward or personal gain, we lend ourselves to every motion of the good will of God, to conscience, to duty, to truth, to our love. Then we feel God within us, then our brightest thoughts come, as if God told them to us; then anxieties and fears vanish and we are at rest, as men who have found themselves. For in every hour of good-will we find God. We are also in communion with all true and good men; our lives move together and in one way.

What I suggest is, whether the word Christ, by one step further in its development, is not coming to stand for the God in us, that is for our own complete personality. In this sense, when I say that I believe in Christ, I simply mean that I believe in the divineness of man; I believe that God is incarnate to-day in thousands of the men of good-will; I believe that I live and move and have my being in God. Do I believe, someone asks, in the divinity of Jesus? Yes, surely; in his deity, if you like to say so. But I find the same deity in Isaiah, in the noble Epictetus, in the great and wise Marcus Aurelius. What else was it that lifted them to the shining heights of heroism? If " Christ " has come to mean the God in man, then I believe in Christ.

More practically, this conception commits those who hold

it, to a perfectly definite ideal of conduct and life. I take Christ to be the name or title of my better, divine or ideal self. If I believe in this nature, I am debarred at once from being mean or selfish. I can stoop to no untruth. I am held up to a supreme standard of generosity and devotion. Show me what my friends, my household, my neighbors, the city, the state, the welfare of mankind demands of me and I am here to do it, as if I held the trusteeship of all the divine resources.

Take the same idea in another form. Suppose I ask what "Christ" would do in certain given circumstances? Would he hold slaves? Would he drink wine? Would he ever tell a falsehood? Would he allow a war? Would he advocate the policy of imperialism? I do not mean, what would Jesus do in the same circumstances. I do not and cannot know what Jesus would do. I really mean: What would my ideal self, the highest possible creation of my ethical imagination, the God in me, do? What he bids, that I must do. I know no law so impressive, inspiring or practical. I do not say that it is infallible, for I am an imperfect intelligence wherewith to contain the divine wisdom. I say that, by the side of this, no other law is so simple, clear or feasible.

We have here a thought of "the person of Christ," which is identical with the ideal personality of each one of us. It is that by virtue of which we are immortal spirits. I believe that I could gather many pages out of the most profound human experience to show that the best thought of Christendom has moved steadily toward this largest and loftiest of all conceptions of the divine human nature; that it is in the straight line of historic development from the early days.

Whether the word Christ is the best name to express this magnificent conception, I do not dare to say. The new use is surely a legitimate development of the history of the word. The word at first, like Master, was the title of one man, a sovereign in the realm of force. It has now become, like Master, the democratic title of respect and honor for all who share our common human nature. In proportion as we honour every man as a Master, a Person, a grown man, we tend to find in him a Christ or Son of God.

If, however, Christ is the best word to fit the fact, it will not be proved so by any urgent insistence that all men must use it. It must be unbound from creedal limits, to win its own free way to common acceptance. It must take its chances with other words and phrases which equally express the same reality. Moreover, its new use, as distinguished from other uses of the past, must be honestly and distinctly proclaimed.

One thing, finally, is certain. The faith, the religion, the life which goes with our thought of the divine humanity, that is, the God in man, or the ideal Christ, is altogether a grander thing than the Christianity of history, of the creeds and of the historic churches. This religion and the ordinary Christianity ought not to be confounded or even to bear the same name. The Christianity of the creeds and the churches has busied itself chiefly with methods of how to evade the Christianity of the ideal Christ. It has dealt mostly in names and symbols and not in realities. It has let men be content to worship Christ, who never had caught the idea of living the life of Christ. If we stand to-day for Christianity, it is a new Christianity, as different from the prevailing religions of Christendom, as Jesus' religion was different from the religion of the Scribes and Pharisees. We want a practical and spiritual religion, new to the world and yet as old as the prophets. The reality is dearer than all names, symbols, flags or sacraments. The ideal Christ before each of us is grander than the holiest man of the past. If any familiar names or words will help us to possess this Christlike type of life, let us lay hold boldly on such words and convert them to this highest use. If they do not help us, if they stand in our way, if they confuse and befog the minds of men, let us set them aside, as the ideal Christ surely commands. The name, Christ, is now on trial before the world. Can it be converted to the service of humanity?

The Atonement

The Atonement

BY

The Reverend Professor FRANKLIN JOHNSON, D.D., LL.D.

AT the close of the nineteenth century and the opening of the twentieth, the Christian world as a whole believes in a substitutionary atonement. This has been its belief ever since it began to think. The doctrine was stated by Athanasius as clearly and fully as by any later writer. All the great historic creeds which set forth the atonement at any length set forth a substitutionary atonement. All the great historic systems of theology enshrine it as the very ark of the covenant, the central object of the holy of holies.

While the Christian world in general believes in a substitutionary atonement, it is less inclined than it once was to regard any existing theory of substitution as entirely adequate. It accepts the substitution of Christ as a fact, and it tends to esteem the theories concerning it only as glimpses of a truth larger than all of them. It observes that an early theory found the necessity of the atonement in the veracity of God, that a later one found it in the honour of God, and that a still later one found it in the government of God, and it deems all these speculations helpful, while it yearns for further light.

If we should ask those who hold this doctrine on what grounds they believe that Christ is the substitute for sinners, there would be many answers, but perhaps in only two of them would all voices agree. The first of these grounds would be the repeated declarations of holy Scripture, which are so clear, so precise, so numerous, and so varied, that they leave no room to doubt their meaning. The other ground is the testimony of the human heart wherever it mourns its sin or rejoices in an accomplished deliverance. The declaration of the Scriptures that Christ bore our sins on the cross is necessary to satisfy the longings of the soul. The Christian world in general would say: " We believe in gravitation, in light, in electricity, in the all pervading ether, because we must, and not because we can explain them fully. So we believe that Christ died instead of the sinner because we must, and not because we know all the reasons which led God to appoint and to accept His sacrifice."

While the Christian world as a whole believes in a substitutionary atonement, the doctrine is rejected by a minority of devout and able men, who present instead of it what has often been called "the moral influence theory." According to this, the sole mission of Christ was to reveal the love of God in a way so moving as to melt the heart and induce men to forsake sin. The theory is sometimes urged with so great eloquence and tenderness that one will fain find it sufficient as an interpretation at once of the Scriptures and of human want.

Now no one calls in question the profound spiritual influence of Christ where He is preached as the propitiation of God, and those who believe the doctrine of a substitutionary atonement lift up the cross as the sole appointed means of reaching and saving the lost. They object only when "the moral influence theory" is presented as a sufficient account of the atonement, to the denial that the work of Christ has rendered God propitious towards man. One may appreciate the moon without wishing that it put out the sun and stars.

The advocates of this theory, in order to make it an adequate explanation of the atonement, must clear the doctrine of substitution out of the way. They attempt to do this by advancing many arguments, only two of which need detain us here, since, these removed, the others, of lighter moment, will fall of themselves.

First, it is said that the doctrine of substitution supposes that which is impossible. Guilt cannot be transferred from one person to another. Punishment and penalty cannot be transferred from a guilty person to an innocent one. An innocent person may be charged with sin, but if so he will be innocent still, and not guilty.

An innocent person may suffer, but if so his suffering will

not be punishment or penalty. Such is the objection: the Christian world, in believing that a substitutionary atonement has been made by Christ, believes a thing which is contrary to the necessary laws of thought.

The reader will observe that this objection has to do wholly with the definitions of the words guilt and punishment and penalty. It is perhaps worthy the serious attention of the theologian who wishes to keep his terms free from offence; but it has no force beyond the sphere of verbal criticism. It is true that guilt, in the sense of personal blameworthiness, cannot be transferred from the wrong-doer to the well-doer. It is true that punishment, in the sense of penalty inflicted for personal blameworthiness, cannot be transferred from the wrong-doer to the well-doer. This is no discovery, and it is maintained as earnestly by those who believe in a substitutionary atonement as those who deny it.

Let us use other words, if these are not clear, but let us hold fast the truth which they were once used to express. The world is so constituted that it bears the idea of substitution engraved upon its very heart. No man or woman or child escapes from suffering inflicted for the faults of others. In thousands of instances these substitutionary sufferings are assumed voluntarily, and are useful. Husbands suffer in order to deliver wives from sufferings richly deserved. Wives suffer in order to deliver husbands from sufferings richly deserved. Children suffer in order to deliver parents from sufferings richly deserved. Parents suffer in order to deliver children from sufferings richly deserved. Pastors often shield guilty churches in this way, and sometimes at the cost of life. Statesmen often shield guilty nations in this way, and sometimes at the cost of life. If now we shall teach that Christ suffered in order to deliver us from sufferings which we richly deserved, we shall avoid a strife about words, and shall maintain that, coming into the world as a member of our race, He suffered to the utmost, as many other heroic souls have suffered in a lesser degree, by subjecting Himself to be a common rule of vicarious suffering, instituted by God in the formation of human society bound together by ties of sympathy and love, and existing in daily operation from the dawn of history till this present time.

The vicarious sufferings by means of which the innocent deliver the guilty from sufferings richly deserved are frequently assumed in the fear that overmuch of grief will harden the culprit and in a hope that a stay of judgment and the softening lapse of time may lead him to better things. May we not believe that Christ was affected by a similar motive, and has produced that delay of the divine justice at which every thoughtful person wonders? But the vicarious sufferings which we observe in the world are frequently assumed for a stronger reason, in the belief that the culprit already shows signs of relenting, and in the assurance that patient waiting, even at great cost, will be rewarded with the development of the tender beginnings of a new life which the thunder-storms of untempered equity might destroy. So it was predicted of Christ before His coming that "He should see of the travail if His soul and be satisfied."

Thus if Christ suffered in order to deliver us from sufferings which we richly deserved, it was also in order to deliver us from sin by reason of which we deserved them.

The second argument by means of which the advocates of "the moral influence theory" seek to refute the doctrine of a substitutionary atonement is equally unfortunate with the first, in that, like the first, it criticizes words, rather than the thoughts which they are employed to express. The doctrine of a substitutionary atonement, it is said, is immoral. Let us inquire what this immoral doctrine is. The doctrine, it is answered, is that our guilt was transferred to Christ and that He was punished for our sins. Here again let us "strive not about words." Let us admit that the theologian might well express himself in other terms, which would create no prejudice against his meaning. But, if he amends his statement, let him retain every part of his meaning. Let him say that

Christ suffered in order that guilty man might escape from sufferings richly deserved. Is this teaching immoral? Then the constitution of the human race, ordained by God, is immoral, for, since its ties are those of sympathy and love, human beings are constantly suffering that others may escape sufferings richly deserved. Then sympathy is immoral, for this is what it does. Then love is immoral, for this is what it does. Then the best persons are the most immoral, for they do this oftener than others.

The objector does not maintain that the doctrine of a substitutionary atonement has equally produced immorality wherever it has been proclaimed. He does not venture to test his charge by an appeal to history. The appeal would be fatal. For nineteen hundred years, the only great moral advances of the human race have been brought about by the preaching of a substitutionary atonement. " A tree is known by its fruits." It is impossible that a doctrine essentially immoral should be the cause of morality among men.

Let us turn now to " the moral influence theory " and consider why it ought not to be accepted as an adequate account of the atonement.

As a complete theory of the atonement it is far too narrowly circumscribed, and too near the surface. Were it universally adopted, it would be the end of thought on this high theme. The substitutionary atonement promises an eternity of delightful progress in study. It cannot be exhausted. All the theories which have been advanced to cast light upon it are valuable, but they leave a whole universe to be explored, and one may hope to extend the field of discovery at any time. To shut us out of this boundless prospect, and limit us to the petty confines of " the moral influence theory " would be to shrivel the ocean to the dimensions of a pond, and bid the admiral sail his navies in it, or to blot out all the worlds save those of the solar system and bid the astronomer enlarge his science.

As the adoption of this circumscribed view would be the end of thought, so it would be the end of emotion. The heart has always been kindled by the preaching of a Christ who bore our sins before God on the cross. By this truth the hardened sinner has been subdued and in it the penitent sinner has found a source of rapture. An atonement of infinite cost, flowing from infinite love, moving an infinite God, and procuring deliverance from infinite loss, melts the coldest heart and inflames the warmest. To preach a lesser sacrifice would be to spread frost instead of fire.

But the will is reached through the reason and the emotions. That which would cease to challenge profound thought and would put out the flames of emotion would fail to reach the will and transform the life. The theory makes the death of Christ predominantly scenic, spectacular, an effort to display the love of God, rather than an offering to God in its nature necessary for the salvation of man. It struggles in vain to find a worthy reason for the awful sacrifice. Hence it may be charged with essential immorality. In any case, the work of Christ, if interpreted in this manner, will not prove "the power of God unto salvation." The speculation is called "the moral influence theory," but when preached as an exclusive theory of the atonement, it is incapable of wielding any profound moral influence. The man who dies to rescue one whom he loves from death is remembered with tears of reverence and gratitude; the man who puts himself to death to show that he loves is remembered with horror.

Still further. The chief failure of those who advance this view is in the sphere of exegesis. The Bible is so full of a substitutionary atonement that the reader comes upon it everywhere. The texts which teach it are not rare and isolated expressions; they assemble in multitudes; they rush in troops; they occupy every hill and every valley. They occasion the greatest embarrassment to those who deny that the relation of God to the world is determined by the cross, and various methods are employed by various writers to reduce their number and their force. They are most abundant in the epistles of the apostle Paul, and some depreciate his authority as a teacher of Christianity. The doctrine is implied in the words which our Lord uttered at the last supper, and some attack these as not genuine. Christ is repeatedly declared to be a propitiation. " Whom God hath set forth to be a propitiation, through faith, by His blood," Rom. 3 : 25. " He is the propitiation for our sins, and not for ours only, but also for the whole world," 1 John 2 : 3. " God sent His son to be a propitiation for our sins," 1 John 4 : 10. " Wherefore it behooved Him in all things to be made like unto His brethren, that He might be a merciful and faithful high priest in things pertaining to God, to make propitiation for the sins of the people," Heb. 2 : 17. Many special pleas are entered against the plain meaning of these declarations. It does not seem difficult to understand them. A propitiation must be an influence which renders some one propitious, and the person rendered propitious by it must be the person who was offended. Yet some representatives of the theory do not hesitate to affirm that these texts regard man as the only being propitiated by the cross. Special tortures are applied to many other Scriptures to keep them from proclaiming a substitutionary atonement. Christ is " the Lamb of God, which taketh away the sin of the world," John 1 : 29. " The Son of Man came not to be ministered unto, but to minister, and to give His life a ransom for many," Matt. 20 : 28; Mk. 10 : 45. " Him who knew no sin He made to be sin on our behalf, that we might become the righteousness of God in Him," 2 Cor. 5 : 21. Such are a few examples of the countless declarations of a substitutionary atonement which the Scriptures make, and with which those who reject the doctrine strive in vain. Any speculation which sets itself against this mighty current flowing through all the Bible is destined to be swept away.

Yet further. A theological theory, like a person, should be judged somewhat by the company it keeps. If it shows an inveterate inclination to associate with other theories which lie wholly upon the surface, which too are easy of comprehension, which sound no depths and solve no problems, and which the profoundest Christian experience rejects, it is evidently the same in kind.

The theory which I am here studying tends to consort with an inadequate view of inspiration, and some of its representatives question the inerrancy of the Scripture, even in the matters pertaining to faith and conduct. It tends to consort with an inadequate view of God, and some of its representatives in praising His love, forget His holiness and His awful wrath against incorrigible wrong-doers. It tends to consort with an inadequate view of sin, and some of its representatives make the alienation of man from God consist merely in acts, rather than in an underlying state from which they proceed. It tends, finally, to consort with an inadequate view of responsibility and guilt, and some of its representatives teach that these cease when the sinner turns, so that there is no need of propitiation, but only for repentance. A distinguished representative of this theory has written the following sentences: "All righteous claims are satisfied if sin is done away." "Divine law is directed against sin, and is satisfied when sin is made to cease." "If grace brings an end of sinning, the end sought by law has been attained. It cannot be, therefore, that, in the sight of God there is any need of satisfying law before grace can save sinners." These words are like the voice of "a very lovely song;" but many a pardoned soul uttered a more troubled strain. A man may cease to sin without reversing the injury he has wrought. In the course of his business, let us suppose, he has defrauded widows and orphans, and they are now dead. Or, in his social life, he has led the young into unbelief and vice, and they now laugh at his efforts to undo mischief, or have gone into eternity unsaved. In a sense his sinning has come to an end, yet its baleful effects are in full career. His conscience tells him he is responsible not only for the commission of his sins, but for the ruin wrought by his sins. In other words, he is responsible for the entire train of evils which he has put into operation. The

The Atonement

depths of his responsibility are far too profound for such light plummets to sound.

These are some of the reasons which lead the Christian world as a whole to reject "the moral influence theory" of the atonement as inadequate.

I shall not attempt to set forth any substitutionary theory of the atonement. It is not absolutely necessary that we have a theory. It may be enough for us to hold the doctrine without a theory. The writers of the New Testament did this. The earliest fathers of the church did it. The world has been profoundly influenced by the preaching of the doctrine before the leaders of the church began to construct a theory. What was done in the first century may be done in the twentieth. We may proclaim Christ as the sin-bearer and win multitudes to Him without a theory. Men will welcome the fact, even in the absence of an explanation, as the famishing welcome water without asking about its chemical composition.

Yet the Christian thinker will never cease to seek for an adequate theory of the atonement, and it may be well for us to consider some of the conditions with which it is necessary for him to comply in order to succeed in casting any new light upon this divine mystery.

Firstly. Any theory of the atonement, to be adequate, must proceed from a fair and natural interpretation of all the Biblical statements on the subject. It must not pick and choose among them. It must not throttle any into silence.

Secondly. It must make use of the thought which other generations have found helpful. It must not discard these old materials. Though they are not a completed building, they constitute a foundation which we cannot afford to destroy. They may be covered over with an accumulation of verbal infelicities from which we must set them free; but who would advance our knowledge of the peace made for us by Christ must not disdain to build upon them.

Thirdly. An adequate theory of the atonement will take

account of all the moral attributes of God, for all are concerned in our salvation. It will find the chief motive of the atonement in the love of God, who " so loved the world that He gave His only begotten Son," John 3: 16. It will find one necessity of the atonement in the righteousness of God, who " set forth " Christ " to be a propitiation, through faith in His blood, to show His righteousness, because of the passing over of the sins done aforetime, in the forbearance of God: for the showing of His righteousness at this present season; that He might Himself be just and the justifier of him that hath faith in Jesus," Rom. 3: 25, 26. It will find one effect of the atonement in the aversion from man of the wrath of God, the product of love and righteousness outraged by sin: " While we were yet sinners Christ died for us. Much more then, being now justified by His blood, shall we be saved from wrath through Him," Rom. 5: 9.

Fourthly. An adequate theory of the atonement will accord with a profound Christian experience. It will not toy with Socinian interpretations of the Godhead, for the doctrine of the trinity is the product not only of a sound exegesis and a sound philosophy, but also of a sound Christian experience. It will not picture God as a Father in a sense which would deny His kinship, as a weak-minded Father who bewails the rebellion of His children but has no courage to wield the rod. It will not cover His face with feeble smiles or inane tears and deny to it the frowns of wrath, for a profound Christian experience pronounces such portraitures untrue. It will not join those excellent Christians who see in sin only a temporary fault, a disease of the surface, the product chiefly of circumstances, and probably a necessary stage in the progress of man to higher things, for these roseate hues are known to be deceitful by all who have entered earnestly into battle with the corruption of our nature and have achieved any great moral triumphs. It will not diminish the guilt of the transgressor, for it is the pardoned transgressor who knows best the awful demerit of his deeds and of the state of alienation from God from which they issued. In short, it will take into account the judgment of those wise souls who have learned "the deep things of God" in much spiritual conflict, and will reach conclusions acceptable to them.

Fifthly. An adequate theory of the atonement will view the sacrifice of Christ as an event planned from eternity, and effectual with God from eternity. He is "the Lamb that hath been slain from the foundation of the world," Rev. 13:8. He "was foreknown before the foundation of the world, but manifested at the end of the times," 1 Pet. 1:20. Sin did not take God by surprise when it entered Eden; He had foreseen it, and had provided a Redeemer before it had led us captive.

Sixthly. An adequate theory of the atonement will take a broader view of the self-sacrifice of Christ than that once presented to us. His self-sacrifice culminated in His death, and we speak of that very properly as His atonement. But His self-sacrifice had other features which we must not forget.

It had two principal moments, one in eternity, and the other in time. The first was the laying aside of some of His divine attributes that He might take our nature; the second was the endurance of the evils of human life and death, which He would not remove from His lot by miracle. Both are brought before us in the statement that, "being in the form of God, He counted it not a prize to be on an equality with God, but emptied Himself, taking the form of a bond-servant, being made in the likeness of men; and being found in fashion as a man, He humbled Himself, becoming obedient even as far as unto death, yea the death of the cross," (Phil. 2:6-8). And all this pathetic history of self-sacrifice is rendered yet more pathetic when we reflect that He anticipated His sufferings from eternity and moved forward in the creation and government of the universe, with the vision of His coming sorrows ever before His eyes.

We can form no conception of the cost at which He laid aside some of His divine attributes to become incarnate. We can form but little conception of the cost at which He died for the world. No mere man ever laid down His life for others in the sense in which Christ laid down His life for the world. Every man must die at some time; "there is no discharge in that warfare." When a man sacrifices his life he does but sacrifice a few days or years; he does but lay it down earlier instead of later. But Christ did not choose between dying at one time rather than at another; He chose between dying and not dying. Thus, viewed in any light whatever, the voluntary sufferings of Christ surpass our powers of thought and imagination, reaching infinitely beyond all human experience.

Seventhly. An adequate theory of the atonement, will make much of the effect produced upon God by the infinite, voluntary, and unselfish sacrifice of Christ for the world. Here all human language breaks down, and it sounds feeble to say that God admires with the utmost enthusiasm this holy and heroic career of suffering for the salvation of man. Yet we must use such words, though they are cold. The Scriptures speak of His attitude toward His incarnate Son as one of unbounded appreciation and approval, and tell us that His voice was heard repeatedly from heaven, saying: "This is My beloved Son, in whom I am well pleased." When we say that the sacrifice of Christ is meritorious with God, we mean that it calls forth His supreme admiration. Such was His feeling towards it as He foresaw it from eternity, such was His feeling towards it as He looked upon it while being made, and such is His feeling towards it now, as He looks back upon it and glorifies Christ in honour of it.

Eighthly. An adequate theory of the atonement will find that the work of Christ has made a vast difference in the relations of God to the fallen world. It was infinite in the love which prompted it and in the self-sacrifice which attended it, and hence infinite in its moral value. We cannot but deem it fitting that it should procure for the world an administration of grace. Provided for eternity and efficacious with God from eternity, it has procured an administration of grace from the moment when the first sin was committed.

No doubt it is for this reason that God has suffered the

world to stand through all the ages of its rebellious history. He has looked upon it from the beginning in Christ, and hence has treated it with forbearance, with love, with mercy. It did not first come under grace when Christ was crucified; it has always been under grace, because Christ has always offered His sacrifice in the plan and purpose of God, and thus has always exercised a propitiatory influence. The grace of God towards man was not fully revealed and explained till it was made manifest in the person and work of Christ, but it has always been the reigning principle of the divine government. Men are saved by grace since the death of Christ, and they have always been saved by grace when they have been saved at all. The entire argument of the apostle Paul in his epistles to the Romans and the Galatians has for its purpose the defense of the proposition that God has always justified men by grace through faith, and that there has never been any other way of salvation. The entire administration of God in human history is set forth, in the light of "the Lamb that hath been slain from the foundation of the world," as one of infinite kindness and leniency, notwithstanding those severities which have expressed His abhorrence of sin.

But if the self-sacrifice of Christ has made a difference in the practical attitude of God towards the world, it has also made a difference in His feeling towards the world. God is one. He is not at war within Himself. He is not a hypocrite. He has not one course of action and a different course of feeling. If He has dealt patiently and graciously with our sinning race, it is because He has felt patient and gracious, and the work of His Son, by means of which His administration has been rendered patient and gracious, has rendered His feeling patient and gracious.

It is to this different administration and to its basis in a different feeling that the Scriptures refer when they present Christ to us as "the propitiation for our sins, and not for ours only, but for the whole world."

The Atonement

The Atonement

BY

The Reverend JAMES MUSCUTT HODGSON, M.A., D.Sc., DD.

THE Life and Death of Jesus of Nazareth are matters of history, the interpretation of which involves problems for Christian Thought of unique interest and importance, but of by no means easy solution. The Doctrine of the Atonement is the attempt to set forth the meaning, purpose, and results of the historical events.

The fundamental distinction between historical actuality and spiritual significance, which cannot but be recognized in this as in every other department of Revealed Truth, has sometimes been inaccurately presented in the form of an antithesis between the *Fact* of the Atonement and the *Theory* of the Atonement. What is really meant by the Fact of the Atonement, in this connection, is the proposition that there is a relation between the Death of Christ and the Forgiveness of Sin and the deliverance of sinners from the practice and power of Sin and their restoration to Righteousness and Fellowship with God. But in making such a statement, we have already passed beyond the facts of actual history to the interpretation of the facts. There is, of course, a difference between the assertion that some relation exists between the Life and Death of Christ and the Forgiveness and Salvation of sinners, and the further attempt to explain the nature of that relation. But the recognition of *any* relation or connection between them itself involves a faith, a conviction which is capable of being set forth in the form of an opinion or a theory. Moreover, the bare assertion that the things are somehow related is of little religious value, and cannot be regarded as materially helping to an intelligent apprehension and adequate appreciation of the historical events.

Dr. Horton has recently said, " The Life and Death of the Saviour we take to be facts; the recovery of men and women from lives of shame and folly, so far as these can be observed, may also be set down in the category of facts. But the connection between these two series traverses a vast expanse of theory. At all events when we are discussing this connection we are moving in that borderland of ideas where fact passes over insensibly into theory." " It is very difficult to say what we mean by the fact of the Atonement if we leave everything of a theoretical nature out of account."

The Doctrine of the Atonement is really the attempt to justify the affirmation that a relation does exist between the Life and Death of Christ and the Salvation of sinners, by the presentation of that which is regarded as an intelligible and satisfactory statement and explanation of the *nature of the relation* in which we are constrained to believe that the one stands to the other.

From the time of the apostles to the present day, it has been the belief and conviction of almost the entire community of Christian people that in Christ we have the ground, the source, the Agent of the salvation of sinners. But in the interpretation and exposition of that relation there has not been by any means the same unanimity.

The apostle Paul clearly and emphatically ascribes all the elements and phases of the process of salvation from sin and of growth in righteousness and blessedness to the work of Christ. The release of the sinner from the bondage of sin, from everything that prevents or hinders him in the attainment of righteousness, which Paul designates by the term " Redemption," is due, according to him, to Christ who " gave Himself as a Ransom-price for all." " The law of the Spirit of Life in Christ hath made me free from the law of sin and death." " The Reconciliation " (or the Atonement, according to the Authorized version in the only passage in which that word occurs in the New Testament), is said to have been " received through Christ." " God was in Christ reconciling the world unto Himself." " It is all of God who reconciled us unto Himself through Christ." As Prof. Adeney says, " Sin consists in a quarrel between man and God, and Christ puts an end to that quarrel, and brings us back into friendly relations with our Father."

Christ, again, is said to have been set forth as a "Propitiation," or Mercy-seat, where God shows Himself to be propitious, favorable, and merciful to men. Under the Old Dispensation, the Mercy-seat was separated from the Outer Court, indicating that the way into the Holiest of all was not yet made manifest; but Christ, the real Propitiatory, is set forth before all, the veil having been rent in twain, and all men are now freely invited to draw near.

Christ, it is also declared, " is made unto us Sanctification;" He is the power by which the progressive development of the Christian's character and life is brought about. "If Christ is in you, the spirit is life because of righteousness." Believers are described, moreover, as being "quickened together with Christ." "Arise from the dead, and Christ shall give thee life."

In short, Salvation, which may be taken as denoting the whole process, combining all the aspects and elements of Christ's work in us and for us, is everywhere, in the Apostle's teaching, connected with the life and work of Christ. "We shall be saved through Him." "Saved by His life." "Christ Jesus came into the world to save sinners." In all respects, in fact, Christ was to the apostle "the Power of God unto Salvation;" His was the only name given under heaven among men whereby we can be saved.

In Paul's Doctrine respecting the Mediatorial Work of Christ special emphasis is undoubtedly laid upon His Death. "Christ died for our sins." "The word of the Cross is the Power of God." "Christ died for us that we should live together with Him." But when we come to ask *how* it is that the Death of Christ helps to effect the salvation of sinners, we do not find in Paul's writings any definite statement or theory. He says that Christ died in our behalf, and on behalf of our sins; but he does not say that He died in our stead, that He was punished instead of us, or that He suffered the death that our sins deserved and made us liable to. He died for our sins; He died that we might live; *that* is as far as the apostle goes in explanation of the connection between His Death and our Forgiveness and Salvation. Love for us was the impelling motive which led Christ to lay down His life, and He laid it down in order that He might deliver us from the bondage and wretchedness of sin and impart to us freedom, and power, and life for righteousness.

Subsequent theologians have proceeded much farther in their efforts to interpret and expound the nature of the connection between the Death of Christ and the Salvation from Sin which is offered to men through Him. Their theories as to what Christ accomplished by dying for us have frequently displayed no little speculative ingenuity,—sometimes affording light and help, but in other cases tending to obscurity and perplexity, and at times even perverting and degrading the subject by the introduction of conceptions essentially immoral and unworthy.

An extraordinary theory which was early formulated, and which for centuries held a place in Christian Thought, was that Christ's Death was the Ransom paid to Satan to secure the release of those who by sin had become his captives.

The Doctrine propounded by Anselm in the twelfth century was a distinct improvement upon this. His contention was that the attribute of Divine Justice demands satisfaction for the sins of men, and that the purpose of Christ's Death was to remove this obstacle to the Forgiveness and Salvation of sinners. Dr. Hodge expresses this opinion when he says, " In the Old Testament and in the New, God is declared to be just, in the sense that His nature demands the punishment of sin; and that, therefore, there can be no remission without such punishment, vicarious or personal."

But what a righteous being must desire to secure in others is their righteousness. Punishment administered by righteous love may be valuable as an instrument and a means towards attaining this end. But a loving and merciful being can have no wish that pain and sorrow should continue when the sin and unrighteousness are abandoned.

A Loving Being, such as God is believed to be, cannot but forgive the sinner who repents and forsakes his sin. So far as the New Testament is concerned, the word "Justice" never occurs, and there need be no hesitation in affirming that the notion that the Justice of God must be satisfied by the infliction of punishment is a non-Scriptural, and, in reality, a purely pagan conception. A righteous being may be regarded as bound to punish sin as a palpable expression of his disapproval of it, and as a necessary element and instrument in the task of destroying sin, of separating the sinner from his sin, and restoring him to the righteousness of loving, trustful loyalty. But when that end has been gained, Righteousness and Justice cannot be thought of as demanding any further satisfaction.

In the seventeenth century, Grotius urged a modification of this Doctrine. Rejecting the idea of the absolute necessity of Satisfaction, he contended for what is described as *relative* satisfaction. It was not, he held, the Divine Nature itself which demanded punishment, but, *as a Ruler,* God could not dispense with punishment without some provision by which the authority and dignity of the Moral Law should be maintained. But this theory rests upon the unwarranted assumption that God occupies a relation to men precisely analogous to that of a human ruler to his subjects. Under human governments, the penal sanctions of the law are an expedient needed for the support of its enactments. But this is a consideration which has no place in respect to the Divine Law. Moreover, human rulers simply seek by the fear of threatened punishments to repress wrong-doing for the sake of others than the criminals; whereas God seeks to subdue the evil in men's hearts and to make them good by inspiring the love of goodness,—an end which punishment alone cannot secure.

A cruder and more offensive type of doctrine, confusedly combining the views of Anselm and of Grotius, has been largely prevalent in Protestant Theology, in which the emphasis has been mainly laid upon the notion of Substitution as a description of the relation between the Death of Christ and the penalties deserved by sinners. Luther, in his commentary on Galatians says, " God " sent His only Son into the world, and laid upon Him the sins of all men, saying, ' Thou art Peter, that denier; Paul, that persecutor, blasphemer, and cruel oppressor; David, that adulterer; be Thou the person that hath committed the sins of all men. See, therefore, that Thou pay and satisfy for them;' And so He setteth upon Him and killeth Him." Dr. Hodge contends that Christ " suffered in the place of sinners. He was their substitute. He assumed their obligation to satisfy justice. What He did and suffered precluded the necessity of their fulfilling the demands of the law in their own persons."

This conception, which unfortunately has obtained popular acceptance, in many quarters, not only assumes that the infliction of suffering and death was demanded either by some principle of abstract justice or by the majesty and authority of the Law, but affirms an actual transference of the penalties of sin and of the Divine displeasure which they reveal, from the guilty to the innocent, which is utterly repugnant to the primary instincts of the Moral Sense and really subversive of the very foundations of Moral Order. As Dr. Dale has said, "If we attempt to construct a theory of the Death of Christ on the hypothesis that it corresponds to what would occur in the administration of human justice if some illustrious man died as a substitute for a number of obscure persons who had been guilty of treason, we are confronted at once by an objection which admits of no reply. Such a substitute could not be admitted. It would be contrary to the principle of justice, and in the highest degree injurious to the state."

Under cover of the term "Propitiation," which has been very freely employed as descriptive of the Work of Christ, another strangely perverted and unworthy conception has been permitted to lay hold of the minds of many. It has been supposed that by the sacrificial Death of Christ, the wrath of God was appeased, and He was induced to extend to sinful men the grace and pity which, without that sacrifice, He would not, or could not have manifested towards them. And yet in one of the two passages in the 1st Epistle of John in which alone the word "propitiation" occurs in the New Testament, the apostle distinctly says, "Herein is love, not that we loved God, but that He loved us, and sent His Son to be the propitiation for our sins." As McLeod Campbell has said, "The Scriptures do not represent the love of God to man as the effect, and the Atonement as the cause, but just the contrary; the love of God as the cause, and the Atonement as the effect."

On the other hand, what is called the Moral Influence Theory of the Power and Work of Christ, whilst true as far as it goes, cannot be regarded as an adequate one. One great purpose and result of Christ's Mission undoubtedly was to reveal the forgiving and self-sacrificing love of God, to "declare the Father's name." Indeed, what sinners need, first of all, is to be assured that God really loves and pities them; that He is willing and waiting to forgive and forget the guilty past as soon as they turn to Him with contrite and obedient hearts; that He is "reconciling the world unto Himself, not imputing their trespasses unto them." And as Dr. Fairbairn has said, "The sufferings and death of Christ are the symbols and the seals of the invisible passion and sacrifice of the Godhead." They exhibit God "as a Being who does not need to be appeased or moved to mercy, but who suffers unto sacrifice that He may save us."

The particular form which the Divine Sacrifice of Love assumed was that of participation with us in the sorrows and pains which are our common inheritance as a sinful race. The various evils which we endure are regarded by us, in our consciousness of sin and guilt, as an experience that is deserved by us, and as the revelation and expression of the displeasure with which God regards our sin. But it is not possible to conceive that to Christ the sufferings which He bore could appear in the light of punishments deserved by Him. No doubt, the burden that He accepted would be recognized by Him as the symbol and demonstration of the wrath of the Holy Father against sin and unrighteousness; and in His human consciousness He keenly realized the terrible malignity of the sin from which He had come to rescue men.

It cannot, however, be supposed that the sacrifice was made, that the suffering and death were endured, simply for the purpose of demonstrating in a dramatic fashion the grief of God on account of sin and His loving pity for sinners. The Divine Love was manifested for a practical purpose,—in order, namely, to the supply of the Power and the Life whereby men may forsake sin and attain righteousness and goodness. The true explanation of the Life and Death of Christ must find in them, not merely a Revelation of the Truth concerning God,— of His forgiving love, but also a truly objective element which is spiritually *vital* and *dynamic*. In fact, whether appeal be made to the teaching of the Scriptures, or to the experience and testimony of those who have been helped, and saved, and blessed by Christ, we cannot avoid the conviction that Christ's work on our behalf, that His redemptive action within us, the help and life of which His Spirit is the source, go far beyond the instruction which His words, or the Revelation which His Life and Death afford, and beyond the moral effects which these may have upon our hearts and lives. "Christ liveth in me." "I can do all things through Christ who strengtheneth me."

Why, in order to the impartation of spiritual life and strength, such sacrificial suffering as that of our Saviour's should have been necessary, we may not be able clearly and accurately to comprehend. It is, in fact, involved, we may well believe, in the mystery in which the nature and the origin of all life are enshrouded. What Christ Himself said of the quickening of spiritual life in dead souls, applies, with at least equal force, to the Divine side of the redemptive, life-giving process. "The wind bloweth where it listeth, and thou hearest the voice thereof, but knowest not whence it cometh, nor whither it goeth; so is every one that is born of the Spirit." If the human and earthly side of the quickening of those who are "dead in trespasses and sins," be so difficult for us to understand or realize, how much more difficult must the Divine and heavenly side be to our comprehension. "If I told you earthly things, and ye believe not, how shall ye believe if I tell you heavenly things?"

We may say, in the words of Dr. Lyman Abbott, that "Self-sacrifice is the Divine method of life-giving;" and, perhaps, that is all, or nearly all, that we can ever hope to say in the direction of explaining why, in becoming "the author of eternal salvation," it behoved the Christ to suffer. "Except a grain of wheat fall into the ground and die, it abideth by itself alone, but if it die, it beareth much fruit." Life comes through death; spiritual life through the suffering and death of loving self-sacrifice. In the death of sorrow to which from love for us He submitted, "the Blood of Christ" was shed,— "the Spirit of Life in Christ Jesus" is now poured forth, in order that by the impartation of that spiritual life to the souls of men, and by its in-dwelling power they may be set free from the bondage of sin and be raised to a life of righteousness and blessedness.

The Atonement

The Atonement

BY

The Reverend HENRY W. PINKHAM

GOD must be at least as good as an average man. Jesus argued, not without humour: "If ye then, being evil, know how to give good gifts unto your children, how much more shall your Father which is in heaven give good things to them that ask him?" The best in human nature truly reveals the divine nature. God is the creator. His creature cannot surpass Him. The fountain must be at least as high as the stream that flows from it. Jesus' argument is conclusive.

But human nature improves from generation to generation. The race is in a process of spiritual evolution. The average Christian father to-day is kinder than was the average Jewish father in Jesus' time. The divine is imaged in the human more and more as the centuries pass. Accordingly, Jesus' theological method of reasoning from the human to the divine leads to ever nobler conceptions of God as the human race itself moves forward. The prevailing theology at any given time indicates a certain stage of moral progress and spiritual experience. A more advanced stage requires a new theology. As a species out of harmony with its environment perishes, so doctrines that have become repugnant to the general Christian consciousness are repudiated.

The moral improvement of man and the progressive enrichment of his spiritual experience evidence the presence of the Holy Spirit. The theological changes that result should not be deplored or resisted but welcomed. Theology must be in harmony with moral ideals, it must correspond with actual religious experience, if it would minister to the religious life; otherwise it is a hindrance and a stumbling-block. Many conservatives do not sufficiently recognize this fact. An undue reverence for the past, a mistaken use of the Bible, an illogical habit of mind, and a deficient sense of humour, combine to make it possible to hold and to advocate doctrines that imply dispositions in God which the average Christian would be ashamed to acknowledge in himself. Once admit that God is no worse than an ordinary human father and—in Jamie Soutar's words —" half o' the doctrines wud hae to be reformed."[1]

The history of the doctrine of the Atonement well illustrates how dogmas that have become repugnant to the moral sense are gradually abandoned for better ones. The ransom theory prevailed for about a thousand years. Jesus had spoken of giving his life a ransom for many; to whom did he give it? To Satan, answered early theologians: by the sin of Adam the human race had become the legal possession of Satan; Satan was willing to give up his claim to mankind if Jesus be surrendered to him as a ransom; the bargain was made; the race was set free; Satan, however, found that he could not keep Jesus; he could torture and kill his body, but, being divine, Jesus himself escaped and returned to heaven. The Atonement was thus a trade between God and Satan, in which Satan got cheated! Served him right, too, for had he not deceived Eve in the first place?

The ransom theory has entirely disappeared. It is a curiosity in the museum of Christian history. Anselm, in the eleventh century, related the work of Jesus with the righteousness of God: the Atonement was a transaction, not between God and Satan, but between the Father and the Son. Anselm's theory has prevailed to the present time. It is the popular view and long will be. Yet, in whatever form presented, —commercial, legal, governmental, or sacrificial,—it is unsatisfactory to many Christians.

It has been taught that the voluntary death of Jesus was a work of supererogation making a vast treasury of merit to be drawn upon by bankrupt sinners, enabling them to square their accounts with God; that God credits the surplus righteousness of his holy Son to the sinners that believe on Jesus. It has

---

[1] "The Days of Auld Lang Syne," by Ian Maclaren, p. 330.

been taught that Jesus bore the penalty of human sin; that God treated his perfect Son as if he were guilty of the world's transgressions and therefore, by way of compensation, will treat believing sinners as if they were as holy as his perfect Son. Such explanations of Christ's work are presented even to-day as the "simple Gospel." They are simple. They are immoral too, and their logical effect is evil. To be sure, the majority of men are not logical, and gratitude to their Saviour leads many to seek personal holiness who stoutly maintain that Christ's perfect righteousness is to be credited to them without regard to their actual merits; nevertheless, the teaching that Christ was the sinner's substitute on Calvary and will be his substitute at the judgment, is hurtful, lulling to sleep many a guilty conscience, and kindling a vain hope.

The truth needs emphasis that salvation is ethical; it is real, not make-believe; not a legal fiction to which God becomes a party. God does not call black white; and if he should, it would not make black white,—it would be simply telling a lie. Righteousness is not transferable like a commodity; it cannot be put on like a borrowed garment. The Bible nowhere says that Christ's righteousness is imputed to the believer. The believer's own faith is counted as righteousness, but that is because faith is potential righteousness. Faith is the constructive principle of character; he who has sincerely given himself to Christ has started on the way to that genuine personal holiness for which there can be no substitute. Nor is moral penalty transferable. Punishment conceived of as an external thing might be visited upon the innocent; it is possible for a man to go to prison, or to the gallows, in the place of a friend who is the real criminal. But the essence of moral penalty is the havoc which sin makes in the moral nature,—the animalism, the depraved tastes, the heartless selfishness, the devilish meanness in which a course of sin culminates, together with remorse and shame and the consciousness of alienation from God and all holy beings. That the sinless Jesus knew aught of such penalty is inconceivable. To punish such as he would be not only unjust but impossible.

Theories of the Atonement which make Christ's sufferings penal leave no place for genuine forgiveness; for how can there be pardon of that whose punishment has already been inflicted? To avoid this difficulty, Grotius, in the seventeenth century, suggested that the sufferings of Jesus were not strictly penal but served the purpose of penalty in expressing to the moral universe God's hatred of sin as well as it could be expressed by the full punishment of every sinner; save for some such expression the offer of forgiveness on the sole condition of repentance might lead men to regard sin as but a trifle, and thus the gracious purpose of God be defeated; for an ethical salvation—and there is no other—requires that the dreadfulness and hatefulness of sin be recognized. This view does not satisfy, for it makes Jesus an actor presenting an impressive object-lesson. Surely God's moral government stands in no need of a dramatic spectacle to keep it from contempt. God's direct dealing with sin, as that dealing appears in individual and social experience, shows clearly enough his estimate of it.

It is true, however, that the history of Jesus affords the most startling and awful revelation of the hideousness of sin. That the one faultless person who has appeared on this earth, that he whose life was an unbroken ministry of love, should be treated as Jesus was by his fellow-men, is an appalling commentary on human depravity. The evil that is in our hearts declares our spiritual kinship with the murderers of Jesus. Here is a man who discovers that he has a taint of leprosy. As yet he suffers not the slightest inconvenience. He would not know that he is diseased save for that faintly appearing spot on the skin. But bring him face to face with one in whom leprosy has run its course, leaving its victim disfigured by its ravages and loathsome with its foulness. He recoils in horror, and shudderingly exclaims, "Great God! Can it be that I have in me that disease? Shall I reach that horrible condition?" So when we think how Jesus was taken and by wicked hands was crucified and slain, we may well shudder; for in our own meanness, cruelty, bigotry,—which we have perhaps esteemed but trifling faults,—we may see the very same seed that bore its legitimate fruit in the murder of the Sinless One. When we are cruel, we join the company of those who pressed a crown of thorns on Jesus' brow, who buffeted him with their hands, and spat upon him. When we are narrow and bigoted, more eager to maintain our petty authority than to know and to obey the truth, we enrol ourselves among the Pharisees and chief priests who plotted to kill the Son of God. When we are false, rewarding trust with treachery and love with scorn, we are claiming as our master Judas Iscariot who betrayed his friend with a kiss.

Moreover, in the spiritual anguish of Jesus as he received the full shock of human iniquity; in his cry of wounded, rejected love—"O Jerusalem, Jerusalem!"—as he wept over the doomed city; in the agony of Gethsemane, we see what sin means to a pure soul, what torture the contact with it produces.

> "My sins, my sins, my Saviour!
> Their guilt I never knew
> Till, with thee, in the desert,
> I near thy passion drew;
> Till, with thee, in the garden,
> I heard thy pleading prayer,
> And saw the sweat-drops bloody,
> That told thy sorrow there."

The work of Christ is sometimes explained in terms derived from the sacrificial system of the Old Testament. Sacrifice is giving to God something precious. The ideas of expiation and propitiation are not necessarily connected with it; a sacrifice may be purely an expression of gratitude and love. But the universal sense of guilt, and the effort to propitiate a remorseful conscience, find expression in sacrifices whose purpose is to conciliate an offended God. If men who have been wronged can be appeased by seeing the wrong-doer give up something dear to him, or by seeing him endure pain,—why not God? An angry man may find relief in venting his wrath even on the innocent, in scolding his wife, kicking the dog, or slamming the door. But God should not be conceived of in forms evidently derived from the moral imperfection of men. In our minds there may sometimes seem to be a conflict between the claims of justice and of mercy, but we cannot think there is any such conflict in the divine mind. God's justice and his mercy have the same object in view, to bring man from sin to holiness. As we become better we find it easier to forgive, on the sole condition of repentance, those who have wronged us, and we scout the thought that we need any propitiation. Jesus bade his disciples forgive a brother till seventy times seven, if he repented. Did he expect them to be more forgiving than God himself. The doctrine that God cannot or will not forgive sinners save on account of a bloody offering is passing away. Taught by the spirit of Christ good men find that they are able to forgive those who have wronged them. They know that God must be at least as good as they are, and will not impute to him a relentlessness of which they themselves would be ashamed.

It should not be forgotten that the Mosaic legislation with reference to sacrifices is regulative rather than mandatory.[1] Time and again in Israel's history prophets' voices were raised in ridicule and scorn of the notion that God could be pleased by the slaughter of animals. The work of men like Isaiah, Micah, and Amos, was not quite completed by the Prophet of Nazareth. The actual offering of animals has ceased indeed, but the idea of a propitiatory sacrifice lingers, and what Bushnell called the "slaughter-house theory of the Atonement" is still preached.[2] Attention is directed to the physical blood of Jesus, as if it had a magical efficacy, until one feels like asking whether, if the Romans had inflicted capital punish-

---
[1] See Dr. Lyman Abbott's Commentary on Romans, p. 65.
[2] Dr. Trumbull's Reminiscences of Bushnell in *Sunday School Times*, Aug. 12, 1899.

ment by the gallows instead of the cross, and not a drop of Jesus' blood had been shed, there would then be no salvation for sinners.[1]

The essence of the Christian revelation is that God is a Christlike being. We should not think of Christ as a protection from God, but rather as the perfect expression of God's real self. Christ did not come to buy us off from divine wrath, but to show us divine love; not to appease God, but to assure us that God does not need to be appeased. It has been said, "God outside of Christ is a consuming fire;" but the Christian knows nothing about any "God outside of Christ;" to the Christian the God that is in Christ is the only God. No one reading for the first time the gospel history and seeing in Jesus a revelation of God, would think of saying, "God is justice;" or, as theologians have said, "God must be just, he may be merciful." One would say, as did St. John, "God is love." Christ's mission was not to change God's disposition and make him willing to forgive, but to demonstrate that he is eternally willing to forgive. The sufferings of Christ find their key not in the justice of God which demands some victim for his wrath, but in the love of God which at any cost seeks to win men to holiness.

Strictly speaking, the death of Christ was not necessary to human salvation. He voluntarily laid down his life, and in so doing obeyed the divine will. But he was not a suicide; he was murdered. To say that his death was an indispensable condition of human salvation is to say that God's grace had to call in the aid of murderers in order that it might find a way to human hearts. I am not willing to acknowledge any indebtedness to Judas Iscariot for the forgiveness of my sins. Whatever necessity there was for the death of Jesus lay not in the justice of God, nor in God's regard for law, but in human sinfulness. The world being what it was when the Son of God was here, the human heart being what it was, it was indeed inevitable that, he whose perfect purity was so terrible a

---

[1] See Abbott's Commentary on Romans, p. 70.

rebuke to all evil should receive the full shock of human wickedness. It was indeed true, in the circumstances, that divine love could find its supreme utterance only through the suffering of God's Son at the hands of sinful men. But we must not charge to the justice of God or the supposed necessities of his moral government that which really belongs at the door of human sin.[1]

That the death of Christ should receive the prominence the New Testament gives it is most natural. The supreme self-sacrifice for which his cross stands, revealed the real spirit of Jesus even more impressively than did his gracious words and kindly deeds. His death in the most painful manner was the lowest depth to which his sacrificing love could take him. Accordingly, the cross has become the symbol of his entire mission, and attention has been fixed upon his death rather than upon the ministry that preceded. His death provided the mightiest of appeals to our sinful hearts. He foresaw that, lifted up, he would draw all men unto him. It is fitting, therefore, to say, in scriptural language, that we are cleansed by his blood, or that he died for us. Yet Jesus freely offered forgiveness to penitent sinners who had no thought of his death. His death may be said to save in the sense that it leads to repentance when perhaps nothing else would. It may be regarded as indispensable in the sense that only by it could God make his mightiest appeal to sinful men. But Jesus clearly made repentance the sole condition of divine forgiveness, and to main-

---

[1] A theological absurdity extreme enough to be worth remembering is the reply a brother minister once made to my contention that unqualified insistence on the necessity of Jesus' death makes murder an essential part of the plan of salvation. "Suppose," said I, "that the Jews had accepted their Messiah, that Pharisees and chief priests had repented and become his disciples as they ought to have,—then there would have been none to murder him. In that case would the divine forgiveness of sins be impossible?" "In that case," was the reply, "it would have been the duty of the high priest, as an official obeying the divine law, without any malice in his heart, solemnly to slay Jesus as the Lamb of God appointed to suffer."

tain that God's grace was blocked until a foul murder had removed an obstruction is utterly foreign to his thought.

"God was in Christ,"—being reconciled to the world? no,—"reconciling the world to himself." Why are we so unwilling to accept frankly Jesus' declaration, "He that hath seen me hath seen the Father?" Do our guilty consciences make us feel it too good to be true? Should we be afraid to trust ourselves directly to the mercy of Jesus, as did the sinful woman in Simon's house? Why need we frame an elaborate "plan of salvation?" Is it not enough to say that God is love, and to see in Jesus an interpretation and a proof of that glorious fact? If "God was in Christ," then Christ's spirit is the Eternal Spirit. Atonement is eternal, the Lamb of God is slain from the foundation of the world. Our sins hurt our heavenly Father. It is he who sacrifices himself for our salvation, because he loves us. It is he who says in his Son:

"I died for you, my children,
And will ye treat me so?"

Christ's passion lifts the veil and shows us the divine heart pierced and wounded by our transgressions. We answer:

"O Lord, with shame and sorrow
We open now the door:
Dear Saviour, enter, enter,
And leave us nevermore."

Why must divine love for sinful man be expressed through suffering? Perhaps no answer can be given, save to say that it is inherent in the essential relationship of moral beings that love in a good person for a bad one involves pain. The fact, at any rate, is unquestionable. The good always suffer for the bad, and in proportion to their goodness is the intensity of their pain. It is the purest souls that feel most keenly the shame of the world's sin. It was inevitable that Jesus, the Sinless One, being in this sinful world, should be preëminently the Man of Sorrows. The ingratitude of man never pierced another's heart as it did his, for none other ever loved like him. The wickedness of man never burdened another's soul as it did his, for none other has had such clear eyes to perceive it in all its hideousness. None other ever felt so keenly the infinite pity of it that man, made in the image of God and capable of high fellowship with God, should choose a brute's life rather than a divine life, for none other has known as he did the full possibilities of human nature. The sinless loved the sinful,—that always means suffering. We may not explain why, but we shall appreciate the fact in the measure that we ourselves suffer as Christ did, bearing in our hearts the burden of others' sins and gladly sacrificing ourselves that we may bring our fellowmen to God.

Not in vain is it that the good suffer vicariously. The cross of Christ became his throne. The blood of the martyrs is ever the seed of the church. Through the sacrifice of the noblest men, the moral progress of the race is achieved. "Vicarious suffering," says President Hyde, "is the price some one must pay for every step of progress and every conquest over evil the world shall ever gain."[1] The cross of Christ is the symbol of a universal law of the moral order. Christ is the Saviour *par excellence*, but every man of Christlike spirit is to a degree a saviour.[2] He makes the world better for his presence, but at cost to himself. He drinks Christ's cup and is baptized with Christ's baptism. He knows the fellowship of Christ's sufferings and fills up that which is lacking of his afflictions. He is made sin on behalf of his fellow-men that they may become the righteousness of God in him.

> "Count me o'er earth's chosen heroes,
> They were souls that stood alone,
> While the men they agonized for
> Hurled the contumelious stone."

The suffering of Jesus is thus not without analogy in human experience. The pious mother who agonizes over her way-

---

[1] "Outlines of Social Theology," p. 228.
[2] The late Prof. Bruce has made what he calls a modest contribution to a scientific theory of progress through sacrifice in "The Providential Order," p. 327.

ward boy, who went down to death's door to bring her child into the world, and who would now gladly have that door swing wide open for her if only she could see her son forsake his sins and become a noble man,—knows the meaning of Christ's passion through her own anguish better than she could learn it from any theological treatise. It is that suffering love that avails to bring back the prodigal sons, and only as parents have it for their children, pastors for their people, friends for their friends, can they be real soul-winners.

The word Atonement might well be abandoned. It is not in the New Testament and the ideas which it suggests to most minds are unchristian.[1] Reconciliation is better. It is more accurate to say that Christ reconciles than to say that his death reconciles. He reconciles because of his divine-human nature. To that statement all true explanations may be reduced. What Jesus did was natural to such a being as he. He has the religious value of God to us, and in him God makes the incomparable appeal of sacrificing love. He is the perfect man; his purity thoroughly exposes and condemns our sinfulness; his nobility speaks to our nobler selves. To love him and to follow his example is to love God and to adopt as one's own God's ideal for man. In moral union with him and spiritual companionship there is that transformation of character from sin to holiness which alone is true salvation. He is the meeting-place of God and man. Not because of some transaction in which he had a part about nineteen centuries ago is Christ our Saviour, but because in him God comes to us, in him we have our access to the Father.

---

[1] "Atonement" occurs in Rom. 5:3 in the Authorized Version. In the Revised Version of 1881, "reconciliation" is properly substituted.

The Lord's Supper: Is It a Church or a Christian Ordinance and Who Should Partake of It?

The Lord's Supper: Is It a Church or a Christian Ordinance and Who Should Partake of It?

BY

The Reverend W. T, JORDAN

THE Church has two ordinances, baptism and communion. Because inseparably related it is not possible to consider them separately. They are of the same authority, dignity and value. One cannot take the place of the other. Each receives its authority and value from the express command of Christ, " Go ye, therefore, and teach all nations, baptizing them." " This do in remembrance of me." Clothed with equal importance each is to continue perpetually. Coupled with the command to preach and baptize is the promise, " Lo, I am with you alway." " As often as ye eat this bread, and drink this cup, ye do show the Lord's death till He come." Looked at from every standpoint, whether in relation to Christ, the believer, the church or the world they are of equal authority and stand or fall together. The same reasons must be given for maintaining one as the other. They can never be changed either in their nature, relationship or design without doing violence to the scriptures, and disregarding the authority of Christ.

What is baptism? What is communion? These questions must be answered together. Baptism is putting on Christ sacramentally.

This is done spiritually in accepting Christ by faith, orally by confessing Him in word (Rom. 10: 10) and sacramentally in baptism, and in baptism only. (Gal. 3: 27). Communion is the continuous confession that the new life in Christ, received by faith and confessed in baptism, is being continued by fellowship with Him. Baptism declares that we have come to Him; communion says we are continuing with Him. Baptism is a confession that we have renounced sin and become separated from the world; communion is the act of one thus separated. Baptism speaks of life accepted in Christ; communion of life lived with Christ. The two ordinances stand as antecedent and consequent, birth and growth.

Each ordinance recalls an historical fact, and each points to blessings yet to be enjoyed. Baptism points back to the death, burial and resurrection of Christ, and forward to the blessings of the resurrection life of the believer (Rom. 6: 4-6). Communion points back to the death of Christ and forward to His coming again and to perfect fellowship with Him in His Kingdom (1 Cor. 11: 26; Luke 22: 16).

If all the scriptures were lost except those which refer to baptism and communion we would still have left a clear teaching upon the fundamental doctrines of Christianity—the death, burial and resurrection of Christ. As the believer is buried with Christ by baptism he is voluntarily placed in the same position in which he will be placed when buried beneath the sod. The hands are folded reverently upon the breast and he is buried under the water in a horizontal position. By this act he says to the world, " I believe that Christ died and was buried." As he is raised up out of the water by the hands of the administrator, he says by the very act, " I believe that Christ was raised *from* the grave by the operation of the Holy Spirit (Col. 2: 12); and since He died for me, was buried, and rose again, I hereby, in my baptism, confess that I have died to sin through faith in His death for me, and by my resurrection from the water I also confess that it is my purpose to live the new, or resurrection, life in Christ (Rom. 6: 4-6). It would be a crime to bury a man who is not dead, and a shame not to bury him when he is dead. Hence a man is baptized, buried, because he has died to sin. In other words he is baptized not to save him, but because he is already saved. As in baptism he confesses his death to sin, in communion he confesses his new life in Christ, and that that life is being sustained by fellowship with Him.

The Lord's Supper

The organization of the church is based upon the ordinances. An organization without them has no more right to the claim of being a church than has a debating society or a literary club. They set forth the very life of the church. They symbolize the very essence of the gospel. They can never be altered or set aside because of the symbols in which they are clothed. The symbols fix their meaning.

But they are more than acts of symbolic meaning. Baptism is the act of initiation into the church. "For in one spirit we all were baptized into one body" (1 Cor. 12:13). To what body does this refer? To the spiritual and invisible body or to the visible body, the church? Certainly to the visible body, the church. It is visible baptism into a visible body. It cannot mean a spiritual baptism into an invisible body. "The New Testament recognizes no visible church outside of visible churches." The Bible teaching is plain that no one is a member of the church until he is baptized. It is baptism that constitutes membership. The New Testament recognizes no baptism except that of believers, and no authority to administer the ordinances except that of a church.

All orthodox churches, or denominations, agree in the practice of admitting none to the Lord's Table until they become members of a Christian Church, and none are considered members of a Christian Church until they have been baptized. This practice agrees with the New Testament teaching. Baptism was instituted before the Lord's Supper, and it was the invariable practice of the apostles to baptize all believers before they admitted them to the Lord's Table. To this practice there is not a single exception. See the account of Pentecost in Acts 2; the eunuch, Acts 8; Lydia and the jailor with their households, Acts 16; Cornelius and his friends, Acts 10; Saul, Acts 9. These were all baptized as soon as they believed, and not one of them enjoyed the communion of the Lord's Supper until after they had been baptized. This practice was strictly adhered to because it was required by the great commission. The order of the commission is, 1. Teach all men to repent and believe on Jesus Christ for salvation. 2. Baptize all who believe. 3. Teach them to observe all things whatsoever I have commanded you.

Among the commands to be observed after baptism is, "This do in remembrance of me." The apostles understood the commission and strictly adhered to it, and the same order has been observed by all orthodox denominations since the days of Christ. To this all the authorities agree from Justin Martyr in A. D. 150 to the present time.

Communion is a privilege of the church. One must be initiated into a society before he can enjoy its privileges; and baptism being the initatory act, therefore it necessarily precedes communion. Thus the position of communion has already been determined by the position of baptism.

It follows necessarily that communion is a church ordinance. Believers are commanded to be baptized; these believers being baptized constitute the Church, and as a Church they partake of the one loaf in compliance with the dying request of Him into whom they have been baptized, and by whom they are now being sustained. The ordinances then set forth the life of the believer and constitute the basis of church organization. Left just where Christ placed them, in the Church, and properly observed, they body forth the very gospel of God's salvation. Taken out of their place, they are stripped of all meaning, and become mere forms without any significance whatever. The harmony of Christian order is broken and only confusion follows. Communion is a Church ordinance because no organization can preserve it in its ordained order except the Church. The ordinances cannot maintain themselves. They were committed to the Churches, and if the Churches do not preserve them who will?

It is clear from the scriptures that the Supper is not an individual or social or family ordinance. For regarding it as a social ordinance the Apostle Paul severely rebuked the Church at Corinth and commanded the members to wait one for another, and, with the whole Church partake of the Supper.

"For we being many, are one bread and one body; for we are all partakers of that one bread" (Cor. 10:17). It is said of the disciples immediately after Pentecost, "And all that believed were together, and they continuing daily with one accord in the temple, and in breaking bread from house to house" etc. (Acts 2:44-46). "They worshipped daily in the temple; they broke bread at home".

Paul says to the Corinthians that he received the information which he gave them concerning the Supper from the Lord Jesus (1 Cor. 11:23). He is writing to the Church as a body and not to individuals. Individuals were exhorted to examine themselves before partaking of the Supper in order to be sure that they were observing it from proper motives, not as a feast but simply in memory of Jesus. Heavy responsibility is placed upon the individual, it is true, but the burden of responsibility is placed upon the Church. If there should be a conflict between the judgment of the individual and his Church as to his fitness, the individual should yield. A Church cannot escape responsibility on the plea that each one must judge for himself. The laws concerning the ordinance have been given to the Church, and it is her duty to enforce them. Paul told the Corinthians not to keep company, not to eat with any brother reputed to be a fornicator, or covetous, or an idolater, or a drunkard, or an extortioner (1 Cor. 5:11). According to the best authorities this means, not to eat at the same table with such: whether the love feast, or in private intercourse, *much more at the Lord's Table.*

"That the man should be a converted man, a baptized man, a Church member, is as plainly declared in the scriptures as that he should be a moral man and just in his deportment. If it is the province and duty of the Church to judge the communicant as to his possession of a part of these scriptural qualifications, and the apostle distinctly asserts that it is, no less can it be the province and duty of the Church to judge the communicant as to his possession of all the scriptural qualifications. And if the Church has not this right, aye, if this duty does not solemnly rest upon her, then the Lord's Table is a prey to designing men, and the Church herself is impotent to determine or preserve her own character." Corrective discipline becomes an impossibility. Many unkind and harsh things are said of those who practice restricted communion on the ground that Christians should not be separated at the Lord's Table. We should remember that the separation does not take place at the table. It takes place at the water. In the beginning it was not so, and for nearly three hundred years all Christians sat down together at the Lord's Table. The division took place over baptism. The Catholic Church arrogated to itself the right to change the ordinance from immersion to sprinkling, and did so. When the ordinances were given to the Church denominations were unknown, and so long as baptism was retained in its primitive purity as a public profession of belief in the burial and resurrection of Christ, no separation at the Table was thought of. But since the change from immersion to sprinkling, Christians have become separated into all sorts of sects and by all sorts of beliefs. So long as these differing sects and opposing beliefs are justified there can be no consistency in objecting to separation at the Lord's Table. If all Christians of all denominations can consistently come together at the Lord's Table, what justification is there for maintaining separate denominations? There can be no real fellowship at the Table unless all who sit down together have the same views of scriptural truth. " How can two walk together except they be agreed?" Oneness of belief is the basis of fellowship. How can there be any real communion when the basis of it is lacking?

When Christians of every denomination shall come to admit what the scriptures clearly teach, and what the scholarship of the world is agreed upon, that the original mode of baptism was the immersion of a believer in water and that baptism is prerequisite to communion, the question "is communion a Church ordinance?" will be no longer asked.

The Lord's Supper: Is It a Church or a Christian Ordinance and Who Should Partake of It?

The Lord's Supper: Is It a Church or a Christian Ordinance and Who Should Partake of It?

BY

The Reverend GEORGE HENRY HUBBARD, D.D.

CHRISTIANITY, as represented by Jesus Christ, was a thing of life. Forces, principles, ideas, were its constituent elements. It was essentially the manifestation of the Christly spirit in all the manifold relations of human society, in all the most commonplace directions of human activity. And it contained within itself the vital power which makes for continuous growth. Spontaneity, elasticity, adaptability, these were the characteristics which revealed themselves in the new religion as it came to men fresh from the hands of the Master, —these, wedded with a divine and transforming power.

The Christianity of the Church, on the other hand, has ever tended towards forms and institutions, *i. e.* towards the mechanical and the lifeless. Indeed, something of this tendency is inherent in the very nature of the Church, which, in its organized form, is itself the first manifestation of the principle of crystallization in religion. There have been periods in Christian history when the Churchly ideal of religion has stood in marked contrast and even antagonism to the Christly ideal, when the disciples of Jesus have striven for the rigid perfection of the crystal instead of the growing perfection of the tree.

We frequently speak of the Church as having been established by our Lord; whereas, in point of fact, the Lord did not establish an organized Church at all. Doubtless an organized Church is the natural, perhaps the inevitable outcome of His work and teaching. But we do well to remember that Jesus Himself only gathered a band of disciples and chose twelve apostles in the most informal fashion, without any definiteness of organization or corporate relation to one another. The only bonds by which He united them were the spiritual and living bonds of brotherly love. The only constitution He gave was the Gospel of human salvation. The only authority with which He invested them was the inherent authority of truth and righteousness.

To these disciples, not as a body of men and women, but as individual followers of the Christ, drawn together by a common interest and held together by a common purpose and loyalty, He suggested certain simple rites as helps in the maintenance and upbuilding of spiritual life in themselves and in the world. The rites themselves were not prescribed in an exact and positive manner. They were not like the metal casting that must conform precisely at every point to the mould in which it is run. Rather were they given and accepted in a very free and natural fashion. And their purpose seems to have been individual, inspirational, educational; not as a badge of separation from the world or of union with each other.

For example, In calling His disciples, Jesus simply uttered the invitation, "Follow Me," and, asking no questions regarding personal character, experience, or belief, imposing no conditions of special or corporate responsibility, He welcomed all who came to the fullest privileges and opportunities of discipleship. Then He held them to Himself and brought them into a growing relation of fellowship with one another solely by the power of personal loyalty. In Himself as the Son of God was the magnetic force which rendered all external bonds superfluous. In all things He was the Leader; and to whatsoever duty or danger or sacrifice or effort He called others, He led the way.

The same elasticity characterizes all His relations with His followers. Take the matter of baptism. Notwithstanding the strenuous assertions of certain theologians and lexicographers, the rite of baptism was apparently administered at the first with great freedom. Its precise form is nowhere clearly defined; and the only absolute prerequisite would seem to be the expressed desire of the candidate. And even this desire was sometimes representative rather than individual; for, while it is not recorded that the disciples under the immediate direction of the Master ever baptized entire households, it is certain that the apostles did so at a later period believing that in so doing they were fulfilling the purpose and command of their Lord.

Again, when His disciples came to Him asking for a form of prayer, the spirit of what He said made so deep an impression upon their minds that the form of words was forgotten, and to-day we do not know what were the words that He taught them. To be sure, the Church has given us a form of words which we repeat on suitable occasions under the title of "The Lord's Prayer"; but the only thing we certainly know about it is that *it is not* the form which Jesus gave at the request of His followers. It is a part of the Churchly crystallization, not the living utterance of the Christ.

The institution of the Lord's Supper follows the same analogy. How utterly informal was that little gathering of Jesus and the apostles the evening before the crucifixion. In preparation for it the householder had made ready the room and the Passover feast, and the company came as his guests. And when they were assembled, Jesus rebukes the spirit of ceremonialism and the strife about positions of honour by taking upon Himself the duty of a servant. And as we read the conversation that took place there, we realize that it was a time of deep feeling not of formality. The Passover feast of the Jews, while it was in a sense a Churchly ordinance, was also a peculiarly family service. It was eaten *in the home,* the members of the family being together, and the father sitting at the head of the table as director of the feast. So this gathering of disciples with Jesus is a sort of *family gathering,* the Master and those dearest to Him and most closely identified with His mission. In view of the fact that Jesus had no home of His own, the occasion and service seem to approach as near to the home conditions as possible.

The natural interpretation of the symbols of the feast is in perfect harmony with the simplicity of its circumstances. The little Christian family is seated about the Passover table. Without introducing any new elements, our Lord makes use of the materials immediately before Him, the simple appointments of the supper, as emblems of His sufferings and death, saying, "As often as ye eat this bread and drink the cup, ye proclaim the Lord's death till He come." He thus turns to spiritual use a *family supper,* to keep His disciples in remembrance of His death. There is no significance in the particular materials, and no emphasis is laid upon them. It was *the consecration of the ordinary articles of daily food* as symbols of the spiritual food of the soul. Christ Himself thus interprets the symbolism, "My flesh is meat indeed, and my blood is drink indeed." The two general classes of *food* and *drink* comprise all that is necessary for the sustenance and growth of the physical system; so the Christ in His fulness furnishes all that is necessary for the sustenance of the spiritual life. This, then is the meaning of the symbols of the Lord's Supper. They are only *representative articles of food and drink;* nothing more.

In this very simple and informal sense of sanctifying the family meal to spiritual uses the apostles clearly received the suggestion of their Lord; for we have no hint of a Churchly interpretation of the ordinance till some years had passed. But immediately after the ascension we find the disciples meeting together in their homes and breaking bread from house to house. As the writer of the book of Acts tells us, "All that believed were together,—continuing steadfastly with one accord in the temple, and *breaking bread at home,* they did take their food with gladness and singleness of heart, etc." In other words, at the common daily meals, and at their frequent gatherings of a semi-social nature, the food became to them a memorial of the Lord's death, and so every such meal or feast was to the spiritually minded a true Lord's Supper.

Soon, however, the Church began to assume a more definitely organized form. This was the almost inevitable result of increasing numbers and geographical extension. But in some respects it was an unfortunate result; since the organization from a very early period manifested a tendency to exalt itself above vital truth, and the means often overshadowed the end. The lines of discipleship were drawn more sharply than Jesus had drawn them. The brotherhood included, not all who wished to follow Jesus, but all who fulfilled certain prescribed conditions of membership, which conditions became increasingly strict and arbitrary with passing years. With the crystallization of the Church came a corresponding change in the rites, which were more and more looked upon as formal sacraments connected strictly with the Church and her services. Exclusion from the Church involved exclusion from the sacraments, until at length these became the exclusive privileges and prerogatives of those who were in full and unquestioned Church membership.

Dr. A. C. McGiffert, in his well known work " A history of Christianity in the Apostolic Age," attributes the consummation of this change directly to the apostle Paul, whom he regards as the originator of the Lord's Supper in its present ceremonial form. He says, " Though the Lord's Supper was everywhere eaten by Christian disciples before Paul, it may be said in a certain sense that it was established by him; for it was he, so far as our sources enable us to judge, who first made it a special meal, and separated it from all others." This view of the matter is deduced from the fact that in his epistle to the Corinthians Paul enjoins upon the Christians to whom he writes the wisdom of eating their regular meal at home before coming together to eat the Lord's Supper, in order that no stress of appetite or undue indulgence in food and drink should lead to excess in the sacred service.

Now, while we may not all agree with Dr. McGiffert in thus definitely fixing the responsibility for the change, the *fact* of the change is self evident. None can read intelligently the story of the formation of the Church as given us in the

New Testament without discovering that this which was given and received at the first as a simple family service observed as often as disciples partook of their food, was gradually transformed into a purely formal and Churchly ceremony.

With the transfer of the ordinance to the Church it lost much of its original significance and freedom, and certain ideas were foisted upon it which probably had no existence in the mind of the Master when He partook of it with the disciples in the upper chamber. The essential thought of a common meal, the partaking of food and drink as necessary to bodily strength and nourishment, was overshadowed by numberless theological fictions such as that of transubstantiation, consubstantiation, and others. The freedom of the family meal has given place to the stiffness of a public ceremonial, and the simple emblems of a supper are transformed into a sort of spiritual charm. In one branch of the Church the bread is displaced by a consecrated wafer which would never suggest the notion of food; and in many others the liquor which fills the "cup" is that which is banished from the home table of most Christians as unfit for common use, hence it cannot stand as a typical article of drink.

The liberalizing and intelligent spirit of the present age has relaxed somewhat of the exceeding strictness which for centuries held the sacraments with iron bands. A Church which insists upon one particular form of baptism no longer refuses to fellowship Churches that adopt other forms, nor denies to the members of other communions the privilege of partaking of the Lord's supper in its circle. The reasonable demands of enlightened common sense coöperating with the spirit of true Christian charity have secured the general introduction of non-intoxicating wine at the Lord's Table in the place of the fermented wine which was so long required, to the unspeakable injury of many a weak disciple. And the common formula used in many of our Churches to-day invites to the Supper "All those who love the Lord Jesus Christ," making no distinctions of Church membership nor even specifying membership as a qualification.

Thus far the advance guards of toleration and Christian charity have come, and the other battalions of the host are following. Still we have no reason to flatter ourselves that the original ideal of simplicity and freedom is restored. We are yet very far from that. True, many clergymen give an unqualified invitation to the sacrament; but they and their people look upon it as a Churchly sacrament none the less, and they do not expect their invitation to be accepted in the same broad and unhesitating manner in which it is given. The invitation says nothing about Church-membership; but if one who is not a Church member ventures to participate in the service there are many expressions of wonder both by look and word; and some may be heard seriously questioning the propriety of the act. Church members generally do not encourage or even permit the children and other members of their families not in the membership of the Church to participate in the Supper. And the modern introduction of individual communion cups is a distinct step away from the spirit of fellowship towards greater formality.

Now the spirit of the broadest modern invitation to the Lord's Supper is undoubtedly the nearest approach to the spirit of the original institution, and ought to become the sincere expression of the Church's desire and expectation. Not one of those who partook of that first Lord's Supper was a Church member in the modern acceptation of that phrase; for as yet there was no church. Furthermore, the Supper as observed in the days immediately following was wholly informal, and there was no " fencing the table." Families gathered together, men, women, and children, so far as the " sources " indicate, and the meal was accompanied with the usual conversation, naturally upon themes connected with the growing kingdom of God.

What should we think of gathering all the families of a Church together at a social feast for pure spiritual and neighborly fellowship and talking over the work and interests of the kingdom of God in the community, and calling that the Lord's Supper? Would it not shock many a conservative disciple? Should we not tremble for the sacredness of the institution? Yet that would truly fulfil the original idea of the Lord's Supper as manifested in the "Upper Chamber" and in the first gatherings of the disciples.

Even the most liberal of modern Christians fears a loss of reverence for the sacrament if it be made too common. But who can ever estimate the loss of spiritual power that has been suffered by taking the rite from the Christian home and limiting it to the Church, thus secularizing the ordinary meal of the disciple? Can anyone doubt that the recognition of every meal in a Christian home as a true sacrament would exert a strong influence upon all who sat at the table? To remind each household thrice daily of the Lord's death could not fail to make a salutary impression upon every child.

Or if the Church made the Supper a real meal, all the members gathering about the tables with their children and guests, not sitting in cold and formal silence, but engaging in earnest and friendly intercourse, drawing together those of different classes as could not be done in any other way, would it be other than a strong force for cementing in the Church the bonds of brotherly love, and attracting the unconverted into its fellowship?

Such a restoration of the original freedom of the Sacrament would relieve our Churches of at least one serious hindrance to their work and progress. So long as the Lord's Supper is held to be a strictly Churchly ordinance, and at the same time a badge or test of discipleship it necessarily follows that every disciple should be admitted to the Church with all possible promptness. Hence it has come to pass that many persons of immature mind and tender years are received into the membership of the Church to their own injury and the retarding of the proper work of the Church. For, whatever may have been its original design, the Christian Church as now existing is an organization charged with the most stupendous duty and the gravest responsibility that ever rested upon any body of men and women. In the matter of responsibility and service no corporation in the world can for a moment be compared with it. Yet we receive into active participation in these duties and responsibilities persons who would not be permitted to share for a day the responsibilities of a banking or railroad corporation. Why is this? Because we have come to believe that to shut them out of the Church is to deprive them of the sacraments and other means of grace which the Church has gradually reserved to herself. When shall we learn that the organized Church is simply a human instrumentality for the accomplishment of a definite work and that we may restrict and limit its membership as the exigencies of that work may demand; but that the real Church of Christ is not organized but organic, living, free, and offers its sacraments and all other privileges and benefits without limit to all who wish to share them?

In some respects we are certainly making progress towards the restoration of the original ideal; but in others we are moving away from it. We shall not stand upon the right ground till we realize fully that the Lord's Supper was given not as a badge of membership in the Church of Christ, not as a medium for the dispensation of a Churchly grace, not as a precise and formal service; but as the consecration of a daily act to a sacred purpose, so linking the most profoundly spiritual element of religion with the most common and vital act of our every day life.

The Sacrament

The Sacrament

BY

The Reverend ROBERT COLLYER, D.D.

I LOVE to muse over those words of Saint Paul touching our Christian Faith and Fellowship, "By one spirit we are all baptized into one body, whether we be Jews or Gentile, whether we be bond or free," and, when I note how we differ in so many ways, to stand free from the letter, so far as I am able to do so, and cleave to the spirit because the letter is so often the line of division we all draw, while the spirit of truth and love is the Divine reality.

For we read the same Bible, turn our faces to the same blessed heavens when we pray, and hold in our hearts the one essential faith that God is our Father, and that Jesus the Christ, the anointed, came to reveal the Father to our human family. While the line of division may mean sprinkling or immersion, prayer from a printed book or directly from the heart, predestination or free grace, the essential or verbal inspiration of the scriptures, trinity or unity, with many things beside on which as my own faith stands no man's eternal welfare ever did depend or ever will. Because the essence of prayer is to pray in the spirit and in truth, with printed words or without them, or with no words at all. And baptism is merely the symbol; so far as the water is concerned, we can use it if we will, or let it alone as the " Friends " do. And the divine inspiration is the holy spirit of truth—of God—in the soul, in the Bible and in all noble and true books; while the Bible is to me the noblest and the best, and predestination or freewill are the centripetal and centrifugal forces in the soul of man as they are in the planets. So turn where we will we find the spirit which giveth life, and turn where we will we can find the letter which killeth; while just as we come into bondage to the letter in doctrine, dogma or usage, and disdain to have fellowship with those who differ from us we make naught of the love of God in its uttermost sanctuary, the heart of His Christ, and are not Christians then but sectarians. Also there is always this deep distinction to be drawn between faith and doctrine no matter where we may stand, that the one is the body at best, while the other is the spirit, the one is the fountain and the other the cistern, the one the garden in which is gathered all I love best, while the other is the great garden of God which belts the world; and doctrines, dogmas and usages are of the seen and temporal, but a living faith is of the unseen and eternal.

I note again when this truth of the spirit touches me to the finer purpose that there is no way open to me if I would be a proper man, let alone a Christian, but this, that I must admit the good, the sincere and the true in all the Churches into my fellowship no matter whether they will take me into theirs or freeze me out. Because I have to remember my dear mother was a Baptist, so that Church is dear to me for her sake and was not a prison but a home to her fine sunny heart in which she found all grace and blessing in her sweet old age. I was also baptized into the Episcopal Church, and so she has a lien on me I cannot and will not deny, while it was very sweet and good for me a year ago to stand close to the old Church far away in England and see them bear me to the Font through the mists of seventy-four years. I was a scholar also for about nine years in a good old-fashioned orthodox Sunday School, the only Divinity school that was ever open to me, and I confess myself a lifelong debtor to that school. In my early manhood I became a Methodist, and for ten years was a local preacher within that pale. She was also my nursing mother; I have still a tender regard for her. She nursed me forth for my ministry of fifty years all told and nursed me well; while my love still takes me back to visit the old home now and then as Mahomet in his last years visited the garden of his youth and said to his attendant, "Pluck me some fruit from that tree; I know it is very sweet and good."

So in all the Churches I have kinsfolk now and friends

whose hands clasp mine in the fellowship of the spirit, while still we differ in dogma, in doctrine, in usage and ordinance, and I can say in all sincerity, men and women good and generous of heart as you are belong to the Church of the Living God, no matter about the name or denomination. You believe in a sight of truth you do not understand as yet, and so do we. We give a greater place no doubt than you do, to what we call reason and perhaps underscore reason now and then with too heavy a line, while we think you underscore faith with too heavy a line in some directions. We think our faith is the best, while you think yours is the best, but I think we should all be of the mind of the old Divine who when a youth that had just chipped the shell said to him, "Sir, I will believe nothing I do not understand," answered, "Then, sir, your creed will be the briefest I ever heard of in my life."

As I said, I was for ten years a Methodist. I have been for more than forty years now a member and minister of the Unitarian denomination. Then I believed and tried to teach the truth held in that church, now I believe and try to teach the truth in the Church of my love and fellowship which still bears the brand of heresy. I did not try to believe in this heresy—so called—any more than I tried to grow to my stature as a man. The striving was indeed the other way. I would fain have stayed in the old warm nest and could not imagine what would become of me if I should push out and try to do for myself. But it was all of no use; the truths I have accepted would haunt me and master me, and so I found I must accept them or I could have no peace, and being in some sort a preacher I must preach what I most surely believed or I could have no honour; so we parted company, the mother and her son, with a tender regret, and I went forth not knowing whither I went to find this home and ministry among the Unitarians.

It was fifteen years after I left England and six years after entering this ministry that I returned to visit my dear old mother and the household. We have a very noble Church in the city of Leeds where her home was then, and they invited me to preach there. My mother went with me to the Church. I was glad and proud to have her go and hear me. We went home arm in arm after the service. She was silent for a while as we walked along and then she said, " My lad, I am not sure that I understood thy sermon or that I could believe as thou does now;" but then she clasped my arm with a loving pressure and said, " thou must be sure that I believe in thee." And I answered, " Mother, that is all I care for, that you shall believe in me."

And now I wonder whether this is not still the best of all both for faith and fellowship among those who differ, that we shall believe each in the other, and that our beliefs this way or that, are far less a matter of our free will than we usually imagine; while if we are true to our own souls and therefore to God, we must believe about as we do.

We cannot always think alike or believe alike in the most sacred relation we can hold toward each other in our homes; how then shall we do this in the great Church of the Living God to which we all belong who are worthy the Christian name?

The oaks grow best alone but the vines need a standard, and as some flowers love a day which is three-quarters shadow and some love all the sunshine the heavens can pour upon them, and as all the herbs and the fruits in a garden are better than any one, sweet and bitter, sharp or mellow. As some love Rembrandt's pictures best with their strong lights and shadows and some Raphael's with their floods of glory and hosts of angels, while no great gallery can be perfected with either school left out, so I think we should make up our minds that any Church which can include these diversities of thinking and believing in a common fellowship must be more Godlike and Christlike than those that insist on the law of uniformity and exclusion and breed in and in, like the fowls in Hawthorne's story, so careful in their breed that in the end there was only one chick to their name and he could not crow, he could only croak.

Does my brother believe then that only the elect shall be saved and like Davie Deans in "The Heart of Mid-Lothian" say, "he only kens of two who hold to the pure doctrine, Davie Dods and ane ither he will not name." And does he want me to fellowship with him on these terms I will say, "Yes indeed I will," and then try to enlarge the boundaries of his faith until they are as broad as my own. Does he say, "I am an atheist, now will you fellowship with me?" I will answer, "That must be at your own option; I will give you my hand and heart and try to have you believe as I do. And then if after all you die an atheist, if you have been gracious and helpful toward your brother man, if you have done justly, loved mercy and walked humbly on your lonesome way, then I tell you, my friend and brother, I for one will stand by your dust if you die first I will say, 'This man was true to himself, to his humankind, to me and mine and to all the truth he could find. Let us thank God for the good atheist.'"

Such are the terms of fellowship I love to hold for one. I would not say, are you a praying man, or are you a believing man? I would say, "Do you want to be a good man?" My faith is that the directest way to heaven lies right through the world we live in, and the best preparation for the life to come is a sound and true life down here, that can be in the world and of the world in clean and wholesome ways. I will welcome a man for his manhood or the budding promise of manhood or the hope that the bud will appear bye and bye. And teach this truth also for faith and fellowship, that we can serve God as truly in the week days as on the Sundays, in the forge, in the shop or in the field as certainly as in the Church. That this world is no dismal prison house in which all the commandments begin with Thou shalt not. We may make it a sweet and gracious home in which laughter shall be as sacred as tears, and a noble ballad when we want to sing one as good in its time and place as a psalm of David.

So runs my faith, that God our Father does not stand burning with wrath, because we do not believe in Him as we should; but that He is long-suffering and gracious, and will find a way to bring us home from our wanderings at last, all the lambs, all the sheep, all the goats. Faith in God, in His Christ, in His Holy Spirit, in His holy truth, in our human mind; faith in the good time coming when shibboleth and sibboleth will no longer be the watchwords or war cries within the Christian fold, but the grace of our Lord Jesus Christ and the love of God, and the fellowship of the Holy Spirit will clasp in all sects of all the churches and all the outsiders, and make us all one, and so usher in God's kingdom on the earth as it is in heaven.

>   The Holy One stood at the open door
>   And His face was fair to see,
>   When one came up the shining way
>   And moaned in his misery.
>   'Twas the soul of Judas Iscariot
>   Stood black and sad and bare,
>   And cried: "I have wandered long and far,
>   The darkness is everywhere."
>
>   And there were those who stood within,
>   Within the blessed light,
>   Who cried: "Scourge thou the traitor soul,
>   Away into the night."
>
>   The Holy One stood at the open door
>   And waved to the man below;
>   The third time that He waved His hand
>   The air was thick with snow,
>   And from every flake of the falling snow,
>   Before it touched the ground,
>   There came a dove, and all the doves
>   Made a sweet and gentle sound.
>
>   The Holy One stood at the open door
>   And beckoned, smiling sweet;
>   'Twas the soul of Judas Iscariot
>   Stole in and fell at His feet.
>   And the Holy Supper was spread within,
>   Where many candles shine,
>   But the Holy One beckoned for Judas to come
>   Before he poured the wine.

The Sacerdotal Conception of Christianity

The Sacerdotal Conception of Christianity

BY

The Reverend P. H. HICKMAN, B.Sc.

LET us see, first of all, what we mean by Christianity.
"Christianity is faith in a certain person, Jesus Christ, and by faith in Him is meant such unreserved self-committal as is only possible, because faith in Jesus is understood to be faith in God, and union with Jesus union with God. 'We know Him that is true, and we are in Him that is true, even in His Son, Jesus Christ. This is the true God, and eternal life.'"

"True Christianity is thus a personal relationship—the conscious, deliberate adhesion of men who know their weakness, their sin, their fallibility, to a redeemer whom they know to be supreme, sinless, infallible."

So it "is the simple verdict of Christian history, that the characteristic fruitfulness of our religion—its fruitfulness in the temper and spirit of sonship—varies with the extent to which Jesus, the historical person, the ever-living person, is recognized as the object of our devotion, and the lord of our life. This is equally true of personal religion and official ministry, for it is converse with the perfect personality of Jesus, which gives the pastor his power to deal with the various personalities of his flock, and the preacher his power to move the wills and consciences of his hearers. It is devotion to Jesus which has been the source of the enduring forms of Christian heroism. It is the same reality of personal relationship which touches the Christian's private life with the brightness of sonship. 'To me,' says Paul the prisoner, summarizing his religion, 'to live is Christ and to die is gain,' for that too is 'to depart and to be with Christ,' which 'is very far better.' 'Eighty and six years,' says the aged Polycarp, again summarizing his religion in response to the demand that he should revile the Christ, ' eighty and six years have I been His servant, and He never did me an injury; how then can I blaspheme my king who is my Saviour?'" (Chas. Gore, M. A., *The Incarnation of the Son of God,* New York, 1891, pp. 1, 2, 6, 7.)

The fact of the Incarnation, that the Son of God, "the Word, became flesh and dwelt among us,"[1] is thus the central fact of Christianity. And the principle and method of the Incarnation, that through the creature, through matter, through "flesh," the invisible God revealed Himself, becomes the governing principle and method of Christianity. The taking of a human body by the Son of God as a means of revelation of God and of the redemption of the world, establishes all the means appointed by Him as essential, not only upon the ground of His authority, but also upon the ground of His method.

He "builds His Church,"[2] He ordains its unity,[3] He trains and commissions a ministry,[4] He establishes a mode of entrance to His Church,[5] He provides a method for the nourishment of its members,[6] and for the repair of their failures.[7] By all these means, He unites His disciples to Himself and provides for their growth into a likeness to Him.

So the first of the great African Fathers, and the first Christian writer in the language of the West, Tertullian of Carthage (writing between 190 and 220 A. D.) paraphrases the institutions of our Lord: "And since the soul is, in consequence of its salvation, chosen to the service of God, it is the flesh which actually renders it capable of such service. The flesh, indeed, is washed in order that the soul may be cleansed; the flesh is anointed, that the soul may be consecrated; the flesh is signed

---

[1] St. John 1:14. (All quotations are made from the Revised Version)
[2] St. Matthew 16:18.
[3] St. John 17:21.
[4] St. Mark 3:13-19.
[5] St. Matthew 28:19.
[6] S . Luke 22:19-20.
[7] St. John 20:23.

(with the cross), that the soul too may be fortified; the flesh is shadowed with the imposition of hands, that the soul also may be illumined by the Spirit; the flesh feeds on the Body and Blood of Christ, that the soul may likewise fatten on *its* God."[1]

If it were possible to deny that the Lord Jesus Christ had founded a Church and established a ministry in it; if it could be denied that the forgiveness of sins was granted in Holy Baptism and by the absolution of His ministerial priesthood and that the souls of the faithful were " strengthened and refreshed by the Body and Blood of Christ " it would be possible to declare that Christianity is not Sacramental and Sacerdotal.

At this point, let us guard against any misuse of terms.

" It is an abuse of the sacerdotal conception if it is supposed that the priesthood exists to celebrate sacrifices or acts of worship in the place of the body of the people or as their substitute. . . . What is the truth then? It is that the Church is one body. The free approach to God in the Sonship and Priesthood of Christ belongs to men as members of ' one body ' and this one body has different organs through which the functions of its life find expression, as it was differentiated by the act and appointment of Him who created it. The reception, for instance, of Eucharistic grace, the approach to God in Eucharistic Sacrifice, are functions of the whole body. ' *We* bless the cup of blessing,' ' *we* break the bread,' says St. Paul, speaking for the community: ' *we* offer,' ' *we* present ' is the language of the liturgies. But the ministry is the organ—the necessary organ—of these functions. It is the hand which offers and distributes; it is the voice which consecrates and pleads. And the whole body can no more dispense with its services than the natural body can grasp or speak without the instrumentality of hand and tongue. Thus the ministry is the instrument as well as the symbol of the Church's unity, and no

---

[1] Tertullian, On the Resurrection of the Flesh, ch. 8, p. 551, Vol. III, Ante-Nicene Fathers, Buffalo, 1885.

man can share her fellowship except in acceptance of its offices."[1]

This sacramental and sacerdotal conception of Christianity prevailed (as no one denies) from the period of the great Ecumenical councils to the Reformation; from the Council of Nicæa, A. D. 325, to the repudiation of the Papal Supremacy by the Church of England in 1534, A. D. It still prevails in the Roman Catholic Church, *i. e.*, speaking generally, among the Latin Nations, who inherited the traditions of the Western Empire. It prevails, also, in the Holy Orthodox Church, both among the Greeks and the Russians, the heirs of the Eastern Empire, and representatives of the four Eastern Patriarchates, Constantinople, Alexandria, Antioch, and Jerusalem.

Was then this prevalence of the sacerdotal conception of Christianity at the period of Ecumenical councils due to the pressure of circumstances, to some evolution of the idea of unity until it became a leading idea of the church's life, or on the contrary is it derived from the authority of the Founder, and does it " stand as a necessary element of the truth from the very beginning?"

The question is put in this form, because the fundamental thought in the sacerdotal conception is the Unity of the Church, as in the Creed we confess: " I believe one Catholic and Apostolic Church " and then " acknowledge one Baptism for the remission of sins."

It is this unity which forms the central thought of the " concluding words of the great High-Priestly Prayer of our Lord Jesus Christ, wherein the exposition and operation of His work is summed up, at the close of the last evening before He died: ' As Thou didst send Me into the world, even so sent I them into the world. And for their sakes I sanctify Myself, that they themselves also may be sanctified in truth. Neither for these only do I pray, but for them also that believe on Me through their word; that they may all be one: even as Thou, Father,

---
[1] Chas. Gore, M.A., The Ministry of the Christian Church, New York, 1889, p. 85.

art in Me, and I in Thee, that they also may be in Us; that the world may believe that Thou didst send Me. And the glory which Thou hast given Me I have given unto them; that they may be one, even as we are one; I in them and Thou in Me, that they may be *perfected into one;* that the world may know that Thou didst send Me, and lovedst them, even as Thou lovedst Me." (St. John. 17: 18-23.)

Thus " the unity which the Church represents is the Unity of God. It is true, therefore, of the Church, in the highest conceivable sense, that her unity is not to be understood as a growth which begins from below, and gradually coalesces; her unity is not the crown of an evolution which starts from disunion; the Church is one in idea whether she is one in fact or not; her ideal unity from the first is inherent, transcendental, divine; she is one essentially, as and because God is One." [1]

Moreover, this unity is visible, organic, binding with moral force and for moral purposes upon every disciple of the Lord. Such is the meaning of the practical appeal of St. Paul to the members of the Church: " I, therefore, the prisoner in the Lord, beseech you to work worthily of the calling wherewith ye were called, with all lowliness and meekness, with long-suffering, forbearing one another in love; giving diligence to keep the unity of the Spirit in the bond of peace. There is one body, and one Spirit, even as also we were called in one hope of your calling; one Lord, one faith, one baptism, one God and Father of all, who is over all, and through all, and in all." (Eph. 4: 1-6.)

Commenting on this passage, says Dr. Hort: " The comparison of men in society to members of a body was of course not new. With the Stoics in particular, it was much in vogue. What was distinctively Christian was the faith in the One baptizing and life-giving Spirit, the one uniting body of Christ, the one all working, all inspiring God. . . . According to St. Paul, as Christ ' is before all things and all things in Him consist ' (Col. 1: 17), so also it was God's purpose in the course of ages

---

[1] R. C. Moberley, D.D., Ministerial Priesthood, New York, 1898, p. 6.

'to sum up all things in Him, the things in the heavens and the things in the earth." (Eph. 1 : 10; cf. Col. 1 : 20.) Part of this universal primacy of His (Col. 1 : 18) involved in His exaltation to the right hand of God as the completion of His Resurrection, was (Eph. 1 : 22, f.) that God ' gave Him as Head over all things to the Ecclesia which is His body, the fulfillment of Him who is fulfilled all things in all; ' or as in Col. 1 : 18) : ' Himself is the Head of the body, the Ecclesia.' The relation thus set forth under a figure is mutual. The work which Christ came to do on earth was not completed when He passed from the sight of men. He the Head, needed a body of members for its full working out through the ages. . . . And on the other hand His disciples had no intelligible unity apart from their ascended Head."[1]

Into this unity, says St. Paul in an earlier Epistle (A. D. 57, 1 Cor. xii: 13), presenting in this passage (vv. 12-28) what is afterward developed in Ephesians; into this unity are we all instrumentally brought: "For in one Spirit were we all baptized into one body, whether Jews or Greeks, whether bond or free, and were all made to drink of one Spirit."

It is not surprising, therefore, to find the Baptismal interrogation in Carthage, under the Episcopate of St. Cyprian (248-258 A. D.) inquiring: "Dost thou believe remission of sins and eternal life through the holy church?" (Ep. 69: 7; cf. Ep. 80: 2, Oxford ed.)

In this "one body," St. Paul claims his office as an Apostle (Col. 1 : 24) : "Now I rejoice in my sufferings for your sake, and fill up on my part that which is lacking of the afflictions of Christ in my flesh for His body's sake, which is the church; whereof I was made a minister;" "an ambassador on behalf of Christ." (2 Cor. 5 : 20.) And this equally with "The Twelve," by a divine Commission, an "Apostle (not from men, neither through man, but through Jesus Christ, and God the Father, who raised Him from the dead)." (Gal. 1 : 1.)

Of this Apostolate, " the fundamental character and war-

---

[1] F. J. A. Hort, D.D., The Christian Ecclesia, London, 1898, p. 147.

The Sacerdotal Conception of Christianity

rant," the divine commission, was given by the risen Lord: "Peace *be* unto you; as the Father has sent Me, even so send I you. And when He had said this, He breathed on them, and saith unto them: 'Receive ye the Holy Ghost; whosesoever sins ye forgive, they are forgiven unto them; and whosesoever sins ye retain they are retained.'" (St. John 20: 19-23; cf. 17: 21.)

The exercise of this *"commission of authority for government"* is constantly illustrated in the Acts (6: 6; 15: 28; 14: 23; 21: 18) and the Epistles (see especially 1 Tim. 2 and 3; Titus 1: 5 f.).

The nature of the ministry thus established in the "one body," by divine commission, as understood by the church at the close of the first century, is set forth by St. Clement of Rome, in his Epistle to the Corinthians, chapters 37 to 44. The letter (A. D. 96) was probably written while St. John was still living at Ephesus. (Bishop Westcott, Speaker's Commentary, Introd. to St. John, p. xxix.)

"All cannot be captains or generals," (I quote the paraphrase of Dr. Moberley, pp. 114-115, Ministerial Priesthood), "but all are arranged from the Emperor downwards, in a completely articulated hierarchical system. So it is with the body and its members, in the language of St. Paul to the Corinthians. And such must be the unity of the Body of Christ—based upon mutual submission, dependence, subordination. Self-assertion and pride are the characteristics of fools. There is order everywhere—order of places, times, persons—as the sacrifices of old had appointed places and times; and the high priest, priests, Levites, people, their distinct and co-ördinate offices, Everything, then, and every one in place and order. God sent forth Christ; Christ sent forth His Apostles. The Apostles, from their converts, constituted bishops and deacons. So Moses of old established a graduated hierarchy and silenced the voice of jealousy against the priesthood by the blossoming

---

[1] See Dr. Moberley, Ministerial Priesthood, p. 127, note 2; and Canon Gore, The Church and the Ministry, p. 229, note 4.

rod of Aaron laid up in the Ark of God. In parallel-wise, the Apostles, foreseeing the jealousies which should arise about ministerial office, did not merely, as has been said, constitute bishops and deacons, but afterwards also made provision, in case of their decease, for a continuous succession of ministerial office. Those, then, who have once been duly constituted ministers, either by Apostles, or by other faithful men after them, with the consent of the whole Church, can never justly be deposed from the ministry which they have so long and blamelessly exercised. Such deposition of men, who without scandal or irreverence have exercised the presbyterial office, and offered the gifts of the Church, would involve the Church in grave sin."

On this exposition of the ministry, Dr. Moberley comments: "I submit that it would be difficult to find a stronger assertion than this, of the principle that ministerial office is an outward and orderly institution, dependent for its validity upon transmission, continuous and authorized, from the Apostles, whose own commission was direct from Jesus Christ" (p. 115).

The teaching of St. Ignatius is well-known. "He is, beyond question," says Canon Gore (The Christian Ministry, p. 292) "the greatest theologian among 'the Apostolic Fathers,' with his deep insight into the Incarnation as a principle, a fact, a doctrine, and with his power to hold in balance its great antithesis in all its applications—the antithesis of the spiritual and the material, of the Word made Flesh." It will suffice to quote from one of his seven Epistles. "See," he says to the Smyrnaeans, "that ye all follow the bishop, even as Jesus Christ does the Father, and the presbytery as ye would the Apostles, and reverence the deacons as being the institution of God. Let no man do anything connected with the Church without the bishop. Let that be deemed a proper Eucharist which is (administered) either by the bishop, or by one to whom he has entrusted it. Wherever the bishop shall appear, there let the multitude (of the people) also be; even as wherever Jesus

Christ is, there is the Catholic Church. It is not lawful without the bishop either to baptize or to celebrate a love-feast; but whatsoever he shall approve of, that is also pleasing to God, so that everything that is done may be secure and valid." (The Ante-Nicene Fathers, Vol. I, pp. 89, 90, Ch. VIII.)

Thus the East answers to the West, Antioch to Rome, at the close of the first and the beginning of the second century.

At the close of the second century, the Church was adorned by the life and teaching of three great theologians; in Gaul, Irenaeus (Bishop of Lyons, 177-202); in Alexandria of Egypt, Clement (head of the famous catechetical school, 190-202); in Africa, at Carthage, Tertullian (190-220). The testimony of these three centres to the Divine Foundation, the Unity, and the Continuity of the Church, and the expression of that Unity in the Ministry, is uniform.

"Is it probable," exclaims the epigrammatic Tertullian, "that so many Churches of such importance should have hit by an accident of error on an identical creed?" (The Prescription against Heretics, Chap. XXVIII. Ante-Nicene Fathers, vol. III, p. 256.)

Clement of Alexandria thus concludes his argument against the "new invention" of "later heresies." "In the nature of the One God, then, is associated in a joint heritage the one Church, which they strive to cut asunder into many sects."

"Therefore, in substance and idea, in origin, in pre-eminence, we say that the ancient and Catholic Church is alone." (The Stromata, Ch. XVII, Book VII, The Ante-Nicene Fathers, Vol. II. p. 554.)

To Irenaeus of Lyons, "The true knowledge" (so he calls the Christian Faith) "is the doctrine of the Apostles, and the ancient system of the Church in all the world; and the character of the body of Christ, according to the successions of the bishops, to whom they (the Apostles) delivered the Church in each separate place." (The Ante-Nicene Fathers, Book IV, Ch. 33, Sec. 8, p. 508.)

In his Prescription against Heretics (Ch. 20, p. 252), Tertullian expands this statement of the bishop of Lyons into a precise and systematic definition.

Thus the sacerdotal conception of Christianity prevails at the end of the second century in the representative centres of the Church and the conception is held as well in the functions as in the foundation, unity, and continuity of the Church.

In the treatise " On Baptism," the earliest treatise on the first Christian Sacrament, the doctrine of Baptismal Regeneration is expressed by Tertullian as clearly and definitely as in the *Book of Common Prayer;* in the treatise " On Penitence," he urged the motives for the use of the " plank after shipwreck " and the benefits of its use (see especially Chaps. IV, IX, pp. 659, 664, A-N. Fathers, Vol. III.). Irenæus holds the doctrine of the Real Presence of Christ in the Eucharist as firmly as St. Paul (1 Cor. 11:29) or Justin Martyr (The Apology, I, 61, 65-67, A-N. Fathers, Vol. 1, pp. 183, 185) :—" The mixed cup and the bread which has been made receives the word of God and the Eucharist becomes the Body (and Blood) of Christ, and the substance of our flesh grows and gains consistence from these. How, then, can they say our flesh is not susceptible of the gift of God, which is eternal life—our flesh which is nourished by the Body and Blood of the Lord, and which is His member." (V. 2, 3, A-N. Fathers, p. 528.)

It was said that in the Church the sacerdotal conception of Christianity prevailed from the period of the great councils to the Reformation (and this no one doubted), and still prevails in the Greek and Roman Churches, and did prevail in the Church of England till the Reformation. It is now clear that it prevailed in the undivided Church from the day of Pentecost to the Nicene Council, and the Archbishops of England declare that it has prevailed in the Church of England since the Reformation and prevails at this day.

The Archbishops declare in their " Answer to the Apostolic Letter of Pope Leo XIII on English Ordinations ": " He declares that we deny or corrupt the Sacrament of Order, that we reject (viz. in the Ordinal) all idea of consecration and sacrifice, until at last the offices of Presbyter and Bishop are left 'mere names without the reality which Christ instituted.'"

"Now, the intention of our Church, not merely of a newly-formed party in it, is quite clearly set forth in the title and preface of the Ordinal. The title in 1552 ran: 'The fourme and maner of makynge and consecratynge Bishoppes, Priestes, and Deacons.' The preface immediately following begins thus: 'It is euident unto all men, diligently readinge holye Scripture and auncient aucthours, that from the Apostles tyme there hathe bene these ordres of Ministers in Christ's Church: Bishoppes, Priestes, and Deacons; which Offices were euermore had in suche reuerent estimacion, that no man by his own private authoritie might presume to execute any of them, except he were first called, tried, examined, and knowen to have such qualities as were requisite for the same; and also, by publique prayer, with imposicion of hands, approued, and admitted thereunto. And therefore, to the entent that these orders should bee continued, and reuerentlye used and estemed, in this Church of England; it is requysite that no man (not beyng at thys presente Bisshope, Priest, nor Deacon, shall execute anye of them, excepte he be called, tryed, examined, and admitted, accordynge to the form hereafter folowinge.' Further on, it is stated incidentally that "euery man which is to be consecrated a Bishop shal be fully thyrtie yeres of age.' And in the rite itself, the 'consecration' of the Bishop is repeatedly mentioned. The succession and continuance of these offices from the Lord through the Apostles and the other ministers of the primitive Church is also clearly implied in the 'Eucharistical' prayers which precede the words, *Receive the Holy Ghost*. Thus the intention of our Fathers was to keep and continue these offices which come down from the earliest times, and 'reverently to use and esteem them,' in the sense, of course, in which they were received from the Apostles and had been up to that time in use."

And, the Archbishops declare: "We make provision with the greatest reverence for the consecration of the holy Eucharist, and commit it only to properly ordained priests and to no other ministers of the Church. Further, we truly teach the doctrine of Eucharistic sacrifice, and do not believe it to be a 'nude commemoration of the Sacrifice of the Cross,' an opinion which seems to be attributed to us by the quotation made from that Council. But we think it sufficient in the Liturgy which we use in celebrating the Holy Eucharist—while lifting up our hearts to the Lord, and when now consecrating the gifts already offered that they may become to us the Body and Blood of our Lord Jesus Christ—to signify the sacrifice which is offered at that point of the service in such terms as these. We continue a perpetual memory of the precious death of Christ, who is our Advocate with the Father and the propitiation for our sins, according to His precept, until His coming again. For first, we offer the sacrifice of praise and thanksgiving; then next we plead, and represent before the Father the sacrifice of the Cross, and by it we confidently entreat remission of sins, and all other benefits of the Lord's Passion for all the whole Church; and, lastly, we offer the sacrifice of ourselves to the Creator of all things which we have already signified by the oblation of His creatures. This whole action, in which the people has necessarily to take its part with the priest, we are accustomed to call the Eucharistic sacrifice."

Divorce and Remarriage

Divorce and Remarriage

BY

The Right Reverend WILLIAM CROSWELL DOANE, D.D.

THE Church represents three distinct shades of thought and conviction upon this very important question. First, of those who are convinced that there can be no remarriage after divorce for any cause during the lifetime of the other party to the marriage. Secondly, of those who so far doubt the *legality*, that they dare not give such a marriage the sanction of the Church, and yet so far admit the possibility of the authenticity and intention of our Lord's words regarding a divorce for unfaithfulness, as to be unable positively to declare its *illegality*. And thirdly, of those who are so clear of the exception as divinely allowed, that they think it warrants the giving of the sanction *and* of the Sacraments of the Church in the case of this one remarriage. Three wide lines of difference, clearly drawn, strongly held, earnestly urged. I believe, however, that more and more examination and education will bring our Church to recognize and realize that the only safety for the sacredness of marriage, the purity of society, the protection of the family and the sanctity of the home, is to refuse the sanction of the Church to all remarriage of divorced persons, guilty or innocent, for whatever cause.

In the study of this subject, before I come to the crucial difficulty of text and interpretations, there are two undisputed and I think indisputable facts, namely, that during two marked and important periods of the history of the Church, the law and use about remarriage are positive and clear. One of these periods is Primitive and the other is English. When Mr. Gladstone said in 1857 that divorce with remarriage was unknown in Christendom for 300 years; and when Mr. Keble wrote and proved that there was almost a *consensus patrum* until A. D. 314 on the absolute inviolability of marriage, they were asserting, after minute investigation, an indisputable fact. The references in Mr. Keble's "sequel to his argument that the nuptial bond is indissoluble" begin with St. Paul's strong statements and end with the forty-seventh Apostolic Canon, including the testimony of Hermas, Justin Martyr, Clement of Alexandria, Tertullian and Origen, so covering "the whole of Christendom" according to its bounds in that age, the East, Egypt, Africa and Rome. Quotations from the canons of Eliberis A. D. 305 to 313, and the canon of Arles A. D. 314, at which council two or perhaps three British Bishops were present, exhibit the same principle acting in Spain and in Gaul. I shall hope to have the opportunity, in some day of larger leisure, to collect and publish these authorities. Meanwhile, because Mr. Keble's statements need no verifying, we may assume them to be true. This brings us down to a marked and momentous period in the Christian Story, which may be variously described as the time when Constantine became Christianized or when Christianity became Constantinized. Certain it is that the first departure from the old rule is to be found in the Divine Institutions of Lactantius, tutor to Constantine's son, which contain the statement that the tie of the marriage covenant may never be undone except when it is broken by faithlessness; and again, that he is an adulterer who, except for the cause of adultery, hath dismissed his wife to marry another. It is to be noted as marking the danger of departure from the strict rule, that within seven years after this, when Constantine promulgated his law of divorce, which was a civil and not an ecclesiastical rescript, it included four other grounds of legal divorce, murder, sorcery, the violation of graves, pandering to unchastity in others. And it is to be noted also that the Bishops most in favour at court at this time, were those who were known either as Arians or Indifferentists.

The second undisputed fact is that the Church of England, in her canons and in her customs, following the course of her Bishops in the Council of Arles, from the Norman Conquest, through the Reformation and down to the present day, has never recognized divorce with the right of remarriage. This was true also of the civil law of England until forty years ago. The primitive and the Anglican authority therefore are in entire accord, and altogether on the side of the indissolubility of the marriage bond except by death. Between these two points, the Primitive and the Anglican, what occurs? In the East, Erastianism, going from bad to worse, from one to four, from four to sixteen causes of divorce. And in the West, what has been called by an admirable collocation of adjectives, though sometimes misapplied, a course of conduct, "Latin and disingenuous." That is, the Roman Church has in the letter of her laws upheld nobly and boldly the sanctity of marriage but, after her manner, she has managed, by the application of the rite of marriages annulled and of Papal dispensations, to make the law elastic and inclusive, through a list of prohibitions, which made marriages unlawful from the first on grounds often unknown to the contracting parties, and so to destroy the practical value of her catholic profession. Alas, it is the old story, *Romae omnia venalia*. One says it with shame and with sorrow because the appearance, the utterance, and in the majority of cases the practical application of the Roman Catholic law, has made divorce difficult and remarriage after it rare. But it leaves the primitive centuries and the English Church for nine hundred years, still, as bearing the most manly and consistent testimony to this great fact. The suggestion that the condition of social morals in Continental countries is an argument against strong laws about marriage and difficulty of divorce has no such application. Because impurity is a matter of climate and race rather than of ecclesiastical relation, as is easily seen by the fact that there are no purer women in the world than the women of Roman Catholic Ireland.

If it is true that prominent ministers of other religious bodies have said openly that they were tired of marrying people whom we would not marry, it means that a strong stand taken by this Church will lift the standard of all religious denominations to a higher level. And the time will not be far distant when we shall have no need to discriminate between those whom we marry and those whom we admit to the Sacraments; because the positive teaching of this Church and its influence elsewhere will go far toward making divorce difficult and remarriage after it a thing unthought of. Meanwhile it must be insisted that our present canon takes higher ground than that which is ordinarily held, in allowing only one cause for divorce with remarriage; that we are not considering the question of legal separation, when living together as man and wife seems impossible; and that no reference can be had, in this argument or in any canon that may be passed, to persons who had contracted marriages, by the express permission of the present canon.

I pass to a brief summary of the grounds on which I hold the view that by the teaching of Holy Scripture the marriage bond is indissoluble, that separation is permitted in one case only, but that no remarriage is possible under any conditions. I speak, not with the authority of a scholar, which I have never had time to become, but of a careful student seeking only truth. The question turns, of course, upon the authenticity and meaning of our Lord's words in the nineteenth chapter of the Holy Gospel according to St. Matthew. Allowing that the words ought to stand, and that they mean what they seem to mean in the English version of the passage, the deduction from them in our present canon, and in a canon proposed in 1897 is based upon a series of inferences. At best they contain a negative non-prohibition, which it is proposed to turn into a positive permission. They refer only to the man putting away his wife, and are inferred to apply to the woman. And they use the word πορνεία which is, to say the least, probably not the same as μοιχεία; the distinction between the two sins being expressed in the English as well as in the Greek by two different words. Then comes the question as to whether our Lord used these words, and *when* He used them, and if He did, and with what intention; about which it must be remembered that in the Sermon on the Mount, as St. Matthew records it, there is no reference to remarriage. The text reads there, " Whosoever shall put away his wife, save for the cause of fornication, causeth her to commit adultery." And the words in the Greek are παρεκτὸς λόγου πορνείας, which certainly means " apart from," " leaving to one side," " not considering the cause." The sentence then would mean, " Whosoever shall put away his wife (I am not speaking of fornication, which if it means uncleanness before marriage is provided for by the permission to annul the marriage; and if it means adultery is provided for by the requirement to put the adulteress to death) causeth her to commit adultery." In the fuller statement that is contained in the nineteenth chapter of the Gospel the expression is apparently different. There is an allusion here to the possibility of remarriage after putting away. " Whosoever shall put away his wife, except it be for fornication, and shall marry another, committeth adultery." The words in the commonly received Greek text are, εἰ μὴ ἐπὶ πορνείᾳ. It is, to say the least, doubtful if our translators render these words accurately, for εἰ μη means probably " if not " or " though not " for fornication, which would make this, not an exception, but an exemplification and illustration. But there is good reason to believe that the case is stronger than this. The revisers in their note say " some ancient authorities read, as in chapter v: 32," that is to say, as in the Sermon on the Mount. So also Lachmann. And the Syriac translation, the famous Complutensian edition, and such editors of the Greek text as Griesbach, Tregelles, Tischendorf, Mill, Burton, such commentators as Grotius and Lucas Brugensis and Selden and before them Chrysostom and Augustine omit the εἰ and read μή, which make synonymous and consistent our Lord's words here and in the Sermon on the Mount.

" Whosoever shall put away his wife (I am not speaking of uncleanness and unfaithfulness, which are provided for by another law annulling or putting away) and shall marry another committeth adultery." And the words, probably, be they exception or qualification, refer not to the marriage but to the putting away; forbidding divorce, that is to say, for any but the one cause, instead of for the innumerable causes allowed by rabbinical accretions and additions to the law of Moses, but giving no permission to remarry. "Is it lawful," the Pharisees ask, "to put away for any cause?" and our Lord said, "No, only for one cause, uncleanness or unfaithfulness."

It is a most weighty addition to this whole argument that all three evangelists record the language of our Lord, as to the remarriage of the person put away or divorced, in the same sweeping terms,—"Whosoever marrieth," not *the* woman put away, which might mean the adulteress, but "a woman," any woman, "put away," or as St. Luke has it "*a* woman put away from *a* husband," committeth adultery. And this being true, it follows, that if no man can marry any woman put away from any husband without being guilty of adultery, it must be because the marriage bond is not dissolved by divorce, because she is still the wife of the husband who has put her away. The man cannot marry because he *has* a wife, and the woman cannot marry because she *has* a husband.

We must add to this the fact that the first words recorded in this nineteenth chapter of St. Matthew's Gospel were spoken to Jews in answer to a particular question, and were intended plainly to limit the loose mode of the Jews of that day in enlarging and distorting the permission which Moses, not God, had granted them because of the hardness of their hearts. But when St. Mark tells the same story he records the fact that, speaking to the disciples in the house, not of the past nor to the Pharisees, nor in regard to Mosaic law, but speaking of the future, to those who were to continue His preaching, and in regard to Christian principle, Christ made the statement simple and unexceptional and clear. "And he saith unto them, whosoever shall put away his wife, and marry another, committeth adultery against her. And if a woman shall put away her husband, and be married to another, she committeth adultery." And when we turn back to St. Matthew's story of the effect thus produced on the disciples, it is quite evident that they understood the saying to mean that no man putting away and no woman put away could marry again, for, they said, "if the case be so of the man with his wife, it is not good to marry," and Jesus said "all men cannot receive this saying," *not* the saying, It is not good to marry, but the saying, Whoso putteth away his wife committeth adultery, and whoso marrieth any woman put away committeth adultery. St. Mark and St. Luke alike omit all reference to any exception to the rule. St. Luke prefacing the unexceptional statement with the words, "It is easier for heaven and earth to pass than one tittle of the law to fail," turns back to another, and the strongest point of all, namely, our Lord's statement of the principle of marriage as a divine institution, which St. Matthew records in full, in the same chapter of his Gospel. The question was, Can a man put away his wife for any cause? and our Lord's answer is unequivocal. "And He answered and said unto them, Have ye not read, that He which made them at the beginning, made them male and female, and said, for this cause shall a man leave father and mother, and shall cleave to his wife; and they twain shall be one flesh! Wherefore they are no more twain but one flesh. What therefore God hath joined together, let not man put asunder." This can mean but one thing, that He who instituted the sacred bond in the beginning, Who made it in the very terms of its institution mystical, reaffirms the fundamental principle of it, monogamy and indissolubility, one man and one woman, one flesh; "what therefore God has joined together let not man put asunder." The passages must be taken together. They relate and refer, all of them, to this restatement, reaffirmation, re-institution, which underlies the natural, the Mosaic, the Christian institution. And we can only so avoid, it seems to me, the fault and failure of the Pharisees, who, "tempting Him," here as elsewhere, tried to "entangle Jesus in His talk." He cannot contradict Himself. Somehow, any seeming contradiction, must be explicable. And the reconciling words, by which the exception which would contravene the principle of marriage, if it were what it seems to be, may be so understood as not to break the law of God;—the reconciling words are "what *therefore*," because they are one flesh, "what therefore God has joined together let not man put asunder."

I do not think that in the ordinary discussion of the scriptural presentation of this matter, attention enough is called to St. Paul's witness. We turn to him constantly about the doctrine of the Resurrection, of the Holy Eucharist and Confirmation, etc., as an outside and independent witness, because he has assured us that his Gospel was not from man nor by man, but that he received it directly and immediately from our Lord Himself. It may of course be possible to push this too far, if we make it apply to every dogmatic utterance of the Apostle, but it is plainly applicable to his two statements about Christian marriage. "And unto the married I command, yet not I, but the Lord, Let not the wife depart from her husband: But and if she depart, let her remain unmarried, or be reconciled to her husband; and let not the husband put away his wife." 1 Cor. 7: 10, 11. In which he says distinctly, Not I, but the Lord. And it is as applicable to what he writes to the Roman Christians as asserting a well known Christian law. "Know ye not, brethren, (for I speak to them that know the law,) how that the law hath dominion over a man as long as he liveth? For the woman which hath an husband is bound by the law to her husband so long as he liveth; but if the husband be dead, she is loosed from the law of her husband. So then if, while her husband liveth, she be married to another man, she shall be called an adulteress: but if her husband be dead, she is free from the law; so that she is no adulteress, though she be married to another man". Rom. 7: 1, 2, 3. So that these two utterances, both unmistakable in their meaning, are not Pauline canons, but restatements and revelations to St. Paul by our Lord Himself, which had passed at that time into a well-known law of the Church, to which the Apostle could appeal, for the fact that only death dissolves the marriage bond.

We are taught to refer in our search for truth to "Holy Scripture and ancient authors." We are told also, as to the teaching of our Church, that the fathers of it in America, and the revisers and compilers of our Book of Common Prayer, and the framers of our canon law, had no intention of "departing from the Church of England in any essential point of doctrine, discipline or worship." And this marriage question touches all these three. It cannot be said that there is consentient doctrine in the Church of England when men like Keble and Bishop Hamilton and Isaac Williams and Dr. Bright are on the one side, and on the other side Lightfoot and Bishop Wordsworth of Lincoln and Bishop Wordsworth of Salisbury and Bishop King of Lincoln. So that one must recognize the honest and somewhat astonished attitude of John Keble, scholar and saint, when he writes "It is notorious that very many having no other wish than to live and die dutiful children of the Church of England, believe, nevertheless, that they see in Holy Scripture all but a direct contradiction of a main principle of our doctrine and discipline of marriage." But about the discipline and worship of the Church of England, her canon law, and her form of service, there is no room for doubt or question. Plainly in her canon law, positively in her long inheritance of traditional legislation, from Arles, from the time of the Norman Conquest, at and after the Reformation, she speaks still with no uncertain voice, in refusing any remarriage after any divorce. And the Office for the solemnization of matrimony, hers and ours, is built at every turn and step upon its indissolubility;—"so long as ye both shall live," "until death us do part," "Whom God hath joined together let not man put asunder." So much so, that to use that office for the remarriage of a divorced person, or to use it with any contemplation of a separation during life of those so married, would be a ludicrous, if it were not a blasphemous, contradiction in terms.

Not least of all the reasons which make for the value of the principle that divorce does not carry with it the right of remarriage, is the great thought of the duty and possibility of reconciliation after repentance. That is a door that ought never to be closed. Even the gravest offense, expiated by bitter remorse, ought to be kept within the reach of forgiveness and restoration. The erring husband or the sinful wife, separated one from the other, ought not to have the barrier of another wife or another husband taken, between them and the possibility of pardon and the renewal of rights and privileges forfeited, perhaps in some moment of unresisted temptation, for which years of misery have made atonement.

I have stated the case in favour of the proposed canon forbidding any minister of our Church to solemnize the marriage of either party to a divorce during the lifetime of the other party, if the divorce be granted for any cause arising after marriage. I am not called upon to make argument or plea for the other side, which has many able supporters, but I am bound to recognize that there is another side,—those whom Mr. Keble describes as wishing "to live and die dutiful children of the Church of England, who believe, nevertheless, that they see in Holy Scripture all but a direct contradiction of the principle of her doctrine and discipline of marriage, namely, that marriage once really contracted is indissoluble by man." They include in our own day the names of most learned and holy men. There has been always a strong array of students of Holy Scripture and canon law, holding to the Divine authority of the one exception which allows remarriage; and the testimony of the Eastern Church since Constantine has been as distinct in this direction and in wide departures from it, as has been that of the Western Church in the other direction. How should this state of things affect our canon law? Plainly, it seems to me, it ought to hinder us from presuming to declare the illegality of this one marriage by affixing to it any ecclesiastical penalty other than (if it be called a penalty) the refusal to give it the sanction of the Church's benediction. The form of the proposed canon purposely avoids declaring such a marriage either legal or illegal. It is in no sense a canon of discipline for the lay people. That matter may be dealt with in other ways and must be dealt with elsewhere; either by such a suggestion as was made in the amendment proposed to the canon, in the House of Bishops, excepting the innocent party to a divorce suit, asked and obtained for adultery, from the prohibition to admit to the Sacraments persons remarried after divorce; or, there may be some wiser and better way to accomplish it. The canon for which I am pleading leaves this question untouched. It is not, and does not pretend to be, a canon on divorce or on remarriage. It is a canon on marriage. At the same time I am free to confess that no canonical enactment would be complete, and no canonical action would fully represent the actual historic attitude of the Church toward this question, which does not somehow recognize the claim of conscience and of scholarship, about that most difficult of all things to define, the innocent party in a divorce suit for adultery. Say what you will about the danger that conscience in this case means often the self-will of passion; think what you will about the clearness of Scriptural principle; it is true that scholars and saints, in all the later ages and in the two great divisions of the Church, Eastern and Western, have been divided and uncertain about this one point. And something that will recognize this, something that will at least exclude from Christian consideration any cause for tolerated divorce *but the one,* must be done. I am only concerned to say that the appeal to the Church on the ground that she is the *ecclesia docens* to decide this question, to teach the truth positively, peremptorily and without a qualification, is asking this American branch of the Church to do what she has no warrant to do, what no general council of the Church has finally settled, and what no uniform consent of her members during these nineteen centuries has been able to accomplish. Her mission, therefore, is to teach what she can most surely find established by the strongest warrant of authority; and if I can read rightly the collected teachings of the centuries, it must be this: That any remarriage after divorce is so far doubtful that she cannot give it the sanction of allowing her clergy to solemnize it; that the rightful remarriage of the man whose wife is an adulteress is so far possible that she dare not refuse to admit this person, remarried, to the Sacraments. The end of this question is not yet. Considering the cardinal and critical consequence of that with which it deals, namely, the primeval and fundamental institution, implied in creation, instituted in the earliest moment of man's being, and certified and sanctified by the teaching of our Lord,—considering its relation to all that most concerns the stability of the family, of society, of the home, of the state,—considering the chaos of confusion, of uncertainty, of levity, of contempt for the sacredness of this holy estate, of divergence in civil laws, of resort to fictions and falsehoods of residence,—considering the influence and power of a declaration in her canon law by this Church, which shall conform it to the constantly increasing power of the teaching of her Book of Common Prayer,—it must be recognized as a burning question in theology, in morals, in discipline. And it is imperative that all should make such study of the facts as they may be able to make, and above all, to pray God to give them wisdom and courage, when the time for decision shall come, to think and to do the thing which is right.

Divorce and Remarriage

Divorce and Remarriage

BY

Justice D. V. BURNS, LL.D.

THE question of divorce is one of the most perplexing of all the social questions. This perplexity, in the minds of many, is greatly increased when we come to deal with the question of the remarriage of divorced parties.

Ours is a Christian Nation. The most profound reverence is, as a rule, paid to the teachings of Holy Writ by our legislators and judges. Great respect is also by them paid to the opinions of the religious element of society. But inasmuch as we have with us no union of Church and State the dogmas of no particular sect are allowed to control either in legislative halls or in judicial forums.

The Founder of the Christian religion never assumed to legislate in regard to purely civil affairs, or to judicially determine matters which properly belong to the State. In all such matters He ever carefully held Himself aloof. He declared Himself to be a King; that He came to set up a Kingdom, but while possibly it was to be begun on this earth, it was not to be of this world. Had He done so, but few would now be found to controvert His authority or challenge the wisdom of His utterances. To the writer His every word is Yea and Amen. But to rightly understand and interpret the meaning of what is said upon any subject, the time and the place of utterance, the persons addressed, and all that is said must be taken into consideration. During His ministry the Great Teacher both by precept and example taught that in all matters of a political character respect and obedience should be paid to established authority. (Matt. 22: 21; Luke 12: 13-14.)

Keeping these things in mind let us proceed to examine the teachings of Our Lord upon this important and perplexing question.

At the very outset He announced that no one could even

enter into His Kingdom or become a subject thereof, until he had been born anew,—born from above. After having so announced, He, in the famous Sermon on the Mount, which has been fittingly called His "Inaugural Address," laid down certain basic principles which are to control in His Kingdom. In the course of such address He mentioned among other things the subject of divorce, using the following language: "It hath been said, whosoever shall put away his wife, let him give her a writing of divorcement; But as I say unto you that whosoever shall put away his wife save for the cause of *fornication* causeth her to commit adultery; And whosoever shall marry her that is divorced committeth adultery." (Matt. 5: 31-32.)

A moment's consideration ought to convince any unbiased mind that the Lord was not then speaking about matters pertaining to civil legislation or civil judicial decision. For in the same discourse He said: "Whosoever looketh upon a woman to lust after her hath committed adultery with her in his heart." "Ye have heard it hath been said, 'An eye for an eye, and a tooth for a tooth:' But I say unto you, That ye resist not evil; but whosoever shall smite thee on thy right cheek, turn to him the other also." "If any man sue thee at the law and take away thy coat, let him have thy cloak also." "Whosoever shall compel thee to go a mile, go with him twain," etc.

The Mosaic law upon the subject which is supposed to have been God-directed, reads as follows:

"When a man hath taken a wife and married her and it come to pass that she find no favour in his eyes, because he hath found some uncleanness in her; then let him write her a bill of divorcement and give it in her hand and send her out of his house. And when she has departed out of his house she may go and be another man's wife," etc. (Deut. 24: *et seq.*)

During the ministry of the Christ there were in existence in Palestine two great rival schools of theology. The one founded by Rabbi Schammai and the other by Rabbi Hillel. These differed widely in their interpretation of the above law.

The question was one of fierce and bitter debate between them. The school of Hillel taught that a man might put away his wife for any cause which seemed good to him. While that of Schammai held that she could only be put away when guilty of an act of unchastity. A delegation from the Pharisaical party sought to entangle Jesus by having Him espouse the cause of one of the parties and thereby incur the opposition of the other. They therefore came tempting Him saying: "Is it lawful for a man to put away his wife for *any cause?*" Discerning their motives, He answered, "Have ye not read that He who made them at the beginning, made them male and female. For this cause a man shall leave father and mother, and shall cleave to his wife; and they twain shall be one flesh. What therefore God hath joined together let not man put asunder." This was equivalent to His saying, You have asked my opinion as to how a mooted question shall be decided in the present disorganized and corrupt state of society, which I answer by calling your attention back to the indissoluble relationship which bound together the first wedded pair as they came fresh from the hands of their Creator. Male and female created He them and indissolubly, so far as the act of man is concerned, joined them together. I am not to destroy, but to fulfil.

His teaching upon this particular subject was so startling and perplexing to the disciples that after His tempters were gone and He had entered a house, they came to Him for further light, saying: "If the case of man be so, it is not good to marry"; to which He answered, "All men cannot receive this saying, save they to whom it is given; there be eunuchs which have made themselves eunuchs for the kingdom of heaven's sake. He that is able to receive it, let him receive it." (Matt. 19: 3-12; Mark 10: 2-12.) He was not dealing with temporalities as earthly law makers and judges are compelled to do. He was laying broad and deep the foundations of a Kingdom which is to be eternal. Those who are fitted to enter it, to them gives He power to receive His sayings and keep them, even to the plucking out of the eye which offends. But not so with the world.

Divorce among the ancient Hebrews was quite a different matter from what it is to-day in our own land and in Great Britain. The husband was the sole judge, and he alone severed the bonds. Such a thing as a wife putting away her husband for any cause was never even so much as dreamed of. The only protection the wife had was that the law of Moses required that the husband upon divorcing her should write out his reasons for so doing, and after having the same attested by witnesses, give it into her possession. This enabled her to show the causes of separation to others, which often carried upon its face her own vindication. If a wife was guilty of adultery a husband need not resort to such a proceeding to rid himself of her. All that he had to do in such case was to deliver her up to be put to death; though, if he was so minded, he might put her away privately as Joseph was inclined to do in the case of Mary.

But among the English speaking people the rights of a wife are as jealously guarded, and in practice more so, than are those of a husband.

In the contemplation of the law there are three parties to every marriage contract: the man, the woman and the State. Likewise, the same three parties are entitled to be present and heard whenever a dissolution is asked. There is no putting away of one by the other at pleasure; nor is a divorce now decreed unless pursuant to some express provision of statutory law.

In England prior to the year 1858 the subject of divorce was cognizable only in the ecclesiastical courts, in which the canon law, *i. e.*, a body of rules and ordinances of Roman Catholic councils and popes, qualified by statute, prevailed. But the evils arising thereunder proved to be so intolerable that in obedience to popular demand and common decency, jurisdiction of the subject was in that year by Act of Parliament taken from such courts and vested in courts of law in which the practice is open to public scrutiny.

In none of the States of the American Union has the canon law ever prevailed. In some of the States divorces were formerly granted only by legislative enactment, but now in all of the States and Territories, save one (South Carolina), divorces are permitted by general law for certain specified causes, as adultery; cruel and inhuman treatment of one party by the other; wilful desertion for a specified definite length of time, usually two years; conviction of a felony followed by imprisonment in a State prison; habitual drunkenness, and failure on the part of an able-bodied husband to make reasonable provisions for the support of his wife and family. In most cases the decree of divorce is absolute as to both parties; while in a few, only the innocent party is permitted to remarry. In all the States having statutes upon the subject both husband and wife are, except as to the cause last above mentioned, equal before the law.

It is the function of human governments to deal only with present physical conditions. They cannot punish the lustful glance, nor unrighteous mental anger not evidenced by physical violence, nor can they suppress the instinct of self defence. If compelled to govern only in accordance with the high principles enunciated in the Sermon on the Mount, they could not under existing conditions maintain their existence at all. They must deal with men as they find them. The brutal and the vicious must be restrained; the rights of the innocent and unoffending must be protected, or such governments must utterly fail of their purpose. When one party so far violates the mutual contract as to render cohabitation intolerable, the other should not be held bound.

Observation and experience teach that many couples who have been wed are not mated; that they have always remained twain and have never become one flesh. Husbands are sometimes bought in the open market as are sheep in the shambles. The marriage ceremony is sometimes performed at the muzzle of the revolver of an irate father or brother. How is the human judge to determine "whom God hath joined together," except from the manifestations of outward conduct?

The ecclesiastical judges were often confronted with such difficult questions as these and often solved them by decreeing that such marriages were void *ab initio*. But not so with our law judges. Every marriage not prohibited by law is treated as valid until dissolved by a decree of a competent court. They do not attempt to read the heart, but deal only with outward conduct, leaving man to be judged by his Maker as to his thoughts and unmanifested purposes. If a man become an habitual drunkard and so unfits himself for procreation or association with his own family; or by his brutal conduct constantly puts the life of her whom he has vowed to love, cherish and protect in jeopardy; or so violates the laws of his country that he is imprisoned for life, or a lesser term; or being able-bodied, refuses to make any provision for his family, ought the State in such cases to say to a suffering, innocent, inoffensive and helpless wife, "The laws of your country can afford you no relief." Would He who ordained and upholds human government for the protection of the weak, the punishment of the vicious, and who lifted up woman, gave her an individuality of her own, crowned her with nobility and placed her upon equality with man, desire that such governments should so utterly fail in their purposes as to leave her a helpless victim to man's inhumanity? In case of severance of the family union by wilful desertion on the part of either husband or wife, the great Apostle to the Gentiles expressed himself thus: "But if the unbelieving depart, let him depart. A brother or sister is not bound in such cases." (1 Cor. 7: 15.)

Upon the question of the remarriage of divorced parties the State utters no voice. Divorces were formerly in many instances granted a *mensa et thoro, i. e.,* from bed and board only. The parties being thus separated were married and yet not married. A man was a husband and at the same time wifeless. A woman was a wife and yet was without a husband. History and experience have shown that such decrees are not conducive to public morals, such is the affinity of the sexes. Therefore the State has found it better, in most instances when it dissolves the bond at all, to dissolve it absolutely, thus leaving the parties in the same condition in this respect, as if neither had ever been married. They are thus left to their consciences and individual judgments as to their future actions. The State does not attempt to legislate upon questions affecting only private conscience.

That much unwise legislation has been had and much looseness of practise indulged in, upon this highly important question, cannot be denied. Scandals have arisen therefrom in many instances which have brought disgrace upon us as a people. No one is more conscious of this evil than are the thoughtful members of the legal profession. All such recognize that the family is the foundation on which rests the hope of the State; and that no nation which willfully disobeys any of the precepts of the living God can permanently endure. But human laws which are much in advance of public sentiment cannot be enforced, and when enacted uselessly encumber the statute books. What is needed is the creation of a healthier public sentiment which shall control in all matters of legislation and in the administration of justice.

The laws upon the subject of marriage and divorce are not uniform throughout the several States. If they were, much scandal would be avoided, for there are now sections where divorce is made easy. The American Bar Association, recognizing the prevailing evils, has taken the matter in hand and appointed a committee which has prepared a stringent code of laws upon the subject which it will seek to have enacted by the various State legislatures. If successful, the present evils will be greatly lessened. But the true solution lies in having the Constitution of the United States so amended that Congress alone can legislate and the Federal Courts alone adjudicate, upon these great questions so vital to our national and moral well-being

Exposition of Christian Science

Exposition of Christian Science

BY

The Reverend O. P. GIFFORD. D.D.

THE purpose of this paper is to give an exposition of Christian Science. An exposition is neither an attack nor a defence but is an attempt to state the subject so clearly that each may attack or defend for himself. Christian Science is a fact to be faced, a force to be opposed or profited by. It is a fact and a force in the religious and the medical world, dealing with the souls and bodies of men. It is a philosophy dealing with God, man and the universe. It is an art healing the body, calming the mind, quieting the soul. It claims to be a revelation. "A final revelation of the absolute Principle of Scientific Mind-healing." As a revelation Christian Science affirms the being and unfolds the nature of God, as a philosophy it formulates this revelation in human phrases, weaving the threads of revelation into a web of complete thought, as an art it applies the truth revealed and thought through to the regulation of life.

Christian Science accepts the Scriptures as the Word of God, a revelation made in times past through holy men by the Holy Ghost; it supplements this revelation with another given through Mrs. Mary Baker Eddy, bound in a volume known as "Science and Health with a Key to the Scriptures." This volume contains the revelation, presents the philosophy, and teaches the art.

GOD.—"God is Spirit, Omnipotent, Omniscient, Infinite, Eternal, Self-existent, Life, Truth, Love, Being, All-in-All."

Christian Science summarizes its creed in four propositions: "I. God is All in all. II. God is good. God is mind. III. God, Spirit, being all, nothing is matter. IV. Life, God, omnipotent Good, deny death, evil, sin, disease.—Disease, sin, evil, death, deny Good, omnipotent God, Life. These may be read forward or backward, they are self-evident propositions."

God is not a person. Personality implies limitation, there may be many persons in one room, there is but one God, therefore He cannot be a person. If it be true that personality implies limitation, and it be granted that God is unlimited then it follows that He is not a person. He may transcend personality as a person transcends a thing; God cannot be less than man, He may be, and is, more than man. In man personality is limited, if we know all that is to be known of personality by knowing man, then it follows that God is not a person. Christian Science claims to be a revelation, if it is what it claims to be, we must accept its teaching concerning God. Though not a person He wills, loves, plans, and these in our thought are the essence of personality.

When it is said that "Matter is nothing, Nothing is matter," the revelation is given from God's point of view. To man Matter is much, it limits us on every side, to God it has no existence, hence it follows that all belonging to Matter, inhering in Matter is also non-existent. Physical Science is teaching (speculatively) that "Matter is a mode of motion". The atom has never been found outside the mind of man, it is a subject of thought, it lies below the horizon of sense. Christian Science teaches that Matter has no existence outside the human mind; as the human breath turns to white mist on a frosty morning and then disappears, so matter is but the breath of mortal mind, has no reality to God. If that be true then it follows that disease in Matter has no real existence, or existence to God, and what is unreal to God is in its essence unreal, for He is the only Reality.

MAN.—Man is God's Idea, expression, reflection, image, likeness. He is as eternal as God is. So long as God thought Man was, for Man is God's thought. God could not be and not think, His thoughts are as real as He is, as eternal, they are the expression of His essence, the image of His being. A Man standing before a mirror sees his own image, it has no being except as he is, it moves toward or away from him as he moves. If it could mirror his mind it would think his

Exposition of Christian Science 371

thoughts. If the man and the mirror and the light were eternal, and the three were externally related the image would be as eternal. God is eternal Being, Man is His eternal image. God is conscious only of Himself and His Image. He is, He is Light, He is His own mirror, and Man is His eternal reflection. Before Man knew time, before time was, Man reflected God, thought His thoughts, lived His life, had only God-consciousness. He came to self-consciousness, how or why we do not know. The writer of the book of Genesis tells the fact in parable form. Man asserted his own will, separated himself from God in thought and purpose. Lost God-consciousness. Thought of himself as an independent being, became self-centered. From being a planet with God as the centre, he became (in his own thought) a sun and evolved a universe to circle about himself. This dream, so real to him, has no reality to God. God sees only His own image and likeness, man still revolves about God, this man-made universe has no reality to God. He sees only truth, and this human attitude of mind is false, He sees only the real, and man's dream is unreal. Man is like one in a dream, when he awakes in God's likeness he will be satisfied, but he is in God's likeness all the time, only not awake to it, hence he is dissatisfied. He is hewing out broken cisterns but the water of Life still flows under the throne. God sees only the river, to Him the cisterns have no existence. The vagaries of the insane are unreal to the sane, sin is insanity, a mental delusion, real to the man who has sinned but unreal to the sinless God.

Having asserted himself, Man makes a new world to fit his new mental state. The human body is real to Man, but unreal to God. It is a burden and a barrier to and between men. We know only so many of each other's thoughts as each sees fit to express; God knows the thoughts and intents of the heart, if the body were as real to Him as it is to us it would be a veil between Him and the soul of man, but it has no place in God's world. Created light casts shadows when it strikes bodies, the uncreated God-Light casts no shadows, shines through matter directly, because to God there is no matter, "Matter is nothing."

Buildings, books, machines, pictures, all that make what we call civilization, are the expression of human thought. Matter is our alphabet, civilization is our literature. None of these things were before man, none of them will last long after man passes from the stage of action. Men think, and thoughts embodied in matter is civilization, laws, institutions, governments are but human thoughts, they come and go like sea-born clouds. But Matter itself, the alphabet, the language is also a product of human thought. Thought wedded to language makes literature, but thought and language are from the mind of man, language is the product of thought. Civilization is thought wedded to matter, but matter is also the product of human thought. There was no matter before man thought it, there will be no matter when man ceases to think it, it has no reality to God. As matter is real God is unreal, as God becomes real, matter becomes unreal. Christ so mastered matter that at the end it had no reality to him. "He emptied Himself, made Himself of no reputation, took upon Himself the form of a servant," then asserted Himself, and mastered His man-made environment, putting sin to death in the flesh, to teach us the reality of God and the unreality of matter. To God matter is as unreal as it became to Christ when He disappeared from man in earth-born clouds. Christian Science teaches that God is the only reality, Man as God's Idea shares that reality, but matter and all it means to us, is unreal to God, for He is Spirit, and only the Spiritual is the real.

SIN.—Sin is unreal to God. It is a mode of human thought. It is a shadow cast by man when he stands with his back to God. It disappears when he changes his mind, or repents. Sin is not a reality, it is simply a mood of mind, a form of thought, a set of will, it disappears when a man faces God and becomes, consciously, God's Idea again.

SICKNESS.—There is no sickness, to God. Thoughts away

from God are unreal thoughts, unrecognized thoughts, as unreal and unrecognized as Aguinaldo's government, we deal with the men who are opposed to us, but not with the government they assume exists. Sickness is simply a human thought, real to the man who thinks it, expressed in matter of man's making, but to the realm in which God lives it has no existence. When man changes his mind, the expression of the thought changes and the sickness disappears.

DEATH.—"There is no Death, what seems so is transition", sings our Longfellow, the song of the poet is the creed of the Christian Scientist. Death is a form of thought, at most it is "shuffling off this mortal coil" which we made ourselves and are trapped in, it is the rolling away of clouds which have risen from the sea of human thought and letting the light of Life shine undimmed.

SATAN.—Satan has no being outside the human mind, he is the child of fear. Once grant that God is All, only God and His Idea are real, and we can see that Satan, not being a part of God's Idea has no real being. He is the pulse beat of the heart throb of human fear, when the throb stops the pulse beat stills. The triumph of monotheism is at last complete. The diverse deities of the unscientific ages have been forced to abdicate. Last to yield has been the notion of the gods of good and evil contending with doubtful issue for the mastery. The modern theory of the universe, as originating in the self-revelation of God, necessarily removes the premises from which such interpretations spring. As the idea of God as universal being excludes the earlier conception of dualism in mind and matter, so the idea of God as universal spirit excludes the earlier conception of the dualism of God and evil spirits.

The malignant form of an arch-spirit of evil, who has cast his baleful shadow over the human mind from the beginning, and who until quite recently, has been an awful terror, freezing the pulses and paralyzing the will of mankind, is forced to yield his sceptre and betake himself to the congenial regions of chaos and old night. The spirit of God, it is at last seen, has not to strive with a spirit of evil so universal, so powerful, as always to hinder and often to thwart the divine effort for human welfare; but instead has but the slowness of moral growth in humanity, and the wilfulness of souls ignorant of their true good with which to contend. The new conception of God as Himself the universe is a proclamation of emancipation from the powers of Satan; it is a declaration that God is always man's friend, it is also a notice that for his own sinfulness man is himself responsible. The Devil is no more."

Matter is not, Sin is not, Sickness is not, Death is not, Satan is not, to God. God is conscious only of Himself and His Idea Man. Whatever is not to God is not in any real sense.

THE ART.—The art of healing is very simple. Accept the fundamental proposition that God and His Idea are the universe, that only Spirit is real, accepting this you are bound to deny the reality of matter, of sin, sickness, death, Satan. Before your affirmation the denial will flee away. The way to cure disease is not to add to the burden of matter by more drugs, the soul is already overburdened with false belief, but to add to the spiritual force of the soul. Bring your positive affirmations and brush away the negations as the sun destroys the clouds. The soul of the patient sits in spiritual darkness, standing in the outer hall press the button, relate the room to the dynamo through the wires and lamps that are unknown to the sufferer, but are known to you. Darkness is the absence of light, a negative, it is not something, but the lack of something, the Christian Scientist carries light by realizing light. Be positive, affirmative, deny the reality of matter, sin, sickness, death, affirm God, Truth, Life, Spirit.

All revelations before this present revelation have been anthropomorphic. God has been conceived of in human terms, the molten metal of Divine Truth has been run into moulds of human thought, the white radiance of eternity has been stained by the many-coloured glass of human thought; God has come to us through the court room as a Judge, through the palace as a King, through the army as a General, through the family as a Father. Christian Science is Theomorphic, it does not set moulds to fashion Truth, but lets it flow on, a broad deep stream of living fire, it does not imprison the race in a temple of human making, domed with human thought, but leads man out under God's blue dome and bids him lift his face and be God-conquered. It does not lead God to man by the way of the court room, the palace, the army and the family, but leads man to God directly; not in mountain nor temple must God be worshipped and served. "God is Spirit, and they that worship Him, must worship Him in spirit and in truth." Accepting God thus, Christian Science accepts the universe and man as He accepts them. Man is God's Idea, and the visible universe is man's thought. Only so far as Man thinks God does he think reality, all other thoughts are unreal.

> "The baseless fabric of this vision,
> The cloud-capp'd towers, the gorgeous palaces,
> The solemn temples, the great globe itself,
> Yea, all which it inherit, shall dissolve,
> And, like this insubstantial pageant faded,
> Leave not a rack behind."

The key to Christian Science is found in the assertion. "God is all," "God and His Idea, Man." God is conscious only of Himself and His Idea. Man lives as God would have him only when his life is hid with Christ in God, and self-consciousness is lost in God-consciousness.

Christian Science

Christian Science

BY

EDWARD A. KIMBALL, C.S.D.

CHRISTIAN Science is to-day engaging the attention of intelligent people on two hemispheres because it is healing the sick, causing the blind to see, reclaiming drunkards, saving sinners and abolishing innumerable ills that have harassed and prostrated a suffering race.

Again it is because a million people who have been thus benefited are insistently bearing witness thereof to the world and impressing upon men the tangible fact that some supreme influence is working out a transforming deliverance for the people of this generation and meeting nearly every conceivable human need. Lastly it is because the person who, earnestly and in good faith, studies this Science learns that he can gain a demonstrable knowledge thereof, whereby he can prove its verity. He finds that it reveals the real nature of God and man and the Science of Being. For him, it effaces mystery and dispels the illusion that the things of God are supernatural and miraculous. It places him on the solid basis of the Science of Life, on which all right reasoning must rest and wherein logic and exact knowledge govern, instead of theory, superstition and mysticism.

All of this has been made possible because Rev. Mary Baker Eddy wrote the text-book of Christian Science—"Science and Health With Key to the Scriptures"—and has taught others the principle of this science; the rules for demonstrating it and the entire modus operandi of its practical application. This book of 600 pages contains an exhaustive and ample exposition of the entire subject, by the only one fully qualified to do it. It would be a work of supererogation for any other person to undertake to answer fully the question, "What is Christian Science?" Every attempt to do so has exposed flagrant plagiarism or a diluted substitution of faulty statements.

The writer of these few pages needs not to apologize for refraining from any such attempt here. He who most wisely meets the question, "What is Christian Science?" will direct the inquirer to that book. There is no better, easier or safer way in which any one may gain a knowledge of the subject.

This book, "Science and Health," which is rapidly approaching its 200th edition, contains the declaration that it is not a presentation of theory or philosophical speculation on the part of Mrs. Eddy, but that it is definite knowledge, or demonstrable science, and that it comes by way of discovery or revelation. This fact that it is demonstrable science greatly simplifies the progress of the investigator, because he can prove that the principle is absolutely true and he does not need to believe what he cannot understand and verify.

Jesus said, "Ye shall know the Truth and the Truth shall make you free."

All truth is divine and the impartation of Truth to man is called inspiration, revelation, perception, discernment or discovery. It matters not what name be given to this but it is essential to know that it means that some individual man or woman has discovered, or as Paul says, spiritually discerned the Truth which must always reach humanity through some one who, voluntarily or involuntarily, has been undergoing a preparation for such revelation or discovery.

The announcement of Christian Science as the Truth, or God's word to this age, is likewise the announcement that Mrs. Eddy is the one through whom this science has been made known.

The special fitness of this illustrious woman for this service is traced from her childhood, indeed Rev. Dr. Hines said of her, "This child was consecrated before she was born."

Her devout parents were of deep religious culture, and a saintly mother, little knowing the vast destiny of her child, trained its moral tendencies heavenward and nourished her in the atmosphere of piety and uncompromising rectitude. While yet a young girl she became a student of philosophy, moral science, theology and metaphysics. In later years she took a thorough course of study in the Homeopathic school of medical theory and practice. In consequence of her experience as a practitioner and her researches in the realm of mental causation and phenomena, she detected the defects of medical theories and abandoned the entire system as being unscientific, and sought diligently to know the Science of Life which is also the Science of Healing.

Her life has been one of unselfish devotion to the welfare of humanity and marked by numberless instances of benevolence and philanthropy. The income from the enormous sale of her books finds outlet in the way of donations which her secretary says have averaged $88,000 annually for the last four years.

For thirty years Mrs. Eddy has been under the public gaze as Author, Minister, Editor, College President and Leader of the Christian Science denomination, and those who have known her best during all these years testify as to her unselfish love for friend or enemy; the manifest purity of motive and judgment; her consummate honesty and ceaseless endeavour to do God's will.

Entrusted with a message of deepest import to the world, she has been faithful to her trust and to-day nearly a million people attest the results of her ministry in the healing of disease and kindred evils. As the century closes, this pioneer in the age of Christian Science stands conspicuously upon the scene of the moral, intellectual and religious transformation which is prevalent, and is inseparably connected with the Christian Science cause and its progress.

Having taken every advancing footstep, she is by the inevitable logic of events the Leader of a religious denomination whose growth has been more rapid than any other known to history and whose works of healing and deliverance are without a parallel since the time of Christ and primitive Christianity.

As a noble, patriotic woman; as constant friend and benefactress; as wise teacher and leader, she is now the object of the esteem, gratitude and affection of millions. Could the imagination depict a more appropriate state of consciousness through which the Truth, long prayed for, should reach humanity.

An erroneous assumption that Christian Scientists are inclined to " deify " Mrs. Eddy is met by her own statements.

" Whosoever looks to me personally for his health or holiness mistakes. He that by reason of human love or hatred or any other cause clings to my material personality, greatly errs, stops his own progress, and loses the path to health, happiness and heaven. The Scriptures and Christian Science reveal the Way, and personal revelators will take their proper place in history but will not be deified."

" To-day though rejoicing in some progress, she (I) finds herself a willing disciple at the heavenly gate waiting for the Mind of Christ."

Revealed Truth always " turns and overturns." It revolutionizes thought; supplants error; reforms and regenerates.

Christian Science is overturning many of the chaotic and grotesque misconceptions of Deity and is destined to supplant the fatal human philosophy of life which always ultimates in death.

In revealing the Science of Being it shows that the all-inclusive God, which is Omniscience or infinite Mind, includes no evil, but is absolute Good. It shows that the individuality of God as infinite Spirit transcends immeasurably the human concept of Him as being but little higher than a corporeal personality or a God with personal attributes.

Mrs. Eddy in her published works writes:

" As the words *person* and *personal* are commonly and ignorantly employed, they often lead, when applied to Deity, to confused and erroneous conceptions of divinity and its distinction from humanity. If the term *personality,* as applied to God, means *infinite personality,* then God *is* personal Being—in this sense, but not in the lower sense."

" The human person is finite: and therefore I prefer to retain the proper sense of Deity by using the phrase, an " individual God," rather than a " personal God."

The proneness of critics to conclude that this reduces the sense of God to an abstraction is corrected by many statements by her like the following:

" Father is the name for Spirit, God which indicates His tender relationship to His Spiritual creation."

" The Fatherliness of God makes His sovereignty glorious."

" Now this selfsame God is our Helper. He pities us; He has mercy upon us and guides every event of our careers. He is near to them who adore Him.

" The desire which goes forth hungering after righteousness is blessed of our Father and does not return unto us void."

The study and demonstration of this science exalts thought to the discernment of God as Spirit and as being good in every phase of His Being and in every manifestation of it. This realization of God which excludes evil from the divine nature and phenomena reveals conversely the actual nature of evil. Deity is either mindless or Mind. The infinite divine Mind could not include anything that is not divine or divinely true and good, and supremely real and permanent.

Evil is the paraphernalia of what the Bible calls the " carnal mind " and what Mrs. Eddy has designated in a somewhat more ample way as mortal mind, because it includes the range and activity of an evil sense of being, which means sin, disease and death. The Bible says, " To be carnally minded is death, but to be spiritually minded is life and peace." This necessarily means that to be carnally minded is sickness and to be spiritually minded is health. Christian Science confirms this with scientific accuracy and shows that evil instead of being of divine ordination is contrary thereto and is abnormal, unlawful, unrighteous and unnecessary,—an unreal, perverted, misconceived sense of life and truth and of the actual facts of Being.

The philosophy, science and theology of Christian Science are based on the spiritual foundation that Deity, which English speaking people call God, is infinite; that God is the infinity of Truth, Spirit, Mind, Wisdom, Intelligence, Life, Good, Love, Harmony; that the power, action and government of the supreme, divine individuality is good and that the law of God to man is the law of life, holiness and harmony. The entire Christian Science structure is absolutely consistent with this divine premise and all of its ideas converge at the Allness of God.

Christian Science leads its student to an accurate discernment of the fact that the Bible contains the word or law of God to man.

It declares without reserve the Messiahship of the Divine Christ and emphasizes the statement that Christ is the only possible way of salvation for all men and all time.

It shows that Jesus Christ is the perfect representative of perfect God, manifesting by His works or demonstrations the divine nature; the spiritual or natural law and the perfectibility of man when governed by the law of Spirit rather than the law of evil.

As the representative of God, Jesus' works are the best interpreters of His mission. He came, it is said, " to do the will of God;" "to seek and to save that which was lost" and "to destroy the works of the devil." He knew more about God and man; more about law and government, the science of Life and the cause and cure of disease, than all of the people that ever lived. He knew the best possible way in which to heal the sick and in doing so, fulfilled the law.

The science of that healing and the fact that it was scientific instead of supernatural and mysterious is disclosed with much amplification by Mrs. Eddy in " Science and Health."

Some of the conspicuous deductions of Christian Science are

that sin is based upon an utterly erroneous and unreal sense and must be wholly destroyed; that all diseases are curable, and that Christian salvation includes salvation from sickness as well as sin and promises the restoration to man of his lost dominion over evil.

Christian Science unlocks the so-called mystery of evil and shows that sin and disease are primarily of mental rather than physical origin and that the only possible way whereby both may be dominated is through the spiritual power of the divine Mind which was also in Christ. It shows the havoc caused by evil thought, acting through the individual and collectively, and it shows particularly that evil thought externalizes itself in human experience as calamity and disease. As a mental remedy for mental causation it heals all diseases where drugs fail, because it is impossible for mindless matter to cope with an ignorant or sinful condition of consciousness. Hence the terms "metaphysical healing" and "Christian Science healing," which has been more successful than any other remedial agency known to man.

Although reluctant to attempt a fragmentary and incomplete exposition of the technicalities of this science, I can with propriety and gladness presume to speak of the vast benefits which are accruing to mankind because of its discovery and of its demonstrable availability. Having been rescued as it were from the grave by Christian Science after all else had failed me, with a deep sense of gratitude I bear witness in behalf of thousands, once dying but now in health and happiness, and whose praises are encircling the world and revivifying the dead hopes of despairing, dying men.

Christian Science declares God aright and reveals Him as Divine Love. This revelation dispels all gloomy, portentous fear of God or His will and law and presents a Heavenly Father that is always good and doeth well. The Christian Scientist learns to turn to this God as an "ever present help," as "the Healer of all thy diseases," and as being ready, willing and able to save unto the uttermost from all evil.

The light which "Science and Health" sheds on the sacred scriptures makes clear the revealed word and presents the spiritual interpretation of the Bible, which is the true saving sense thereof. Christian Scientists cling steadfastly to this book without fear of criticism, changing creeds or the clamor of the hour.

Christian Science brings to light the real divinity and Messiahship of Christ, so that the disciple no longer gropes amid the mysterious, but knows just why and how Christ is our Saviour, not alone after sin, sickness and death, but *from* these evils. Christian Scientists gladly learn the way of this Saviour, and strive for the life that is in imitation of His purity and goodness.

Christian Science encourages prayer without ceasing, and its followers are learning the prayer that is answered and which heals the sick. It inculcates the highest conceivable morality. It shows that the only possible escape from the penalty for sin is to stop sinning. It cancels temptation and rationally inclines the sinner to the abandonment of evil; not because of fear or threat but because of a new-born and natural affection for goodness and holiness.

It enables mortals to master fear, worry, care, grief and all kindred offspring of the carnal mind or evil sense of life.

It leads its follower to a spiritual height where true Christianity, logic, reason and science coincide. It releases him from the intolerable demand that in order to be saved he must have blind faith in an unknowable God, a mysterious and supernatural Saviour and an impenetrable plan of salvation after death. Jesus said, "Ye shall know the Truth and the Truth shall make you free," and this promise is being practically fulfilled, now.

The infidel or agnostic, who has been amazed and repelled by the myriads of fabulous conceptions of Deity which men have been pleased to say were God, has learned through Christian Science to know God aright, to worship and love Him.

Thousands of drunkards in the bondage of hereditary or

acquired vice have found that Christian Science does two things that neither drugs nor resistance have ever done. It destroys appetite and reinstates lost will and control. No drunkard is ever safe until thus transformed by the renewing of Spirit.

Christian Science has healed thousands of instances of disease that have been pronounced incurable by eminent medical authority. It is making people happier, better and healthier. It enables them to cope more successfully with fear, pain, sickness and all the vicissitudes of life. It adds impulse and energy to all righteous endeavor. It increases the capacity to do business and control circumstances and is of assistance and help in every department and circumstance of life.

The man who is touched by its influence finds himself more devout but less gloomy; more confident and self-reliant but less conceited and vainglorious. He loses the pleasure of sin and finds the satisfaction of right living. He becomes more tolerant, just, upright and pure. He learns the art of loving his neighbour and learns to be merciful and forgiving. He experiences a yearning for a higher and more spiritual life and the Mind of Christ which overcomes sin, heals the sick and establishes the Kingdom of Heaven within.

If the world lived up to the highest teachings of Christian Science, sin and sickness would be abolished and the millenium would be at hand.

Christian Scientists rejoice in the knowledge that they are proving its verity and realizing in a measure the fruition of the promises which have been the hope of ages.

These are some of the fruits, the indisputable facts, which are in manifestation of the boundless good of Christian Science.

I submit to the consideration of every well ordered mind, the proposition that they are like unto the results of Christ's ministry and in keeping with the commandments, the Sermon on the Mount and the highest conceivable ideals of Christian life, the welfare of man and the reign of God on earth.

Christian Science

Christian Science

BY

The Reverend WILLIAM H. P. FAUNCE, D.D.

ALL persons familiar with the intellectual life of our time are conscious of a wave of "new thought" now sweeping over this country. This thought assumes Protean forms, and manifests itself in a mass of literature of all shades, from the sublime to the ridiculous. The movement has a twofold origin. On the one hand, it comes from the German idealism of Hegel and Fichte, which (mediated by Thomas Hill Green) has at last filtered down through all the strata of society and reached the average man. On the other hand, it comes from contact with the religions of the Orient, and a new appreciation of their mystic peace and brooding calm.

A foretaste of this "new thought" appeared in the New England Transcendentalism of fifty years ago; it achieved its brightest literary expression in Emerson, and its passing embodiment in the Brook Farm experiment. But that movement was chiefly confined to New England. The present movement—a reaction from the deistic view of the world which has long pervaded both science and theology—covers the entire country, and is putting forth a quantity of literature of whose extent few are aware. The philosophy underlying the whole is optimistic and idealistic, and often claims and produces large results in bodily healing. Mrs. Eddy is only one—the most successful one—of scores of teachers in this country who are now insisting on the power of thought to change life, and the immanence of God in such a sense that pain and grief and sin can be practically ignored.

*Reprinted by permission of Fleming H. Revell Co; Copyrighted, 1899, Goodman & Dickerson Co.

A CRUDE IDEALISM

Most of these teachers are destitute of philosophical training, and are putting forth crude systems more wonderful than Joseph's coat which was *not* " of many colours." " They have been at a great feast of languages and stolen the scraps." They strongly antagonize each other, and unite only in antagonizing both materialism and scholastic orthodoxy. Oriental importations, the flotsam and jetsam of the Parliament of Religions, wander through the country, unfolding outworn theories of the Orient as the latest fad of the Occident. Indian Swamis enter Boston parlors and instruct companies of adoring women in the science of mist and moonbeams. Some of Mrs. Eddy's pupils, weary of her personal control, have revolted and set up schools of their own. "Metaphysical healing" is largely practiced in the eastern states by those who utterly reject Christian Science. On a much higher intellectual level are the books of Dr. Dresser, Ralph Waldo Trine and Henry Wood, all having an extraordinary sale, all insisting that "there is nothing either good or bad but thinking makes it so," all giving an idealistic and spiritual interpretation of the universe, and all succeeding in lifting from scores of weary souls a burden of care and fear and pain which we have been taught is inalienable from human life. All of these teachers unite in rejecting the eighteenth-century conception of God as an "absentee," or as an "occasional visitor," or as a "magnified Lord Shaftesbury;" and when they are theists in any real sense, affirm that God is immanent in the human soul, and that if we will but "practice His presence" we shall be delivered from all the ills consequent on faith in a distant deity. We may at least rejoice that the tendencies of our time are no longer toward disbelief in a spiritual world. So far has the pendulum swung, that the same popular literature which, thirty years ago, was trying to believe that "thought is a secretion of the brain," now gravely affirms that the brain is a figment of thought!

What, now is the particular phase of this thought embodied

in "Christian Science?" We are concerned now only with its philosophy, which is most certainly a rare collection of shreds and patches. Among the many notions inconsistently united we may distinguish a few dominant thoughts.

1. The idealistic conception of matter. A modern teacher has called Christian Science "an incomplete misconception of Berkeleyanism." But good Bishop Berkeley's faith in Christianity was not hindered in the least by his philosophical explanation of the material universe. In order to combat atheism and materialism, he asserted and believed that the apparently external world exists only in our own idea, and that minds alone have real existence. This is a philosophic view which will always have its advocates, and need not be discussed here. All human beings must *act as if matter did exist,* and the speculative denial has little influence on life. If the Christian Scientist wishes to build a house, he must treat bricks, mortar and timber just as every other man treats them, even though he honestly believes that the bricks are all in his own brain. Only in the treatment of the human body does the idealism have practical consequences. If a man believes that his body is the pure expression and even the creation of mind, he will certainly endeavour to shape and control that body mainly through the maintenance of mental conditions.

2. A monistic conception of God and His world, ever verging into pantheism. The publication of Dr. Strong's "Ethical Monism" was one of the most significant events in the history of Christian thought in this country. It showed how great is the present reaction from a mechanical and external theology, and how even the thinkers who have stood most stoutly for the reality of the soul, of sin, and of redemption, are now passionately demanding some unifying conception of the world-order. Dr. Strong is abundantly able to safeguard his monism; but Mrs. Eddy goes straight over into the camp of those who deny personality to God, and all real freedom and responsibility to man. She explicitly denies that God is personal. Her denial is meant as a protest against anthropo-

morphism; but it goes so far as to make God a metaphysical abstraction or principle.

DENIES DIVINE PERSONALITY

A young man recently came to me who had gone through Christian Science into Atheism. I asked him to describe the path he had passed over. He answered: "The Christian Science teacher began by thoroughly persuading me that God is not personal, but is pure 'Principle.' After some months I accepted that, and then I said to myself: 'What is a principle? Does it have real existence? Is it an entity or reality?' I soon saw that a 'principle' is simply an idea of my own mind, and when the Scientist dissolved my God into 'principle' I ceased to believe in any God whatever. I now believe simply in myself."

Mrs. Eddy answers the question, "What is God?" as follows: "God is divine Principle, supreme incorporeal Being, Mind, Spirit, Soul, Truth, Love." At the head of this confusing list of alleged synonyms she puts Principle, as being the most thoroughly de-personalized term, and hence best suited to her purpose. But let us ask her to define more closely. Does her God possess consciousness, will, purpose? Is He so like to the noblest earthly father that our highest name for him is Heavenly Father, and that we can commune with Him, pray to Him? To all this Mrs. Eddy must answer, No. To her God one must not pray, for that would be to acknowledge Him as personal. While one might in an unwary moment call her God "Father," yet that term is omitted from her definition of God. Her God is "Being," but being need not be conscious of its own existence, or of ours. Her God is Truth; but truth is destitute of volition or affection for man. Her God is Life; but life in moss and tree is unconscious and unintelligent. Her God is Love; but not the love which can answer any request for aid. Her God is Mind, Spirit, Soul, provided that we interpret those words as synonyms of unconscious "principle."

ELASTIC TERMS

Much of the success of Christian Science is due to the fact that its vague phraseology is equally acceptable to the evangelical Christian and to the atheist. The average Christian, approaching the Christian Science creed on one side, hears that God is "Spirit, omnipresent and eternal," and at once accepts the teaching. The atheist, coming up on the other side, hears that the only God is "principle, truth, harmony," and he can accept it without the slightest change of position. I would not charge conscious duplicity upon Christian Science teachers. But I do know that they will say to the simple-minded Christian: "We of course believe in prayer, and we use the Lord's prayer at every service;" while to the antagonist of Christianity they will say: "You know in what sense we believe in prayer—it is by affirming Principle."

When Mrs. Eddy in her reaction from deism joins Theodore Parker in denying personality to God, she makes her capital blunder out of which all other blunders spring. She thinks personality means limitation and corporeality. But Dr. Martineau has well said: "You cannot deny God's personality without sacrificing His infinitude; for there is a mode of action—*the preferential*—the very mode which distinguishes rational beings—from which you exclude Him." Since Mrs. Eddy's deity is incapable of preferring and willing and seeking moral ends and communing with His children, since He is *less than personal,* He is less than the Christian God, the Father of our Lord Jesus Christ.

3. Of course such a faith must issue in optimism. Pain vanishes, since God is incapable of pain, and God is the only reality. Mrs. Eddy is as contemptuous toward pain as was Marcus Aurelius when he wrote: "Do not suppose you are hurt and your complaint ceases. Cease your complaint and you are not hurt." Indeed, her steadfast denial, *i. e.,* her determination to ignore, has close affinity with ancient stoicism. There is nothing new under the sun. The Emersonian oracle has long been telling us that " good is positive, evil only pri-

vative"; Browning has long been crying, "All's right with the world." But what the stoics and the poets have always affirmed as ideally true, Christian Science turns into bald prose propositions, telling us that, by refusing to think of the ills that flesh is heir to, we may destroy their phantasmagorial existence.

Still further goes this optimism. It denies that sin exists, save in our thought of it, *i. e.*, in " mortal mind." It declares that " man is incapable of sin, sickness and death, inasmuch as he derives his essence from God, and possesses not a single original, or underived power." Here again we are misled by alleged synonyms. Certainly man has no " underived " power; but has he no " original " power? Has he no power to originate action, to determine some events, to choose between good and evil? If not, we are landed at once in the pantheism where good and evil coalesce in universal being. The Christian Church has always believed in a God not to be identified with His own creation, a God distinct, though not separate from His children, a God with power

> "To create man, and then leave him
> Able, his own word saith, to grieve him."

Mrs. Eddy denies that man is able to grieve God, both because God is incapable of grief or any other emotion, and because all human sin is apparent only, and in reality does not exist. Such teaching is exceedingly perilous to the moral life. It coincides with the teaching of the English Antinomians of the seventeenth century, who affirmed that " the feelings of conscience, which tell them that sin is theirs, arise from a want of knowing the truth." In view of Christian Science, since man is incapable of sin, conviction of sin is a dream, and redemption from it an impossibility. Christ therefore is the " Way-shower," no longer Himself the Way. When a leading Christian Scientist said to me: " Mrs. Eddy is the way to God," I answered, " I thought Christ was the Way." " But Christ, you know, is dead," she answered, " and Mrs. Eddy is now alive." "But Mrs. Eddy must soon die, and who then will be the way?" "Well, we do not think that Mrs. Eddy will—what you call *die;* we expect she will—dissolve—into—the life of the universe!" Could optimism further go? Yet men call this age—the age of Keely and Mrs. Eddy—a materialistic age!

TWO TRUTHS AFFIRMED

Let me now mention briefly some of the strong and the weak elements in this strange Christian Science creed.

It is strong in its clear realization of the immanence of God. God is not only "in His heaven," but God is in His world. The average Christian Church is still shy of the doctrine of the Holy Spirit, leaving that to Northfield and Keswick, and believes only in a far-away Deity who occasionally has interfered with His world to work a miracle. The average Christian Church believes in an inspiration which ceased about 100 A. D., and miracles which ceased about 300 A. D., and in an interpretation of the Bible which makes it the story of what was but no longer is. Christian Science affirms that God is as near His world to-day as in any age, and performing all the wonders now that He ever performed. In this it agrees with the Roman Catholic Church, and is a standing reproach to Protestant unbelief.

Christian Science has undoubtedly gotten hold of a great truth in its affirmance that the best way to heal the body is through the mind. The principle which underlies all these various forms of healing, "metaphysical," "mental," "faith," or "Christian Science" healing, is the same, as Dr. Buckley has clearly shown, or Mr. Hudson in his "Law of Psychic Phenomena." If we believe that the mind is more than the body, and that all our minds are in contact with the infinite Mind, why should we not, when afflicted with bodily disorder, go first, not to the druggist, but to some friend of strong mental and spiritual powers? If we believe in prayer, why should we not pray to that Spirit in which we "live and move and have our being"? Medicine has long treated the mind through the body; now let it show as much zeal in treating the body through the mind. It is for this reason that Prof. James, of Harvard University, has recently defended the Christian Scientists against the enaction of an oppressive law by the Massachusetts Legislature—not because he can accept their bizarre philosophy, but because he believes that the power of the mental over the physical life is greater than any accredited philosophy has been willing to admit, and that the possession of a medical diploma does not entitle any man to a monopoly of healing.

The weakness and danger of Christian Science are to be found, especially, in the following points:

1. In a quite unwarranted use of the Bible. Mrs. Eddy professes greatest attachment to the scriptures, and her followers are constant readers of the Bible. Yet she selects only certain portions of the Bible, and commends those portions only when interpreted allegorically and arbitrarily. Thus, in commenting on Gen. 2:7, she mildly queries: "Is it the truth? or is it a lie, concerning man and God? It must be the latter, for God presently curses the ground." Mr. Ingersoll, in elucidating the "Mistakes of Moses," never condescended to such language. But not content with the charge of falsehood, she proceeds to a little exegesis of her own. In order to prove that "Adam" is merely a name for the "matter" which opposes "mind," she suggests to her obedient followers a short and easy method with the skeptics: "Divide the name Adam into two syllables, and it reads, *a dam* or obstruction." And the book which contains this sample of exegesis is supposed to be addressed to sane men and women!

The Bible flames from beginning to end with a passion for righteousness, and an indignation against iniquity. To say that man is "incapable of sin" is to stultify the noble army of martyrs, to discredit all the prophets and apostles, and to make the life and death of Christ farcical. Men may believe that sin is temporary, that at last God shall be all in all, and still follow the Christ. But to say that man is "incapable of sin" is to rob man of real freedom and responsibility, and make Christ only a "Way-shower" instead of the Way.

2. Another danger lies in a dissolving of God into a misty, unconscious abstraction. In her attempt to get rid of anthropomorphism Mrs. Eddy denies personality. But John Fiske has truly said: "We are bound to conceive of the Eternal Reality in terms of the only reality that we know, or else refrain from conceiving it under any form whatever." To ascribe human weakness and limitation to God, is indeed an error and a folly. But all the objects we know are either persons or things. Which is Mrs. Eddy's God? Does she believe in the thingness of God, or the *personality* of God? The answer of her books is clear—she believes in the *thingness* of God, in a Substance like that of Spinoza, incapable of purpose, choice, or consciousness, a Being whose shadowy self is best described as "Principle."

MONEY IS NOT DESPISED

3. A danger in this movement, which perhaps has not yet developed, is the confusing of moral distinctions through the denial of the reality of evil. I gladly bear witness to the personal nobility and high-mindedness of many Christian Scientists. I rejoice to find beauty in lives whose creed I cannot accept. Yet the Scientists are often sorely put to it to explain how Mrs. Eddy could charge each pupil $300 for twelve lessons, or what she does with the vast revenues which constantly come into her hands. The usual explanation is that any sum is small in comparison with the benefits received, and that "all that a man hath will he give for his life." In absolute religious despotism, combined with the belief that one is "incapable of sin," however we may explain the words, danger always lurks. The latest step in this line, and perhaps the most surprising, is the publication in the Christian Science Weekly for January 19 of the following card concerning "Christian Science Souvenir Spoons": "On each of these most beautiful spoons is a motto in bas-relief, that every person on earth

needs to hold in thought. Mother requests that Christian Scientists shall not ask to be informed what this motto is, but each Scientist shall purchase at least one spoon, and those who can afford it, one dozen spoons, that their families may read this motto at every meal, and their guests be made partakers of its simple truth. (Signed.) Mary Baker Eddy." Probably one outside the mystic circle should not " ask to be informed " as to the price of these precious spoons; nor as to the object of the sale; nor as to the proceeds of the sale, if every Scientist of the 300,000 claimed in this country were to purchase one or one dozen; nor as to the results if " every person on earth " should seek after this talismanic motto; nor whether the " Christian Science Souvenir Company " is identical with the " Church of Christ, Scientist." But even one outside the circle may think, and marvel, and wonder if all the followers of the " Mother " will approve. " Beloved, believe not every spirit, but try the spirits whether they are of God."

The Church and Ethical Leadership

The Church and Ethical Leadership

BY

The Reverend WILLIAM E. BARTON, D.D.

THE Church exists for ethical ends. However much the purpose of the Church may transcend what superficially is called "mere morality," its reason for being is in the ethical nature of God. Its purpose, therefore, in doctrine, in ritual, in preaching, is ethical, and must be judged by its ethical bearing. The twentieth century will not easily tolerate a Church which forgets or neglects these ethical ends.

There is no danger more real or insidious than that the Church may come to consider as an end what are in fact but some of the means to this end. The history of Israel abounds in illustrations, and the writings of the prophets are largely made up of protests against the constant tendency of organization to a conservatism which regards its own machinery as more sacred than that for which the machinery exists. The history of the Christian Church has illustrations also of the danger which tempts the Church to believe either that ritual on the one hand or dogma on the other is the real end of the Church. To-day as ever the real answer to the question, "Wherewith shall I come before Jehovah?" is the declaration that the sum of God's requirement is that man shall do justly and love mercy and walk humbly with their God. To this end is the Church established, and to this ultimate test must all her effort be brought.

Now, in so far as the Church has failed in ethical leadership it has been through failure to keep this end constantly in view as the real end; the ethical end has been an end often with something that to the unenlightened mind seemed superimposed. The Church has thought at times that, important as it has always considered righteousness, it was rather an incidental than an end of religion; that righteousness is salvation is a proposition which must be explained to be accepted even now by many Christians.

It is not my purpose to dwell upon, nor even to specify, the failures of this kind. Let him who will, read them in Old Testament history and in the records ancient and modern of the Christian Church. Suffice it to say, the failures, when there have been failures, have been of this sort. Rather than dwell upon these failures, let me suggest the other, the better, the truer aspect of the truth.

How much the world owes for its ethical ideal and purpose to the leadership of Israel. We have been discovering many things in the ruins of ancient cities; we have not found many decalogues. We know more than we once did about comparative religion, and we have found that the Jews held this rite which we have thought distinctive in common with the Egyptians, and that doctrine which we have supposed their monopoly with the Assyrians, and that in perception of yonder truth the ancient Persians were their superiors; but we have not found any ethical ideal which dispossesses this ancient nation from its title to leadership. Buddha's five commandments are as good, and I doubt not as truly from God, as the corresponding five of Moses' ten;—but it is not Buddha but Moses who has led the world's most enlightened nations in their legislation, in their conception of duty to God, and their ideal of honesty and virtue and holiness among men. Their hard legalism had its limitations, their narrow bigotry wrought monumental folly,—for there is no bigotry like the bigotry of enlightenment,—but their stern monotheism linked to its pure worship a pure family and social life, and their high thought of God co-ordinated with it a high thought of human duty. That " the law was given by Moses " is no disgrace either to Moses or to the law, but an everlasting honour to the great personality that stamped contemporary and subsequent legislation with his immortal name, and to the law which, with all its imperfections, is the world's schoolmaster to bring it to Christ and the ethics of His religion.

When we come to early Christianity there is yet more to be said. Nor need we care to say more than has been said by Gibbon of the purity of the life of the early Christians in an impure age as one of the five causes of the spread of Christianity. Nor can this century afford to forget its obligations to those ages when Christianity was getting its depth and its ideal. There is much to be read with sorrow. There are ages of dreary controversy over *homoousian* and *filioque* and other matters when the battle waxed hot in proportion to the destiny of human ignorance, and the assurance of the contestants was in inverse ratio with the clearness of Divine revelation; but still there was the preservation and transmission, and even the clarification of an ethical idea.

Even in what we call the dark ages the Church did not wholly lose its leadership in ethics. Even when the Church was elaborating its ritual till the soul of piety died out of it, and emphasizing the value of its sacraments till grace became mechanical and artificial, it did not wholly lose its thought of the preeminence of duty and of personal piety. Side by side with the movement which made the church great as a visible organization and throned it in Rome with power and splendour, grew the other movement which sought God in the desert and the cave, and there, with splendid inconsistency, was shown the grace of the Church. For, when her pontiffs and councils were saying that men must be saved by her sacraments, she was also canonizing the names and honouring the lives of men who cut themselves off from the sacraments, and preserved and manifested the ethical ideal in isolated but holy lives. That the system was abnormal, that monasticism had its ethical dangers, we may and do readily admit; yet we ought to remember that the Church honoured and favoured its ethical ideal and advanced its leadership in the very age when personal piety and quiet of soul with God seemed lost in the world movements of a vast politico-religious organization.

If we examine the results which the Church has accomplished in the world as proof of its ethical leadership we shall find, what Dr. Storrs so ably set forth in his lectures on "The Divine Origin of Christianity Indicated by its Historical Effects." The Church has set forth, as is nowhere else exhibited, the basis of ethics, and a new conception of duty, of worship, of the moral worth of man and of the being and relation of God. It has given us a new ideal of childhood; it has brought a new glory to womanhood; it has ameliorated the conditions of slavery and prepared for emancipation; it has reduced the occasions for war, and introduced some element of mercy even into that barbarity, and has given to the world a hope, which as yet is only a hope, but a hope that will not confess itself a vain one, of universal peace. It has inspired in men a belief in the moral value of being that has created a hope which is one of the most potent of all influences for good; and which may be measured either against the hopelessness of the world before the Church had gained a footing, or the hopelessness of non-Christian lands and faiths, or the hopelessness of un-Christianized Christendom. In all this, which exhibits leadership of the first order, the Church has won its record for nineteen centuries of progress and of hope.

It is now intently inquiring how its activities and philanthropies may not simply relieve poverty, but hasten its removal; and how by encouraging right relations between man and man it may aid in bringing in a better social order. If it does this with even partial success it deserves glad recognition and encouragement.

But we should remember that the Church is the real leader in not a few ethical movements which in popular thought exist outside its organization. The Church has been blamed by zealous opponents of the anti-slavery cause because it did not always denounce slavery with their own unsparing severity; but the Church was the real leader in the anti-slavery crusade. Even the zealous abolitionists who called themselves "come-outers" got from within the Church the love of men for Christ's sake which made their own protest effective, and their less intense, but no less efficient brethren within the organized Church formed the real body that brought slavery to its end. Yet, had it not been so, and if men had been compelled to go outside the organized Church to realize the ethical ideal which they received within it, it would still deserve to be remembered that the Church is much more inclusive than the sum of the Churches.

At the present day there are reformers whose name is legion, and they bombard the study door of every pastor asking permission to "present the cause" of this or that on next Sunday, or to take a collection for some more or less worthy philanthropy. If the pastor could make room for them all, he would seldom need to appear in his own pulpit. To the multitude of good and earnest men whose real or imaginary call is to one of these special reforms, and to the greater throng of visionary enthusiasts, the Church often seems cold and heedless of great and important interests; and no one claims for it perfection. But these same causes, so far as they are sane and hopeful and truly benevolent, have their hope in the Church. The social reformer, the political temperance orator, and the man who prays daily for the restoration of the lost tribes of Israel may find the Church too little moved by their appeals. But without the support of the Church the efforts of true reformers are hopeless. Indeed the Church is often overworked by its too zealous members in the interests of their special causes.

Again the leadership of the Church must not be forgotten in those agencies which, while independently organized and controlled are yet integral parts of the active life of the Church. The Young Men's Christian Association, the Salvation Army, and all like causes, cannot be lost to the Church by any mere form of organization. The spirit of Church life is in their wheels, even though the method of operation is foreign to the accustomed method of the organized Church. It is the spirit, and not the form; the soul, and not the accident of organization that makes and identifies the Church.

Still again, the leadership of the Church must be recognized in agencies over which the Church no longer exercises organic control, but which it founded and established, and whose genius and spirit it created. Popular education in America is of this sort, and is a mighty example of the leadership of the Church. A single denomination founded the five historic New England colleges, and that and other religious bodies have given and are giving princely sums for the support of these and other schools. Now, the leadership of the Church is by no means limited to those organizations which it directly controls. It is felt in the entire school system which has grown up around and out of these institutions. The same is true of hospitals, reformatories and asylums. Many of these under private or State control owe not only their existence, but much of what is best in their conduct, to the Church and its spirit in the life of the community.

Even when the individual who gives his life to these causes exhibits least contact with the Church as an organization, he is not outside its spiritual pale. The man who gives his days and nights to the scalpel and the microscope, working sometimes in peril of his life that he may discover a deadly germ and its antitoxin, may not count himself a Christian. He may live in some respects a very un-Christian life—more's the pity! But still I thank God that even such a man may become inspired with the love of men and their good which is the spirit of Christ, imperfectly transmuted through the Church. Even if he himself is purely mercenary—which I greatly doubt—he is straining himself to reach the ethical ideal of the best men in his profession and the community; and the presence of that ethical ideal bears witness that the Church has not lost its leadership even here. Nor must the Church forget that this man who has so strained his sight looking into the microscope that he can no longer see God or providence, but only physical causes and effects, is still using the unatrophied part of his soul—his alert mind and his professional skill and sympathy—for ends which are one with those of the Church.

The ethical leadership of the Church is thus of the broadest possible sort. It may be that a political campaign will turn now and then upon the activity of the Church as an organization, effected through resolutions and caucuses; but the larger leadership will be in exalting the ethical ideal in politics until that ideal takes shape in the entire community within and without the Church. The Church may provide, and often ought to provide, wholesome entertainment and amusement, but a larger proof of its leadership will be found in the type of amusement which is patronized by the body of those whom its influence reaches. The Church may in special exigencies provide wood-yards and working men's restaurants for the relief of the poor, but a better and larger proof of its leadership will be the infusing of the spirit of Christ into the business world, so that wood-yards and restaurants shall be maintained in righteousness and at fair profit. Then the wood-yard man and the restaurant man and each of the rest will be, not a salaried official of the Church and subject to suspicion if he conducts his business at a profit, or to imposture if he conducts it as a charity, but a Christian man of affairs, testing every theory by its workability. In the long run men must get a living while they theorize; and the Church will do its best ethical leading by showing men how they can at once be Christian men and live in a world and amid social conditions still far from the ideal for which they strive.

It is the mission of the Church to transform society, or as we sometimes say, to prepare the world for the coming of Christ. That coming will be the advent and triumph of his spirit in all social relations. This is the essential thing in its leadership. It is not to establish beneath its own roof every sort of commercial and social activity; it is to inspire the community with an ideal which shall realize itself in the world of commerce, of politics, of amusement, of literature, of art.

If the Church does not always realize fully its opportunity; if it fails adequately to interpret the meaning of its transitions, —it does not yet become reprobate. Yet enlargement comes through another place,—God raises from the stones children unto Abraham—and the thing for which the Church has come to the Kingdom is delayed, or is poorly done, or if well done is done by another agency which for the time more truly interprets the spirit of the Christ. And if the goal is far off, and the progress toward it in the Church is slow, still the Kingdom is coming, and he that believeth shall not make haste. The holy city, whose pattern and ideal is coming down out of heaven, is being builded slowly but stably in brick and stone and human institutions, and the tabernacle of God is with men in the Church. Thus shall be " gathered together in one all things in Christ, both which are in heaven and which are in earth."

The Place of the Church in Modern Civilization

The Place of the Church in Modern Civilization

BY

The Reverend C. R. HENDERSON, D.D.

THE student of society, asked to estimate the value of the Church as he would that of any other institution, may be affected by the bias of friendship or of indifference or of hate. The present writer must confess at once his partiality for the Church. Those who feel it their duty to hold a brief for the opposition must do their work, and the more freely and openly they show their cards the sooner will the answer come. But affection has some advantages over hostility and indifference in an attempt to give an exposition of an institution. Only one who has a deep care for religion will devote adequate time to the consideration of its phenomena. The hand is more skilful which is guided by love and obeys its behests. Revelation of spiritual values comes in through the eyes of sympathy. The *odium anti-theologicum,* as Mr. Spencer has said, is as evil in its way as partisan sectarianism. Religion must be studied from the inside. It is not worth while to pass the Louvre or Uffizi gallery after a long and costly voyage and return home without entering the halls where hang the masterpieces of the painters. The pictures are on the inside, and those who merely pass along the street know not their glory and beauty. Only the lovers of music know the value of music. " Amateurs " are they called; and to loving admirers the artists owe their power to exist and work and create.

Only the pure in heart see God. He that is willing to do God's will has entered the path which leads to knowledge. No one can criticize Christianity except the Christian. All other criticism is external, superficial, dealing with accidents and not with essences.

The material resources and cost of the Church can be approximately set down in terms of money. The financial exhibit is impressive and compels attention, even of enemies. An institution which can show in the United States 165,177 organizations, 111,036 ministers, and 20,612,806 communicants and members, cannot be ignored by the worldly statistician, although he may be inclined to regard the data as very imperfect and not always honourable to the intelligence and honesty of the members and leaders. An institution which can open 142,521 houses of public assembly, with a seating capacity of 43,564,-863 is, indeed, a light set upon a hill. Religion is not near becoming obsolete when it can command the use of property worth $679,630,139, the result of the gifts of belief and love, unconstrained by the legal power of the tax gatherers. Similar statistics might be gathered from a wider area; these serve the purpose of illustration.

Dr. Thomas Chalmers believed, early in his life and early in this century, that the Church must be supported by the State because religion, unlike commercial products, is not wanted and must, therefore, be upheld by the strong arm of law. Before he died he had grand occasion to revise his fallacious argument, and he may be supposed to rejoice in the success of the voluntary principle in the United States, where it has been tried without the hampering bonds of tradition and custom. The figures cited are not beyond criticism, and our information betrays much weakness and defect in consecration; but even as they stand we have in them a revelation of a stupendous social phenomenon for which we must, as social students, give an account and which deserves our study.

The characteristic and essential contribution of the Church to civilization is its religious ministration. Many of the marks which were once supposed to distinguish man from other animals have been found not to be characteristic; but certainly religion is peculiar to humanity as it is practically universal. That which marks man as man is the peculiar province of the

Church. It honours man by offering a form of satisfaction which pays homage to his highest nature and powers.

To the sincere believer religion is a good beyond question. It is a state of his consciousness; it is to his soul bread and light and air. He cannot state his valuation in money terms, any more than he can fix a price upon the love of his wife and children. Love is not for sale; it is not quoted in the market lists. But no goods whose prices are quoted on 'change would be good if love were not.

> "The light of a bright life dies,
> When love is done."

The estimate which sincere believers actually set upon this highest good is obscured by a thousand conflicting elements. Millions of the poor find in the hopes and encouragements of their faith a joy and satisfaction to which their narrow and meagre means give scant possibilities of expression. Only the Lord, sitting over against the sacred treasury, and omniscient, could discover to the ages the secret of the devotion symbolized by the two mites which the poor widow cast in, while the purse-proud looked contempt. Heaven has a refined calculus for the registration of the recording angel.

On the other hand we may express a charitable judgment of the inadequate contributions of some rich Christians. Surely they value religion at a higher rate than some of their money gifts would suggest. Then we cannot estimate the religious satisfactions of rich men by the amount of their contributions to the Church, because all that one does in Christ's name, for charity, for education, for patriotism, for the community, may be an evidence of the gratitude and devotion of a follower of Christ. The preacher is sometimes tempted to gauge the religious consecration of wealthy laymen by the amounts contributed to salaries of clergy, Church edifices, missions and other ecclesiastical causes. This ecclesiastical and professional bias needs correction; it blinds us to important evidence of the real appreciation which rich men may feel for religion.

The man of classical culture, rather ignorant of economics, is tempted to join the unthinking and envious throng who damn the rich for being successful and refuse to believe that one may sometimes do the greatest good, and do it out of genuine purpose, by investing in and directing productive enterprise rather than by bestowing alms. One may show his faith in a far purer and more useful way by directing wealth than by surrendering it to less efficient hands. A rich man finds it difficult to make others believe that he is in business with any such purpose. Usually he does not claim to be dominated by philanthropy and religion. But this consecration of capital as well as of alms and gifts is possible, ought to be universal, and will become more and more the rule as we insist on it and show our appreciation of it. It we could get at the real heart of a genuine rich Christian, in his somewhat isolated position, we might often find more of the spirit of the good widow than is generally thought possible. Jesus said it was impossible for men, but not impossible with God, to make even a rich man show his love of God by his personal use of wealth.

It is open to the sceptic to sneer at this claim; easy for cynicism to find hypocrisy everywhere. It is open to the agnostic to question the subjective estimate of the personal valuations of religion. The caviller may admit that we are honest but mistaken; that religion, as a sweet delusion, is to the dreamer all that he thinks it to be,—while he dreams. To him, the illuminated and disillusioned, the Church offers nothing but visions; nothing but unfounded promises. He declares that we are trying to cheat him out of the pleasures of this world by offering to buy them all up with checks on the bank of heaven, checks signed and endorsed by the spectral hands, payable at an unknown date in an unknown world.

A superficial answer to this cavil would be that our delusions and visions are very pleasant to us, that we cherish them as real, and that we do not thank any rude person who interrupts our dreams. We might, in a moment of weakness, claim rights for our reveries which break the hard routine of drudging life with enjoyments of the imagination. But a rational Christian will refuse to be content in this lazy attitude of repose. He will not put the pangs of doubt to rest with logical opiates and sleep out the years of self-deception. A comfortable lie is no solace to the man who would choose to perish forever rather than devote one year to a charming falsehood.

If religion is false the Church has no social use. It is a thief and a robber. There are without it institutions of justice, of money-making, road-building, arts and science, recreation and amusement. Even charitable relief might be provided by the State. The sole final justification for a Church is that it gives men religion and that religion is true. Therefore we owe it to ourselves and society to prove religion to be based on reality. If we cannot do that we should withdraw our finance committees and turn over our buildings and funds to valuable human uses.

The books on apologetics, with their array of evidences, external and internal, have their reason for being. They are the answer of the intellect of the Church to the demand for evidence. We ask for money-service, time, energy; we must justify this claim as a reasonable service. It is vital that this issue shall not be hidden by pious exclamation. If the Church rests its claim primarily on its educational, economic or other secular contributions to civilization it has lowered its flag and confessed its cause to be lost.

The evidences of Christianity are not all in the books of the apologists. They must be in life before men can recite their history. The lives of Christians are the living epistles which all men read and understand. One must already care a good deal for religion before he can be induced to read an ordinary book on the evidences, in these busy and crowded days.

Here the human services of the Church are significant. We dare not urge, for example, that our philanthropies and our schools establish the claim of the Church to support. It is not because we make real estate bring higher prices in a locality that we ask speculators to assist in the support of ministers. We do not ask help for foreign missions because they will enlarge markets for our mills and diffuse respect for our flag. And yet all such services are evidences of Christianity; they reveal the essence of the divine life; they symbolize the love of God and the spirit of goodness. Good in themselves, they convince the doubter that they are signs of a spring of deeper good. The cup of water given in the name of Christ is soon drunk dry, and the recipient is as thirsty as before. But when the cup touched his parched lips and the name of Christ was spoken as an explanation of the motive in the act, the soul of the thirsty man made an eternal acquaintance, and found its own way to a well of living water, eternal life. This is the true mode of making the argument for religion by works done in His name.

The Church is, indeed, a powerful economic factor and contributor to wealth. It enriches men. The economists discuss the production and the distribution of wealth. Under the head of production they assume the presence of wants and desires which urge men to industry. The queer animal once called " the economic man ", all self and that self stomach, does not exist. The real economic man works to satisfy all his wants. If he is a miserable primitive man, just above the gorilla, he may be satisfied with the gratification of two or three bodily appetites, and when these are glutted he quits labour. Industry under these conditions has a short-hour day. But the civilized man, heir of classical and Christian culture, has a multitude of wants, and he is impelled to work early and late, all the year through, with far-seeing providence, with vast schemes and systems, in order to gain the means of satisfying these endless cravings. Religion, acting through the Church, awakens the highest wants, stirs intellect and heart, asks beauty for temple and home, creates a market for architects and painters and poets and musicians, excites men to industry by appeals to every capacity of his nature. Hence the influence of the Church on production of wealth.

Christianity profoundly influences the distribution of wealth, and again, by this indirect route, promotes production. The doctrine and feeling of brotherhood and equality have gradually uprooted slavery and even made all society feel that what the ruler and the rich really need for completeness is also the right of the peasant and mechanic. The common man is exalted by the fundamental doctrines of Christianity. He is made to feel that he has a rightful place, and not as a suppliant, at the banquet of life. The product of industry is the product of a coöperating community. It belongs to all. Before trades unions were so powerful as they are now, and before the wage workers could make their voice heard through universal suffrage, Shaftesbury and Macaulay appealed to these religious doctrines, and asked for a fairer apportionment of worldly goods, and shorter strain of wasting and exhausting toil, and not altogether in vain.

The ancient slave received nothing but his subsistence and his all belonged to the master. The wage worker is not yet at the end of his demands, but he already has a larger share of the product and owns himself and his increasing leisure. And as he can buy more he can spend more. His larger purchases open new factories, mines and stores. Having more education he has multiplied desires. Being in the vast majority he furnishes the widest market. Productive energies are set free and the world grows richer. Deep down in the whole process is the awakened and erect common man, with his finer nature, his willingness and ability to work steadily in prospect of varied and elevated satisfactions. The Church has a share in this process and its results.

In this entire system of industry order is assumed to be essential. There is no liberty of movement, no security of life, property and investment, unless the respect for social order is deep in the common conscience. Laws are things of straw unless they represent the convictions of the people. Where brigands infest the roads, or debauched legislatures seek, with shortened vision, to cheat their creditors, there capital is timid and the founders of industry are paralyzed. Texas and other Western regions owe to the pioneer missionaries a debt beyond calculation. The border ruffian was not only cowed but converted by the brave preachers of righteousness.

Among soldiers, sailors, politicians and merchants we are hearing more than formerly of our national duty to the weaker races. We are told that we must rouse ourselves, break the barriers of nationality, and make our civilization known beyond seas. Cynicism mocks at this crusade of culture carried on with pike and gun; foreigners sneer at the pretension which seems to them to cover the mean old vice of greed. Granting that the unworthy forces are not quite extinct and that commercial earth-hunger may account for some of the new interest in cosmopolitan civilization, it remains true that there is an element of good intention in the talk. But the idea itself is not novel, except to those who have refused to listen to the pleas for foreign missions. This whole vocabulary of world-conquest has been familiar in the Church during all this century. There it is natural and absolutely above suspicion of sinister purpose. There it is certainly pure self-sacrifice. There is room for discussion and even honest difference of judgment in relation to conquest of weaker races by force of arms; there is no room for doubt or hesitation about the value and duty of Christian education and evangelization. This is the doctrine of the Great Commission. Commercial, military and political extension must at best be limited in area; but for Christian culture the field is the world.

The educational function of the Church fills a chapter in the history of civilization. Jesus was the Teacher; His followers are disciples; His Church is a school. The very genius of Christianity is educational. The light which illumines every man arouses the intellect. In all ages the clergy have been custodians of culture, and from their ranks the modern profession of teaching has been evolved by specialization and differentiation. The hood and the gown are memorials of the monastic origin of academic dress, and they remind the world of the debt which culture owes to the Church. This stream of religious culture has enriched the field of secular education, over-flowing the banks of ecclesiastical control. The public school has generally abolished Bible reading, but it cannot without suicide expel the Word as it is incarnated in good teachers. The literature of the public library, charged with the finest expressions of Christian thought and ideal, is bringing back in poem and declamation, the sublime expressions of the faith. If a window is left open for air and light the music of social religion floats inward and steals its way to the heart. Christianity cannot be excluded from the public schools.

Volumes have been written to illustrate these varied and important ministries of Christianity to culture and amelioration of the lot of man on earth. The eloquent pages of Storrs, Brace, Dennis, and the rich treasures of the literature of missions might furnish illustrations that would give convincing power to the suggestion of argument here indicated. Every decade of missions and of Christian education adds substantial and material evidences of the fruitfulness of the Christian agencies of promoting welfare. The force is not near to exhaustion but promises perennial supplies; the spring draws its pure waters from mountain heights and ocean depths.

But we must return a moment to the beginning of our statement; the best gift of the Church to civilization is not economic and cultural blessing; and the best gift of Christ is not the Church and the institutions which it creates or uses for social betterment in the lower sense. Thanks unto God for His ineffable gift,—Himself. The bouquet of flowers sent to the room of the invalid by a thoughtful friend is worth far more than the florist was paid; the petals will wither and decay; but the friend is immortal and his friendship remains forever, a joy and a solace.

The Adjustment of the Church of the Future to the Life of the Future

The Adjustment of the Church of the Future to the Life of the Future

BY

CHARLES F. THWING, D.D , LL.D.

THE Church is Christianity incarnate. Christianity is humanity living in, and for, and by Christ. Christianity is truth, but truth means a mind to understand. Christianity is duty, but duty means a doer. Christianity is doctrine, but doctrine implies a will to believe. The Church is a religious, an ecclesiastical person. The Church is therefore to adjust itself to truth, to duty, to doctrine. The Church is to adjust itself to life. The Church is to adjust itself to the future. The question, therefore, is: The Adjustment of the Church of the Future to the Life of the Future.

The Church of the future will adjust itself to the material conditions of the future. The present age is a material age. The future age is also to be material. The material character arises in part from the newness of the country. The woodsman's axe precedes the sculptor's chisel. Often we lament that the time is so material. We regret that absorption in things is so deep. We should not regret: we should not lament. The Church should find its mightiest triumphs in such a time. For to the Church, as it stands for Christ and for Christianity, a material age turns. A material age is restless; Christianity stands for peace. A material age is full of disappointment; Christianity stands for hope and fulfilment. A material age recognizes the brevity of its own duration, the lowness of its own ideals, its powerlessness to satisfy the dearest wishes of the human heart. Christianity stands for the infinite and the permanent satisfaction of life. Lament that the Church is flung into a material time? Nay, rejoice! As from the crude products of petroleum are made the brilliant dyes, rivaling the colours of the rainbow, as from dark caves is plucked the sunshine of the diamond, so from the hard materialism of our time is to come forth a Christianity more vigorous, more spiritual, more triumphant.

To this fact of materialism is the Church to adjust itself. The Church is to give up no one of its doctrines. She will still hold the faith once, once for all, delivered to the saints. She will not surrender one of her wise methods. But this materialism may cause her to hold her truths in different relations. The perspective of truth will change. The materialism of our time demands that the Church be a working Church, that Christianity be a very practical Christianity. The age demands what the Church can do. The Church will write not new creeds, but will inaugurate new methods. The Church will add not new intellectual forces, but rather will add a new force to all old forces. The Church will develop not the prayer-meeting, but the city mission. It will offer, not mysticism, but intense practicalism. Its hero is not Madame Guyon, but Clara Barton and Florence Nightingale. Its symbol is less the golden cross flying on the spire of a building than the simple red cross glowing over the heart. This working Church has small patience with feelings as tests of Christian character. It abominates cant phrases. It asks, "What are you doing in Christ's name?" It fastens its eyes more on the words, "He went about doing good," than on the words, "He opened His mouth and taught them." It fixes its eye on the Christ going about doing good rather than on the Christ standing resplendent upon the Mount of Transfiguration. The Church adjusting itself to the future age will be intensely, mightily practical.

We shall get a new conception of the Christ, of Christianity, and of the Church, through such an endeavour. The Church has been developed more on its philosophical, doctrinal side, than on its practical. Our creeds are a good deal better than our practice. We are now to see a development on the side of life. The Church coming to a material age and giving it of its life will receive a clearer thought of the Christ, more real, more vital, more personal.

The Church of the future is also to adjust itself to the intellectual conditions of the future. These intellectual conditions represent, for our present purpose, a demand that the Church shall emphasize the reason of and for things. The Church must stand ready to answer that little, that infinite question, " Why? " The Church is most happy to do its best to answer that question. The Church must address herself more and more to the reason of men. It no longer bases its claim for the receiving of its beliefs upon its own *ipse dixit*. It demands that the ground of faith be examined. It asks that truth be tested, and that whatever part is proven false be flung aside. It believes that the Bible is the Book of God, but it is eager for the reasons of the belief to be declared. It believes the doctrine of the creed, but it asks that each soul be able to say " credo " for reasons convincing to itself. For, Christianity is according to reason. Christianity is not anti-reasonable; it is not opposed to the fundamental principles of thought. Christianity is super-reasonable; it is in certain respects above reason; it is divine. Christianity is also sub-reasonable; it goes below the ordinary principles of the human mind; it is divine.

The Church, in addressing the reason, is not to make undue demands. It is to respect the conditions for receiving evidence, and the conditions of evidence itself. It is to recognize that the evidence, Biblical and rational, for certain truths is stronger than the evidence for some other truths. The evidence for the being of a God is stronger than the evidence for the being of a triune God. The evidence for the person of the Christ on the earth in some human form is stronger than the evidence for the presence of the Christ on the earth having a double nature. The evidence for the double nature of Christ is stronger than the evidence for any theory of future punishment. Such gradations of evidence the Church has not always recognized. Such gradations of evidence the Church does not now recognize as it should, but the Church of the future, with a discrimination keener, a philosophy profounder, and a loyalty to the Bible no less loyal, will recognize these conditions and these limitations.

The Church of the future and the intellectual conditions of the future meet in their closest relationship in the pulpit. The pulpit of the future Church must be a great pulpit. Its message is to be addressed to the reason as well as to the heart, to the conscience as well as to the will. This pulpit will be broad without being superficial; deep without being narrow; high without losing itself in clouds of philosophic dreaming. Its truths will be more intuitions than inductions or deductions. It will be Biblical, for it will be true; it will be rational, for it will be addressed to rational beings. It will be eloquent with all the warmth which a love of God and a love to man inspire, but its eloquence will be touched by the dry light of truth rather than moved by the heat of passion. It will be great in its themes. Its themes will be the themes which underlie and fill every great utterance, whether made in history, or song, or story,—love, self-sacrifice, virtue, bravery, duty, holiness, faith, peace. It will be a pulpit as diverse in the forms of its utterance as the character and conditions which it addresses, and it will adjust itself to the special conditions and in every utterance and through every message will be heard the one fundamental note of a supreme love to God and of love to the brotherhood of man. It will be great in its aims. Its aims will be none other than the highest to make men highest. It will be great in its conceptions. Its conception of man will be that man is of infinite value. No increasing power of the book, no increasing prevalence of the newspaper, is to narrow the place of the pulpit. No decline of eloquence in the senate or at the bar shall promote the decline of its persuasive, living speech. It is still to be the place in which man is to testify to the glory of the service of God, to the obligation of human duty. It shall paint the wickedness and the wretchedness of sin, the beauty of holiness, and with tongues of fire call upon men to live for God and to die in the grace of His Son. So long as life is life, so long as truth is truth, so long will life and truth in the pulpit give truth and life to men.

The adjustment of the Church of the future to the intellectual conditions of the future will promote a union between ethics and Christian doctrine. The history of the divorce of ethics and of Christian teaching is a sad chapter in the history of both ethics and Christianity. The science of ethics the philosopher has developed, but he has too often developed it without reference to the relations divine and eternal. Christianity has been developed into creeds and formal statements, but these creeds and statements have too often been formed with reference to the other world, not to this. Christianity has been saying, " Thou shalt love the Lord thy God with all thy heart, and with all thy mind, and with all thy soul, and with all thy strength," but it has sometimes forgotten to add, " and thy neighbour as thyself." Ethics has declared, " Thou shalt love thy neighbour as thyself," but it too often has forgotten to command supreme love to the Supreme. The Church is to be a Church of this world and also a Church of the other world. It is to be a Church of the present and of eternity. It is to be Christlike in its comprehensiveness. The Church is to make ethics Christian. The Church is to make Christianity ethical. The Church is to tell men that righteousness is but " rights " writ large, that graciousness of man to man is but grace humanized, and that faithfulness is the eldest daughter and sometimes the beautiful mother of faith. Let men be taught by the Church that the man who is most in the world is the most Christian, and that the man who has most of the spirit of Christ will be most in the world. Let men learn that the steps on the stairway of the right slope upward in both night and light to the throne of God. Let men know that the Incarnation makes the simple right Christian. Let it never again be possible for a thinker, aiming at truth, to say, as said one of the great thinkers of the century; " If to hell I must go for doing right, then to hell I will go." No. The man who is doing the right is the man whom Christ takes to his own great heart of love, to His own great conscience of supreme devotion to the right. Thus the Church of the future may minister to the intellectual conditions of the future by making ethics Christian.

The Church of the future is to adjust itself to the social conditions of the future. This is the most important of all these adjustments. We are living and we are to live in a time when the foundations of human society are to be tested. Socially, is the family to remain the social unit? Industrially, are capital and labour to remain as armed neutrals? Economically, is competition to remain the method of trade? Is the present condition of human society sound? Nature represents the rule of the strongest. The fittest survive. The unfittest and unfit die. Does the phrase, "To him that hath shall be given, and he shall have abundance, but from him that hath not shall be taken away even that which he hath," represent what is and what ought not to be, or what is and what ought to be? Is modern society founded on the basis of the Sermon on the Mount? Are the meek inheriting the earth? The American people are going through a transformation from a small, widely scattered agricultural people of similar aims, methods, and conditions, to a great people, crowded into towns, having diverse employments, having aims, methods, and conditions very unlike. It is no wonder that we hear the cry of poverty, the cry of suffering childhood, the cry of wronged innocence. The "song of the shirt" has ceased to be a song and has become a cry, a moan wrung from the heart. The labourer feels that he becomes labour simply and his manhood becomes less than his work; his soul goes into a spade. The hoe owns the man rather than the man the hoe. The capitalist knows that he must buy labour and every other commodity in the cheapest market and sell his product in the highest. All this represents the fields of the modern Church. The Church has converted the individual. Can it convert society? The Church has caused private trusts to be well administered. Can it cause public trusts also to be well administered? The Church has helped poor men. Can it remove poverty and the causes of poverty? The Church has been conservative. Can it become aggressive? The Church has been led. Can it become a leader? The Church has been and is a great social force. Can it become a great sociological force? The members of the first Church at Jerusalem had "all things common." Communism there failed. Can the modern Church be fitted to some form of socialism and not fail? The Church has been at some times inclined to hold itself aloof from life. So far as the Church has been remote from life, so far has it been powerless. The Church must keep itself in touch with life. Whatever interests man cannot be foreign to the Church. The Church may or may not approve of many socialistic movements. The Church may or may not approve many movements to improve society through the statute-book. But the Church must know these movements. The Church must be ready to pluck the one sweet drop of truth and beauty from the thorny-rose-bush of public debate. Emotional extravagances, intellectual eccentricities, sensationalism, emotionalism, should not prevent the Church from knowing that humanity is more or less expressive in its feelings, more or less eccentric in its thoughts, more or less fond of receiving and of giving sensations. The Church should take humanity as it is and make humanity what it should become. An age which sees the Salvation Army going on its triumphant march round the world should not fail to impress the Church with the duty of knowing and of using every movement of the age for the impression of human kind and for the improving of human kind by any agency, which may impress or improve.

> "New occasions teach new duties;
> Time makes ancient good uncouth;
> They must upward still and onward,
> Who would keep abreast of Truth."

I do not forget that this adjustment of the Church to the material, the intellectual, and the social conditions of the future may oblige the Church to alter somewhat its own constitution. Indeed, the Church already shows its capacity for this adjusting of itself to those to whom it is to minister. For no less than three types of the Church are now emerging. One, the Church of the family. It is placed in the midst of homes. One also, which may be called the institutional Church, placed in the midst of a neighbourhood composed partly of families and largely of single men and women who are in a certain way homeless. One also, the Evangelistic Church, placed in the midst of great tides of population. Each of these Churches has its means and methods. The family Church consults the fitness of good taste. Its services are orderly and decorous; its methods are stable and conservative. The institutional Church employs many agencies in carrying on its work, teaching trades and arts, seeking to amuse as well as to convert. It is a genuine "fisher of men," using books of all kinds and baits of all sorts in this holy angling. The evangelistic Church is content to preach the gospel and to minister to individual men. Each of these types is to be found in every well equipped city. Each of these types has its special work and for each of them a large opportunity is waiting. The Church of the future is to be one of these three types or a combination of these three types according as its special constitution can best serve its constituency.

This adjustment will give to the Church a new sense of life. Coming into life, life will come into the Church. That Church which is remote from life is a Church dying. Its temples may be splendid, its services ornate, its wealth great, its past stored with stories of prophets and martyrs, its palaces hung with the glories of the Old Masters, but remote from present life that Church is dead, thrice dead. But the Church which has a message for men, for men here and now, a message of hope, for the despairing, a message of guidance for the lost, a message of inspiration for the careless, a message of love for the indifferent,—such a Church, as humanity seems to come into it, goes forth to humanity. Let us never forget that the Christ who came to humanity came into humanity. "He became man."

It is also to be said that this adjustment of the Church to the varying conditions will give to us great denominations; it will give us great and noble divisions of the Christian forces. It will give to us denominationalism without sectarianism. For life is infinitely diverse and the Church should minister to the infinite diversity. The monarchical system of Roman Catholicism, the oligarchical system of the Episcopacy, the republican system of Presbyterianism, the democratic system of Congregationalism, will each find a devout acceptance. The system of doctrine which begins with the severity of God will find a hearty reception in minds inclined to the monarchical system of ecclesiastical rule. The system which begins with the authority of the human will, will find acceptance with those who are inclined to emphasize the republican or democratic method. The system which is the more systematic and orderly and logical will appeal the more strongly to minds of a certain type, and a system which is not systematic but a series of actions, which is content to bind Christ's two commandments upon its brow, will seem to minds of another type more acceptable. A philosophy of the Holy Spirit will be to some helpful and to some harmful. A service composed of prayers which the lips of saints have said, a service inlaid with psalms and hymns which martyrs have sung, rich in historical associations, suggestive of the glories of a noble past, will be to some more pleasing; but a service which is simple, direct, plain, will have to others the richest value. The appeal of the Church to life will give diversity in unity, and also, it may be added, unity in diversity.

I fear that I may have given the impression that the Church is in peril of breaking into fragments through this bending of itself to the needs of men. Someone may ask, " Is the fable of Osiris to be repeated; are the Christian forces again to be scattered?" Let me at once say; The Church is one. Christianity is complete and whole. The Church is one, but the Church is great in power and large in relationships. Truth is complete and comprehensive; but because it is so comprehensive it will minister to diversity of condition and to variety of need. The

Christ is unchanging, and the unchanging Christ is to be preached to changing man under constantly changing conditions. The substance of the gospel lasts, but methods change and means vary as conditions are altered. This universe of ours so far as we know it, is subject to constant change. No two tides ever sweep up the beach in the same orderly ripple, no two spring-times dawn in the same form, after winter's long night, no two summer-tides blush toward the autumn in the same tints of beauty; but the great earth itself still swings to and fro, jarless and noiseless. The great sun is still found in his appointed place at the proper hour, and the whole universe moving through infinite space keeps harmony with itself. So Jesus Christ is the same, "the same yesterday, to-day, and forever." So the Christianity of Christ is the same yesterday, to-day, and forever. So the Church, founded by the Christ, and by Christianity, is the same yesterday, to-day and forever.

The Sabbatic Principle in Modern Society

The Sabbatic Principle in Modern Society

BY

The Reverend ALBERT E. WAFFLE, D.D.

EVERY age has its peculiar characteristics. It is not always easy to define and describe them, for human nature is always the same, and every age is, in some respects, like every other. And in other respects it is often only a difference of degrees. For example, there has never been a civilized country in which love of money, greed for gain, was not a prominent characteristic; but it has not been the predominating spirit in every country in every age. In Sparta the love of military glory was a stronger passion; among the Puritans religious zeal overmastered it. There is always a probability of making a mistake in stating the characteristics of an age. The ignorance of the analyzer—his inability to know about his own age as compared with others—and his personal bias will have their effect upon his judgment. But in spite of these difficulties, there will be a general agreement about the leading characteristics of this age.

It is an age of *intense activity*. In the development of natural resources and in the multitude and magnitude of the enterprises on foot man has never before displayed such mighty and restless energy. In manufactures, in mining, in agriculture, in commerce, in building, in teaching and studying, in purveying to the love of pleasure, and in other pursuits we are as busy as bees and ants on a summer day. This is especially the characteristic of European and American life. We live at fever heat. We are a nation of "hustlers," and the ability to "hustle" is the talent most admired. The rush and roar and clatter of city life is appalling, when one stops long enough to contemplate it. Quickness in manufacture and speed in transportation are the first considerations. Even our pleasures must be done with intensity or they are not worth while. We have little respect for dignity, repose and quiet thoughtfulness, but reserve all our admiration for the energy and activity which bring things to pass.

It is an age of *practical materialism*. It would be absurd in the face of patent facts to assert that our age ignores the moral and spiritual. Never before was better effort made for world-wide evangelization; never was money more freely and lavishly given for the support of Churches and schools; never did states give so much attention to the education of the people; never were so many books and periodicals printed and read. Nevertheless, it remains true that devotion to material good is the most prominent characteristic of our age. The prodigious energy which the age puts forth is incited to activity mainly by the hope of material gains. Our boast is of our inventions, our vast wealth and resources, our cities, farms, machinery, factories, railroads and ships, and our luxuries and comforts more than of fine characters and of noble productions in literature and art. There is a general demand that education shall be " practical ",—that is, that it shall fit men and women to earn more money,—and study of the natural sciences and of engineering crowds out the studies that make for character and culture. The money-power is largely dominant in our Churches and Christian missions commend themselves to many minds mainly on the ground that they promote discovery and trade. Men contribute to build houses of worship because their presence will enhance the value of real-estate. Everywhere, on the streets, in hotel lobbies, on railway cars, the conversation among men is about business and the different ways of making money. In our own country for many years political stump-orators have appealed only to the pockets of the people, and have asked for votes on the ground that their party in power would improve the financial conditions, and the voters have not been insulted by the assumption that they have no moral sensibility and no convictions. Ask if a man is " good " and the answer relates wholly to his financial standing. The ideal of success and prosperity is that we shall have money for our comforts, luxuries, pleasures and pride.

It is an age of *religious doubt.* Dr. Van Dyke publishes a book of lectures on *The Gospel for an Age of Doubt.* That characterization of the present age is certainly not unfair. Since human history began no age has been so marked by unbelief in the supernatural. That statement relates in no way to the acceptance or rejection of Christianity, but solely to faith or unbelief in some power above nature and in a life beyond the grave. The progress of scientific knowledge dispels superstition; the old gods depart from the stage of human thought; but natural science does not, as yet, foster faith in God and in the spiritual life. The materialism of the age is both a sign and a cause of the decay of faith. People who believe strongly in God will not become absorbed in the pursuit of material advantages. On the other hand people who devote themselves to that pursuit are almost certain to forget the existence and the moral government of God. The boastful scientific spirit of our age produces its natural fruit in agnosticism. The more men pride themselves on knowing the present world, the more willing they are to confess that they know nothing of the world to come. Of course, if anything could be known they would know it, but nothing can be known. The tendency of practical materialism, of devotion to material good, is to crowd out of mind and heart all thoughts of God and of the spiritual life. Of the vast majority of the people in the present age, it may be truly said that " God is not in all their thoughts." They have ignored Him and His claims, and He has left them to their idols. It is inevitable that such habits of life should be productive of religious doubt.

It is an age of *lawlessness.* This statement will not apply to every country; it has a special application to our own. Neither is it meant that there is among us a general disregard of civil law, and that we are given over to anarchy and disorder. The reference is to respect for divine law and those phases of conduct which grow out of it.

The causes of this lawlessness are not difficult to discover. A prominent characteristic of our age is the tendency to exaggerate individualism. We have carried this so far that the average man has come to feel that he is a law unto himself. Ours is an age in which the individual has a great conceit of himself. He has little reverence for God, little respect for rightful authority, and little regard for the rights of others. Practical materialism and religious doubt have also helped to make ours an age of lawlessness.

This spirit manifests itself in the common disregard of parental authority on which every one comments but for which no one seems able to suggest a remedy; in the evident tendency to substitute sentiment and personal preference for obedience to Divine law; in the impatience of all restraint in the Churches; and in the general feeling that one should be allowed to live out his own nature, following his own impulses and passions.

In such an age as this one would not expect to find much regard for the Sabbath. The spirit of an age affects all of its institutions, and unless one be illogical enough to argue that what works against a thing will promote it, he would look for a decline of Sabbath-observance in this age. The restless activity of the age is against it. Men claim that they have not time for it; that it is too much to expect that for one-seventh of the time they will abstain from the absorbing pursuit of money-making. The practical materialism of the age is against it. The proper observance of the Sabbath pre-supposes some interest in spiritual things. It demands a pause from secular activities in order that attention may be given to the interests of the soul. It implies that after six days have been devoted to the interests of the present life one shall be taken to consider the future life. To men of a secular spirit this will seem like a waste of time,—like devoting a day to the cultivation of dreams and the pursuit of shadows. Religious doubt is against it. The Sabbath roots itself in the idea that there is a God who has been immanent and regnant in the affairs of men. In its relation to the past, it is a memorial of supernatural events; in its relation to the future, it points to a supernatural life. Men of doubt may want it for a holiday, but they will see no significance in it as a holy day. Lawlessness is against it. The observance of the Sabbath rests upon a Divine command. It involves restraints. It bids men pause in the pursuit of money. It bars them from indulgence in sensuous or worldly pleasures. It constrains them to bring their minds and hearts to the consideration of religious truths. It insists upon the performance of duties which are not pleasant to the natural heart. Against such restraints a lawless age revolts.

And yet, this is just the kind of an age that most needs the Sabbath. The perversity of human nature is such that men always despise and reject their greatest blessings, the things of which they stand in the greatest need. They stoned the prophets and crucified the Saviour. Man has always needed the Sabbath. It makes provision for some of the deepest needs of his nature. "The Sabbath was made for man." Its establishment by Divine authority was a benevolent act. It is among the good gifts which God has bestowed in such abundance upon the race. It was not intended to be a restriction or a burden, but a blessing. That "the Sabbath was made for man" does not imply that he is to take one day in seven and use it according to his own pleasure. If he receives the gift at all, he must receive it as God gives it. If the institution is to be a blessing to him he must suffer himself to be blessed. Man's need is not met in a Sabbath which he adjusts to his own desires or observes according to his own opinions of what is best. The same Lord who made the Sabbath made man, and the two are fitted to each other. The reception of the gift implies submission to the authority of him who bestows it.

I have said that man has always needed the Sabbath; but in this age he specially needs it—needs it more than ever before. The very characteristics of the age which incline him to neglect or misuse it, but increase his need of observing it with the greater strictness. He needs the Sabbath for rest. The strain, and fret, and worry, and competition of modern life make it especially imperative that one day in seven we should be free from all secular activities and worldly burdens. The rush and fever of present day activities will soon destroy us unless we preserve the regular rest-day. It has been proved by experience that among an active and industrious people the weekly rest is essential to the preservation of health and to the greatest accomplishment. Man does better work, lives longer and has better health working six days in seven than when he works every day. The need is intensified as the activities of life become more intense.

In an age of practical materialism, man needs the Sabbath to remind him of God and of spiritual realities. The original purpose of the Sabath was to remind man that there is a God who created the heavens and the earth and rules over them. To the Jews it was also a memorial of their deliverance from Egypt by the power of Jehovah. Among Christians it especially commemorates redemption as consummated in the resurrection of Christ. But in any case it is a reminder of God. When those who revere Him pause in their work and Church-bells ring, and the people gather in their houses of worship, the world is reminded, as it could be in no other way, of the Creator and Redeemer. The Sabbath thus stands as a bulwark against the strong and ruinous tendency of a materialistic age to forget God. It is certainly a ruinous tendency. " The wicked shall be turned into hell, and the nations that forget God."

Man needs the Sabbath for religious culture. If he forgets God, he will also forget the interests of his own spiritual nature. So far as the present age is not materialistic, it is intellectual. Reverence decays, religious fervor is despised, the Bible is studied as literature, preaching must be intellectual or it will not attract hearers; meanwhile spirituality shrinks and shrivels. Faith, power of vision, spiritual insight, communion with God, recognized answers to prayers, conscious peace, the joy of the Lord are unheeded by the mass of professing Christians, to say nothing of the world, or are thought of as the vagaries of wild fanatics or mystical enthusiasts. The Sabbath rightly observed, used as a day of worship and religious meditation and prayer, will be a means of cultivating man's religious nature. Thus observed it will be an antidote to doubt and the promoter of faith.

Man needs the Sabbath as a cure for lawlessness. One day in seven he needs to be reminded that he has obligations and duties as well as rights and privileges. Remember, says the law, that the Sabbath is to be kept by " not doing thine own ways, nor finding thine own pleasure, nor speaking thine own words." Such restraints are certainly good for men in an age of self-conceit, arrogance, and headlong disregard of any law higher than one's own inclinations.

It may be objected that in basing the claims of the Sabbath upon man's needs it is placed upon a low foundation. But this was the method followed by our Lord when he said " The Sabbath was made for man; not man for the Sabbath." Moreover, it is the claim most likely to be heeded. If men can be convinced that strict observance of the Sabbath is for their own good, they will regard it.

It is argued that in our day man needs a modified Sabbath. There is a certain amount of truth in the contention. Undoubtedly the Christian Sabbath is, in important respects, different from the Jewish. Contingencies arise out of the methods of modern life in which it may be difficult or quite impossible to observe the Sabbath as our forefathers did, or even according to an ideal standard. But plainly it is not for man to modify the Sabbath to suit his own desires or conveniences. That is the tendency of our times even with those who have some regard for the Sabbath. It is a dangerous tendency. It is our business rather to adjust ourselves to the law of God. There may be questions of interpretation and application which cannot be settled off-hand. But those who have teachable and obedient spirits need not experience serious difficulty in learning the mind of Christ. He has claims which must be respected. If we disregard them, the result will be our own undoing.

The obvious conclusion of this brief discussion is that there is in our times an imperative demand for strict Sabbath observance. Christian people should give special heed to its requirements. Instead of relaxing their observance of it in deference to the spirit of the times, they should be more than usually careful. The Sabbath was never in such danger; the Sabbath was never so much needed. Who shall rescue it from the danger, who shall conserve and foster this institution so fraught with blessings to humanity, if not the people of God?

Revivals in the Light of the Present Day

Revivals in the Light of the Present Day

BY

The Reverend GEORGE A. HILTON

THROUGH over-wrought imagination, and defective conception, the actual meaning of a Revival has almost disappeared. "The thought of foolishness is sin," and sin means death to right thought as it does to all else it touches. The wages of sin is death "—death to all righteousness, including righteous thought. The subject of revivals is in no sense exempt from foolish thought. A man supposedly drowned is frequently resuscitated if heroic remedies are applied early enough. Thus a man, insensible to and apparently dead in sin, if brought within the reviving range of God's power, through the preaching of the word and the quickening influence of the Spirit's presence, is awakened from the sleep of death; the deadly opiate of sin finds its antidote—" old things are passed away " and " all things are become new ".

As there is joy in the home when the new babe is born, so there is joy, not only upon earth, but " among the angels of heaven ", when a soul is born. Sometimes joy is excessive, and exciting, and if there is anything on earth that ought to produce excitement, it is the bringing to life of a dead soul. In many minds the great exhilaration accompanying some conversions is mistaken for the conversion itself, and hence a revival season has by many thoughtless ones been regarded as a time of fanatical excitement and emotional excess—and consequently shunned.

The history of the Church is a history of revival. From the beginning the wandering mind of sin has been drawn by revival from its spiritual paralysis to the Church and the objects for which it was established. The history of revival seasons has been too ably and exhaustively recounted to need any repetition here. All along the line stands the monumental work of revival, and blessing through revival. The work of David, Jehoshaphat, Hezekiah, Joshua, Ezra, The Disciples, Luther, Bunyan, Owen, Baxter, Wycliffe, and later Wesley, Edwards, Whitefield, Porteus, Fuller, Hill, Finney and so on until this day. The "Hand Book of Revivals", by Henry C. Fish, D.D., deals thoroughly with the periods of revivals.

The very nature and environment of man demand seasons of revival. The human nature constantly seeks for that which will supply human needs and desires. The human nature craves that which will give physical comfort, pleasure, peace. They are sought for through channels of human organization and perpetuation. The pressing necessities of temporal life, must be supplied. The absorbing business of life is to sustain life in its physical nature. The mind is active, and frequently over-active, in the great study of how to live. The daily life becomes for the masses a tread-mill grind for existence, and its thoughts are in but one direction. The natural man seeks first the needs and joys of temporal life, not the "kingdom of God". "That the just shall live by faith", has no practical value to the world. That "Godliness is profitable unto all things", including business and pleasure, is an unlearned lesson.

Man cannot see faith, and as faith has no apparent commercial value, he gives no consideration to the things that "shall not pass away". Humanly speaking, "Business is business". No business means no bread. The schools of this day have not taught that "man shall not live by bread alone". This is a day of concentration, concentration of activity, worldly thought, business, sin, capital, selfishness, and covetousness: but not of righteousness. It is a day of startling events, in war, in discovery, invention, in everything that appeals to the mind simply human. Few things old or ordinary arrest the attention. Something more than ordinary is necessary to head off the on-rushing tide of humanity, and bring it up to the dead-line of thought, regarding spiritual matters and the things of eternity. Concentration of prayer, burden for lost souls, unselfishness, sacrificing effort, real love for our neighbor, intensified Christ-life, more love for the upbuilding of the Heavenly Kingdom, rather than denominations, will result in genuine revival. The genuine is never mistaken for the artificial, even by the world. It is this genuine revival that the oppressed of humanity is suffering for to-day.

Referring to a revival in a Canadian town six years ago, where in three weeks, over six hundred souls were brought to a saving knowledge of Christ, a *secular* paper of the town says,—

"The union of the ministers and churches excited a moral force of great magnitude on the public conscience. If in nothing else, *the moral value of this movement as an object lesson, teaching the exceeding worth of co-operation in Christian work by all the churches, is beyond computation. There is no doubt that many have been savingly impressed in the recent movement who could not have been influenced but by the spectacle of earnest men of all churches uniting as if one family* in the effort."

Just so long as the potent agencies of evil multiply as they do in this day, to the promotion of sin in the evil heart; so long as the enticing allurements of the world continue to enfeeble the Church: just so long will revivals be necessary: and never in the history of the Church, so necessary as in this opening of a new century.

One of the agencies operating against the successful ingathering of souls is the adherence to set methods for reaching those interested,—methods used because once used with success. Any reasonable method for reaching the souls of men is justifiable; for nothing weighs with God as does the soul of man, and it is unwise for the soul-winner to be tied down to any set form, simply because one is used to it. The Spirit-led worker must be free from conventional ways and means, that the Holy Spirit, and not habit, may lead. It is a sad but indisputable fact, that the Church has not kept pace with the world in progressive ways and means, to accomplish its great work; and God has therefore set His seal to agencies without the organized Church to seek and to find the lost. Notably does this apply to the Salvation Army, and Gospel Missions. It is singular that the Church has been so long in recognizing that something is wrong with present Church methods for winning souls.

The Methodist Episcopal Church, a denomination, possessing in the past, the revival spirit to greater extent than any other, is at last awakening to the fact, as set forth in the following utterance of the committee appointed by the Board of Bishops:—" To-day our Methodism confronts a serious situation. Our statistics for the last year show a decrease in the number of our members. Year before last our advance was checked. Last year our advance-column has been forced back a little. The lost ground is paved with the dead. We are surrounded by powerful enemies. The attack is on every side. It is high time for every Methodist to take himself or herself to prayer, to call mightily on God for help."

It is also true beyond question, that more effort has been put forth in the building of Church edifices, than in building up souls for God's Kingdom. Costly edifices have been multiplied, monuments of stone and brick, frequently only pride-stimulators, while the greater work of securing through an equal effort, monuments of God's grace, has been neglected. The Comptroller of New York City, an honored member of the M. E. Church, has sounded a true note,—" If the Churches are to be successful in raising the twentieth century offering, to my mind they must convince the people that the money will be used to the best possible effect. I believe the great masses of the people in our great cities are away from the Churches simply because the Churches are away from them. It is a waste of money to build a two-hundred-thousand-dollar Church and then use it only once or twice a week. These immense auditoriums that we now own should be thrown open for educational as well as religious teaching. There should be libraries connected with every Church, and certain educational work should be started."

This is a bugle blast in the right direction. Above all other educational work to be done by the Church is Bible education. The ignorance that exists regarding the Word of God by those occupying Church pews is shameful and sinful. The soul is starved and the Church weakens and dies. "Study to show thyself approved unto God, a workman that needeth not to be ashamed". There is much that the Christian Church should be ashamed of to-day, and it comes through lack of study. Yet it is sad that not more shame is felt at conditions so brought about. Much study is given to the most approved methods of promoting worldly interests, and we are justly proud of our educational systems for promoting mental and physical growth. But what a lack of spiritual education. Should not every Church be a Bible Institute in itself? The candidate for Church membership publicly vows to "renounce the world, the flesh and the Devil",—would it not be well to impose a vow upon candidates to "search the scriptures" in home and Church? Consecration is not only to set apart from sin—but to set apart unto God.

May we not learn another lesson from that same Comptroller who says,—"A man who tries to handle a primary, first gets acquainted with everybody in his district. He knows everybody, their relations, their business, their habits and all about them. So it seems to me that Churches should follow that line. Churches do not do this, because they do not seem to have the same personal interest as do the politicians. Some of our people do not use the same amount of persuasion to get people into the Church that the politicians do to get them into politics."

If the Church really believe that "Godliness is profitable", let it be proven that it is "unto all things", and that it has "promise of the life that now is", as well as of "that which is to come". The whole secret of favorable conditions and results in revivals as related to the Church, is found in the method of Jesus, " He took him by the hand and lifted him up and *he arose.*" It is sometimes a matter of wondering comment why there are not more converts in the season of special evangelistic work to-day; but the reason is to be found in the fact that the Church is not equipped for the work of harvesting souls. A minister of celebrity in a large western city recently said in a ministerial gathering—" I should not know what to do if a season of revival came to my Church."

Is it not true, as has been stated, that the student for the ministry has not, in his seminary course been practically taught that " he that winneth souls is wise "?—and that this most important of all teaching for successful ministry, is left to be supplied by the chances of after life? If a pastor be not practically furnished with the whole armour, surely it cannot be expected of the people. The most difficult work of an evangelist in this day is to convince a Church membership that it has any part in seeking out the lost, and bringing the unsaved within sound of a saving gospel. The revival most needed to-day is in the Church and among its members; and the part of the Church in revival work in the coming years must depend upon the courage manifested in the breaking away from the traditions of men, and dealing with existing apathy and worldliness in the true spirit of righteous desire. " When a man's ways please the Lord, he maketh even his enemies to be at peace with him."

Common decency is shocked not only at the open and barefaced disregard of civil law, but far more at the studied effort to bring God's law into disrepute. Not much improvement can be looked for among the evil and immoral classes so long as learned professors in colleges and learned ecclesiastics in pulpits publicly hurl ridicule at the Word of God. If supposed ambassadors of Christ pronounce God's Word, *not* God's Word, but simply human tradition, what regard for godly things can be looked for from the unchurched masses?

The world is a keen sighted critic and sums up pretty accurately, "By their fruits ye shall know them", and the religion that shows itself once in the week is not practical for a lost world. The non-Christian laughs at spasmodic piety,—forced rest from dissipation for a season,—repentance as guaged by what one eats for forty days, and turns loose with the world, the flesh and the devil three hundred and twenty-five days,— when "good form", not "good Lord" reign supreme. It is a problem what part revivals will have in the future of the Church. From existing indications the outlook is not encouraging.

If a business man received so little compensatory result for his capital and effort as the Church by its present methods receives, through its vast means and available appliances, he would consider his business a failure and seek compromise with his creditors. No more beggarly interest is paid to-day than that paid to the Lord by the Church, when its vast resources of opportunity, privilege and means are considered. If the world were to be converted to Christ by present Churchly methods, human conception could not number the years it would take. Comparatively, how few Christians there are capable of sitting down beside a neighbor, and with God's Word in hand, piercing through the sinful thought and desire of "the heart that regardeth iniquity". Indeed there are not over-many ministers can do it. They are not educated to it. It is not in general a part of the seminary course. The Word of God must be used to build up Christians as well as to stir out of the sleep of death, the sinner. The Word of God is still "sharper than a two edged sword", if it be used, and the Holy Spirit is the agent in the use of that mighty weapon. But the Holy Spirit in person, presence and power, is minimized. Ear—eye—man—stomach—worship, is the order of the day, and the Spirit is grieved.

"Let no man deceive you, by any means, for that day shall not come, except there come a falling away first, and that man of sin be revealed, the son of perdition; who opposeth and exalteth himself above all that is called God, or that is worshipped; so that he as God sitteth in the temple of God, showing Himself that He is God." There is great speculation as to the possibilities of the coming century; not excepting the part that revivals shall have in the future of the Church. Possibly it will be but a little part. There may be no coming century by human measurements, for seeing the hopelessness of life and methods in present conditions, the coming Lord may come to the rescue and do what this age cannot do. " Therefore let us not sleep as do others, but let us watch and be sober."

Revivals in the Light of the Present Day

Revivals in the Light of the Present Day

BY

The Reverend SAMUEL McCHORD CROTHERS, D.D.

THE term "revival of religion" is often used in a narrow and technical sense. As a matter of fact, all forms of religion are subject to fluctuations of feeling. A period of coldness and indifference is followed by a new access of spiritual energy. Respectable formalism gives way to a fresh enthusiasm; old words take on new meaning, and there is a great awakening. Chrysostom, St. Francis of Assisi, Savonarola, Jonathan Edwards and Theodore Parker were revivalists. Widely as they may have differed from one another in theology, they were alike in their power to startle those who had been content with the conventionalities of religion. They were enemies to spiritual mediocrity. The profession of religion was not enough for them; they insisted upon a real personal experience. Under the influence of their preaching, old truths appeared in new relations, and were seen to involve a new way of life.

Such men have always introduced innovations; they have been open to the charge of sensationalism. When they preached, they expected something to happen,—and something did happen. The pious routine was broken up, and those who had indulged an easy faith were sent forth to strenuous service. The result of such presentations of the power of religion has always been a conflict with worldliness. What sympathy could the fervent follower of Wycliffe expect from the merry friar, when:

"Ful swetely herde he confession, and pleasant was his absolution."

When, therefore, I am asked to write in criticism of the revivals of religion in our modern evangelical Churches, I must disclaim any objection to revivals, as such. I should as soon object to the spring-time.

The last half century has shown in many respects a marked improvement in the character of religious revivals. The appeal to fear has very largely been given up; we no longer hear of those physical contortions which were in the early part of the century mistaken for the movings of the spirit; and above all we must acknowledge the increased emphasis upon conduct and character. Upon certain obvious moral conditions, the influence of an evangelical revival is good. The emphasis is laid upon temperance and the virtues of domestic life. The convert is likely to be awakened to his duty to his family and to his neighborhood, as well as to his Church.

To the man who has been living a worldly, careless life, the orthodox revival is indeed a " means of grace ". It brings to him the realization of the spiritual nature with which he was endowed. But, how far does the revivalist impress him with the thought that he has made only the beginning, and that he must make progress in the life which he has begun? What encouragement does he give him to add to faith virtue, and to virtue knowledge?

Here is the weak point in the popular " revival." There are elements in the finest religious life of to-day, which, so far from being revived are actually discouraged in the ordinary revival efforts. One of these elements is the love of truth. Many years ago, James Martineau wrote:—

" The rarity with which doctrines connected with morals and divinity are looked at with a single eye to their truth or falsehood, is disheartening to those who know what this symptom implies. The fear of doubt is already the renunciation of faith. With all the talk of infidelity in this age no one has more certainly a heart of unbelief than he who cannot simply trust himself to the realities of God; who cannot say—' If here there be light let us use it gladly, if otherwise let us go into the dark where Heaven ordains; ' owning our helplessness, we shall feel the Invisible Presence near us keeping His Holy watch; but pretending that we see we shall be left to a bleak and lonely night."

Our age is familiar with the severe standard of veracity set by the man of science in his laboratory. How careful he is to free his mind of every prejudice that might obscure his judgment; how intent he is in his observation, how watchful over his own words lest he misreport the facts. The demand is that the same high standard be applied to religion.

How far does what is commonly known as a revival issue in a finer sensitiveness to the claims of truth? How far does it develop what has been termed "the piety of the intellect"? A test of this may be found in the effect upon the study of the Bible. Here is a field wherein reverent scholarship has been at work, seeking only to find the truth. In almost every case the so-called revivalist uses his influence in behalf of an unscholarly dogmatism rather than in behalf of genuine truth seeking. The career of the late Henry Drummond gave promise of a new kind of evangelist, whose zeal shall be according to knowledge.

Another element which is insufficiently exhibited in the ordinary revival is that of justice as between man and man.

We hear much of justice as a divine attribute, and much denunciation of human sinfulness; but the revival methods tend to blur those distinctions between the just and the unjust which are necessary in a well ordered society. Justice is only attained through the habit of discrimination; and the revivalist is apt to be indiscriminating. He is likely to mistake sweeping denunciation for prophetic fervor. In particular, he is likely to fail in discriminating between intellectual differences and moral obliquity. After a revival of religion in a community there are too frequently found heart burnings and misunderstandings which have come because the new fervour has not been properly tempered by a judicial fairness of mind.

The most serious defect in the ordinary revival of religion lies in its lack of spiritual elevation. To popularize religion is a worthy aim, but those who attempt to do it often succeed only in vulgarizing it. Reverence is an essential quality which is too often sacrificed to a flippant familiarity with sacred things. Here we must, of course, not be too fastidious, and we must remember that what may seem to one cheap and unworthy, may to another be a symbol of the highest ideals. Doubtless, to many an inhabitant of the slums the tinkling tambourines of the Salvation Army have brought holy thoughts and suggestions of a higher sphere of life and thought. So long as they actually do this they are justified by their results.

But the point is this,—the methods of religion must always be such as to produce the religious attitude. The preaching, the symbolism, the discipline, must all be on a little higher plane than the ordinary life of those who are to be reached. The essential thing is that they must look up. The religious teacher must present an ideal which commands their reverence.

The sad thing is to see apparent success attained by the appeal to something less than the best. Religion then becomes a satisfaction in the actual rather than a striving for the ideal. Thus presented it becomes a reactionary rather than a progressive force.

In what I have written I have had in mind the genuine, though imperfect revival of religion. In so far as it is a revival of any of the elements of religion it is worthy of our sympathy. A rational criticism is directed not toward its excess but toward its defects. The danger is not that there may be too much zeal, but that there may be too little clear thinking, discriminating judgment and passion for ideal perfection.

It is necessary to add but a word in regard to the pseudo revival. In the acts of the Apostles we are told of the preaching of Philip in Samaria, and how "there was much joy in that city". In the very next verse we are made to see the ugly face of Simon Magus giving out to the people of Samaria that he himself was some great one; to whom they all gave heed from the least to the greatest, saying, "This man is that power of God which is called Great." It was not easy for the simple minded believers to discriminate between the genuine and the false. For " when they believed Philip preaching good

Revivals in the Light of the Present Day

tidings concerning the Kingdom of God and the name of Jesus Christ, they were baptized both men and women, and Simon also himself believed, and being baptized he continued with Philip."

There does not exist a more despicable creature than he who sees in the holiest emotions of others only a power to further his own fortunes. In our days the experience of the Apostolic Church has often been repeated. It is pitiful to think of the slowness with which good people perceive the difference between a godly sincerity and a simulated zeal. Much of the discredit thrown upon the earnest expression of religion, comes from the honest revulsion of feeling from those who have made the revival of religion a trade. The very name "revivalist" has often taken an unworthy meaning.

At no time is it so necessary as in a period of universal religious interest, to have as leaders in the church men of keen insight into character, and courage to expose the pious fraud. It is the time for Peter to say to Simon Magus: "Thou hast neither part nor lot in this matter; for thy heart is not right before God."

The New Orthodoxy

A New Orthodoxy

BY

The Reverend DANIEL EVANS

THE subject pre-supposes that there are changes in Theology. This is not surprising, for Theology is called upon to interpret the Divine Revelation in Nature, Man and the Christ. While it deals with realities eternal, and with truths illimitable, its interpretation is progressive and partial. When we consider the abundance of new material brought to us by the different sciences, it is only natural that changes should occur. There are constant advances in the physical sciences. The Science of Biology has changed, not only our theories, but also the very spirit of our thinking. The growth of historical research necessitates new conclusions as to God's action in the historic process. The comparative study of religions furnishes us with data which demand a larger view of the providence of God and the spiritual nature of man. The critical study of the Bible imposes new tasks on Biblical Theology and necessitates revision of opinion as to the nature and method of Revelation. Philosophy is still hard at work in its endeavour to unify all our knowledge. Equally potent in the production of changes in Theology is the realization of the truths of Revelation which hitherto have been too often neglected. These truths in the Bible which require new ages and new conditions for their full appreciation—we need but instance the new emphasis on the sociological significance of Paul's truth of "the body and the members" and the ethical significance of Christ's words in the 25th chapter of the Gospel according to St. Matthew. We are not, therefore, going beyond, but deeper into revelation, in our changes in theology.

I. The change which may be characterized as " the new theism."

This is seen in the stress laid upon the truth of the immanence of God. This truth we constantly meet in the best literature and philosophy of England and America; it has been the vital element in the philosophic thought in Germany for a century. No longer do we think of God as separate and far removed from His world, rather, we think of God as related to the world in much the same way as the soul is to the body. Here the relation is vital and organic. The soul vitalizes the body. The body is not the soul, nor does it exhaust or express all the thought, love and purpose of the soul; the world is not God, nor does it exhaust the thought, love and purpose of God. This immanent God is ever and everywhere operative. With the abandonment of the idea of an "absentee God," has gone the idea of an "otiose Deity." Science is the sermon on the words of Christ: "My Father worketh hitherto, and I too work." God himself is ever active in His world. Nothing is delegated to "angels," "aeons," "laws," "forces," or "evolution." God's action is immediate. Everything thrills, pulsates with energy and movement. There is no dead matter—all is alive with power. Every atom, process of nature, as well as the course of planets, bear witness to God's ceaseless activity. God is not so much the first cause, as the constant cause and eternal ground of all. God is the binding and unifying power of all. Everything is related; the blade of grass is dependent upon all nature for its life; so intimately allied are all things in nature, that every science, however specialized it may become, is closely connected with all the other branches. Departments of knowledge so far apart as physiology and philology are related to each other. Man too finds that he is a part of, and in, the great whole. He comes from it and lives in it. But in virtue of his personality he sustains a more intimate relation to the ground of the unity. He is more akin to God. There is an original and indestructible and personal relation of man to God and union with Him. God is the binding tie of all. In Him all things cohere. Their manifestations are the expressions of the inner life of God. Nature is the utterance of the thought of God.

This truth of unity of the world reveals to us the extent and significance of law. Law is everywhere, for God is everywhere. Law is the habitual method by which God works. It is His rational way of doing things. There is no place for chance in His rational universe. Everything is rational and law-abiding. The freedom of God is the freedom of Law. There are no contradictions in nature, for there are none in God. What is now inexplicable is not irrational, but unexplained. The inexplicable will one day be interpreted, as were the hieroglyphics of Egypt, and mind will converse with mind. Our deepest faith manifests itself to-day in taking God's universe as it is, in conforming to His laws in nature and in allowing God Himself to conform to them, rather than change them at our suggestion. God has realized His thought and purpose in the world by a gradual and organic evolution. From atom to mind, we read progress. There are gaps in our knowledge, but the law of evolution holds so far, and goes so deep, that thought demands the rational continuity of the same method. Everything that comes after stands in an organic relation to what has preceded. It is not claimed that man came from any animal, but from God along the pathway of the animal creation. He is no more a *special* creation than anything that preceded him. His pre-eminence is that by virtue of his personality he is the highest product of the evolutional process and the most adequate expression of the thought of God. He is therefore the goal of the process. The soul in nature is deep in slumber; in the animal is dreaming just before the dawn; in man is awake. Man alone stands erect, God-conquered, with face to heaven upturned.

This new theism yields significant results. Perhaps the greatest result, though least palpable, is the new spirit, the new mental attitude toward all subjects. It is what Balfour calls "the psychological climate." It is the spirit that loves facts first and theories afterward. It creates a strong faith in the rational. It looks for God, not in the gaps of our knowledge, in the things which Reason cannot at present explain, but in the whole process and in the explicable. God is not brought in where evolution apparently breaks down, but He is found everywhere in His world and everywhere in the process of the evolution of the world. Another result is seen in the way that we all try to abolish the hard opposition made between the natural and the supernatural. We see now that the partisans of Science created a false separation between two realms when in reality there can be no separation. They separated the natural from the supernatural, suffered no unusual action by God in the realm which they arrogated to themselves, and ever added to it more territory from the realm of the supernaturalists. The supernaturalists, on the other hand, were wrong in their admission and in their contention, when they conceded to the scientists their claim of a separation between the natural and the supernatural and demanded the right for God to interfere in the realm of the natural by violence without regard to the laws already in force there. We deny the right of the claim to separate the natural and the supernatural. We see in the miracle, not something that interferes with order, but the working of God in accordance with a higher law. We ascribe far greater powers and possibilities to nature than either the naturalists or supernaturalists are wont to. We regard nature as a sphere in which the law-abiding God manifests Himself. Everything from one point of view is supernatural; from another everything is natural. Since God's power is in nature and works according to law, we may call it natural; since the power is not of nature, but of God, we may regard it as supernatural. " The budding of a rose and the resurrection of Jesus are due to the same power." " There is no division of labour between God and law." All is of God, according to law, and the law itself is of God. The new theism brings to the soul a present living God. It feels that it is here and now in God's world—everything witnesses to His presence—the Burning Bush is a symbol of His presence in every bush. The God whom it feels in the depths of its own life, is one who not only spoke, but speaks; who not only acted, but acts; who not only inspired, but inspires. This conviction is the vitalizing power of our best literature, philosophy and life.

2. *The change in our thought of Revelation and the Bible.*

Revelation is a living possession of the soul which may or may not be written and the whole of which never could be written. The Bible is the literary record of a part of the Word of God. The Bible is no more coterminous with Revelation than it is synonymous therewith. We hold firmly to the reality of the inspiration of the men through whom the revelation came. We find inspiration, not in the collecting and compiling of documents and such like verbal matters, but in the activity of the souls of these men. Inspiration, since it is of the soul, must be in accord with the laws of the activity of the soul. When the soul's activity is at its highest and best, then it sees clearest. And since the mind does not generate the truths from within itself, but from contact with the Eternal Mind, and since the consciousness of man is deeper than its explication to the intellect, every inspired man grasped truths, the full significance of which he himself did not comprehend. The evidence of inspiration we find in the content of the message of the inspired. We note it in the strong conviction on the part of the historian that God is in the history of man; we feel it in the psalmist's experience in finding peace in God. We perceive it in the prophet's vision of God, in the strong insistence on the social nature and ethical character of religion and in the hope of some coming One who would redeem the nation. We see it in the majestic struggle of Job for the solution of the problem of human suffering. In the New Testament, we find it in the sublime life of the Christ, in the new characters He has created, which give rise to new thoughts and ideals, and in the manifest consciousness of God. We hold that the scientific description of the data brought to us by the critics, no more explains them in any deep philosophic way, than the description of the scientists explains in any ultimate way this world of ours. The great souls of the Bible have not returned to us with messages from some "Weissnichtwo," but from contact and communion with God. This conviction, however, carries us one step farther.

We recognize that if the content of revelation is the criterion, then we must conclude that the activity of the spirit of God was not confined to the Hebrews. Men have come into relation with the same reality elsewhere than in Palestine. A study of the religions of the world leads us to believe in an "ethnic inspiration." Religion is as wide and deep as humanity. The unscientific statement that there are peoples without religions is gone, and fast following it is another equally unfounded statement—that all other religions than the Christian are false. There is no such thing as false religion. There are false elements in religions, but the power of those religions for righteousness has been in virtue of the true in them and in spite of the faults. No longer can we characterize religions as true and false, revealed and natural, but as perfect and imperfect, as absolute and relative. The imperfect and relative religions have been working out by sweat of brain and pang of heart the argument for the existence of God which we now think out in our studies. And if they had not worked them out in the past we would not be thinking them out in the present. "The history of religion is the explication of religion." They all have a real, if inadequate, knowledge of God. The founders and continuators of those religions were in contact with the same Reality as the prophets of Israel. Christianity acknowledges their truths, relates them to others of which they were not cognizant and points them to the One Person of all history who revealed and embodied all these truths in virtue of which He is the Life and the Light of the World.

3. The changes in our thought of the Christ.

Dr. Fairbairn says: "The most distinctive and determinative element in modern theology is what we may term a new feeling for the Christ." There is a new personal feeling for the Christ. Men now think of Christ as a real human being.

There is a great desire to know more about His human life, to see Him among men. This interest is seen in the great sale of popular lives of the Christ, in the abundance of pictures of the Christ in the magazines and in the applause the name of the Christ receives in the great conventions of the working people. There is also a feeling for the Christ which we may characterize as the historical. The real motive of most of the critics who have concentrated their attention upon the gospels is the desire to see the Christ Himself directly, rather than through the eyes of the Church, the Apostle Paul or the immediate circle of disciples. It is the effort to see what the Christ was, so that we might know what original Christianity was. It is the attempt to trace the mighty Christian river to its source, rather than explore tributaries. If the Ritschlians merit criticism for their depreciation of God's world, they merit praise for their study of God's word. But there is a deeper feeling for the Christ which we may characterize as the ethical. We see how great was His soul, what profound thoughts were in His mind, what pure feelings in His heart, what great purposes were His for which He gave His life,—we confess Him one in thought, in sentiment and purpose with God. He is the King of our souls in virtue of His character. Never as much as now did the moral ideal of Jesus and His character have such a place in the life and thought of people. Still deeper is the feeling for the Christ which may be characterized as philosophical and religious. We believe in the word made flesh. We rejoice in this varied interest in the Christ, but ours goes deeper. It is not enough for us to say that He was the greatest of men, the divinest of seers. We accept the statement of the gentle Charles Lamb and apply it in all comparisons between Christ and other masters. "If Shakespeare was to come into the room, we should all rise up to meet him; but if that person (the Christ) was to come into it, we should all fall down and try to kiss the hem of His garment!" We respect Shakespeare; we pray in the name of Christ.

The central fact in the Christian faith is the Incarnation.

The universal and the particular here meet in perfect accord. There is perfect response between the Christ and God. God fills the field of His consciousness, but the personality of the Christ is maintained in its strict integrity. The one is not sacrificed to the other, but finds in the other the object it longs for. If we are not satisfied with the creedal expression of our faith in the person of the Christ, it is because of its inadequacy, not its overstatement. The psychology of the creeds is discredited, —the person of the creeds lives and is credited with more of thought, personal power and character than ever before. If we can no longer speak of two separate, distinct natures, out from either of which he may speak at will, now as man, now as God, we do recognize the truth which they were striving to express by these terms. As we no longer seek for God, outside or alongside, but in His world, so we no longer seek for the divinity of our Lord in two separate natures, but in the one living, thinking, feeling and willing Personality. And we cannot think this Personality to the roots of His being, we cannot sound the depths of the basal union of this soul with God and express the result in terms less significant than the confessions of the Scripture, the symbols of the Church and the hymns of the Faith. However great and sublime the thought of the Incarnation, it is easier for us of to-day to understand than for those of other days. History shows that Christ is the moral leader of mankind. The new evolutional construction of our world makes it easier to think of the Christ as the disciples, especially Paul did. The larger significance of the Incarnation makes the thought reasonable.

The deeper thinking of the New Testament correlates Christ and the Creation. He is the head of all. The purpose of God which found its first manifestation and imperfect realization in the evolution of the world, a fuller manifestation and a more perfect realization in the arrival and ascent of Man, finds at last in the Christ the adequate manifestation and complete realization. Creation is the first and Christ the final term of the Purpose of God. In like manner, the deeper thinking of the

New Testament correlates Christ and Humanity. He is the Head of humanity. He is the person who unifies all men in a social fellowship in which each finds himself in a right relation to his brother-man. The full explanation for the existence and nature of man is given in Christ alone. Men, therefore, do not explain Christ,—He explains them. As man is the final end of nature and therefore is the principle to explain the power at work in nature, so Christ, seeing that He is the final end of all men, is the principle to explain the existence, nature and destiny of man,—verily, He is the Light of the World. We find the rationale of the Incarnation in the nature and the purpose of God, rather than in the sinful condition of man. Sin may have changed the time, condition, incidents of the Incarnation, but sin was not the ground of it, nor was its removal the final purpose of the Incarnation. There was something in the thought of God prior to the thought of reconciliation. It was the end for which both nature and man should exist.

There is something deeper than the sin of man. It is the original and indestructible union of God and man. There will ever be in process a deeper realization of the purpose of God, when sin will be but the faded recollection of the past. The soul must ever find its life in relation to God and man through the eternal Christ. Christ is the end of all and in relation to Him do we find our eternal salvation.

The Incarnation is the final principle for the interpretation of the character of God as revealed in Nature. The heart of the Universe is like that which beat in the bosom of Christ. "Ours," as Dr. Gordon says, "is a Christological universe." We moralize the eternal energy of which Spencer speaks. The Power not Ourselves, on which the late Matthew Arnold discoursed, we know as the eternal God, the basis and pledge of the realization of all righteousness. We baptize our "new theism" into the name of Christ. We are thus saved from the vaporous and immoral pantheism of Pope expressed in the line: "Whatever is, is right." In like manner, Christ becomes the final principle for the interpretation of the character of God as revealed in human life. Christ's words are taken in their full meaning: "He who hath seen Me hath seen the Father." God is Christlike. Christ is Godlike. The profoundest interpretation of the character of God is in the term, Father. The Fatherhood of God is grounded in His nature. It is not conditioned by the attitude of men. It means an everlasting interest in every soul. The interest never changes, for God cannot deny Himself. We cannot ascribe to God anything which we would not ascribe to Christ, nor respect in man. However powerful God may be, He must be love. However sovereign He is, He must be righteous. In the same way Christ becomes the criterion for the determination of revelation. We make the Christ the sole authority for the truth within or without the Bible. The validity of any part of the Bible as authority for faith and conduct is determined by its germinal or developed congruity with the thought and life of Christ. We are beginning to feel how unfortunate is the use of the term Infallibility as applied to the Bible. When applied to the whole Bible, it is an undue use of the principle of extension. Every book and part of the Bible must bear its own burden. The actual carrying into life of principles found in the Bible irrespective of their relation to the Christ, the sole final authority, has resulted in most unChristlike acts. Furthermore, while Catholicism is the religion of the Church and Protestantism the religion of the Bible, Christianity is the religion of the Personal Christ. Jesus did not come to give us another code for conduct, but a new Spirit for life. The Bible is indispensable in its place, but when it is in the place of Christ, it is out of place. It ever points us beyond itself,—to the flowers, sun, moon and stars, to men, institutions and nations, and to the Christ, to find therein the same God whom those men found who gave us the Bible.

4. The Change in our thought of Atonement.

We are emphasizing the fact that the love which finds its expression in the atonement is an eternal love. The work of

Christ on the earth is not regarded as manifesting a new disposition of God toward men,—but as the new and most effective demonstration and realization of an eternal disposition and determination of God for His children. We see in Christ's work a demonstration, in the highest terms, of the truth that in the very nature of God, Atonement had everlastingly its potential and efficient foundation. What the Christ was and what He did on earth was the time-focussed expression of what God eternally is and had been partially realizing in nature, more fully in man, and absolutely only in the Christ. The Law of Sacrifice is fundamental. It is adumbrated in nature, it dawns with human life, it is in its noontime glory in the life of Christ. Christ is not the only expression of the love of God, but He is the only adequate expression of that love. The Atonement is by the living personality of Jesus rather than by some specific act in His life. It was first a fact in His own life. He Himself was always at one with God. His whole life, therefore, with all its wealth of thought and sentiment and personal power, and all the incidents in that life, is the saving power. He reconciles because He was Himself ever reconciled and because He knows best the soul of man. Because He Himself was in communion with God, He brought others into communion with Him. The effect of the love and service of Christ is the reconciliation of man to God. Christ is not better than God, but is the expression of the love of God. God does not stand off, demanding some appeasing of His wrath before He will have aught to do with man. Christ did not first have to reconcile God. Nor did Christ come to save man from suffering, from punishment, but from sin. He saves man to all that is in God, to His wrath no less than to His love. He brings the soul into its native environment, for as the air is the environment of the bird, so God is the environment of the soul. Only in right relation to God does the soul realize its true life. The man with whom God has ever been in union, now holds communion with Him.

5. *The Larger Conception of Salvation.*

Salvation is interpreted in the terms of ethics as well as in the terms of religion. We are asking what is the nature of the man reconciled to God and are recovering our renewed human life with all its wealth of thought and sentiment, social relations and institutions. There is at present great interest in the study of ethics and this study has yielded us a far richer conception of the nature of man. Ethics speaks of divine possibilities in every soul, knows nothing of a lost original endowment, smiles at the idea of a fall of the race in any individual in the far barbaric past, who has imposed upon us all the task of the recovery of what he lost. Ethics finds in the man the nature which needs realization. Man's salvation is not in getting something *ab extra* but in the realization of his human nature. Salvation is self-realization. Human goodness is Christian goodness. "Oh to be nothing" is not a healthy human sentiment. "Oh to be something," is. The task of the Christian is not the annihilation of any part of his being, but the realization of all that is within him. We are recognizing that the body plays an important part in our life. It is a divine work and a human necessity. There is a physical basis of the mental life. Talents are God-given and are for use. Culture and religion are friends. Since salvation is self-realization, it is a progressive thing. It begins in an act of will, it continues as an eternal process. The progress is not, however, a running after "a flying goal," but it is life within the sphere of all that is ethical and spiritual. We progress *in*, rather than *toward*, the goods of the soul. Man is social. He is made for others as well as for himself and for God. Therefore salvation is social. This truth is now strongly emphasized. It is one of the dominant ideas of our time. In our study of the thought of the Christ, his idea of the kingdom is playing its important part. Man lives in relations. These relations produce and necessitate certain institutions and interests. All are being ethically interpreted. The progress of ethical thought is finally illustrated by a comparison of Adam Smith's Political Economy with that of Professor Marshall. We are placing the same moral estimate on the family, the neighbourhood and the state. All the vital interests of men are regarded as the legitimate concern of the theory and practice of Christianity. There can be no division of life into the sacred and secular, however much the priest would like the one and the man of the world the other. The things necessary for life are facts and factors in the kingdom of God.

I have endeavoured to trace some of the greater changes in the theology of to-day. All these changes result from and bear witness to a deeper change in thought. The fundamental truth which we find in literature, no less than in theology, is the inherent and organic unity prevailing everywhere and controlling all things. This explains our new theism. Everything in nature exists because of its vital relation to God, no less the moat that floats in the sunbeam than the sun itself. This explains and is evidenced by our new thought of revelation. Every truth that quickens the mind and thrills the heart of the reader of the Bible first quickened and thrilled the mind and heart of the man who gave it to the world, and he obtained it because of the realization of his vital relation to God. This explains and is evidenced by our thought of the Christ. He was the human realization of God. Fellowship with Him then and now, uncovers to man the eternal union of his soul with God and secures a spiritual communion between the child and the Father. So with our larger thought of salvation. The whole man lives and moves and has his being in God. In every point of his being there is a meeting ground of God. And no less true is it that He stands in the same vital relation with men. The same is true of our thought of the continued moral opportunity for the salvation of men. The vital and organic relation of man to God is not grounded in the phenomenal, in the temporal, but in the essential and eternal nature of the man himself and in the nature of God.

The Trend of Theological Thought in England

The Trend of Theological Thought in England

BY

The Reverend R. A. ARMSTRONG

TO discriminate and state the Trend of Religious Thought in England at the close of the Nineteenth Century is no easy task. To make the statement in the limits assigned to this essay is harder still; and the statement when made can be no more than a very general indication, and will necessarily be tinged by the personal idiosyncrasies, beliefs and interests of the writer. My only excuse for making the attempt is a profound interest in the problem together with the fact that I have for more than thirty years made perpetual endeavour to read the signs of the times and to understand the movements of thought around me.

The main difficulty lies in the complexity of the facts to be observed. There appears such confusion in the religious world. There seem to be so many cross-currents. In a caldron of seething waters it is hard to discern a stream. Yet one has seen such boiling masses in the narrows of some mighty river, and one has known that in spite of their sweltering chaos, those waters were really hurrying to the sea, and in what point of the compass that broad sea lay.

To what distant ocean, then, is the religious thought of England moving, caught in the resistless undercurrent, though seeming a mere whirlpool with disordered waves flung objectless from side to side?

There are some four or five obvious phenomena which have to be co-ordinated, their common measure found.

First and most obvious of these is the Ritualist and Sacerdotal movement.

To a somewhat superficial observer this might well seem the

one characteristic religious phenomenon of our time. It is but a few years since the Protestantism of England was an incontestable fact. *Paterfamilias* hated priestcraft, whether he cared much for Evangelical teaching or not. Ritualism has come in with a rush. The appeal to the senses, by music, by vestment, by incense, has fairly conquered the Church of England, and even in the most moderate parishes practices are familiar now which would have scandalized almost every one a generation ago. And far graver than the Ritualism is the Sacerdotalism. Not only is spiritual doctrine symbolized to the eye, to the ear, to the nose, but the man stands between the worshipper and God, the supernaturally endowed priest, holding the keys of Heaven, and compelling the approach of the worshipper to God, and even the approach of God to the worshipper, to pass through the doorway of his own person; all other communion between God and man is barred. It is a tremendous revolution, but it is a revolution which has been ruthlessly carried out over large areas of England in the last quarter of the Nineteenth Century.

Side by side with the Sacerdotal development has proceeded the intellectual decay of Evangelicism. In spite of its scorn of "carnal reason" Evangelicism in the past has produced doughty and vigorous theologians. It is now in England without great scholars or strong thinkers. Its polemics are extraordinarily feeble, its reasoning degenerating often to mere shrewish scolding. It still gathers in its thousands and tens of thousands, still arrogates to itself the exclusive title of "orthodox", still lets the Catholic, the Ritualist, the Unitarian, the Agnostic know what it thinks of him in terms not marked by courtesy nor always by humility. But the looker on, I think sees pretty clearly that as an orthodox system it is rapidly relaxing, that where it still retains the nominal allegiance of thinking men, those men have practically slipped the creeds and fallen into certain veins of somewhat loose and formless liberalism which really present no permanent foothold for the religious life.

Among these somewhat loose and formless veins of liberalism, the most interesting is that which may be summed up in the phrase so common on many lips of late, "Back to Jesus." When the Reformation of the Sixteenth century ploughed its way through the Catholic Church, the Reformers, feeling that the authority of the church had broken down, simply fell back on the authority of the Scriptures.

They felt no need to construct any theory to justify the assumption of that authority. The atmosphere around them made that unnecessary. It was the natural retreat for men who had abandoned the infallibility of the church and it was accepted without challenge or question. And just so now, when men bred in Evangelical associations discover that the absolute authority of all parts of Scripture can be maintained no longer, they are simply falling back on the authority of Jesus Christ, and especially of the spoken words of Jesus Christ. Nor do they in their turn feel any need to construct a theory to justify the assumption of that authority. They breathe an atmosphere in which that seems quite unnecessary. The authority of Jesus is the natural retreat of men who have abandoned the infallibility of the Scriptures, and it is widely accepted without challenge or question. And the men of the "New Orthodoxy" do not appear to see that there is a profoundly difficult critical question to be solved before we can with a sense of repose adopt their attitude;—namely, "How are we to know which are actually the spoken words of Jesus?" —or that there lies behind that the still more difficult and fundamental question, "Why are we to accept the authority of Jesus Christ at all?" And so for the moment this school flourishes. It is not without seduction for refined and spiritual natures. It has cast away all that was ugly and repulsive in the narrow bigotries of earlier Evangelical and Calvinistic schools. It robes itself with all the gracious and gentle emotion indissolubly associated with the name of Jesus. But it is without a philosophical or intellectual basis. It is even without the sense that it has any need to found itself on such a basis.

Therefore, at any rate in my view, it is without a future, and marks merely one of the current forms of spiritual transition.

And then side by side with the growth of Sacerdotalism, the intellectual decay of Evangelicism, and the temporary popularity of the broad and liberal "New Orthodoxy", there is the steady march of that Agnosticism which has grown in so extraordinary a degree during the second half of the Nineteenth Century. Whether we like it or not there is no use in disguising the fact that large numbers of men and women are more and more giving up, not only the official creeds, but all positive and definite religious belief. I do not refer now to the careless, the flippant, the superficial, but to men and women among the most thoughtful, the most earnest, the greatest lovers of goodness that exist. Perhaps few men have such opportunities of guaging the extent of this special type of Agnosticism as a minister of the communion itself wholly outside the ranks of reputed orthodoxy. Neither the Church of England, Priest, nor the preacher of salvation through the blood of Christ, is likely to receive quite such frank confidences in this matter as he receives. And profoundly as I believe in God, in Prayer, in the communion of the human soul with the Eternal and All-Holy, I am prepared to say that it is among the very best and noblest men and women whom I know that scepticism about all this is commonest and deepest.

Now for all these very marked yet on the surface very diverse trends of religious thought in England of to-day there must be, I think, some deep underlying common cause; and I believe that I can dimly discern its nature and its workings.

It is a commonplace to point out that the past half century has been marked by the most penetrating revolution in thought that the world has ever known. That method of thought of which the watchword is Evolution has indeed its roots far back in the history of the human mind. Its beginnings may be traced in the infancy of philosophy. Its influence emerges again and again in the successive interpretations which observers and thinkers have given to the universe. But it is nevertheless true that only within the memory of living men has it saturated the common consciousness and become even the unconscious organon of average men and women. Among English-speaking peoples this vast and sweeping change of conception is indissolubly connected with the names of Charles Darwin and Herbert Spencer. And there are millions of persons who have never read an essay or an article by either of those two great masters, the language of whose minds has nevertheless been translated into a new vernacular through the influence of what those masters have observed and thought and written.

The result is, that while to our fathers different departments of knowledge appeared to present no common elements, and jumps, jerks, gaps, lacunæ, in the succession or co-ordination of phenomena occasioned no intellectual uneasiness, the typical man of to-day instinctively wants to find all departments co-related and all progressions offering a smooth and unbroken continuity. His mind is not in equilibrium until he can grasp the unity between phenomena the most diverse; and the belief in that underlying unity is the master instinct of his understanding.

But what does that instinct mean in the sphere of religion? It means in the last resort that there is no ultimate difference in kind between Divine revelation and the revelations of human inquiry, between the Sacred Scriptures, and the general mass of human literature, between Jesus Christ and other mighty prophets and teachers of mankind. And that means that the whole outworks and bulwarks of orthodox religion break down.

I say that at least a vague consciousness of this lies to-day at the back of every educated mind. What then is the result on various classes of mind in the matter of religion?

In some it wakens an instinct of opposition and resistance lest religion itself should be done away. And that is the source of the temporary strength and vigor of the Ritualistic and Sacerdotal movements. Ritual is a series of outworks thrown up to retard the advance of the invading host. To keep the battle from the inmost fortress, and in half conscious recognition that the fortress cannot, at least with the old weapons, be any longer held, symbols of the spiritual are multiplied to occupy the imagination and to divert any wakening suspicion of the emptiness of the central shrine. It is men whose faith has become dim concerning the inmost spiritual sanctities, the veritable touch of the individual human soul with God, that erect images appealing to the senses to engage the attention and feed the spiritual life. And in like manner all attempts to concentrate the consciences of men on the priest and his spiritual thaumaturgy are instinctive efforts to hold back the public mind from inquiry as to the veritable reality of the unseen God. The Holy of Holies in the Jewish cult retained its awful sanctity only by being guarded and surrounded by court after court of the Temple with its ceremonials and its sacraments. Once let the layman pierce through and open the door of the Ark itself, and the solemn sanction would be gone. In like manner, I believe that the whole High Church movement though among its leaders and its servants are men of the loftiest devotion, is unconsciously at bottom a movement of the profoundest scepticism which cannot trust the soul to find its pilgrim way to the breast of the living God.

And the intellectual decay of Evangelicism, which I have noted as the second broad fact in the present religious movement in England, is due no less to the hold that the great Evolution idea has got on the English mind. For the "Scheme" the "plan", the contrivance of a special mode of salvation which is the very basis of the so-called Evangelical Christianity is the flat contradiction of the Evolution conception. Evangelicism is in its essence a system of the special, the unique; but the Evolution idea discourages belief in the special, the unique. It views history as a drama slowly unrolling from primordial beginnings in the birth of time. But Evangelicism asks for belief in a sudden and extraordinary revolution in the history of mankind at a particular moment in the centuries,—

an absolute and penetrating change in the very relation of God to man,—to say nothing of its affirmation of a special and miraculous scripture and a unique Son of God without a brother in the universe. I do not say that Evangelicism is impossible to a mind that has grasped the conception of Evolution. But I do say that that conception puts the greatest obstacle in the way of Evangelicism and weakens its hold on cultured men.

That " New Orthodoxy ", that " Back to Jesus ", movement to which I have referred as the third element in the contemporary religious movement finds its origin in the same intellectual phenomenon. It is the attempt of Evangelicism to throw off its impedimenta, or as many of them as may be possible, while still retaining its characteristic attitude towards Jesus. For a time it will serve. But it has only pushed the difficulty back a little way. And it cannot be long before it feels itself confronted by the like unescapable dilemma as the full " orthodoxy " which it endeavors to replace.

It needs no proof that the Agnosticism enumerated above as the fourth among the characteristics of our time is due to the strength amongst us of the doctrine of Evolution. There is indeed no real incompatibility between the fullest acceptance of Evolution and the deepest and loftiest religious faith. But the Churches have so inextricably involved religion with ideas which the Evolutionist cannot digest that few minds are able to undo the tangle, and for a while religious faith goes overboard along with the unscientific view of human history Ecclesiastics have propounded. I would only observe that, while a generation ago, in the first passion of revolution, scientific thought drifted continually towards a dogmatic materialism, it is even now becoming conscious of hints and suggestions in the womb of nature, herself, which the materialistic hypothesis can never meet.

And this is the turning point of our diagnosis. The expressions of awe and wonder, as in the presence of an unsolved mystery, which escape more frequently from the lips of scientific men are the first bits of drift-wood seen making strange headway against what seemed the strongest set of the current, and revealing a yet stronger current underneath.

The sketch which my few paragraphs have given of sundry movements of our time might seem to indicate that scepticism, the essential spirit of unbelief, is the master force of our age. A closer examination reveals that it is not so. From the depths of the consciousness of the community there is emerging more clearly every year a profound demand for positive religion and a waxing faith that there is religion for us yet. It is coming to be dimly felt that the religious life is as essential to man as the physical, the intellectual, or the ethical, that the spiritual element in humanity cannot be neglected or ignored, and that corresponding to that element in man and meeting that demand there must be and is provision in the spiritual universe outside the human soul. And the more that spiritual fact which is to satisfy the perennial craving takes to itself form and color, the more it is discerned that it is no other than the existence of an Eternal Being who may be dimly suggested by such words as " Father " " Holy Spirit " " God ",—One, who whatever else He be, is the Great Deep in whom we all live and move and have our being, and who bestows on us, His creatures and His children, the wondrous gift of Eternal Life, which may brighten out into conscious and blessed communion with Him.

The sceptical movement—strong as it has been and is—yet is in a sense superficial. It has cleared and is clearing away elements which have served their purpose, many of which doubtless helped to conserve the precious essence through ages of storm and stress, but have no place in the permanent life of religion. Religion has been throwing off ingredients which marred its purity and must ultimately, if, retained in the system, have imperiled its life. It will show itself presently the sounder and stronger for the process.

The Trend of Religious Thought in England is, through a searching and sometimes dark and painful scepticism, towards that "Absolute Religion", that communionism of the soul with the Heavenly Father, which gave the predominant note to the Gospel of Jesus of Nazareth nineteen hundred years ago.

The Modern Trend in Eschatology

The Modern Trend in Eschatology

BY

The Reverend HUGH O. ROWLANDS, D.D

THIS paper does not purport to give the writer's own views on the subject discussed; much less is it a defense of, or an attack on the opinions of others. I shall endeavour to give as an observer what seems to be the drift of modern Christian thought on this great question, such part of it as concerns the doom of incorrigibles, or the "unsaved," after death. I shall not burden the paper with references to authors and books. Usually the preacher and the author are special attorneys pleading for one side of the case or attacking the other.

The newspaper, the novel, the sermon, and magazine discussions of the question, are evidence of the deep and often unconscious faith men have in future immortality, as shells and pebbles on the beach are proofs of the inrolling waves from the deep and mysterious sea.

The very existence of different views and conclusions among the learned, the good, and the great in all ages should preclude intolerant dogmatizing. Reverent Bible students, men profound in the history of Christian Dogmatics and zealous propagandists of the Christian faith, whose piety and devoutness were unquestioned, have been far from being unanimous in their understanding, deductions and conclusions respecting this question. This fact shows conclusively that the revelations of the Sacred Scriptures are not so full and clear as to put the question beyond controversy. Hence the need of charity and catholic toleration; reverent and unobstrusive doubt of any position should place no one outside the pale of Christian fellowship. It should not be made a test of fitness —or unfitness—for church membership. I could conceive of conditions where it ought not to be made a test for an ordination to the Christian ministry, or an appointment to the missionary field.

I name a few of the "trunk lines" of various beliefs that prevail and the favor in which they are held, or considered by different "schools" of Christians.

I. THE "ORTHODOX"

I place the word in quotation marks to save myself from a charge of assuming that the views inculcated under that name are the *right teaching*. The man who dies unrepentant and unsaved is irretrievably and everlastingly lost to blessedness and happiness; this lost condition is one of conscious, unutterable, and endless anguish in the torments of hell. No mercy will be ever offered, and if it were offered the very capability of the lost soul to profit thereby is destroyed.

This condition is not so much the provision of divine justice; but the wilfully chosen self-banishment of the sufferer from God. It is Hell because he is out of harmony with his Environment—God. No one is lost but out of wilful rejection of Jesus Christ who is the Light and Life of men. Hell is both retributive of sin and exhibitive of divine justice, hence it is subjective and objective in its elements.

Theories of the methods and nature of future retribution such as "lake of fire," "brimstone," etc., must be eliminated from the teaching of modern orthodoxy; they are the remnants of a by-gone literalistic, materialistic age and of the legalistic, Latinic church in distinction from the spiritual Greek church. They are associated with orthodoxy by its adversaries for the purpose of caricature and ridicule. That a sporadic few "orthodox" people believe in those lurid details is possible; but no party should be judged as to its principles by the extravagancies and frenzies of a few of its least representative adherents, nor by the caricatures of its opponents. It is needless to write that the orthodox view of this question is professedly got from the Scriptures; on them entirely its supporters depend for authority.

COMMENTS

Does the Bible teach such a dogma? It certainly appears so to a multitude of zealous and pious Christians. Revivals, missions, the impassioned appeals of great evangelists have been greatly quickened, inspired and intensified by this dread belief. The strange parable of the "sheep and the goats" recorded in the Gospel according to Matthew seems to teach this doctrine explicitly; so also Matthew 18:8, 9; other passages from the Scriptures seem to teach or imply the sentiments with more or less clearness.

However, let it be remembered that a large number of holy, learned Bible students believe that those parts of the Scriptures on fair exegesis are capable of other and widely different explanations and construction.

Moreover, there is an irrepressible rebellion in the heart and consciousness of man against the orthodox deductions from Scriptures on this subject. The "intuitional intelligence" of the soul protests against them. Look at it! think of its dread, unutterable meaning! The lost soul (numbered by the millions), by virtue and authority of an irreversible law in his nature, which is a Divine fiat, is devoted to a condition in which with every pulsation of existence he becomes more guilty and depraved. Farther and farther from holiness, from God, and from hope he sweeps like an anarchistic comet of perdition. With every throb of being he becomes more satanic in ambition, more infernal in passion, and more hateful toward his Creator; bloating with the unending torments of fermenting remorse; this process going on for one year, for a century, for ten thousand—ten millions of cycles of the eternal æons; let each second of those periods represent so many æons still coming, and when those dread eternities are spent the lost soul is only on the threshold of its existence careering into ever-deepening Endlessness. If at the close of a million times those periods we could discern a gleam of hope hinting that in a nameless future there was an end to the foaming, gurgling misery of the lost it would be a satisfaction; but no! the darkness is denser and murkier as we look ahead! And all of this for the glory of a Heavenly Father and the satisfaction of a justice whose ideal and embodiment is Himself! It would not seem possible that men could believe such a doctrine and teach it as within the limits of a benevolent God's government The trend is away from it. The evangelical pulpit is slow to preach it. Evangelists do not appeal to it as did Edwards, Swan, Knapp. Moody never preached it. In cold, logical controversy it may be stoutly defended; but in the message of the pulpit it is held as a " background of mystery."

UNIVERSALISM

Old-fashioned Universalism has in later years taken upon itself the hue of restorationism. Formerly it was taught that men are adequately punished in this life for all their sins; death ended all suffering as the result of transgression, and was the strait gate that led into blessedness and bliss. The pains of the final dissolution were the Jesus that redeemed the soul and not the Jesus of Calvary. The dying transgressor took a draught of Lethe, and was at once relieved from the guilt and memory of sin and entered the abode of the Holy and Good.

So contrary to Scriptures, so repugnant to reason, and so repellant to every intuition and instinct of justice was that teaching that intelligent Universalists no longer teach or father it. It was the extreme swing of the pendulum from the Edwardian Eschatology of New England—one as repugnant as the other. Restorationism qualifies Universalism. Men shall reap what they sow. All wrong-doing shall be punished here or hereafter. The incorrigible soul at death enters "hell"; but this is not retribution; it is a purgatory, a condition of discipline and reform where under new masters and discipline, in better environments, he is educated, disciplined, and finally delivered. Time is no element of the disciplinary course; it may be an hour or an æon; but it will be a constantly progressive process of purification and perfection. At last all men will be restored into the image of God, into holiness and blessedness; God will be all in all. The whole race of man redeemed and glorified.

COMMENTS

This view has never taken a firm hold on the conscience and conviction of the Christian world. It has been popular in the measure the opposite extreme was urged. It has been a hope and sentiment rather than a conviction or a statement of revealed truth; it is a protest rather than a vigorous, constructive faith.

The teachings of Scriptures are not favorable to it; the great majority of its ardent advocates fail to accept the Scriptures as infallible authority of truth; it is considered by many of its advocates as extra-biblical, an evolution of moral consciousness; a sentiment of the benevolent heart rather than a deduction from Holy Scriptures.

Many oppose this view because, as they claim, it is contradicted by all analogies of the material and physical world wherein violations of natural laws are venial only to a certain point; beyond that suffering is not remedial, but retributive Illustrations of this principle are,—transgressions against the laws of the body which may be forgiven to a certain mark of severity and persistence, beyond which they are fatal. True that natural, or psychical laws may not be identical with the spiritual, yet there is a close analogy—some scholars claim identity. This principle of irremediableness is recognized in the sociological, or legal phrase,—*degenerates*. The great poets, dramatists and novelists recognize the fact of irremediable depravity by consigning their villains to final destruction. Furthermore, it is claimed that acceptance of this view is usually associated with a low estimate of holiness and a light estimate of the guilt and virulence of sin. Its opponents say " it cuts the nerve of missions by making sin an error of ignorance, or the blunder of weakness, rather than a guilty violation of the law of justice, holiness, and benevolence as manifested in God. It is claimed that the implications of this view are injurious to morals; it eliminates the element of *prudence* as a motive of right living; while that is not the highest motive still it is a proper one, since it is implanted in human nature.

This view is an argument that God does not in the present life and world furnish the strongest influences for the redemption of men from sin; for, if men who refuse to repent and be converted here under the preaching of Christ and influences of the Holy Spirit are saved after death, it must be there are more favorable environments in waiting after death. Stimulated by this delusion men adjourn the care and preparation they should give their spiritual conditions. Hence "liberal" churches are barren of converts. They seldom bear offspring; but their membership is often of the "lost, strayed, or stolen" of evangelical homes and churches.

"NEW THEOLOGY"

This is an annex of Universalism. It claims that those who have not heard of Christ during their earth-life shall have an opportunity after death; hence there is a future probation for the heathen. This view rises from the unreasonable and unscriptural hypothesis that all to whom Christ has not been preached are lost. Whereas final condemnation is not based on unbelief; but on dis-belief. Men will be condemned not because they received not the Light, but having received it they rejected it, and loved and chose the Darkness. The heathen are not without the Light (the most catholic title of Jesus), for "He lighteth every man that cometh into the world," and they like all men will be judged according to the light they received.

ANNIHILATION

This view is accepted by many as the best solution of the problem. It is argued that it is a scriptural solution; that it is in harmony with the laws of the natural universe, and that it is an escape from the burdens other creeds place on the human heart and reason. This view claims that God alone hath immortality (1 Tim. 6:16) inherently and naturally. Man's assurance of immortality at his creation was conditioned on his being in harmony and union with God; that lost—death seized him. Christ came to restore man into peace with God, hence to reattain the lost life. By faith in Him men are reunited to God and the life of God enters them. Thus the lost immortality is found in Christ who came that " men might have life and have it more abundantly "; and they who accept Christ, though spiritually dead, shall live again in Him.

On the other hand sin is corruption and death, and the soul that sinneth shall die. As disease destroys the physical life so sin destroys the spiritual. The process of destruction may be slow,—but the end will be the annihilation of personality and identity. At last, since sin has no identity, *per se,* and is but the disposition of the sinner, it will be utterly destroyed with him; righteousness and truth shall fill the earth, and to Him every knee shall bow and tongue confess. Those of this faith claim that it avoids the "enervating heresies of restorationism" and the terrible forebodings of endless torments. It is a theory that prevails widely in England, especially among Congregationalists. The last utterances of Henry Ward Beecher on this subject partake of this conclusion. Preaching on the text, " Be not deceived: God is not mocked ", etc (Gal. 6:7-9), he said: " He that lives to the flesh shall of the flesh reap corruption—*shall*. It is sure to come. What shall it be? Future torment? No, I do not mean that; I mean that he that cultivates his lower nature, mere animal nature, with the animal perishes. . . . It is to my mind a relief that if a man never rises any higher than the animal life—the Universe will never see a God enthroned that looks down upon the infinite and prolonged torments of an unconceived number of men shut up simply for the purpose of suffering. If there be anything more infidel than that I do not know what it is, or anything which more effectually blots out the possibility of respecting and loving any God than this,—continuing to create men with some foresight of their perpetual suffering." Felix Adler in one of his lectures said that there are " men incapable of religion which of course makes them incapable of the crowning blessings of religion—eternal life; the end of such men must be death."

THE TEACHINGS OF CHRIST

With those various theories contrast the sublime awfulness and simplicity of the teachings of our Saviour. He spoke as "one having authority," and not like theorizers, and theologians; and from His revelations solely can the knowledge of this subject be secured. The sacred Epistles only echo His words. He certainly did not intend the symbols He used to be interpreted literally, for often they are destructive of each other. His words do not determine the nature, the methods, or the duration of retribution. He emphasized the fact with incomparable strenuousness; He closed none of His great sermons without referring to it; He stood beneath the " cope of the eternal world " and removed the curtain, then He pointed to the two great facts of the future of men,—Rewards and Retribution. He did not argue about them, nor explain them nor reconcile them with divine benevolence, but declared them to be verities as real as man's immortality. So vivid were the awful facts to Him that His eyes moistened and His lips quivered when he urged men to be prepared to meet God in peace. He claimed He had come from His Father's bosom to earth's sorrow and death, not to teach theology, not to establish a church, but " to seek and save the lost." He taught sublime morals, gave new ideals of manhood; He revealed the fatherhood of God, and blessed the world with a new religion, —but all this was to save men from sin and its unspeakable consequences. From the teachings of Jesus I conclude that the retribution of sin is " eternal." How explain that term? I do not explain it. Is there probation after death? Christ gave no message to that purpose. Is the penalty of sin endless torment? The heart and reason of man protest against such a dispensation. Then will sin at last utterly destroy ($απολυειν$) the identity and personality of the incorrigible soul? This is not clearly revealed. A vital element of the awfulness and dread of retribution is the impenetrable mystery which hides from us its methods and nature,—the FACT alone is unmistakably and emphatically revealed, the silence of the Holy Scriptures about its nature, methods, and duration makes it more sublimely grand and dread. The known truth with its application on this subject is summarized by an ancient evangelist in these words: "For we must all appear before the judgment-seat of Christ that every one may receive the things done in the body according to that he hath done, whether it be good or bad; knowing therefore the terror of the Lord we persuade men." II Cor. 5: 10, 11.

Progressive Liberalism in the Closing and the Opening Century

Progressive Liberalism in the Closing and the Opening Century[*]

BY

CHARLES W. ELIOT, LL.D.

THE first thing to be observed about progressive liberalism in the closing century is that it is characterized essentially by a series of slow, gradual, and related developments, and not by a succession of sudden, spasmodic, and unconnected shocks. In the opening century it is sure to be characterized by a slow quiet, giving effect to a few ideas not new in themselves, but new in respect to diffused acceptance. I shall deal with only four aspects of the broad subject.

1. One deep-striking change to which liberalism has contributed is the change in Protestant opinions concerning the Bible. The Reformation substituted for the infallibility of an institution and its official representative—an institution vast, varying, complex, pervasive, and, on occasion, vague—another infallibility,—namely, the infallibility of a small, unchanging, compact, apprehensible collection of ancient writings—the Bible. Contending vigorously against the infallibility of the Church and the Pope, it set up the verbally-inspired, inerrant Bible as infallible authority. Fortunately the Reformation taught that the humblest Christian might have direct access to this infallible Scripture; and, therefore, it ultimately set up the human reason as the legitimate interpreter of this new infallibility. Now the human reason since the Reformation has not only added wonderfully to its stores of knowledge, but has also developed greatly its penetrating and exploring power. Some new sciences have arisen; the old sciences of philology and history have made astonishing progress; and the general

---

[*] This essay has no application whatever to the great Greek and Roman communions, those Churches being founded on an unqualified authority which does not recognize the right of private judgment. It relates exclusively to the Protestant communions.

method of inductive reasoning has been applied during the nineteenth century more widely and with much greater success than ever before. The languages of Scripture and the literatures written in those languages are far better known now than they were before the present century; the other sacred writings of the world have become known to the Christian nations; the history of Egypt, Palestine, Greece, and the Roman Empire has been illuminated by modern archæological research; and the natural sciences have demonstrated countless facts, and have established a few general principles, which throw a flood of light backward on to the beliefs and practices of former generations and the real history of the human race on this earth. Gradually there has appeared a new critical spirit towards the Bible and the supernatural side of religion. What is called the higher criticism is nothing but the application to the Bible of methods of research which have been successfully applied to other bodies of ancient historical and literary compositions.

Naturally, the influence of these new powers and new growths is to-day felt chiefly by scholars and reading people; nevertheless, the popular mind also is not without preparation for the acceptance of new views concerning revelation and supernaturalism in general. In the first place, all people have gradually learned to look always for a natural explanation of the marvellous; and secondly, they are thoroughly habituated to incomprehensible or mysterious effects which they firmly believe to be due to natural causes, although they do not in the least understand the modes in which the effects are produced. Thus, the comet and the eclipse have lost their terrors even for the most ignorant. All men are persuaded that these phenomena portend nothing, being due to natural, though uncomprehended, causes. The entire audience at a magician's show is firmly persuaded that there is no magic in the performance, but only skill. The familiar miracle of driving a street car by an invisible force, brought miles on a wire, though entirely incomprehensible to the common mind, is universally believed to be a purely natural phenomenon. In short, many effects once called miraculous or magical, are now accepted as purely natural; and on the other hand, many effects known to be natural are just as mysterious and wonderful as most of the occurrences described in former centuries as miracles. This state of the popular mind, which has been chiefly developed during the nineteenth century, has prepared the way for the acceptance of new views concerning the Bible and the supernatural in religion.

Again, all through this closing century the relative importance of fact in comparison with theory or speculation has been mounting. Down to the present century the prevalence of myth, fable, and imaginative narration has characterized the most precious literatures; and even history until lately has had highly imaginative elements. Of late years history has become realistic, and even fiction is photographic in quality. This preference for facts has grown stronger and stronger during the closing century, and is likely to be still more characteristic of the opening. Indeed, theory and speculation are almost discredited, except in a hypothesis which temporarily or provisionally explains or correlates a group of facts. Even in such cases the hypothesis is avowedly accepted on sufferance and with suspicion.

Still further, we observe that in the present generation, broad and hasty generalizations from few particulars, and immense superstructures on small, slight foundations are in modern instances almost universally derided. They do not excite indignation or scorn; they excite ridicule and contempt. Now the hugest superstructure ever reared on a diminutive foundation, and the most formidable speculation ever based on a minimum of doubtful fact, is the Augustinian systematic theology, resting on the literal truth of the story in Genesis about the disobedience of Eve and Adam in the Garden of Eden. The whole superstructure of the generally accepted Protestant systematic theology is founded on the literal acceptance of the Scriptural account of the fall of Adam and

Eve. If this account is not a true history, then the whole logical system built on it, including the doctrines of original and imputed sin, of the plan of salvation, of grace, mediation, and atonement, of blood satisfaction and blood purchase, and of regeneration, falls to the ground.

Hear Dr. Charles Hodge, the great Presbyterian theologian, writing about 1870-71, on the nature of the connection between the above doctrines and the account in Genesis of the Fall of Man.

"Finally these facts (the Garden of Eden facts) underlie the whole doctrinal system revealed in the Scriptures. Our Lord and His Apostles refer to them not only as true, but as furnishing the ground of all the subsequent revelations and dispensations of God. It was because Satan tempted man, and led him into disobedience, that he became the head of the kingdom of darkness, whose power Christ came to destroy, and from whose dominion He redeemed His people. It was because we died in Adam that we must be made alive in Christ. So that the Church universal has felt bound to receive the record of Adam's temptation and fall as a true historical account."

Hear Dr. Hodge again when he describes what the system is which is built on this indispensable foundation:

"In the Old Testament and in the New, God is declared to be just, in the sense that His nature demands the punishment of sin; that, therefore, there can be no remission without such punishment, vicarious or personal; that the plan of salvation symbolically and typically exhibited in the Mosaic institution, expounded in the prophets, and clearly and variously taught in the New Testament, involves the substitution of the incarnate Son of God in the place of sinners, who assumed their obligation to satisfy divine justice, and that He did in fact make full and perfect satisfaction for sin, bearing the penalty of the law in their stead; all this is so plain and undeniable that it has always been the faith of the Church, and is admitted to be the doctrine of the Scriptures by the leading rationalists of our day."

Assuming the infallibility of the Bible, the Augustinian systematic theology starts from the Fall of Man as recorded in Genesis, and then by a strict, logical process proves its appalling doctrines from the usage of words, the habitual forms of expression, and the pervading modes of presentation in the infallible Scriptures. All its doctrines are proved by explicit statements or assumptions made in the Bible, or by inferences from these statements or assumptions. The process involves something beyond the infallibility of the Scriptures themselves,—namely, the unerring interpretation of the Scriptures. In the centuries since the Reformation, and particularly in the nineteenth century, the human reason, enriched by new stores of knowledge, equipped with new methods of incisive inquiry, and fired with a new zeal for truth, has gradually undermined the faith of the majority of Protestant scholars, first, in the unerring interpretation, and secondly, in the infallibility of the Bible itself. These scholars no longer believe in the Fall of Man, or in the fabric of doctrine which a purely human logic has built on the Fall. When men begin to protest, or resolve, that they believe a given doctrine, it is a sure sign that real belief in that doctrine is fading away. Among the masses of Protestants some belief in the infallibility of the Bible still survives; but the opening century will doubtless see the gradual surrender of this transitional belief throughout the Protestant world. The controversial writings of St. Augustine have dominated Christian systematic theology for 1500 years. Luther, St. Augustine's disciple, prepared the ruin of his master's system when he declared the Bible infallible, but opened it to the individual inquirer. The nineteenth century has seen the foundations of the structure undermined; the twentieth will see it given over to the bats and the owls, so far as Protestants are concerned. It is not however the real Bible which is thus losing its hold; it is the inferential structure which has been built around and over it.

If it be said that though implicit faith in the Bible as an infallible revelation of literal truth be lost, the real foundations of the old dogmatics will remain unshaken, because they rest on human nature and experience, the answer is that civilized society's convictions about human nature and human conduct have undergone profound modifications during the nineteenth century, and are manifestly undergoing still further modification. Thus, instead of attributing sin in the individual to the innate corruption and perversity of his nature, modern society attributes it in many instances to physical defects, to bad environment, to unwise or wrongful industrial conditions, to unjust social usages, or to the mere weakness of will which cannot resist present indulgences even when the cost in future suffering stares the victim in the face. With this fundamental reconsideration of the whole doctrine of sin goes grave discussion of the till-now-accepted ideas of justice, punishment, and reformation. The theologians used to be sure that they perfectly understood God's justice. The jurists and legislators of to-day are not at all sure that they understand even what human justice ought to be. On the whole the nineteenth century is the least presumptuous of the centuries—the twentieth will be more modest still. Calvin and Jonathan Edwards imagined that they perfectly understood the objects of the eternal, hopeless agonies of the damned. In contrast listen to what a poet-physician says about the mystery of occasional pain in this world.

> "One stern democracy of anguish waits
> By poor men's cots—within the rich man's gates.
> What purpose hath it? Nay, thy quest is vain:
> Earth hath no answer: If the baffled brain
> Cries, 'tis to warn, to punish—Ah, refrain!
> When writhes the child, beneath the surgeon's hand,
> What soul shall hope that pain to understand?
> Lo! Science falters o'er the hopeless task,
> And Love and Faith in vain an answer ask,
> When thrilling nerves demand what good is wrought
> When torture clogs the very source of thought."

2. It is not the authority of the Bible only which has declined during the closing century; all authority has lost force—authority political, ecclesiastical, educational, and domestic.

The decline of political or governmental authority since the Reformation is very striking. The present generation received with derision the sentiment attributed some years ago—incorrectly in all probability—to the present Emperor of Germany—salus populi regis voluntas;—yet at the period of the Reformation nobody would have questioned that sentiment. Ecclesiastical authority has declined in a still more marked degree; and whereas the Church used to rule not only the consciences and opinions, but the daily habits of all Christians, there is now even among devout Catholics the sharpest demarcation between the limited province in which the Church is absolute and the large secular rest of the world. In education the whole conception of the function of the teacher has changed within fifty years. He no longer drives his pupils to their tasks, but leads and inspires them; he no longer compels them to copy or commit to memory, but incites them to observe and think. Instead of imposing on them his opinions, tastes and will, he induces them to form their own opinions, studies their tastes, and tries to invigorate their wills and teach them self-control. But in no field is the diminution of arbitrary authority more striking than in the family and the home; and in no field has the law more clearly recognized the new liberty than in the domestic relations.

What authority is taking in some measure the place of these declining authorities? I say in some measure, because the world has had too much of authority and not enough of love and freedom. There is an authority which during all the closing century has been increasing in influence; it is the developing social sense, or sense of kin. On the negative side, the restrictions which this sense of social solidarity and mutual accountability impose are in some ways extraordinarily comprehensive and absolute. The conviction that one must not do anything which can be offensive or injurious to one's associates is highly restrictive,—especially when this conviction becomes common and gets incorporated in statute law. Thus it may be doubted if any autocrat ever imposed on a population such a personal restriction as the prohibition of spitting on sidewalks and in public vehicles; yet this prohibition is a public regulation in Massachusetts and many other parts of the Union, although it springs solely from the social sense that the individual must not do what might propagate disease from himself to others. In many parts of modern society the social sense plays the part of a very arbitrary ruler; as appears clearly in the surrender to trades-unions of the most important elements of their personal liberty by hundreds of thousands of persons. On the positive side, this social solidarity is quite as effectual to procure affirmative action as it is to secure prohibitions. The British navy used to be recruited by the press gang,—that is, promising young sailors were seized by force in the coast towns, and dragged on board the ships. Now, Kipling and his kind write ballads, and the newspapers, pulpits, and popular meetings arouse a gregarious enthusiasm which sends thousands of young men to labor, suffer, or die in South Africa. It is the sense of common cause which supplies the impelling motive. Would it not be hard to state this doctrine better than it is stated in the brief phrase,—" No man liveth to himself, and no man dieth to himself"?

Another manifestation of the power of the new social solidarity is the tendency in democratic governments, and in some measure in all governments, to relieve the necessities and increase the satisfactions of the poorest classes on the one hand, and on the other to appropriate in part, and to divide anew as soon as possible, large accumulations of property in single hands. The recent legislation of Switzerland, France, England, and the United States illustrates the strength of this new authority—particularly the laws of these countries concerning progressive income taxes, succession taxes, and hours of labor, and for the protection of workmen against accident, and of women and children against overwork. Much of the legislation stigmatized as parental is really due to this strong sentiment of social solidarity. It has all sprung up in the nineteenth century, and it will doubtless grow rapidly in the twentieth.

3. The nineteenth century has seen the rise of a new body of learning called sociology. It is a body of doctrine clearly founded on the ethics of the New Testament; but it is at present in a confused, amorphous state. One of its characteristics, however, is hopeful—it aims at the prevention rather than the cure of sin and evil; just as preventive medicine aims at the prevention of disease both in the single individual and in society at large. The Old Testament relies chiefly on prohibition and penalty. It says, " Thou shalt not." For breaking this command, so much penalty is imposed. " In sorrow shalt thou bring forth children all the days of thy life." " Thy seed shall be cut off forever." " Visiting the iniquity of the fathers on the children unto the third and fourth generation of them that hate me." Now, faith in penalty as a preventive of wrong-doing and evil has rapidly declined during the nineteenth century; and this is equally true of penalty in this world and of penalty in the next. Barbarous punishments have been everywhere abolished in the civilized world, or are used only in moments of panic or delirium; and barbarous conceptions of punishment after death have been everywhere mitigated or abandoned. The new sociology, based on the Gospel doctrine of love to God and love to man, seeks the improvement of environment, the rectification of vice-breeding evils and wrongs, and the actual realization of the ideal— " Thou shalt love thy neighbor as thyself."

Sociology rejects also a motive which systematic theology has made much of for centuries,—the motive of personal salvation, which is essentially a selfish motive whether it relates to this world or to the next. Certainly it is no better a motive for eternity than it is for these short earthly lives of ours. The motive power of personal reformation and good conduct, and the source of happiness must always be found in love of others and desire to serve them, self-forgetfulness and disinterestedness being indispensable conditions of personal worth and of well-grounded joy. Sociology perceives that the multitude can no longer be reconciled to a state of misery in this world by the deceptive promise of comforts and rewards in the next. It sympathizes with them in loudly demanding joys in this world. The promise of Abraham's bosom after death should not reconcile Lazarus to lying at the gate full of sores now. The multitudes themselves perceive that wretchedness in this world may easily unfit them for worthy enjoyments either now or hereafter; since it may dwarf the mental and moral faculties through which high enjoyments come. Sociology is of the mind of the angel who bore a torch in one hand and a vase of water in the other, with the one to burn Heaven, and with the other to quench Hell, that men might be influenced neither by the hope of the one nor the fear of the other.

4. What effect will the great changes in public opinion about revelation and religion which the nineteenth century has wrought and the twentieth will spread, have on the estimate which the next two or three generations will place on the character and life of Jesus of Nazareth? We have already learned that the fundamental ethical conceptions recorded in the Gospels had all been anticipated. The fatherhood of God, the brotherhood of man, the conception of God as a spirit, and the Golden Rule,—to name some of the most fundamental of these conceptions,—all occur in writings earlier than the Gospels. But what of that? The true reformer is not he who first conceives a fruitful idea; but he who gets that idea planted in many minds, and fertilizes it there through the power of his personality. Such a reformer was Jesus. He spread abroad, and commended to the minds of many men, the loftiest ethical conceptions the race had won. He vitalized them by his winning and commanding presence, and sent them flying abroad on the wings of his own beautiful and heroic spirit. In a barbarous age he was inevitably given the reward of deification, just as the Pharaohs and Alexanders and Cæsars were; and his memory was surrounded by clouds of marvel and miracle during the four or five generations

which passed before the Gospels took any settled form. The nineteenth century has done much to disengage him in the Protestant mind from these encumbrances; and the twentieth will do more to set him forth simply and grandly as the loveliest and best of human seers, teachers, and heroes. Let no man fear that reverence and love for Jesus will diminish as time goes on. The pathos and the heroism of his life and death will be vastly heightened when he is relieved of all supernatural attributes and powers. The human hero must not have foreknowledge of the glorious issue of his sacrifices and pains; he must not be sure that his cause will triumph; he must suffer and die without knowing what his sacrifice will bring forth. The human exemplar should have only human gifts and faculties. If these principles are true, the more completely progressive liberalism detects and rejects the misunderstandings and superstitions with which the oral tradition and written record concerning the life of Jesus were inevitably corrupted, the more will love and reverence grow for the splendors of truth and moral beauty which, as a matter of indubitable fact, have shone from the character and teachings of this Jewish youth. Already we see many signs of the approaching fulfilment of Whittier's prophecy,—

> "Our Friend, our Brother, and our Lord
> **What may thy service be?**
> Nor name, nor form, nor ritual word
> But simply follow Thee."

The Effect of Recent Theological Discussions on the Upper Classes of the Anglo-Saxon Race

The Effect of Recent Theological Discussions of the Upper Classes of the Anglo-Saxon Race

BY

The Very Reverend F. W. FARRAR, D.D., F.R.S.

THERE can be no question that great changes have come over the views of thinking men in the upper classes with regard to theological questions during this century. It does not fall under my subject to consider how far these altered and advancing views have affected the opinion and lives of the masses of working-men; but we may feel sure that convictions filter downwards, and that views which have become prevalent in higher circles are sure in time to spread imperceptibly, and to affect those who would not have had sufficient education or thoughtfulness to arrive at such opinions for themselves. There is nothing to regret in the fact that advancing knowledge alters the complexion, and shifts the perspective, of long current beliefs. It is inevitable that it should be so; for

> "We know that through the ages one increasing purpose runs,
> And the thoughts of men are widened by the progress of the suns."

Nor is it only *inevitable*, it is also most *desirable* that the general advance in knowledge and in insight should shed fresh light—not indeed on the eternal and essential elements of religion, which have *remained* the *same* in all ages, but on the point of view under which we regard, and the manner in which we formulate and explain, the statements of theology. The light of all real knowledge is light from heaven, and it cannot lead any faithful soul astray. Nothing can be more fatal, even to moral growth and spiritual progress, than a stereotyped immobility;—that blind and narrow stagnation in the infallibility of optional ignorance, which delivers brawling judgments all day long on all things, unashamed, and which has always been as characteristic of imperfect and narrow religionists as it was of the "priests and Pharisees and hypocrites" in the days of our Lord. The example of those days, even if they stood alone, would be sufficient to show us that men, in the *name* of religion—and even whilst they claim to be the sole faithful supporters of true religion,—are capable of committing, in the *name* of the religion which they profess, the deadliest of crimes. If any other instances were wanting, we may see them in the deadly guilt of Inquisitors, who, in the name of the Lord of Love, blackened the blue of heaven with the Tophet-smoke of their bale-fires of hell, by burning many a dear saint of God, who held the truth which, to their own perdition, *they* rejected; and who lived lives transcenddently holier and purer than their own. In a milder form we may see the same pernicious results of incompetent religious arrogance in the fact that some of the best, wisest, most earnest and most brilliantly gifted Divines of our own day— men like Professor Maurice Kingsley, and F. W. Robertson, and Dean Stanley, and others—were all through their lives the favourite victims of the venomous attacks with which the so-called "religious" press of party Church newspapers is rife. Like Wesley and Whitefield, like Luther and Melancthon, like Savonarola and many more, these men—owing to the refusal of "priests" to accept the new truths—which shake their usurped authority, and expose the ignorant baselessness of their "infallible" judgments—have stood up.

"The very butt of slander, and the blot of every dart that malice ever shot." An unprogressive religion is a decadent and dying religion; a religion which refuses new light is a dead religion. Such forms of belief will inevitably sink into abject and priest-ridden superstitions, or into the cumbersome paraphernalia of externalism, which thinks that God cares for the murmuring of rites and ceremonies, whereas, he has again and again taught us that He requires our hearts, and that without heart sincerity all else is but as the small dust of the balance.

Let me point out one or two respects in which the thoughts of men respecting the truths of religion have been enlarged and changed.

1. It is so as regards our conceptions of God.

One of the most competent of living men of science—Mr. Alfred Wallace—in his very interesting book " This Wonderful Century," estimates that this century has made greater advances in science, both theoretical and applied, than all the centuries of the past put together. Now science has revealed to us immeasurably more of the laws of nature and of the infinitude of the Universe than was ever remotely dreamed of in past ages. The nature of the relation of God to man cannot be quite the same as it was when man regarded the earth as the centre of the whole universe, and thought that the sun and the moon and the starry heavens only existed to give it light. A Greek philosopher defined the stars as " golden nails fixed in the crystalline sky." We now know something of the immeasurable, inconceivable vastness of God's universe, and we know that the earth is but as a speck in the intense inane, a mote of dust in the streaming of infinite light. We can no longer rest in schemes and systems which professed to speak of God " as though he were a man in the next room; " or which proceeded on the conviction that " man's nothing-perfect " could comprehend " God's all-complete." We have learnt more modesty and humility, more awful reverence for Him " whose ways are past finding out." We are no longer content to employ our days in the elaboration of " schemes " and " systems " and " philosophies " of the plan of salvation; and in thus dropping buckets into empty wells, and growing old in drawing nothing out. We are content with holier modesty, to lay our hands upon our lips and to say:

> " So runs my dream :—but what am I?
> An infant crying in the night,
> An infant crying for the light,
> And with no language but a cry."

Changed modes of expression, changed points of view, which—though they do not affect any radical and essential view of religion—seem to require changed methods of expression may partly account for the deep and growing dislike to the use of the so-called "Athanasian" Creed in our public services. The Church of England is the only Church in all Christendom which recites this creed in common worship. The American Church has wisely discarded the practice, as also has the Irish Church. The dislike to it does not in the least spring from any lack of orthodoxy respecting the doctrine of the Trinity, but from the scholastic form of the creed, with its repetition of technical words—like "incomprehensible," "substance," "person"—of which not one person in a hundred knows the true and technical meaning. It also rises from the damnatory clauses, which no honest or enlightened man can repeat without the *subauditur* of large exceptions and explanations, and which the multitude usually understand in a false sense, and in that sense rightly repudiate as unscriptural and false. The narrow and anathematizing pseudo-orthodoxy which vehemently insists on the retention of this creed in public worship is extremely harmful to the Church of England and alienates multitudes from her worship. Late, very ill constructed, harsh, and superfluously verbose, the creed is not in the slightest degree necessary, since the whole Catholic faith is amply and far better stated in the "Nicene" and the "Apostles'" creeds. It was once my curious fortune to stand in church facing a seat on which were seven or eight men of universal fame in Art, in Literature, in Science, in public life. The expression of weariness and dislike upon the face of every one of them while the creed was being repeated was a lesson to me; for each one of them was not in any sense a sceptic, but a Christian and a communicant. All of them felt how utterly unlike was the form assumed by this creed to the general teaching and method of Holy Scripture. Not one of them doubted, so far as I knew, the doctrine of the Trinity, but they all felt that the harsh, formal and technical dogmatism of the creed added nothing to true faith: while—since so few are capable of grasping its real significance—it tends to minister directly to popular error. It is, however, doubtful whether at this moment there is enough of progressive open-mindedness in the English Church to follow, in this particular, the wiser example of all the other churches of Christendom in not demanding the constant public recital of this late and technical creed.

2. Another subject on which there have been great changes of view is the Atonement. I believe that, not only in the upper classes, but in all classes, men believe as firmly as ever they did in the Lord Jesus Christ, the Saviour of the world, by whose blood—that is by whose essential *life* divinely imparted to us—we are cleansed and saved. But they do not believe—and they rightly do not believe—in the hideous travesties of the doctrine which have been intruded upon mankind by an ignorant and systematizing theology, based on the distortion and the misinterpretation of isolated metaphors, or the extravagant forcing of emotional language to impossible logical conclusions. They repudiate, and rightly repudiate, the blasphemy of representing God, the Father, as all wrathful and inexorable justice, and God, the Son, as all loving mercy. They accept no violent disintegration of the persons of the blessed Trinity in the work of man's salvation. They toss aside the age-long absurdity which represented God as paying to the Devil (!) the ransom of Christ's death. They no less reject the *forensic* theory by which St. Anselm replaced the old error—a theory which dwelt on the " exact equivalent " of " vicarious substitutions," and which foisted into scripture a mass of colossal or self-contradictory inferences, elaborated into a " philosophy of the plan of salvation," which relied exclusively on passing illustrations, and resembled a pyramid built upon its apex. Men have become impatient—and rightly impatient—of " the ever-widening spiral *ergo* drawn from the narrow aperture of single texts." They are more than content to know and be sure that " God is love," and that " God *in Christ* "—not as it is erroneously translated in our Authorized Version " God *for*

Christ's sake" forgives us our sins, when, by the aid of His Holy Spirit, they are repented of. The clearing away from the doctrine of the Atonement of the gross anthropomorphism introduced into it by the language of self-satisfied theologians, ignorant preachers and impassioned hymns, so far from tending to *unbelief,* has left men more humbly and deeply convinced that God, by his infinite love and mercy, has granted us pardon in Christ, a newness of life, even though we cannot understand his mysteries, and cannot measure the arm of God by the finger of man.

3. Again, there has been a decided change in the thoughts of Christians about Eschatology. They now see that nothing in Scripture necessitates the crude and glaring horrors, the ghastly and revolting misrepresentations of one or two Scripture metaphors, which have been consolidated into the doctrine of "Hell-fire." I have in my possession a revolting little picture which used to be given by Romish priests to children and women, representing a human being standing naked in red flames, of which the black smoke is smeared with hideous blood gouts, while loathly serpents are twining round and round him, burying their fangs in his convulsive face, and their forked tails into the flesh of his arms; while underneath is written in old French, *" Pour n'y avoir pont pancé."* Strange that Christians could really believe on the strength of a grossly misrepresented metaphor which there is no more excuse for taking literally than there would be for taking literally the metaphor of "Abraham's bosom "—that a God of Love could be happy while the creatures of His hands were writhing hopelessly and for ever in unutterable material torments! Yet that they could maintain such conceptions is sufficiently proved by Dante's Inferno, as much as by endless hymns and religious manuals. There has been a decided and a blessed change of view as to these cruel imaginings. When my " Eternal Hope " was published, I lived for weeks and months amid a hailstone of anathemas. Now the majority of thinking and educated Christians hold the view which I there maintained—that sin

indeed is always punishment; but that there is no proof that repentance and pardon will not be always possible; and that we may trust in the mercy of God "for ever and ever"—or as it is, literally, in the original, "for ever and beyond." We have learned—or at any rate all thinking and educated men have learned—that "everlasting" (ἀΐδιος) which occurs but twice in the New Testament is not a synonym of "eternal" (αἰώνιος) but the direct antithesis of it; the former being the unrealisable conception of endless time, and the latter referring to a state from which our imperfect human conception of time is absolutely excluded.

4. Once more, there has been a radical and most imperatively called for change in the old superstition of what is called "verbal inspiration." We know that God speaks to us out of His holy book; we know that it contains His revelation of Himself; we know that it is as a whole the most supreme of collected literatures; we know that all the rest of the literatures of the world put together could not supply its place; but we know also that it is a plain positive duty to consider it in the heaven-sent light of advancing knowledge; we know that *all* its incidental utterances are not final or infallible; we know that some of its books are composite in structure and that some were written in times much later than the authors whose names they bear; we know that the Old Testament—as in the books of Daniel and Jonah and in the sublime story of the Fall—admits (as our Lord's parables also consecrated) the use of *Haggadah,* or "moral allegory;" we know that the divine enlightenment, which we call "inspiration," did not exclude the human element in the imperfect medium by which it was communicated; and that, in unimportant and minor matters it left the possibility of error; we know, above all, that Scripture is the true sense of scripture, as St. Augustine says; that Scripture is, and only is, what scripture means; that it must be interpreted as a whole; and that the totality of its teaching must not be perverted by insistence on the interpretation which we, for party and for other purposes, may choose to distort out of its

isolated and incidental phrases. Our reverence for Holy Scripture has not been diminished, but has been indefinitely increased by the study and the criticism and the progressive enlightenment which have led us to a truer estimate of its place and meaning in the dealings of God with men.

On the whole, then, I am hopeful as to the stability of our Christian convictions in the minds of men of all classes. The leaders of intellectual research may not be "orthodox" in the old, narrow, arrogant, stereotyped sense of the word, which imposed a yoke of bondage on the free necks of Christians, who are all God's priests; but they believe in God, the Father, and in Jesus Christ, His only Son, our Lord; and in that Holy Spirit which he made to dwell in us and who yearneth jealously and tenderly over all whom God hath redeemed.

The Religious Condition of the Working Men in America and the Effect of Recent Theological Discussion Upon Them

The Religious Condition of the Working Men of America and the Effect of Recent Theological Discussion Upon Them

BY

SAMUEL M. JONES, Esquire

THE religious condition of working men and of all other men is practically the same. Society is a unit. Man is a social being, and the fact that one is asked to write under a title such as forms the head of this article, is one of the evidences that we are not yet free from the most deadly form of scepticism; that is unbelief in one's fellows, the evidence of the unbelief being manifest in the suggestiveness of the title indicating that the idea that man can be dealt with as classes has not yet disappeared from the public mind. I do not accept the class idea at all. In my own life, I have been a working man, a superintendent, a business man, a manufacturer and a mayor, and in all of these various relations to society I cannot see that I was anything other than a *man,* always, to a very great extent, moved by the same impulses, inspired by the same hopes and ambitions and subject to the same disappointments, failures and conflicting emotions.

The very idea that we must deal with people as classes, in addition to being irreligious, sceptical and atheistic, is misleading, confusing and almost an absolute hindrance to one's usefulness as a factor in the educational work that is carrying the race forward to larger liberty.

The religious condition of the working men in America must, of necessity, be the reflex of the religious condition of the business men and the professional men, or the men who do not work. If anything can be said to be *social* rather than individual, it must be our religion, for there is no way in which our religion can find expression except in social relation; for if a man love not his brother whom he hath seen, how can he love God whom he hath not seen? It follows then that my religious condition will be reflected in the condition of those most closely related to me; under the existing capitalistic system, these are the working men, commonly called my employees, upon the fruit of whose toil I may be living an entirely idle and wholly useless life; to such an extent as I am so living, my life is an immoral one. I am not eating my bread in the sweat of my face, but rather I am eating bread produced by the sweat of another man's face, and that other man my brother. And it is as certain that the immorality which I am practising by using my fellow men as mere instruments to gather profit will be reflected in their lives as the virus of small-pox is certain to show itself when injected into the human body.

I have said that I have been unconscious of being anything but a *man* in the various conditions of life through which I have passed, and I know that I get closer to the God in my fellow men when I meet them, treat them and deal with them as equals, as integral parts of a social whole, as *people*, than I could possibly get by, as it were, putting them under a microscope and studying them as classes or as representatives of a class.

So to those who want to improve the religious condition of the working men of America I think I can safely say, first " remove the beam from thine own eyes, then shalt thou see clearly to remove the mote from the eye of thy brother." As the God in us finds opportunity for more perfect expression through more and more just dealing with our fellow men, our eyes will be opened and we will see our fellow men, not as classes or separate and distinct individuals, the highest duty according to prevailing notions being material interest, being the getting of things, property, for himself; but we shall look upon society as a human whole and we shall find our chief joy and delight in doing as a *duty* our utmost to contribute to the happiness of the whole social body. Such a title as the one under which this article is written will have fallen into disuse, the term working men will have become obsolete, for when all are religious then all will work, for nothing can be more irreligious than to live an idle and useless life; every one that so lives, every one that does not render to society useful service is living a useless life and living upon the toil of some other one.

We reach the conclusion, then, stated in the form of a proposition in the beginning of this article that the religious condition of the working men is the religious condition of all men, and we understand more clearly than before that "no man liveth to himself." Of course, I have not used the word religious in any narrow sense; I have rather used it as including all that is best in man. In the narrow and technical sense, I presume the business and the professional classes are more religious than the working men; that is, that in a larger proportion they are Church members and attend the "means of grace," and so on. But the Church itself, no longer deceived, is coming to see that there is a difference between Pharisaism and religion, that there is no real difference between love to God and love to man, and that the only way of expressing one's love to God is in one's dealings with men. And I believe that in the evolutionary processes that now distinctively mark this present epoch, we can see the transformation that is taking place inside the Church that will one day lead the Church to take the high place that must be held by some form of institution, whether you call it "hall of reason" or Church or what not, where men and women will gather together and dismiss their cares and "shake their hearts out together" as the Germans say, in fellowship one with another. When those better days come, we shall see days that are less strifeful for we shall have learned that "life consisteth not in things" but rather in being, in doing, in giving, instead of in getting.

The one hopeful sign of the times that bids us all take courage is seen in the growth of the religious sentiment—I mean the sure enough *religious* as separated from the pietistic notion—for, in the best sense of the word, the movement for social reform is a religious movement. The growth of the idea of the Unity of the entire race is full of encouragement to all lovers of righteousness. No one can be truly religious who does not accept this important fundamental, for the thought of oneness is as scientific as it is religious. If God is All-Father then "it follows as the night the day" that all mankind are brothers. This lesson is being taught in many ways. The true spirit of Socialism, that has grown so marvelously in our country during the last few years, is the spirit of Brotherhood, is religious, and while there are many advocates of Socialism who are yet teaching according to the narrow conceptions of individualism as it finds expression in the party idea in our politics, yet I believe that the day is not far distant when all will see that this teaching must give way to the logical interpretation of the broad principle towards the realization of which humanity is progressing. Socialism is growing among all so-called classes—perhaps among working men faster than anywhere else.

The complaint of the party socialists is directed wholly against the competitive system, and the competitive system is, of course, a system of warfare. We can easily see that competition is wrong in economics, in material things; that the system can never bring peace to the world; that it means the survival of the strongest; in short as has been many times said, competition is war. The awakening of the social conscience and the religious impulse within us will bring us to see that if competition is wrong anywhere, then the competitive principle must be wrong everywhere. But we are not led to see this great truth by the appeals that are made to our material interests, but only as the appeal comes to the religious instinct; that is, to the idea of Brotherhood and duty. All will admit that natural brothers ought not to fight either for trade, advantage, through the methods of business, or for any other advantage by the fiercer methods of warfare. The competitive spirit is the spirit of murder, and it is evident to observing persons that the workers of the world must lead in spreading this great truth. Jesus has told us that a knowledge of the Truth will make us free, and to me there is something like pathos in the thought that there is absolutely no other way for the soul to realize freedom except through a knowledge of the Truth. But there is no cross lots or short cut way. "Ye must be born again" is as literally true to-day as when Jesus uttered the words. There is no middle ground. The scientific principle must rule and does rule, else there is no hope in the world. Love is the only basis upon which we can hope to build an enduring state or secure any sort of permanent social order. The race is struggling as never before to realize this truth in all of its wonderful depth of meaning. We see it in the great growth of fraternal organizations that have characterized the history of the last few years; we see it in the great trade union movement that has fraternized and co-ordinated great bodies of working men; we see it, in the countless number of societies, clubs, lodges, institutions and brotherhoods that are springing up all over the world. In the narrower sense, these movements are individualistic, but in the broader and deeper sense they are social and religious. It is an expression of the longing for Brotherhood, for fellowship, and this awakened social conscience is the very force that will produce the enlightened intellect that will lead these numberless organizations to see and to understand the folly of the unbrotherly method and lead them finally into one grand Brotherhood—the good of all being the music that shall sing the world to its work.

> "We know that by and by a brighter day will come
> When hate and strife shall die and each man own his home;
> When mine and thine are ours, and every law is good,
> And all are pure as flowers in one grand Brotherhood."

I am satisfied that "all things work together for good to them that love God;" that is, to them that love the good. And blessed are we that our eyes see this day, the day of hope and good cheer that none of the epochs of the past have seen; for we are in the beginning of a movement that is finally to culminate in a great revival of real religion that shall exclude none, include all, and that shall open the eyes of our understanding to the real meaning of the life and words of Christ, whom we profess to love, and that will be the beginning of the Kingdom of Heaven on earth.

The Effect of Recent Theological Discussion on the Lower Classes of the Anglo-Saxon Race

The Effect of Recent Theological Discussion on the Lower Classes of the Anglo-Saxon Race

BY

Brigadier S. L. BRENGLE

I. *The Present Spiritual Condition Of The Lower Classes.*

CHEERY old Dr. Theodore Cuyler, after nearly two score years of Christian work in the second Anglo-Saxon city on the planet, looking out upon the Church and world from his watch tower announces himself an optimistic pessimist, and after twelve years of work as a Salvation Army officer among the lower classes of the Anglo-Saxon race, it seems to me that the wisest mental attitude toward their spiritual condition is that of optimistic pessimism.

The present religious condition of these lower classes is far above what it was when Wesley and Whitefield began their mighty labours but it is yet so pitiably low that, but for the abounding sympathy and grace the Saviour bestows, the hearts of those who daily confront the desperate and increasing spiritual need, would well nigh break or become hopeless and hard as stone. They are not generally atheistical or sceptical, but on the contrary are keenly susceptible to religious influence and teaching and ready to receive the gospel, even the most besotted of them on the Bowery in New York or on Clark street, in Chicago, and yet they are not largely reached by the Church. They are not exactly alienated from the Church, but are rather like children whose mother spends her time in reading novels and going to the theatre, or in efforts to reform social customs or civil laws while neglecting her own household. They are not cared for, and so they go their own way, thinking but little of the Church because, as they suppose, the Church thinks little of them; they are restless and unsatisfied, and filled with a hunger for they know not what.

In this particular, Protestant Christianity might learn much from Roman Catholicism, which boasts that the poor have ever been looked upon by them as the little children of the Church; and much more from Jesus, who preached the gospel to the poor, and presented this fact to John the Baptist as the final credential of His divinity, His Messiahship. Effective efforts on their behalf by Protestant agencies are largely confined to the work done by the Salvation Army and the numerous and increasing rescue missions. In fact, these special agencies to reach the lower classes are largely a product of the last third of this nineteenth century, as foreign missions are practically a development of the last hundred years, and unless the Church devises practical methods and means to meet the need, these agencies will necessarily increase in number as the population increasingly pours its tide into the cities.

Saloons, cheap theatres, brothels and low clubs helped by a mighty flood of impure, demoralizing, and debasing literature are bidding for and capturing the lower classes in a way to fill with gravest concern thoughtful Christian men and women who are face to face with the facts; while the children that swarm the streets by day and night, with no man to care for their souls, growing up in densest ignorance of Christian truth, familiar with brutality, vice and sin from babyhood, given to profanity and Sabbath-breaking, early forming the drink and cigarette and worse habits, thereby wrecking their health and laying the foundations of physical weakness and mental, moral and spiritual imbecility for future generations, are in many instances developing into as real a moral heathenism as can be found in mid Africa. I assume that the lower classes of the Anglo-Saxon race are mostly found in the city, and it is a fact patent to all that, with but few exceptions, the Churches follow the avenues and boulevards, erecting magnificent buildings which both in locality and cost of attendance are beyond the reach of the poor, while no adequate provision is made for the crying spiritual needs of the unnumbered thousands left without shepherds in the slums and poverty

Effect of Recent Theological Discussion 539

stricken portions of our cities. In this way a great gulf has been digged between the Church and the lower classes which from the side of the poor, the ignorant and the vicious is practically impassable, but which can be and sometimes is bridged from the side of the Church.

II. *The Effect Of Recent Theological Discussions Upon The Lower Classes.*

Recent theological discussion has not affected the relation of the masses to the Church so much as it has affected the relations of the Church, and especially of the theologians themselves to the masses. The masses never have and never will and, I had almost said, never can seek the Church, but the Church is under solemn obligation and command to seek the masses, and whenever the faith of the Church is undimmed and its love aflame it does seek and has no difficulty in finding them, and at such times the poor, the ignorant, the sinful and the needy flock as doves to her windows.

The common people, the lower classes, are deeply interested in bread, but know little and care less about scientific dietetics, and so they know and care but little for systematic theology as taught by the schools and discussed by the clergy, yet they are more deeply interested than many suppose in theology as taught by Jesus, and Luther, and John Bunyan, and George Fox, and John Wesley, and General Booth, and Billy Bray, Jerry McAuley, and Mr. Moody. They still hear such teachers gladly. Generally speaking, they know and hear nothing of theological controversies, or where they do, it is only as they hear of cabinet discussions of finance or foreign policy, or as peasants hear rumours of distant war, considering them all to be matters in which they have little or no concern.

They receive the Bible roughly as the word of God; they care no more for higher criticism than for higher mathematics, and they pay little more attention to discussions about inspiration, verbal errancy or inerrancy, the theories of evolution and kindred subjects than they do to Laplace's theories of the cosmic universe, Gladstone's Homeric discussions, or Müller's studies in the Hindoo Vedas.

They are more keenly alive to the doctrines of eschatology, though that word would dumfound them. The future life, with its rewards and penalties in heaven and hell is usually a reality to them, though they would like to doubt hell, and if the doctrine is presented baldly, simply to the intellect, they will argue as Napoleon told Josephine he did, like devils against it. But a direct, manly assault upon their sins, "a centre rush" for their conscience, an earnest appeal to their common sense, their better judgment, their highest interests for eternity, together with an affectionate disclosure of the long suffering love and mercy and abounding grace and goodness of God in Christ to penitent, believing souls, and "the severity of God" to incorrigible sinners and moral law breakers, are sufficient to dispel their hazy doubts about hell by convincing them of the unchangeable enmity of the carnal mind toward God; the need of forgiveness, the new birth, and the sanctification of the indwelling Holy Ghost in order to bring them into harmony with God and fit them for heaven.

They cannot long be frightened by lurid word pictures of the fiery torments, the intolerable tortures of the damned such as our forefathers painted for their terrified hearers, but their moral sense healthily responds to a plain, earnest, honest declaration of the certain and terrible sequence of sin and suffering such as is being so generally recognized by the masters of modern literature, but neglected, shall I say? almost criminally neglected, by the pulpit, where the danger signals should never be lowered, but where the dark and awful reality can be relieved by heavenly flash lights of the pitying compassion and forgiving love of the Father through the Eternal Son

"Before the world's foundtion slain."

They do not worry their minds over subtle definitions of the Holy Trinity, but very readily accept Jesus Christ as Saviour and Lord, as Prophet, Priest and King when once convicted of sin and convinced that there is no help in themselves or in man, but only in the condescending grace of God.

The immediate effect of such discussions upon the masses is scarcely perceptible, but where it does affect them it tends for the time rather to relax and weaken the influence of the Church upon them than otherwise. To their minds controversy, even in non-essentials, implies uncertainty in fundamentals, and they in common with the higher classes are altogether too ready to grasp this supposed uncertainty and construe it into a reasonable excuse to relax the strenuous watchfulness and self-denial and sobriety necessary to obtain and maintain deadness to the world, and an active faith in, a steadfast devotion to, and a vivid vision of unseen, eternal things. Where they are religiously inclined they cling tenaciously to the old truth, for adjustment to new truth or to new statements of truth, like adjustment to a new shoe, is inconvenient or even painful, and such is the sluggishness of the average mind, and such is the lack of intellectual equipment among the lower classes and such their mental preoccupation in their struggle for bread that they will often discard both the old and the new and walk forth in dogged and naked indifference or defiant scepticism rather than put themselves to the trouble of praying and thinking through to the solid certainty and assurance of truth.

Theology as taught by Jesus and His disciples was adapted to the lower classes and it should ever be so. Just as men have for ages made and eaten bread and lived thereby though they were utterly ignorant of its chemical constituents, its scientific properties, just as they have for milleniums rejoiced and walked in the light of the sun though unacquainted with the spectrum analysis, so men, humble men, whose hearts and spirits were broken and contrite, and who have dared to trust their heavenly Father and follow Jesus Christ as their Saviour and Lord, have feasted on the Bread from heaven and walked in the light of the Sun of Righteousness though utterly ignorant of the high disputes and hairsplitting distinctions of either deductive or inductive, conservative or progressive, orthodox or heretical theologians.

III. The Effect Of These Discussions Upon The Theologians And Churches In Their Relation To The Lower Classes.

Dr. Dollinger said (referring to his "Checks to Antinomianism") that John Fletcher of Madeley had produced the only Protestant work of theology of value during the latter part of the eighteenth century, and Dean Alfred declared that these "Checks" for the time being drove Calvinism out of England. And yet so saintly was this ready and invincible controversialist that John Wesley declared it to be his opinion that he was the holiest man who had lived since the apostle John. So flaming was his evangelistic spirit that he transformed the parish of Madeley and won its lowliest and vilest people to the Cross, so that Mr. Wesley asserted that if he had given himself up to evangelical work he would have surpassed Whitefield. And so humble was he, and so zealous for the salvation of the lower classes, that he would take a bell on Sunday morning and ringing it from street to street he would call them to worship.

While Albert Barnes was being tried before the ecclesiastical courts for heresy, the Church of which he was pastor was aflame with revival fire, and so in touch were he and his Church with God and with the people that the gracious outpouring of the Spirit and the ingathering of souls continued right through the trial.

Judged by the standard set by these two men, the discussions of the present day have not been favourable to the theologians or to the Churches in their relations to the lower classes.

When Luther preached he declared that he paid no attention to the fifty doctors of theology who were in his congregation, but sought only to reach the heads and hearts of the two thousand common people.

"Depend upon it," said the father of Archbishop Benson, "Depend upon it, the doctrine of apostolic succession is everything for a man's own encouragement and help in dispirited hours, but it is not a doctrine to preach to the world." But it does not seem safe to draw comfort from, nor wise to weary one's self with, doctrines and controversies that cannot be preached. Speculative theology is dangerous to the spiritual life of the Church and when the children cry for bread, woe to them, but more still, woe be to their teachers, if their cry is answered with the stones of speculation.

Would it not be well then for our controversial theologians to remember that "knowledge puffeth up, but love buildeth up" and after many heart searchings and much prayer to test their views and prove their arguments by going with them and preaching them to the frank, childlike, and yet strangely acute lower classes, with the purpose to find out whether they are really the power of God unto salvation or not, and unless they bring about the conversion of men as did the doctrines preached by Paul and Luther and Wesley and General Booth, then cast them aside as vain babblings?

There is the frankness of children among the lower classes. They are conscious of sin, and they do not slip into the kingdom of heaven unconsciously. There is a crisis in their lives that ushers them into this blessedness, and it is the preaching not of negations and doubts and vast ignorance and theological novelties and guesses, but of positive truth, the things we know and are assured of that bring about this crisis. Baxter and Wesley were the great Doctors in practical theology. They were vigorous and undaunted controversialists, but they were also mighty soul winners, for in all their discussions that was the end they sought. They applied doctrine to Christian experience, and Christian experience to doctrine. They proved the experience by the word of God, and they proved the correctness of their interpretation of the word by the experience it produced when preached to humble people.

I would not discredit our theologians, nor discourage discussion. Our fathers have asked questions and answered them in that way which brought rest to their minds. But we have not attained unto knowledge when we have learned the definitions of the fathers. We must needs ask the questions over again for ourselves, and seek answers that bring rest to our minds and peace to our hearts. But the rest and peace are false, if faith's vision is not more clear and love's devotion not more ardent and the sheep for whom the Shepherd died not sought after with more lowly, self-consuming zeal. And these results do not seem so far to have followed recent theological discussion.

Arminius was not an evangelist, but his discussions were so relevant to salvation that he cleared the way for the large freedom of Wesley and Fletcher, and they wrought so mightily as not only to change the spiritual condition of the Anglo-Saxon race, but in a large measure to such a recasting of its theology that has transformed it and made it quite a different thing in this century from what it was in the last.

Theological discussions growing out of active work and burning passion for the immediate salvation of men such as those of Paul and Luther and Knox and Wesley and Fletcher will draw the leaders closer to the common people, but those of this age are not of that kind, and the leaders in these discussions are not leaders in any sense of the word for the evangelization of the masses. While Paul and Luther and Wesley combined broad and accurate scholarship and heroic controversial combativeness with a flaming spirit of evangelism that led them to the lower classes, the evangelistic leaders of to-day are not theologians on the one hand, and the theologians are not evangelists and soul winners on the other.

This may in some measure prove to be unfortunate. There will be discussion. There is a needs-be that the foundations of old beliefs be examined by each succeeding age, and theological formulas changed and readjusted to increasing light. But the crying creed of Christendom to-day, and especially of the lower classes, is not so much for more elaborately equipped theologians, nor for a restatement of theology, as for lovers of souls, and mighty knee-workers and determined wrestlers with God, men steeped in the spirit and skilled in the high yet humble art, the holy science of prayer, who know the secret of the Lord and can bring down the fire of heaven upon the cold and darkened altars of earth.

Date Due

Library Bureau Cat. no. 1137